A ROYAL "WASTE" OF TIME

A Royal "Waste" of Time

The Splendor of Worshiping God
and Being Church for the World

Marva J. Dawn

WILLIAM B. EERDMANS PUBLISHING COMPANY
GRAND RAPIDS, MICHIGAN / CAMBRIDGE, U.K.

© 1999 Wm. B. Eerdmans Publishing Co.
255 Jefferson Ave. S.E., Grand Rapids, Michigan 49503 /
P.O. Box 163, Cambridge CB3 9PU U.K.

Printed in the United States of America

04 03 02 01 00 99   7 6 5 4 3 2 1

Library of Congress Cataloging-in-Publication Data

Dawn, Marva J.
A royal "waste" of time: the splendor of worshiping God
and being church for the world / Marva J. Dawn.
p.   cm.
Includes bibliographical references.
ISBN 0-8028-4586-X (pbk.: alk. paper)
1. Public worship.   2. Public worship — Sermons.
3. Sermons, American.   I. Title.
BV15.D39   1999
264 — dc21   99-19405
CIP

The author and publisher gratefully acknowledge permission to reprint material
from the following:

"Blest Are They" by David Haas. © 1985 GIA Publications, Inc. Reprinted by per-
mission.
"Christ High-Ascended, Now in Glory Seated" by Timothy Dudley-Smith. © 1984
Hope Publishing Co., Carol Stream, IL 60188. All rights reserved. Used by per-
mission.
Excerpts from Douglas Coupland, *Generation X: Tales for an Accelerated Culture*
(New York: St. Martin's Press, 1991). Reprinted by permission of the author
and St. Martin's Press.
"God's Word Alive and Active" by Gladys G. Moore. Reprinted by permission of
the American Bible Society.

This book is dedicated to
composers and poets creating new forms, new images, new sounds
to give us more of God,
preachers endeavoring to speak the Word faithfully in a contrary world,
musicians diligently offering their best gifts in spite of critical attacks,
artists sculpting and dancing and painting to the glory of God,
worship participants yearning for depth and excellence,
congregations struggling to be genuine communities,
thinkers naming the perils of our dying culture,
teenagers searching for significance in the Church,
children needing to be formed in the language of faith,
parents seeking to nurture their children in Christian habits,
pastors concerned for the many in our culture who hunger to meet God,
worship planners asking for better questions to avoid needless conflicts —

and, most of all, to Myron,
whose love of music and royal gardens and faithful care
help me to waste time in the splendor of worshiping God.

Contents

Contents

PART II
WORSHIPING GOD: THE SPLENDOR
OF OUR INFINITE CENTER

PART III
BEING CHURCH: BUILDING COMMUNITY

PART IV
BEING CHURCH: FORMING CHARACTER

CONTENTS

PART V
BEING CHURCH: CHOICES

PART VI
FOR THE WORLD: CHALLENGES

1

Introduction

Ascribe to the LORD the glory of his name;
worship the LORD in holy splendor.

Psalm 29:2

To worship the LORD is — in the world's eyes — a waste of time. It is, indeed, a *royal* waste of time, but a waste nonetheless. By engaging in it, we don't accomplish anything useful in our society's terms.

Worship ought not to be construed in a utilitarian way. Its purpose is not to gain numbers nor for our churches to be seen as successful. Rather, the entire reason for our worship is that God deserves it. Moreover, it isn't even useful for earning points with God, for what we do in worship won't change one whit how God feels about us. We will always still be helpless sinners caught in our endless inability to be what we should be or to make ourselves better — and God will always still be merciful, compassionate, and gracious, abounding in steadfast love and ready to forgive us as we come to him.[1]

---

1. Out of my concern to reach the widest audience possible, I have chosen to refer to God with the pronouns *he, his,* and *him,* which I have always understood as gender-neutral — and yet personal — when used in connection with God. I apologize to anyone who might be offended by my word choices and pray that you will accept my decision to use our inadequate language as carefully as possible to speak to the widest audience. Certainly God is neither masculine nor feminine, but more than all our words can ever connote. Would that we could all join the Hungarians in having pronouns for the third person singular that connote both masculine and feminine at once. Would you be able

1

Worship is a royal waste of time, but indeed it is royal, for it immerses us in the regal splendor of the King of the cosmos. The churches' worship provides opportunities for us to enjoy God's presence in corporate ways that take us out of time and into the eternal purposes of God's kingdom. As a result, we shall be changed — but not because of anything we do. God, on whom we are centered and to whom we submit, will transform us by his Revelation of himself.

To understand worship as a royal waste of time is good for us because that frees us to enter into the poverty of Christ. We worship a triune God who chose to rescue the world he created by means of the way of humility. God sent his Son into the world to empty himself in the obedience of a slave, humbling himself to suffer throughout his entire life and to die the worst of deaths on our behalf. He did not come to be "solving the world's problems in any sense that the world could understand."[2] Worship of such a God immerses us in such a way of life, empowered by a Spirit who does not equip us with means of power or control, accomplishment or success, but with the ability and humility to waste time in love of the neighbor.

We will explore our title's themes more thoroughly below when we look more closely at the subtitle of this book. First, however, it is necessary to sketch the reasons why this book came into being.

Baring/Bearing My Soul

I never intended to write a book about worship. My first one on the subject, *Reaching Out without Dumbing Down: A Theology of Worship for the Turn-of-the-Century Culture,*[3] arose out of what seemed a strange call. I became increasingly concerned as churches in which I served as visiting theologian or guest preacher made decisions about worship without much theological re-

---

to follow this book if I used *ő* to mean he/she, *őt* to mean him/her, and *övé* to mean his/hers? Great thanks, *köszönöm*, to Kati Kovacs, formerly a student at Regent College, who taught me these pronouns. Another possibility would be to join the Chinese in having one character that denotes he/she/it and is joined by a specific sign that means "God." Thus the pronoun is distinctly God's pronoun.

2. Quotation from Simon Tugwell, *Prayer,* cited in *A Guide to Prayer: For Ministers and Other Servants,* ed. Rueben P. Job and Norman Shawchuck (Nashville: The Upper Room, 1983), p. 294.

3. See Marva J. Dawn, *Reaching Out without Dumbing Down: A Theology of Worship for the Turn-of-the-Century Culture* (Grand Rapids: Wm. B. Eerdmans Publishing Co., 1995).

flection, or stayed stuck in traditionalistic ruts (notice that adjective carefully), or constantly increased the hype to keep folks interested, or withdrew into musical snobbery. Meanwhile, I was enjoying immensely training the choir I directed in musical skills and an awareness of the broad range of repertoire — and they seemed to enjoy it, too — so I was surprised when these attempts to teach the music of the whole Church were labeled as elitist. I was deeply troubled that in all the controversies churches were losing what it means to be part of the whole community of the Church.

My field of research is not liturgy, so it took me a long time to recognize that my work in the Scriptures and Christian ethics, with an emphasis on cultural analysis and character formation, had given me the background necessary to answer the call to write that was generated by these worship issues. My childhood in a very musical home where we were always making up new songs and treasuring old ones gave me the desire to be a bridge between opposing factions in the escalating conflicts.

I certainly never intended to write a second book about worship. This one arose out of superb conversations with church leaders across the denominational spectrum, out of excellent comments from thoughtful people at conferences, out of the experience of a diversity of models of people leading worship attentively and astutely. Moreover, the reaction to my first book amazed me; the book seems to be useful in helping people think theologically about worship. Many people from a diversity of denominations expressed gratitude for, and asked for more of, the criteria *Reaching Out* poses by which to evaluate new music and new worship forms. One evangelical radio broadcaster even said that she hoped evangelical churches would rethink their worship using the liturgical issues I raised. Numerous people share my primary concerns that the worship of all denominations lead to genuine adoration of God and faithful formation of his people — so this book provides further elaboration of these topics.

Perceptions that there was more for me to write on the subject of worship began to stir early. Various journals asked me for articles on worship and thereby forced me to ask different questions. Then my favorite radio interviewer, Char Binkley of WBCL in Fort Wayne, Indiana, asked me soon after *Reaching Out* came out what I would add to the book if I wrote it over, and already then I knew that I needed much more study of postmodernism, for it seems to me that postmodernity (often unrecognized) is increasingly the most forceful cultural attribute affecting those to whom the Church seeks to minister (see Chapters 4 and 5 below). Let me also thank those who gave good criticisms in reviews of the book. These greatly contributed to my teaching, and I am grateful.

However, this book also arose out of people's pain. I was shocked at the reaction to *Reaching Out*. Suddenly I was receiving calls of anguish from clergy and musicians across the theological/denominational spectrum. It seems that conflicts over worship are presently a universal ecclesial plague. Increasingly I was hearing despairing stories of pastors seeking diligently to bridge opposing sides in congregational conflicts and yet finding the people progressively more polarized and intransigent, tragic stories of gifted musicians wounded by pastors telling them their loving service was no longer desirable, searing stories of faithful church professionals being dismissed because their congregations were not mushrooming into mega-churches, horror stories of congregants whose brand-new pastor abruptly threw out all the worship practices that were so meaningful to them (see Chapter 17).

The amount of flak people are getting is appalling. How can we learn to talk together as a community instead? This book is an earnest attempt to stand as a bridge, to offer tools for conversing together across differing viewpoints, and to urge churches to ask better questions before making decisions. Most of all, I pray that we can all learn better to hear first what God is saying.

Flak Is Good for Me

It's the "God" part that is the hardest. We are all too human — and, as a result, even if each of us is trying to hear what God is saying to the churches, we will still misunderstand each other. We will still get flak.

For example, a few reviewers of *Reaching Out* flabbergasted me with their vitriolic response. Even as I inwardly complained about their misreading of my book, however, I realized that if they couldn't see the bridges I was trying to build, then certainly part of the fault was mine.[4] It is hard to pose dialectical poles and urge balancing between them without both sides (in this case, those favoring "contemporary" and those preferring "traditional") reacting critically. So here I will try to offer some bridge boards again.

More important, I will try more truly to serve God by learning that the flak always has merit — to put me in my place at God's feet, to immerse me in the Scriptures afresh, to teach me what I've been overlooking, to raise new questions, to drag me away from stubbornness, to critique my tactlessness, to open up new areas of research, to understand better the pains of those bruised in the battles.

---

4. The description on the back cover of the book in its first printing didn't help either, because it seemed to be one-sided instead of conveying the tone of bridging I was trying to communicate.

Rev. Greg Asimakoupoulos specifically and kindly commented in a written interview that I seemed to emphasize the traditional side more than the contemporary in my efforts at bridging, and he thereby indirectly invited me to be more careful in my explanations. I have certainly never advocated "traditionalism" as some reviewers have charged; that is not my "solution" at all (see Chapter 11). Rather, *Reaching Out* (and this book more so) calls for a process, a discernment by the community, a sorting of the best of new and old. However, because tradition is so often thrown out without much thought or consideration, I have tried to demonstrate its beauty and validity and importance for our times in order to counterbalance the overaccentuation on the "contemporary" in current discussions.

Invaluable Help from the Community of Faith

Still I didn't intend to write another book about worship; I was too busy working on one as an encouragement to church professionals and another on ethics as character formation.[5] But things were not progressing very well with my writing, and my wise friend Marguerite Johnson urged me to take a spiritual retreat and be willing to let God take away these books if they were not the projects in which my time should be invested.

Meanwhile, I had been invited to speak for chapel and to give an endowed lecture at Westminster Choir College in Princeton, New Jersey. There a student's question, "Are we wasting our time here?" in light of declining interest in church organs and choirs led me to entitle my chapel address "A Royal Waste of Time" (see the following chapter). Then Sue Ellen Page, who sang a solo exquisitely in the chapel service, asked me afterwards whether "A Royal Waste of Time" might be a book title some day. My spiritual retreat three and four days later joined her question, prayer and Bible study times, and all the mental rumblings of the previous two years together into the conviction that indeed God was leading me away from the books I had been working on and into another volume on worship. The strongly positive reactions I received when I mentioned it at various conferences during the next few months convinced me that another book was indeed needed. Visiting Ms. Page's masterfully directed choir practices also had assured me that our churches can in-

---

5. These will, I hope, be finished next. They will also be published by Eerdmans and are tentatively entitled *The Sense of the Call: Kingdom* Shalom *for Those Who Serve the Church* and *A World of Difference: An Easter Ethic of Biblical Formation.*

deed teach children good habits of singing, acquaint them with a wide variety of musical styles, and meanwhile deepen their faith and love for God.[6]

I loved the title, *A Royal "Waste" of Time*, with all the focus on the word *royal*. However, such a title can be misunderstood, so the publisher and I went through a long process of experimenting with different titles until we finally came back to *A Royal "Waste" of Time* with a subtitle that will, we pray, prevent any misunderstanding of my intent. I am profoundly grateful to the following persons who were my primary companions in that lengthy process of wrestling through to new insights that made possible the present naming: David Lee Brown and Larry Olson of "Dakota Road," David and Susan Palo Cherwien, Sam Eerdmans, David Hendricksen, Eugene Peterson, my husband Myron Sandberg, and my editor Jennifer Hoffman. Let me add extra thanks for the latter because Jennifer is always able to preserve my theological concerns and my word crafting while still catching and inviting me to correct what is not clear. I am grateful for her diligent work on my manuscript in the midst of her eager anticipation of, and joyous care for, her new child, Thomas William.

Besides all the people named in this introduction, many others have contributed to this book, too many for me to thank them all by name. Countless participants in clergy and musicians' conferences in numerous denominations and locations have asked questions, criticized my lectures, protested my ideas, and grieved with me over the state of Christianity in these times. I have learned much from those who have loved the Church and me enough to pursue conversations, and I pray that in this book I have taken both your disagreements and your stories of woundedness seriously enough to be helpful.

This book is not like any of my others; it is not a developed demonstration, nor a sustained theological argument, but instead a sampling of responses, advances, new ideas from all those discussions since *Reaching Out* came out. Some chapters are expanded versions of articles previously printed; some are essays attempting to explicate a bit of the truth of a particular topic;[7] some are more expressionistic, seeking to give vision and Joy to — and perhaps even an articulation of grief needed by — those who serve the

---

6. Two CDs of children singing hymns well (accompanied by organ, oboe, and/or recorder) are available from St. Paul Lutheran Church, 1126 S. Barr St., Fort Wayne, IN 46802. "O Lord, Open My Lips" and "My Mouth Will Declare Your Praise" are intended to be teaching tools and utilize liturgical elements and hymns from the church year.

7. This wording draws on Wendell Berry's definition of an essayist as "literally, a writer who attempts to tell the truth." Wendell Berry, "Christianity and the Survival of Creation," in *Sex, Economy, Freedom and Community: Eight Essays* (New York: Pantheon Books, 1993), p. 93.

Church. As a result there occurs occasionally (and purposefully) a wee bit of repetition. Some of that duplication has been retained because the article is more cohesive in its original form, which seemed necessary to be preserved even though an idea in it might also appear elsewhere. Some of the repetition has been accentuated because these are ideas not being paid much attention in many worship discussions. The advantage of this book's structure is that it is more flexible so that the reader may skip around to peruse whatever is of greatest interest.[8] The introductions at the beginning of each part will explain why various pieces have been included and how they cohere.

God's Splendor

For a while this book was called *Immersed in Splendor.* I love the baptismal imagery in that phrase — like a plunge into a sapphire mountain lake on a hot day. Even so, worship is a cascade into the ever-flowing surprises of encounters with the immensity of God's magnificence and sublimity and radiance. We have retained the word *splendor* in the subtitle because worship that is a *royal* waste of time will immerse us in the fullness of God's sublime attributes and actions. That is why worship must be filled with all kinds of sounds, new music and old, faithful fountains of praise, powerful retellings of the biblical narratives, an ever-widening river to convey the grandeur of God.

Surely one of the greatest problems of our times is that we have become so nonchalant about the Lord of the cosmos. Certainly if we were more immersed in God's splendor we would find ourselves thoroughly "lost in wonder, love, and praise."[9] With all the amazing sights and sounds of our cyberspace world, however, many of us no longer recognize that if we but catch a glimpse of *GOD* — the imperial Lord of the cosmos, the almighty King of the universe — we will be compelled to fall on our faces. Our awareness of God's absolute otherness would give us the sense that we could die now because we have seen God. We would shout with the prophet, "Woe is me, for I am annihilated" (Isaiah 6:5, Martin Luther's rendering).

The awe and astonishment of God's presence so far beyond us is so immense that we could hardly react with anything less than fear and trembling and the sacrifice of all our lives. Our superhyped culture makes it difficult for

8. I should emphasize, however, that a previous acquaintance with the main contents of *Reaching Out* would be most helpful so that the reader can build on the proposals, questions, and research summarized in that volume.

9. This line is from Charles Wesley's glorious hymn of 1747, "Love Divine, All Loves Excelling."

us to take the immense sovereignty and preeminence of *GOD* seriously; we find it hard to realize that his infinite splendor would overwhelm us if he weren't so gracious as to give us samples of it in small morsels. As with Moses, we really see only God's "back" or the *glory* of where he has been and how he has worked (see Exodus 33:17-23).

Such taking God seriously is, however, decidedly countercultural. We live in an age and a culture that want instead to turn the worship of God into a matter of personal taste and time, convenience and comfort. Consequently, we need the biggest dose of God we can get when we gather for worship on Sunday morning — to shake us out of this societal sloth and somnambulism and summon us to behold God's splendor and respond with adoration and service and sacrifice.

Taking God seriously, being immersed in his splendor, unites us with a community that practices the alternative way of life of following Jesus, of participation in the kingdom of God. That is why I use the phrase *being Church*. When we come to belief or are baptized (my concern here is not to deal with denominational doctrinal differences), the eternal reign of God begins in our life. Thus also begin both the transformation of our character and the responsibility for the whole community to nurture our eschatological life (see Chapters 23 and 31).

Worshiping God

My primary concern in various churches' and denominations' struggles over worship is that so many decisions are being based on criteria other than the most essential — namely, that God be the Subject and Object, the Infinite Center,[10] of our worship. This is the main focus of this book: if we keep God as the center of our worship life and worship-full lives, then we will find

---

10. I am grateful to poet Susan Palo Cherwien for this wonderful paradoxical phrase from one of her hymn texts (not included in her wonderful collection, *O Blessed Spring: Hymns of Susan Palo Cherwien* [Minneapolis: Augsburg Fortress, 1997]). It reminds me of the children's experience when they get to "the real Narnia" in *The Last Battle*, the final book of C. S. Lewis's children's stories about Aslan, who is God in lion form. As they enter this heaven of Aslan's country, they discover that the further up and further in they go, the larger it is.

My addition of the idea of "Infinite Center" to my usual description of God as the Subject/Object of our worship was affirmed recently when a "generation X" young woman questioned my use of the latter in light of postmodern literary theory's rejection of subject and object. I was amazed when she readily accepted my use of "Infinite Center" instead.

countless possibilities, endless resources, innumerable ways to encounter and express God's infinite presence. If our congregations earnestly enter the adventure of weekly gatherings to waste time royally as we explore God's unceasing revelations, then we will stop fighting over the wrong questions, the marketers' opinions, cultural pressures, unbiblical solutions.

Part II of this book includes several chapters calling for renewed centering on God. One of my hopes is that these might lead to a resurrection of wonder in the Church. The society around us certainly does not lack for spiritual yearnings these days; what is missing (even in churches) is the realization that the God of the Bible is infinitely interesting in being uniquely both the source and the goal of those longings.

Being Church

Frequently I find myself saying, in answer to questions at conferences, "Do you see, once again, that the root problem is the lack of genuine community in our churches?" In our highly technicized, scandalously superficial, inordinately busy, and extremely mobile culture, our congregations are fighting tremendous odds against being able to build the kind of community the worship discussions need and the Bible describes — in which we truly live "in common" with each other, growing through being formed by the Scriptures, wasting time to bear each other's burdens, and struggling together to overcome all barriers between human beings.

Parts III through V of this book address the need to learn to BE CHURCH. I use that phrase studiously because the bad theology of our saying "I'm going to church" has affected how Christians live. "Church" has been turned into a place, a building, a duty, an hour on Sunday mornings, rather than *what we are* as "those called out" *(ekklēsia)* by Christ into a way of being in the world to the glory of God for the sake of others. Being Church is living as the Scriptures form us and being part of a community which nurtures that alternative way of life.

We will learn to BE Church more faithfully if we keep God the center of our worship. Then the texts that reveal him will mold us to be his people and his community in his image. Part III, "Community Building," and Part IV, "Character Formation," will discuss some of the issues that need to be reflected upon if the Christian community wants to be a truly alternative society, nurtured in its way of life by the Scriptures.[11] These matters of training

---

11. Other aspects of community building and character formation are addressed much more thoroughly in my books *Truly the Community: Romans 12 and How to Be the*

9

and equipping must be examined before we can engage in the processes of "Choices" outlined in Part V.

For the World

Many of the conflicts concerning worship in churches arise because of differing perspectives on how we can best minister to the world. Some insist that our worship should appeal to the culture; others recognize that we serve our neighbors best by truly being Church and that worship that royally wastes time is one element of the community's life which contributes to equipping us for that service. Part VI will focus specifically on the "Challenges" of being formed and living as Church for the sake of the world.

The world for which we care has to be more thoroughly understood by all of us so that our love can be directed in the best possible ways. For that reason, Part I of this book paints some broad sketches of a few aspects of the culture that make worship in our times both difficult and urgently necessary.

Sample Sermons

Each section of this book begins with a sermon, except Part I (which does not contain one since I believe that sermons should be primarily about God and not about the culture). I inaugurate each major topic with a sermon, not to claim that my sermons are superior, but in order to start our thinking about the topic with God's Word and also to offer suggestions, encouragement to readers, and examples of preaching that are more directly scriptural. What makes the Church unique is that we are formed by the Revelation of God. It seems to me that I don't have very much to say if my preaching, as well as my writing and teaching, does not flow osut of immersion in God's Word.

The sermon that follows this introduction is the one that gave this book its title. Though it was particularly addressed to church musicians, its exhortations apply to all worshipers, so I encourage readers who are not necessarily

---

Church (Grand Rapids: Wm. B. Eerdmans Publishing Co., 1992; reissued 1997) and *Is It a Lost Cause? Having the Heart of God for the Church's Children* (Grand Rapids: Wm. B. Eerdmans Publishing Co., 1997), respectively. In this book I will occasionally footnote my other books to encourage pursuing topics more thoroughly. Since the royalties of all my Eerdmans books are given away for scholarships or to ministries that help the poor, your extended reading will also support this aid.

worship leaders to apply these words to their own engagement in worship, whatever form that might take.

Martin Marty told me recently that Romano Guardini calls worship *"zwecklos aber doch sinnvoll"* — "pointless, however still full of meaning/ signs." This entire book is intended to help us never to lose sight of that paradox, but the initial sermon concentrates on the *"zwecklos"* side. "A Royal Waste of Time" intends to counteract the current push for worship to be the means by which people are attracted to God. Of course, people will be attracted when we worship well, but if we make such *appeal* the focus of worship, then *God* will no longer be. Worship is idolatry unless it is a total waste of time in earthly terms, a total immersion in the eternity of God's infinite splendor for the sole purpose of honoring God. It is my prayer that the One whose splendor fills our corporate praise will draw us through the pages of this book to worship him extravagantly and, as a result, to be his people more faithfully and to serve our neighbors more lavishly.

2

"A Royal Waste of Time": A Sermon for Church Musicians on Colossians 3:12-17*

One of the best habits that we have had in the Church for hundreds of years is using the set of phrases, "The Lord be with you. And also with you." When we say these phrases in worship, we enfold the leader in our prayers and recommit ourselves to the responsibility to support him or her in the ministry he or she is undertaking. Meanwhile we remind ourselves that we are a community together. Since I can't preach well if you don't listen well, please answer my blessing, "The Lord be with you," with a response, "And also with you," that sounds like you mean it. I look forward to your participation with me in this sermon.

The Lord be with you. [Response: And also with you!]

Let us pray: Triune God, illimitably beyond our comprehension, teach us to worship you in Spirit and in truth. We know that we will never be able to praise you as you are worthy to be adored until we join the angels and martyrs of heaven in the eternal bliss of worshiping you. Till then, guide us to faithfulness and fill us with the Joy of your presence, especially in the community gathered at this place and time. May we listen now to your Word, so

*My sermon at Westminster Choir College in Princeton, New Jersey, on January 22, 1998, proceeded somewhat like the following. Since I do not preach from written manuscripts and that sermon was not recorded, this approximation from my outline and memory cannot capture the Spirit of the moment, but it will, at least, set the theme for this book.

12

that we will be changed ever more into the likeness of Jesus Christ our Savior, in whose name we pray. Amen.

It was good that I had the opportunity to be on the Westminster Choir College campus yesterday to get to know some of you and to observe your choir rehearsals so that my words today could be more appropriate to the issues and struggles of this place. Two things happened yesterday that changed how we will listen to the text, Colossians 3:12-17, which you heard a few moments ago.

First, at a lunchtime discussion with Sacred Music Department students, one of you asked, "Are we wasting our time here?" In the light of rapid changes in congregations' attitudes toward worship and of numerous controversies over styles and substance, one might wonder if preparing to serve as a church musician is a waste of time. Why study the heritage of Christian worship music if many congregations are throwing out everything from the past? Why learn to play the organ, to direct a choir, and to sing skillfully if these abilities are no longer useful or desirable?

Second, I watched as a choir practiced and heard its conductor rebuking the singers for losing the glow in their eyes. What will help us regain the fire or spark that comes from enthusiasm for what one is doing? We certainly can't crank up eagerness for something if the ardor isn't there. Too much forced fervor wears us out and lessens our zeal even more.

Because we are Christians we have a better option than pushing ourselves to perform, a choice superior to pretending that we are avid when we really are arid. Our text for today will show us that what we are doing in worship and in preparing to serve churches in worship is, indeed, a royal waste of time — but pay attention to that adjective *royal* — and we will see that this waste of time will light the fire in our eyes and equip us with an unquenchable passion.

Colossians 3:12 begins by naming us the "chosen ones of God, holy, and beloved." What a grace-full trio! God, out of the immensity of his fatherly care and wisdom, has chosen us to be his own and to serve his purposes. He has set us apart as holy instruments through the life and suffering, death and resurrection of Jesus Christ on our behalf. The Holy Spirit has been poured out into our lives and our communities to teach us that we are the beloved of God.

We are not chosen because we are great; we are not holy because we act like it; we are not beloved because we have earned it. God is the one to choose, to call, to sanctify, to grace us. We start with this awareness today because it makes everything we do a *royal waste* of time. *Nothing* that we do, no matter how wonderful we are as musicians or as persons, will change one whit how God feels about us!

As a consequence, we worship God. We respond to the enormity of his grace with praise and skill, with lives of service, with the best music we can make. And that is the most wonderful waste of time possible. It is a lavishing of our lives that fills us with fire. We sing our greatest music, play the new songs of heaven to surprise others and ourselves with the overwhelmingly wonder-full, stunningly awe-full grace of God. Focusing on such a subject, how can we help but be passionate?

We choose the most excellent music we can find. We sing or play it with the finest skill we can gain through practice and development as musicians. We do all that we can to enable all the participants in worship to join in the music of the congregation as fully as possible — but it is all still a waste of time. God will not love us any more or favor us with any greater blessings if we pour out our lives for him, for he already loves us infinitely and blesses us abundantly, far more thoroughly than we could ever imagine or desire.

It is a *royal* waste of time because we are participating in the kingdom of God, into which we have been born and borne by our baptism. God has chosen us to be citizens of his kingdom, set us apart for its purposes, and made us beloved members. And it is a royal *waste of time* because we have to die to ourselves and our egos, our purposes and accomplishments to live now in God's kingdom. As Matthew 10:39 reminds us, only in losing our life — wasting our time — do we truly find it.

After the trio of names for us, Colossians 3:12-15 invites us to put on Christian virtues of compassion, kindness, humility, gentleness, patience, forbearance, forgiveness, love, peace, and thankfulness. How odd we are to be characterized by such attributes! Compare these qualities with their opposites prevalent in the professional world of music. The Trinity forms us with guts of compassion (that is what the Greek literally says) in contrast to the one-upmanship of performers, with kindness rather than the rudeness of some who are famous, with humility instead of arrogance, with love rather than indifference, with forgiveness instead of vengeance, with peacefulness and peacemaking rather than the injustice and conflict that competition breeds, with thankfulness instead of narcissism.

Such virtues certainly are a royal waste of time! They won't get you anywhere in a dog-eat-dog, I'm-more-famous-than-you-are, striving-for-success, got-to-get-ahead world. Gentleness and patience, humility and thankfulness, compassion and kindness, love — these are totally irrelevant in the culture that surrounds us. But they are the language of grace, the culture of faith, the characteristics of the kingdom.

We are formed with such virtues when, as verse 16 invites, the Word of Christ dwells in us richly. What is that Word, and how does it dwell in us, and how do we dwell in it?

Of course, the Word is first and foremost Christ himself, and he dwells in us richly by the power of the Spirit. For us to dwell in God's presence and thereby to be given over to God's presence dwelling within us is to waste our time. Ephesians 5 contrasts it with being filled with wine, which is a totally different kind of time wasting, the life-wasting of debauchery.

One way that we enter into God's presence, of course, is by worship, both personal/devotional and corporate/congregational. Why waste the early morning hours (or whenever) reading your Bible and praying? Why waste Sunday mornings in public worship? Why waste your life practicing to extol God more artistically, or composing new music to celebrate his glory, or rehearsing a choir to lead the congregation's praise? There are a lot more important things to do — relevant work, timely work, work that will get you somewhere. But, my dear brothers and sisters, what a glorious lavishing of our lives we engage in when it is the King of the Universe we are seeking to laud! And all of our music helps us abide in him; our practicing and music analysis and preparation, as well as our reading and studying and praying, all lead us into the splendor of his presence.

There are many fights in churches these days over what kind of music to use, but I am convinced that most of those fights could be avoided if we faithfully reflected upon the questions given to us by the text before us today. Instead of asking what kind of music will appeal to the world around us, we must ask, What will enable us most deeply to dwell in God's Word? What will best express that Word? How will the Word's beauty and mystery, its infinity and generosity be best conveyed?

Verse 16 of Colossians 3 gives us several other questions to eliminate conflicts over worship — and they all relate to this wasting of our time that we are celebrating this morning. If what we are doing by worshiping and by becoming and being church musicians is a waste of time, why do we do it? Verse 16 tells us that it is so that every one of us in the congregation can in all wisdom teach and admonish each other in the Christian community. We are formed by the Word in which we dwell to have the virtues of the previous verses and thereby to be a community that cares about each other. You and I — in relation to those searching for God, in relation to the parishioners we serve — offer the wisdom of our training in order to teach and admonish them. We engage in music that will not only enfold the congregation in the grace of the God who chose us, but that will also instill in them an understanding of what it is to worship that God. Our music will instruct, educate, nurture, cultivate, rebuke, exhort, discipline, warn, delight, enlighten, edify, develop. We waste our time so that others in the Christian community can be more profoundly immersed in the Word, can become more deeply formed, can more thoroughly join us in praise. Others in our churches might not be ready to waste their time; that is why you musicians have to be here — to help them give up control and become immersed in Christ.

With what kind of music do we do this? Again our text frees us from conflicts, for verse 16 urges us to teach and admonish with psalms, hymns, and spiritual songs. Rather than letting us debate about styles, this text suggests a wide range for our faithfulness. The word *psalms* undoubtedly refers to the origins of our Christian worship in the First Testament[1] poems, written for synagogue and Temple (as indicated by the frequent title, "To the Chief Musician") and collected primarily in the book of Psalms (and also in other poetic portions, most notably Isaiah). The new Presbyterian hymnal, as one example, contains a wonderful array of settings for most of the psalms.

Next, we are urged to use hymns, a word that points to the development of specifically Christian songs in the traditions of faith. The New Testament contains many of the earliest hymns, such as Philippians 2:5-10 ("Let the same mind be in you that was in Christ Jesus . . ."), 1 Timothy 3:16 ("And by common confession, great is the mystery of godliness . . . ," NASV), 2 Timothy 2:11-13 ("It is a trustworthy statement . . . ," NASV), perhaps John 1:1-14 ("In the beginning was the Word . . ."), and of course all the hymns in the book of Revelation ("Worthy is the Lamb that was slaughtered to receive power and wealth and wisdom and might and honor and glory and blessing!" [5:12]). But these are just the first in a long and magnificent line of hymns, from all epochs, including our own.

Finally, what are spiritual songs? Were they new expressions of praise composed at the moment — or ecstatic utterances? We cannot be certain, but what we do know is that God cannot be contained in what we already know. There is always a need for new compositions, new settings of old texts and new texts for old melodies, new arrangements, new instrumentations, new expressions of the infinitely incomprehensible God. Our choices and creations will be guided by the exhortation in Colossians 3:16 that we use these spiritual songs to teach and admonish each other. All our music will help believers learn the language of faith and what worship is.

---

1. I prefer to call the first three-fourths of the Bible the "First Testament" or the "Hebrew Scriptures," to avoid our culture's negative connotations of the name *Old* Testament and to emphasize both the consistency of God's grace for his people and the continuity of the covenants in the Bible with Israel and then also Christians.

Another conflict over worship is prevented — and another waste of time outlined — by the final phrase in verse 16 persuading us to sing with gratitude in our hearts. It is important to recognize that the word *heart* in the Bible means much more than emotions. The New Testament writers would use the word *bowels* if a greater emphasis on feelings was intended (and the First Testament writers would use the word *kidneys*). The word *heart* connotes instead our will and intentionality. Thus, this phrase suggests that we can sing praise to God whether we feel like it or not, that we will deliberately celebrate who God is simply because he is worthy of our adoration. It doesn't say anything about whether we even like the song or if it makes us feel good!

Moreover, the phrase tells us to sing "under the inspiration of grace" (as the French Bible renders it) and not with vocal chords. The original Greek might be translated "singing with your wills to God in his grace." This is important, for it prohibits us from performing, from glorying merely in the holiness of the beauty we produce, rather than the beauty of God's holiness. The former is mere aestheticism for its own sake; the latter is beauty in order to display the splendor of God.

Finally, Colossians 3:17 says, "whatever you do, in word or deed, do everything in the name of the Lord Jesus, giving thanks to God the Father through him." That is a supreme call to wasting our time and to passion, for words and deeds said and done in the name of Jesus signify exhibiting his character — and he was indeed the supreme waster of time, condescending to give up his equality with God to humble himself and become a servant all the way to the point of dying an ignoble and excruciating death. We are invited to waste our time dying to ourselves and then using our training and skills to gift the Church with the finest music by means of the character — the openness and hospitality and generosity — of Christ. It is the ultimate time waster — that we engage in music not for ourselves and our fame and fortune, but for the glory of God.

Worship is a royal waste of time that spirals into passion for living as Christians and back into more passionate worship. It is totally irrelevant, not efficient, not powerful, not spectacular, not productive, sometimes not even satisfying to us. It is also the only hope for changing the world.

PART I

For the World: The Culture

Ascribe to the LORD the glory of his name;
worship the LORD in holy splendor.

Psalm 29:2

Each part of this book will consider an aspect of the theme verse above because to worship in such a way will truly be the royal waste of time the
LORD calls forth. It may seem strange to begin with observations concerning
the culture, but if we think about all that God is, we recognize the immensity
of his love for the world. If by our worship we want to immerse our neighbors
in the lavish splendor of God, then we must understand them more deeply
than we often do. Many of the bad decisions that are made about worship
touch only the surface needs of our society and not the hidden influences or
powerful forces that make true worship both difficult and essential.

If we understand the genuine needs of our neighbors, we will see that
the best gift we could offer them is our faithfulness in royally wasting our
time in worship. To be immersed in the prodigal splendor of God will lead us,
in turn, to lavish extravagant care on the world.

In this section of the book we will ask crucial questions about the kind
of culture in which we live. My book *Reaching Out without Dumbing Down*
broached the subject of our television, boomer, postmodern culture, but its
introduction to the issues raised by the media and postmodernism barely
scratched the surface. We can't do a full-length treatment of these cultural
subjects here either, but at least we will explore further some dimensions of

the world around our churches. First, in Chapter 3 we will listen to a "generation X" writer describe in fiction form the deepest needs of human beings in our culture — and we will note the Church's gifts in response to those needs. Then Chapters 4 and 5 will examine more closely our postmodern society's need for a master narrative, for truth, for genuine community.

Chapters 6 and 7 will discuss more thoroughly the destructive effects of television and consumerism on our churches and their worship. These chapters will call for setting limits and, beyond that, for the Christian community to be an alternative society that offers other possibilities to our neighbors.

3

The Needs of Our Being

"For God so loved the world that he gave his only Son, so that everyone who believes in him may not perish but may have eternal life."

John 3:16

L et us take seriously the immense love of God for his cosmos and discover how best that love can be displayed, explained, and incarnated so that our neighbors can be immersed in it. How will our worship be part of that enfolding?

Many of the arguments in congregational conflicts over worship are raised in terms of the needs of our neighbors and how churches can meet those needs. Some of those usually listed are such things as the need for the music to be totally accessible to everyone, for the absence of anything like the mention of sin that might alienate anyone, for attractive nursery facilities, and for adequate parking. (Other needs not related to worship that are usually listed are support groups for young mothers, a "dynamic and exciting" youth program, day-care services, and plenty of entertaining events for young adult singles.)

I do agree that we need to consider such options (with the exception of avoiding any mention of sin), and if true love for our neighbors is best manifested through any of them our congregations would do well to pursue them.

However, in all the fuss over such surface needs, we often miss the deep spiritual needs of all human beings.

In an article on "Cross-Multicultures in the Crossfire: The Humanities and Political Interests," Martin E. Marty suggests that multicultures within the larger society are "products of response to [the following] four needs in the late modern world":

> *identity:* the need to answer, "who am I?" . . .
>
> *loyalty:* the need to spell out, "to whom do I belong?" Whom shall I trust? . . .
>
> *values:* the need to answer, "by what shall I live?" What do I pass on to my children? What would I like to see prevail in respect to the true, the beautiful, and the good? . . .
>
> *power:* the need to answer, "how can I protect myself?" or "how can I make my way over against others?" How do I throw off the oppressor and how can I be free?[1]

I have not included Marty's descriptions of how these needs are met by subculture groupings because I am convinced that even such communities are in the end insufficient, for this list of four designates some of the deepest human yearnings, which can be satisfied only by the One who has created them.

As St. Augustine said so long ago, "Oh, Lord, Thou hast made us for Thyself, and our hearts are restless until they rest in Thee." It seems to me that this list of four needs is a good beginning for considering why the Church has before it an opportune moment as we serve the world of the twenty-first century. However, I feel compelled to add three more needs to the list:

> *a master story:* the need to answer, "how does it all fit together?" or "to what larger narrative do I belong?" How can I have an extended history, a longer story than my own by which to get my bearings?
>
> *meaning:* the need to be able to answer, "why should I live?" What really gives my life purpose, so that it is worth the effort?
>
> *hope:* the need to answer, "how can there be a future?" What enables me to cope with the economic and political messes of our times, the tensions of my own life, the struggles to go on?

1. Martin E. Marty, "Cross-Multicultures in the Crossfire: The Humanities and Political Interests," *Christianity and Culture in the Crossfire,* ed. David A. Hoekema and Bobby Fong (Grand Rapids: Wm. B. Eerdmans Publishing Co., 1997), p. 17.

These three and the four that Marty identified seem to me to be the core questions of human existence. Everywhere they are manifested — in movies, novels, rock songs, and conversations on airplanes, in good and bad methods of responding to them, in the poignant cries and nihilistic despair of those who can't find any answers.

To give us a deeper awareness of the universality of these seven questions, we need to hear from a candid conversation partner, so I will use excerpts from Douglas Coupland's *Generation X: Tales for an Accelerated Culture*.[2] The book jacket declares that this is a novel about the "underemployed, overeducated, intensely private, longing for a home" generation, but the undergirding longings demonstrated could be equally illustrated by remarks from the unemployed, the undereducated, gang members, those with exclusive homes or the homeless — and also by literature from any other generation.[3] I am convinced that worship immersed in God's splendor will meet these deep needs, especially if that worship entails the whole Church as a true community and the whole of the Scriptures as they form us with all their depth.

1. Identity: Who Am I?

Coupland's novel is an account of three people in their 20s and 30s — Andy (the narrator), Claire, and Dagmar (usually called Dag) — who have left their previous jobs for reasons of disillusionment and disgust. They wind up in the same community and become a true family to each other, but as the novel opens they have shared an afternoon together, though they all remained somewhat aloof. Afterward, Andy remarks concerning such looking at life from a distance that

2. Recently, when I tested this chapter at a professional church leaders' conference by reading some of the following excerpts and discussing them in terms of the Church's gifts, six young pastors and pastoral interns — all members of "Generation X" — affirmed this use of the literature and exclaimed that they see in their friends and other peers the yearnings these excerpts display.

3. Please note that I am not advocating dividing ministry by generations (see Chapter 15 especially). I simply use this literature as one example. When an older pastor at the conference mentioned in the previous footnote inquired if Generation Xers are simply louder whiners than other generations, I realized that their basic needs, though the same as those of other generations, arise from different cultural pressures and are expressed in different ways. A primary difference is that their cultural milieu is postmodern (see the following two chapters), whereas all older generations grew up primarily in the modern (and even premodern in some aspects) world.

The carapace of coolness is too much for Claire, also. She breaks the silence by saying that it's not healthy to live life as a succession of isolated little cool moments. "Either our lives become stories, or there's just no way to get through them."

I agree. Dag agrees. We know that this is why the three of us left our lives behind us and came to the desert — to tell stories and to make our own lives worthwhile tales in the process.[4]

One need hardly comment on the deep yearning depicted in these paragraphs.

What we must note instead is the way churches are failing to enfold worship participants in the sense that their identity can be found best if God is the focus of their existence. Against all the pressures in our culture — in advertisements, status, position, power, or whatever else — to find ourselves, the most beautiful identity imaginable is that of the baptized child of God. How profound it is if our worship conveys deeply to all the participants that they are the beloved of God!

Of course, we don't convey that simply by declaring that God loves us. We learn it from the details of God's interventions on our behalf — for example, that "God so loved the world that he gave his only Son." We know it best, as the first letter of John tells us, through the cross. "In this is love," the epistle says, "not that we loved God but that he loved us and sent his Son to be the atoning sacrifice for our sins" (1 John 4:10). When our worship services are filled with particulars about God's splendor, then those who are present find their "own lives worthwhile tales in the process" of discovering God's presence in them.

A wonderful story is told of a wealthy Scottish nobleman, richly attired, who was riding his magnificent horse and came beside a poor peasant, dressed in rags, who was kneeling in the mud and praying. "You must be close to God," the lord scoffed. "Aye," the peasant responded with unmistakable bliss, "He is very fond of me." What Joy worship bestows when it conveys this identity!

2. Master Story: How Does It All Fit Together?

The answer to the question "who am I?" is made deeper when we are part of a larger story stretching through time. Jean-François Lyotard, one of the pre-

4. Douglas Coupland, *Generation X: Tales for an Accelerated Culture* (New York: St. Martin's Press, 1991), p. 8. Page references to this book in the rest of this chapter are given parenthetically in the text.

eminent postmodern philosophers, emphasizes that the postmodern condition increasingly manifest in our world includes three transformational trajectories, only one of which concerns us at this point. (The other two are the changes in the directions of the aesthetic and the political.) Our concern here is for the present course of epistemological perspectives (dealing with the question of "how we know what we know"), for our times are characterized by great incredulity toward meta-narratives (or master stories; see Chapter 4 below). Lyotard notes that instead of entailing larger stories, contemporary life is reduced to many language games, with the result that history is slashed into ambiguity and time into chaos.[5]

This searching for a larger story is demonstrated especially in two incidents in *Generation X*.[6] In the first, Andy, at home (where he would really rather not be) for Christmas, has bought an enormous number of candles and arranges them, lighted, throughout the living room early on Christmas morning. As his family enters the room they react with immense wonder.

> "Oh, Andy," says my mother, sitting down. "Do you know what this is like? It's like the dream everyone gets sometimes — the one where you're in your house and you suddenly discover a new room that you never knew was there. But once you've seen the room you say to yourself, '*Oh, how obvious — of course that room is there. It always has been.*'"
>
> Tyler [Andy's brother] and Dad sit down, with the pleasing clumsiness of jackpot lottery winners. "It's a video, Andy," says Tyler, "a total video."
>
> But there is a problem.
>
> Later on life reverts to normal. The candles slowly snuff themselves out and normal morning life resumes. Mom goes to fetch a pot of coffee; Dad deactivates the actinium heart of the smoke detectors to preclude a sonic disaster; Tyler loots his stocking and demolishes his gifts. ("New skis! I can die now!")
>
> But I get this feeling —
>
> It is a feeling that our emotions, while wonderful, are transpiring in a vacuum, and I think it boils down to the fact that we're middle class.
>
> You see, when you're middle class, you have to live with the fact that history will ignore you. You have to live with the fact that history can never

5. See Jean-François Lyotard, *The Postmodern Condition,* trans. Geoff Bennington and Brian Massumi, Theory and History of Literature 10 (Minneapolis: University of Minnesota Press, 1984).

6. In responding to these excerpts, my "generation X" conversation partners at the clergy conference emphasized that Xers never had, as their parents did, a master narrative to rebel against. Many of them don't even want any sort of larger story because such stories seem only to cause enormous pain.

champion your causes and that history will never feel sorry for you. It is the price that is paid for day-to-day comfort and silence. And because of this price, all happinesses are sterile; all sadnesses go unpitied.

And any small moments of intense, flaring beauty such as this morning's will be utterly forgotten, dissolved by time like a super-8 film left out in the rain, without sound, and quickly replaced by thousands of silently growing trees. (146-47)

How different it is to know that all our moments of intense beauty or repulsiveness, sadness or gladness are known to God in the master story of his people. God cares about the depression of Elijah (1 Kings 19) and tells us about it to give us insight for the practical gifts to offer (food and rest and hope) to those who are despondent. God cares intimately for our tears, and they are never forgotten, for they are stored in his bottles (Psalm 56:8).[7]

In the second incident, Andy and his brother visit the Vietnam Memorial in Portland, Oregon, and he is surprised at the potency of his sentimental reaction.

Okay, *yes,* I think to myself, they *were* ugly times. But they were also the only times I'll ever get — genuine capital *H* history times, before *history* was turned into a press release, a marketing strategy, and a cynical campaign tool. And *hey,* it's not as if I got to see much real history, either — I arrived to see a concert in history's arena just as the final set was finishing. But I saw enough, and today, in the bizarre absence of all time cues, I need a connection to a past of some importance, however wan the connection. (157)

But Andy has contradicted himself. Earlier in the book, when he describes the event that triggered his escape from his excellent job, he recounts,

Breathing stentorously, as though I had just vandalized a house, I fled the building, without even collecting my things . . . and that night I packed my bags. . . . Two days later I was back in Oregon, back in the New World, breathing less crowded airs, but I knew even then that there was still too much history there for me. That I needed *less* in life. Less past.

So I came down here, to breathe dust and walk with the dogs — to look

7. These passages are explicated in chapter 10, "Emotional Rest," of Marva J. Dawn, *Keeping the Sabbath Wholly: Ceasing, Resting, Embracing, Feasting* (Grand Rapids: Wm. B. Eerdmans Publishing Co., 1989), pp. 72-77, and in chapter 10, "Our God Records Our Tears," of Marva J. Dawn, *I'm Lonely, Lord — How Long? Meditations on the Psalms,* rev. ed. (Grand Rapids: Wm. B. Eerdmans Publishing Co., 1998), pp. 65-70, respectively.

at a rock or a cactus and know that I am the first person to see that cactus and that rock. And to try and read the letter inside me. (58-59)

It is painful history, disillusioning history that Andy rejects. He needs a hopeful history that gives him a viable frame of reference for learning who he *identity* is (the letter inside of him).

What good news it is for those searching for connections to hear that they are part of a wonderful history of grace, a genuine meta-narrative (see Chapter 4) of a promising God who always keeps his promises! Our worship is the practicing of our history by a people who remember, and this master story (of which we declare some of the parts each week) gives us, over time, a frame of reference in which to understand ourselves and to know more profoundly the splendor of God's presence in our worship and lives.

3. Loyalty: To Whom Do I Belong? Whom Shall I Trust?

The master story of God and his people convinces us that God can be trusted, that belonging to him will be fulfilling and salutary and gratifying. Furthermore, the master story invites us to trust God's people and to belong to his community, for even in their failures there is an antidote in repentance and forgiveness.

Generation X, in contrast, records the agony of those searching for intimacy. Andy declares early in the novel,

All looks with strangers became the unspoken question, "Are *you* the stranger who will rescue me?" Starved for affection, terrified of abandonment, I began to wonder if sex was really just an excuse to look deeply into another human being's eyes. (30)

The novel is a truly postmodern book with various kinds of typefaces lumped together and all sorts of captions and boxes on the side with definitions that don't necessarily tie in with the story. Several of these annotations, of which the following are samples, demonstrate the immense human need for loyalty and the overwhelming failure of our present society to build genuine intimacy:[8]

---

8. On this point, see chapters 1 and 2, "Our Society's Pain and Its Sexual Coping" and "The True Source of Pain," of Marva J. Dawn, *Sexual Character: Beyond Technique to Intimacy* (Grand Rapids: Wm. B. Eerdmans Publishing Co., 1993), pp. 3-19.

CULT OF ALONENESS: The need for autonomy at all costs, usually at the expense of long-term relationships. Often brought about by overly high expectations of others. (69)

TERMINAL WANDERLUST: A condition common to people of transient middle-class upbringings. Unable to feel rooted in any one environment, they move continually in the hopes of finding an idealized sense of community in the next location. (171)

Surely the most poignant expression of the yearning for intimacy in Douglas Coupland's novel is Andy's closing description of the day when he joined a large number of cars in stopping by the highway to look at the contrast between fire-blackened fields and a "cocaine white egret" that had come for the reptiles the charred fields would bring forth. Soon the people watching were joined by a dozen mentally retarded teenagers and their driver.

The bird was circling the field, and it seemed to me to belong more to the Ganges or the Nile rather than to America. And its jet-white contrast with the carbonized field was so astounding, so extreme, as to elicit gasps audible to me from most all of my neighbors, even those parked quite far down the road.

Then the reactions of my giggly, bouncy teenage neighbors became charmed and unified, as though they were watching a fireworks volley. They were *oohing* and *aahing* as the bird and its impossibly long hairy neck simply *refused* to land, circling and circling, effecting arcs and breathtaking swoops. Their enthusiasm was contagious, and I found myself, much to their great pleasure, *oohing* and *aahing* along, too.

And then the bird circled in retreat, westward, just down the road from us. We thought its culinary meditations were over, and there were mild *boos*. Then suddenly, the egret altered its arc. We quickly and excitedly realized that it was going to swoop right over *us*. We felt chosen.

One of the teens squealed alarmingly with delight. This caused me to look over in their direction. At that very moment, time must have accelerated slightly. Suddenly the children were turning to look at *me*, and I felt something sharp drag across my head, there was a *swoop swoop swoop* sound. The egret had grazed my head — it [sic] claw had ripped my scalp. I fell to my knees, but I didn't remove my eyes from the bird's progress.

All of us, in fact, turned our heads in unison and continued to watch our white visitor land in the field, occupying a position of absolute privilege. We watched, entranced, as it began to tug small creatures from the soil, and such was the moment's beauty that I essentially forgot I had been cut. Only when I idly reached up to brush fingers over my scalp to bring down a drop of blood on my finger did I realize the directness of the bird's contact.

I stood up and was considering this drop of blood when a pair of small fat arms grabbed around my waist, fat arms bearing fat dirty hands tipped with cracked fingernails. It was one of the mentally retarded teenagers, a girl in a sky blue calico dress, trying to pull my head down to her level. I could see her long, streaky, fine blond hair from my height, and she was drooling somewhat as she said, *urrd*, meaning bird, several times.

I bowed down on my knees again before her while she inspected my talon cut, hitting it gently with an optimistic and healing staccato caress — it was the faith-healing gesture of a child consoling a doll that has been dropped.

Then, from behind me I felt another pair of hands as one of her friends joined in. Then another pair. Suddenly I was dog-piled by an instant family, in their adoring, healing, uncritical embrace, each member wanting to show their affection more than the other. They began to hug me — too hard — as though I *were* a doll, unaware of the strength they exerted. I was being winded — crushed — pinched and trampled.

The man with the beard [their driver] came over to yank them away. But how could I explain to him, this well-intentioned gentleman, that this discomfort, no this *pain*, I was experiencing was no problem at all, that in fact, this crush of love was unlike anything I had ever known.

Well, maybe he *did* understand. He removed his hands from his wards as though they were giving him small static shocks, allowing them to continue crushing me with their warm assault of embraces. The man then pretended to watch the white bird feeding in the black field.

I can't remember whether I said thank you. (178-79)

That is how the novel ends, except for three pages of statistics such as these:

% of men aged 25-29 never married in 1970 = 19
% of men aged 25-29 never married in 1987 = 42. (181)

% of U.S. 18-29 year-olds who answered "no" to the question, "Would you like to have a marriage like the one your parents had?" = 55. (183)

And that *is* how the book ends.

Many young adults in our society, having grown up in broken or angry homes or with parents who were more concerned to make money than to nurture their children, are starved for the true love that only God can give. If our worship is truly immersed in the splendor of God, then his love for everyone will be readily apparent to all who come searching for it. If our congregations can truly be Church — that is, genuine communities of the beloved of

God — then we have immense gifts to offer those yearning to be enfolded in trustworthy intimacy.

4. Values: By What Shall I Live?

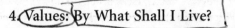

That many young adults in our society are disgusted with the rampant consumerism of our culture is evident in many incidents in *Generation X*. At one point one of the characters asks,

> "You mean to tell me we can drive all the way here from L.A. and see maybe ten thousand square miles of shopping malls, and you don't have maybe just the *weensiest* inkling that something, somewhere, has gone *very very* cuckoo?" (62)

Similarly, many of the side-boxed definitions and aphorisms reveal the author's contempt for contemporary values and his yearning for some alternatives. Here is a sampling:

> YUPPIE WANNABE'S: An X generation subgroup that believes the myth of a yuppie life-style being both satisfying and viable. Tend to be highly in debt, involved in some form of substance abuse, and show a willingness to talk about Armageddon after three drinks. (91)

> You must choose between pain and drudgery. (62)

> RECREATIONAL SLUMMING: The practice of participating in recreational activities of a class one perceives as lower than one's own: *Karen! Donald! Let's go bowling tonight! And don't worry about shoes . . . apparently you can rent them.*
> CONVERSATIONAL SLUMMING: The self-conscious enjoyment of a given conversation precisely for its lack of intellectual rigor. A major spin-off activity of *Recreational Slumming.*
> OCCUPATIONAL SLUMMING: Taking a job well beneath one's skill or education level as a means of retreat from adult responsibilities and/or avoiding possible failure in one's true occupation. (113)

In the book's narrative, when Andy finds himself stuck in his parents' home with nothing desirable to engage his attention, he complains,

> The phone is no friend; Portland is Deadsville at the moment. My friends are all either married, boring, and depressed; single, bored, and depressed;

or moved out of town to avoid boredom and depression. And some of them have bought houses, which has to be the kiss of death, personality-wise. When someone tells you they've just bought a house, they might as well tell you they no longer have a personality. You can immediately assume so many things: that they're locked into jobs they hate; that they're broke; that they spend every night watching videos; that they're fifteen pounds overweight; that they no longer listen to new ideas. It's profoundly depressing. And the *worst* part of it is that people in their houses don't even *like* where they're living. What few happy moments they possess are those gleaned from dreams of *upgrading*. (143)

We might label Andy's comments as arrogant and contemptuous,[9] but we can't help but hear in them the cry for something besides possessions to offer one a worthwhile way of life.

On the same page as the "Yuppie Wannabe" definition above, the book's narrative involves Elvissa (the name given her by Andy) asking a small group of companions,

"I want you to tell me something first: after you're dead and buried and floating around whatever place we go to, what's going to be your best memory of earth? . . . What one moment for you defines what it's like to be alive on this planet? What's your *takeaway*? . . . Fake yuppie experiences that you had to spend money on, like white water rafting or elephant rides in Thailand, don't count. I want to hear some small moment from your life that *proves you're really alive.*"

After a long, thoughtful silence Claire answers, "Snow" (91). Then almost all the persons gathered go on to tell stories — each one involving a time of genuine intimacy with someone in their childhood. The point is obvious: the way of life for which so many search is one embracing very real relationships and providing the opportunity to develop them. Moreover, one's way of life must set a person free to use his or her gifts and set suitable priorities.

Being Church offers such a way of life — developing the believers' character rather than simply talking about values. I have never liked the word *values,* probably because in my earliest years of working for churches the latest fad (already fading) was to do "values clarification" exercises with our

9. As my young pastor friends stressed in conversations, these comments certainly don't condemn house-buying in general. What young people resent in their peers is the smug "I've made it; I've got enough money" or even "I've done better than you" attitude that buying a house frequently implies. They also object to the isolation of watching videos, of "cocooning."

youth groups, and I discovered that no values were clarified. Instead, young people were merely encouraged to pool their ignorances, rather than being mentored by those experienced in the faith to know the wisdom and wealth and wholeness of following Christ.

If our worship is continually focused on God as the Center of our existence, then those of us who are gathered learn the habits of God's people — practices like generosity, nonviolence, hospitality, and the thoroughly royal time wasting of Sabbath keeping. There is no need for "slumming" in this way of life, for we are set free to use our gifts without fear or hiding. Those who participate in this way of life are really alive (not at all stuck in Deadsville) because of the Resurrection and all its implications for daily living. Sharing in the reign of God, we cultivate the beliefs and ethics of his kingdom.

5. Power: How Can I Protect Myself? How Can I Make My Way over against Others?

Participating in God's reign also comforts us with the assurance that we do not need to protect ourselves, that instead God will make a future for us. In contrast, many of the incidents and definitions in *Generation X* demonstrate two major fears on the part of its protagonists.

The first is our society's undergirding fear of nuclear war (which hasn't lessened, of course, with the downfall of the Soviet empire, since so many smaller powers are itching to display their weaponry and engage in terrorism). The long account at the end of section 3 above began with Andy seeing a large mushroom cloud, which he thought signaled the end of the world until he discovered that it was caused by the burning of the fields. Similarly, one of the side-boxes defines "MENTAL GROUND ZERO" as "The location where one visualizes oneself during the dropping of the atomic bomb; frequently, a shopping mall" (63).

The other major fear in the novel is of the pain that vulnerability might entail. These definitions express the anxiety:

KNEE-JERK IRONY: The tendency to make flippant ironic comments as a reflexive matter of course in everyday conversation.
DERISION PREEMPTION: A life-style tactic; the refusal to go out on any sort of emotional limb so as to avoid mockery from peers. *Derision Preemption* is the main goal of *Knee-Jerk Irony*.
FAME-INDUCED APATHY: The attitude that no activity is worth pursuing unless one can become very famous pursuing it. *Fame-induced Apathy* mimics laziness, but its roots are much deeper. (150)

It is those deeper roots in fear that only perfect love can cast out (1 John 4:19). The Good News of the kingdom is that our power for survival is the power of truth and forgiveness, that our freedom is not set over against others but is for their sake. Our master narrative shows us repeatedly how God delivers his people from their terrors and tempters, their foes and fears. Furthermore, we are part of an entire community of caring, members of the body formed to be Church, so that we will be supported in very practical ways through the various struggles of our lives.

6. Meaning: What Is the Purpose of My Life?

Human fears are also directly related to the quest for meaning. We fear most what will rob us of purpose in our existence. *Generation X* includes this report of a dream about the final nuclear bomb attack:

> "And that's that. In the silent rush of hot wind, like the opening of a trillion oven doors that you've been imagining since you were six, it's all over: kind of scary, kind of sexy, and tainted by regret. A lot like life, wouldn't you say?" (64)

The lack of answers to the previous five questions in this chapter also contributes to the poverty of purpose in our society. Having no trusted mentors to guide them, not knowing who they are or how they fit into a larger story, many young people search in vain for a reason to live. Andy gives this description of Dag's arrival after Dag has been missing for awhile (the typesetting eccentricities here are those of the novel):

> Dag has just driven in and looks like something the doggies pulled out of the dumpsters of Cathedral City. His normally pink cheeks are a dove gray, and his chestnut hair has the demented mussed look of a random sniper poking his head out from a burger joint and yelling, "I'll never surrender." We can see all of this the moment he walks in the door — he's totally wired and he hasn't been sleeping. I'm concerned, and from the way Claire nervously changes her hold on her cigarette I can tell she's worried, too. Still, Dag looks happy, which is all anyone can ask for, but why does his happiness look so, so — su*spicious?* ¶*I think I know why.* ¶I've seen this flavor of happiness before. It's of the same phylum of unregulated relief and despondent giggliness I've seen in the faces of friends returning from half-years spent in Europe — faces showing relief at being able to indulge in big cars, fluffy white towels, and California produce once more, but faces also gear-

ing up for the inevitable "what-am-I-going-to-do-with-my-life?" semi-clinical depression that almost always bookends a European pilgrimage. ¶*Uh oh.* (73)

What will we do with our lives? When God is the Infinite Center of them, we discover unequivocally that our purpose is "to love God and serve him forever." Our worship and adoration form us then to be Church in order to reach out to the world. Our work, even if not the most suitable to our skills, becomes an opportunity to spread the reign of God; our leisure activities become filled with the delight of participating in foretastes of God's perfect Joy. There is no lack of meaning in anything if our lives rest in God's hands.

7. Hope: Why Should I Go On?

The threat of nuclear annihilation has been one of the most important sources of our culture's hopelessness, but even that anxiety points to other reasons for our society's nihilism and despair, as these conversations from *Generation X* reveal:

> "You know all of this sex gossip and end-of-the-world nonsense, I wonder if they're really only confessing something else to each other."
> "Like?"
> "Like how scared sick they all are. I mean, when people start talking seriously about hoarding cases of Beef-a-Roni in the garage and get all misty-eyed about the Last Days, then it's about as striking a confession as you're ever likely to get of how upset they are that life isn't working out the way they thought it would." (37)

> [Andy in conversation with Dag about his parents:] "Accept them as a part of getting you to here, and get on with life. Write them off as a business expense. At least your parents talk about Big Things. *I* try and talk about things like nuclear issues that matter to me with my parents and it's like I'm speaking Bratislavan. They listen indulgently to me for an appropriate length of time, and then after I'm out of wind, they ask me why I live in such a God-forsaken place like the Mojave Desert and how my love life is. Give parents the tiniest of confidences and they'll use them as crowbars to jimmy you open and rearrange your life with no perspective. Sometimes I'd just like to mace them. I want to tell them that I envy their upbringings that were so clean, so free of *futurelessness*. And I want to throttle them for

blithely handing over the world to us like so much skid-marked underwear." (86)[10]

[Tyler questioning his brother Andy:] "What do you *do* down there, anyway? You don't have a TV. You don't have any friends —" ¶"I do, *too*, have friends, Tyler." ¶"Okay, so you have friends. But I worry about you. That's all. You seem like you're only skimming the surface of life, like a water spider — like you have some secret that prevents you from entering the mundane everyday world. . . . [after a bit of interchange] *Just don't leave me behind.* That's all. I know — it looks as if I enjoy what's going on with my life and everything, but listen, my heart's only half in it. You give my friends and me a bum rap but I'd give *all* of this up in a *flash* if someone had an even remotely plausible alternative."

"Tyler, *stop.*"

"I just get so *sick* of being jealous of everything. Andy —" There's no stopping the boy. " — And it scares me that I don't see a future. And I don't understand this reflex of mine to be such a smartass about everything. It *really* scares me. I may not look like I'm paying any attention to anything, Andy, but I am. But I can't allow myself to show it. And I don't know why." (149-50)

Into the midst of such disillusionment, hopelessness, jealousy, and futurelessness, the Church speaks the alternative Word of eschatology — a dependable story about the future and the meanwhile. Instead of "hoarding cases of Beef-a-Roni in the garage," God's people lay up treasures for themselves in heaven, "where neither moth nor rust consumes and where thieves do not break in and steal" (Matt. 6:20) — nor do bombs detonate.

The modern scientific age rather completely chased heaven out of the Christian vocabulary, but it seems to me that now is a critical time to recover this "word of power," for God's heaven is neither fairy-tale nonsense nor the illusion of the simple. Paradise is the promise of the One whose presence creates it. It is the perfect fulfillment of the genuine hope our world craves.

The seven needs introduced in this chapter are incontrovertibly not superficial, for they manifest the deepest human search for God.[11] Nor are the an-

10. Of course, all generations have complained and blamed their troubles on the previous generations. One difference now is that young people today live in constant awareness that the bombs of Hiroshima and Nagasaki ushered us into an entirely new era characterized for the first time by the possibility of destroying the whole world.

11. See the explication of *Sehnsucht* (or "longing") in chapter 6, "The Cry of Human *Sehnsucht*," in Marva J. Dawn, *To Walk and Not Faint: A Month of Meditations on*

swers in the Christian faith merely cursory, though my mention of them has been just a brief sketch in order to delineate themes to be developed in future chapters of this book. In the next chapter we will look particularly at the attempts generated by our postmodern times to satisfy spiritual needs and how we must be Church in response. If our worship of God will ultimately serve the world around us, then we dare not give its participants any less than the fullness of God, the faithfulness of God's people, and the future of God's story.

Isaiah 40, 2nd ed. (Grand Rapids: Wm. B. Eerdmans Publishing Co., 1997), pp. 33-44, and throughout my book, *Is It a Lost Cause? Having the Heart of God for the Church's Children* (Grand Rapids: Wm. B. Eerdmans Publishing Co., 1997).

4

Pop Spirituality or Genuine Story?
The Church's Gifts for Postmodern Times*

> Those who believe are the descendants of Abraham. And the scripture, foreseeing that God would justify the Gentiles by faith, declared the gospel beforehand to Abraham, saying, "All the Gentiles shall be blessed in you." For this reason, those who believe are blessed with Abraham who believed.
>
> Galatians 3:7-9

W e hear or see the word *spirituality* thrown around frequently in conversations and in the media these days, but that term has become so ambiguous as to be meaningless. How would the various forms of popular spirituality in our culture compare with the faith of Christians, who consider

---

*The original edition of this article appeared as "Practical Theology for a Post-Modern Society," *Ung Teologi* (Oslo) 4 (1996): 5-15; and an adapted version appeared as "Pop Spirituality or Genuine Story," *Word and World* 18, no. 1 (Winter 1998): 44-56. My thanks to editors Torbjorn Olsen and Frederick J. Gaiser, respectively, for permission to publish this expanded version here. Also, many of the ideas in this article were elaborated previously in Marva J. Dawn, *Is It a Lost Cause? Having the Heart of God for the Church's Children* (Grand Rapids: Wm. B. Eerdmans Publishing Co., 1997), but this topic is so important for understanding the needs for worship in the present epoch that I have amplified them again here.

themselves grafted on to God's promises to the Jews as they worship the tri-une God? And what might that comparison mean for Christians' desire to be Church in order to serve their neighbors? What is happening spiritually in our culture, and how can we best respond out of our love for God and our love for others?

We live in a society that seems to have lost its way and is scrambling to find it by resorting to a wide variety of spiritualities. As one type of the many we could choose for examples, let us consider the "religions" presently finding their way into cyberspace. Stephen D. O'Leary examines some religious ritu-als found on computer networks and predicts that

> we will continue to see old and new religions jostling for attention in the cultural marketplace and using available technology to reach new audi-ences. If current trends hold, computers and computer networks will play an increasingly significant role in the religions of the future.[1]

What will characterize these "religions of the future"? O'Leary recog-nizes the following aspects in almost all of the transcripts he studied:

1. "an attempt to recreate or simulate real space in virtual space and to sanctify a portion of this space as a theatre in which spirit is mani-fested";
2. an emphasis on the difference between this space and the world outside or other places in cyberspace;
3. "an assertion of the power of language to bring about wish fulfillment through the verbal act of declaring the wish within the ritual circle."

These observations lead O'Leary to conclude that the cyberspace rituals

> appear as attempts to fulfill authentic spiritual needs now unmet by the major institutions of religious tradition. Yet there is an irreverence to these discourses . . . ; they are ludic and playful, they revel in pastiche and parody, and they make few (if any) cognitive demands upon the participants. This conjunction of reverence and irreverence seems to me to be in some way characteristic of the spiritual situation of postmodern culture, which can neither dismiss religion nor embrace it wholeheartedly, but which ulti-mately leads to its commodification along with every other product and

---

1. Stephen D. O'Leary, "Cyberspace as Sacred Space: Communicating Religion on Computer Networks," *Journal of the American Academy of Religion* 64, no. 4 (Winter 1996): 805-6.

project of the past that is not doomed to be discarded in the ash-heap of history.[2]

As Christians, we have to ask why religious traditions are not meeting the "authentic spiritual needs" of these rituals' participants. What is the "spiritual situation of postmodern culture," and how should Christians respond to postmodernism? What are the needs and concerns of those who live in the postmodern condition as exemplified in pop spiritualities? How can Christians love our neighbors who might dwell in that condition? What might it take to offer a Christianity that could be embraced wholeheartedly?

So that we can understand much of pop spirituality and the needs of people in our culture, this chapter will investigate the postmodern condition and assess the spiritual needs it creates. We will find that one great challenge for people in our times is the lack of a genuine story, one that is coherent and gives meaning to their lives. Bear with me as we trace the roots and some of the aspects of postmodernity in order to see what the Christian community can be in the midst of it and what we have to offer in terms of the larger story that we all need and that calls forth wholehearted commitment.

Does This Really Matter?

The term *postmodernism* is used in a wide variety of ways and covers a wide variety of ideas as postmodern worldviews, attitudes, concerns, and results spread rapidly throughout the world and enter every major aspect of contemporary life. In university history departments, postmodernism leads to revisionist accounts of events and an ever-increasing fracturing of society into victim groups demanding their own stories. Postmodernist philosophers absolutize the relativity of truth, stress playfulness, and speak in random aphorisms. English teachers and visual artists who accept postmodern theories claim that there is no meaning in texts or paintings except what the reader or viewer brings to them.

Though postmodern thinking was once confined to these university humanities faculties and the intellectual elite, now even the sciences are exhibiting effects of postmodern thinking. Recently, at a small college in Washington State, a guest lecturer insisted that Newtonian physics (emphasizing such natural laws as the law of gravity) was simply the product of male op-

2. O'Leary, "Cyberspace as Sacred Space," p. 803.

pression (a typical postmodern tenet) and should, therefore, be replaced by an openness to other perspectives. A female professor, failing to get him to see reason, sarcastically responded that perhaps, then, this lecturer should demonstrate non-Newtonian physics by jumping *up* from the edge of a twenty-story building!

We are not concerned so much here with the philosophical and academic manifestations of postmodernism, but with the effects of postmodern thinking on the average person, for even young children now experience and react to postmodern conditions. My concern here is for how postmodern notions — often without our awareness — hit the streets, create our children's worldview, and influence the people in (or absent from) our churches' pews. How do these notions impact the basic presuppositions and attitudes of those to whom the Christian community seeks to minister? My remarks will not detail aspects of the condition itself, but will paint a broad picture of the general social fabric so that we can then consider what Christianity has to offer in response and what leaders of churches can do to prepare their congregants for mission in the postmodern world. It is essential that you and I, as we seek to be Church, know all that we can about what drives the despair and nihilism in our culture and how we can genuinely care for those who suffer in the midst of its postmodern condition.

Leszek Kolakowski describes the disastrous despair generated by late modernity's and postmodernity's flight from the past and from meaning as follows:

> Culture, when it loses its sacred sense, loses all sense. With the disappearance of the sacred, which imposed limits to the perfection that could be attained by the profane, arises one of the most dangerous illusions of our civilization — the illusion that there are no limits to the changes that human life can undergo, that society is 'in principle' an endlessly flexible thing, and that to deny this flexibility and this perfectibility is to deny [humanity's] total autonomy and thus to deny [human beings themselves].
>
> Not only is this illusion demented, but it sows a disastrous despair. The omnipresent Nietzschean or Sartrian chimera which proclaims that [human beings] can liberate [themselves] totally, from everything, can free [themselves] of tradition and of all pre-existing sense, and that all sense can be decreed by arbitrary whim, far from unfurling before us the prospect of divine self-creation, leaves us suspended in darkness. And in this darkness, where all things are equally good, all things are also equally indifferent. . . . But this is a belief that cannot be accepted in good faith and can only give rise to a desperate flight from nothingness to nothingness. To be totally free

with respect to sense, free of all pressure from tradition, is to situate oneself in a void and thus, quite simply, to disintegrate.

To reject the sacred is to reject our own limits.[3]

The Movement to Postmodernism

We can best understand the present postmodern condition and its disintegrating pressures by tracing its roots in three particular themes of premodernity and modernity. We will limit the discussion to these three themes not to be reductionistic about the complexities of postmodernity, but because it will be especially helpful for our purposes here to focus simply on each epoch's understanding of God, authority, and truth.[4]

In the premodern world, everyone believed in some sort of god or gods. To understand the immense world alteration brought about by the modern epoch we must comprehend that, prior to the European age of Enlightenment which ushered in modernity, all cultures were devoted to their gods. All societies recognized the superior power of some kind of *supernatural* (theme A). Moreover, in premodernity those who were the bearers of knowledge about the specific culture's gods served as that society's *authorities* (theme B). They taught the rest of the people how to worship or appease the gods; they were thus the agents of truth, its promoters and practitioners. Truth was understood as *absolute* (theme C) because it came from god, and it was thought to be reliably transmitted by the shaman, priest, or witch doctor.

The development in the Enlightenment of science and reason (partly as one attempt to end the religious wars destroying Europe) turned the center of societies from the supernatural to the *natural* (A). We have to recognize what a mammoth change it was when the locus of authority shifted from persons who

---

3. Leszek Kolakowski, *Modernity on Endless Trial* (Chicago: University of Chicago Press, 1990), pp. 72-73.

4. Some excellent resources for further study of postmodernism and, in some of the following, of how the Christian faith can respond to it are Diogenes Allen, *Christian Belief in a Postmodern World: The Full Wealth of Conviction* (Louisville: Westminster/John Knox, 1989); Brian D. Ingraffia, *Postmodern Theory and Biblical Theology: Vanquishing God's Shadow* (Cambridge: Cambridge University Press, 1996); John O'Neill, *The Poverty of Postmodernism* (London: Routledge, 1995); Timothy R. Phillips and Dennis L. Okholm, eds., *Christian Apologetics in the Postmodern World* (Downers Grove, IL: InterVarsity Press, 1995); Anthony Thiselton, *Interpreting God and the Post-Modern Self: On Meaning, Manipulation, and Promise* (Grand Rapids: Wm. B. Eerdmans Publishing Co., 1995); Merold Westphal, *Suspicion and Faith: The Religious Uses of Modern Atheism* (Grand Rapids: Wm. B. Eerdmans Publishing Co., 1997).

passed on the truth of god to the scientific method, by which the truths of the natural world could be objectively discovered. Of course, there is nothing wrong with science — the first scientists were, generally, faithful Christians — but science increasingly displaced the supernatural, especially for those people who had only had a "god of the gaps" before the onslaught of scientific disproof. Those who attributed to God only whatever was not otherwise understood thus thought they had a decreasing need for the God of the Bible as science filled in more and more of the gaps. With the progressive ascent of technology, human beings assumed increasingly that they could control their own futures, that with just the right technological fix they could solve all their problems. Consequently, a "Tower of Babel" was built on the ground floor of science, with technology and economics comprising the next two floors. Science provided the insights, technology the power, and economics the wealth to combat ignorance, superstition, and poverty in a never-ceasing spiral of progress.[5]

Instead of trusting authorities, human beings insisted increasingly on their *autonomy* (B), and all truth, including what could be scientifically determined, became *relative* (C). Now God was no longer absolute, and religion was marginalized to the private sphere. People could simply say, "Christianity might be true for you, but it is not true for me."

Development of the postmodern spirit was really inevitable, since modernity believed so firmly in the faulty Enlightenment idolatry of Progress. With the rise of science and technology, economics and communications, this modern myth insisted that everything would get better and better — that we could solve the problems of the world with enough scientific discovery and technological fixes. However, this modern fantasy was built on shaky foundations, without adequate checks on who controlled the power. The euphoria of the myth of progress began to give way to the despair and hopelessness of grave anxiety as the twentieth century unfolded into major world wars, severe economic depressions, the callous violence of Hitler, the world-changing terror of Hiroshima, the assassinations of leaders and massive betrayals by government in the United States, the environmental destruction and relentless dread of the Cold War, the *Challenger* explosion and Chernobyl and Bhopal, the recent frenzy of ethnic cleansing and tribalism in Africa and the Balkans, growing economic tyranny by major corporations and massive global unemployment, the emptiness and ennui of entertainment that continues to escalate its graphic violence and blatant immorality, the salient loss of any moral

---

5. Some of my general understanding of postmodernity and specifically this image of the Tower of Babel in modernity came from J. Richard Middleton and Brian J. Walsh, *Truth Is Stranger Than It Used to Be* (Downers Grove, IL: InterVarsity Press, 1995).

consensus or commitment to the common good. Through all these graphic contradictions to "progress" the move to postmodernism has accelerated.

Postmodern theorists recognize that science had degenerated into a scientism that needed to be deconstructed. Technicism and economism also were idols, as were the grand narratives of truth, justice, freedom, and beauty. All these gods must be debunked; their proponents must be unmasked for the oppressive authorities that they are as they use these narratives merely to gain power. Thus, both the gods of the premodern supernatural worldview and the various modern myths of progress in the natural world are attacked by postmodern *deconstruction* (A), which leads to constant suspicion, loss of meaning, and rejection of any fixed point of reference.

Postmodern art uses a haphazard mixture of different methods and modes ironically juxtaposed; its literature uses amalgamations of various styles, genres, and even typefaces.[6] Channel surfing with the remote control illustrates the postmodern condition: from a distance the viewer experiences no plot, but merely disconnected images and smatterings of feelings.

The failure of "progress" thus has led to postmodernist spirals of despair and hopelessness. The poor outlook for finding meaningful jobs leaves young people without any reason to learn, even as their entertainments deprive them of the brain space or skills to do so.[7] We might as well amuse ourselves to death.[8] One very visible indicator of postmodern anomie is the immense proliferation of gambling casinos and lotteries.

As many scholars in the United States have noticed, postmodernism has moved young people from the alienation of the 1960s to the schizophrenia or multiphrenia (a legion of selves with no constant core of character) of the 1990s and 2000s.[9] Having no point of reference, no overarching story, no master narrative, people don't know who they are. Constantly shifting their image of themselves to fit in with the fads and fashions of the times, young folks especially lack a nucleus of identity, a personality that has been formed by moral authority and mentoring models. Furthermore, since they have no sense of themselves, they are unable to make commitments to another person

---

6. We saw these sorts of amalgamation in *Generation X* in Chapter 3. See especially Philip Sampson, "The Rise of Post-modernity," in *Faith and Modernity*, ed. Philip Sampson, Vinay Samuel, and Chris Sugden (Oxford: Regnum Books, 1994), pp. 29-57.

7. See Jane M. Healy, *Endangered Minds: Why Our Children Don't Think* (New York: Simon and Schuster, 1990).

8. See Neil Postman, *Amusing Ourselves to Death: Public Discourse in the Age of Show Business* (New York: Viking Penguin, 1985).

9. See, for example, Louis A. Sass, *Madness and Modernism: Insanity in the Light of Modern Art, Literature, and Thought* (New York: BasicBooks, 1992).

in marriage or friendship or to a job, a vision, a vocation, a religion. Their subconscious cry often becomes, "Keep entertaining me, so that I don't have to face the absence of my self." Religion, in the form of pop spiritualities, is merely another technique for entertainment. Thus, the postmodern condition has moved people from both the premodern confidence in authorities and the modern confidence in self (autonomy) to the *decentering* (B) of both self (incoherence) and society (fragmentation) in contemporary culture.

Most important of all, the failure of the hyped-up promises of science and technology accentuates the loss of truth already inherent in modernist relativizing and in the rejection of authoritative structures or persons with moral authority. Consequently, the major characteristic of the postmodern condition is the *repudiation of any Truth* (C) that claims to be absolute or truly true. "Christianity might be true for you, but not for me," our children used to say with modernist relativity — but now they are learning in their schools and from the media that any claim to truth is merely a means of hiding an oppressive will to power. The result is the malaise of meaninglessness, the inability to trust anything or anyone, the loss of any reference point or "web of reality" by which to construct one's life.

As Edward Farley explains, many of our current social problems arise partly as

> the result of a loss or diminishment at the very heart of culture — some would say the loss of culture itself — namely, a loss of the society's powerful deep symbols. Without such things a society becomes alienated from past wisdom, develops institutions that have little connection with sources of humanization, and instigates styles of everyday life whose primary function is ephemeral entertainment and trivial comforts. The diminishment and sickness of all deep symbols, that is, constraining and guiding words of power, is at least one of the things at work in the larger societal infirmity.

He notes that the postmodernism that has led to such a loss of deep symbols refers

> to the way institutions of leisure, buying and selling, governmental, educational, and corporate bureaucracies dominate and set the tone of everyday urban and suburban life. Alienated from the interhuman and from communities of human intimacy, these institutions are fairly emptied of moral, normative, and aesthetic dimensions.[10]

10. Edward Farley, *Deep Symbols: Their Postmodern Effacement and Reclamation* (Valley Forge, PA: Trinity Press International, 1996), p. x.

Though the philosophers use words like *random, playfulness,* and *banter* to describe their assessment of, and approach to, postmodern life, the effects on young people seem more like catastrophe, confusion, and chaos. Lacking authorities in the modern world to guide the formation of their moral character, now children lack basic resources of principled disposition to know how to find delight in what is beautiful, to have compassion for those who suffer, to develop goals for their work and lives. Distorted by the entertainment mentality of their parents, a large proportion of the young people in my husband's fifth-grade classroom have little desire to learn, insufficient conscience calling them to civility and propriety, hardly any sense of meaning and purpose in life, no sense that there is any truth except what they create for themselves.[11]

Dutch theologian Arend van Leewen heightens the radical difference between our times and the previous theocentric world by suggesting that there have been only two basic eras in all of history, which he calls the ontocratic and the technological eras. In the former, life was inherently a cosmic totality, in which belief in a God or gods transcendent to the natural world and to the life of human beings held together the contradictory and confusing elements of that life and world. However, comparatively abruptly, within the last three hundred years or so, this unifying notion has been rejected for "a multiform system of relationships, with no specific cornerstone, no single integrating element which gives all other things their reason for being."[12]

The Denial of Meta-Narrative

Perhaps the most important aspect of various kinds of postmodern thinking for our practical theological purposes here is this loss of an integrating element, this general rejection of meta-narrative. The term *meta-narrative* refers to an overarching story that gives focus, cohesion, commonality, and meaning to life. When I lectured at a seminary in Oslo last year, we acknowledged that Norway's meta-narrative includes the sagas of the Vikings; the grievous domination by both Denmark and Sweden; the courage of church and government leaders, of fishermen and schoolteachers in resisting Nazism; and, in

11. For an overview of manifestations of the postmodern ethos in popular culture, see Stanley J. Grenz, *A Primer on Postmodernism* (Grand Rapids: Wm. B. Eerdmans Publishing Co., 1996).

12. This description is from William F. Fore, *Television and Religion: The Shaping of Faith, Values, and Culture* (Minneapolis: Augsburg, 1987), p. 27. See Arend van Leewen, *Christianity in World History* (Edinburgh: Edinburgh Press, 1964), and the works by Jacques Ellul listed in the bibliography.

the present day, the people's respectful relationship to the king, their leadership in world-class skiing, and their careful stewarding of oil reserves for the nation's future. These and many other elements of that nation's story link the people together and give them common understanding of, and pride in, themselves and their heritage.

In contrast, the United States displays much greater postmodern breakdown and fragmentation as various interest and victim groups compete with one another. The larger, overarching worldview of the United States — including its founding by religious groups, the heroism of the pioneers, the splendor of its democratic vision, the nobility of its leaders — has in recent years given way to small stories of anger over the brutality of the first explorers and settlers against the native tribes, resentment against a government that has betrayed its people, indignation toward religion, and fear of the crimes and violence of our neighbors. Of course, much of this postmodern critique is justified. But the fact remains that we have lost much of our common, unifying story.

Postmodernism especially rejects the meta-narrative of Christianity and claims that it is violent and oppressive. It is alleged that in a pluralistic world no religion can be seen as universal. Meanwhile, retaining the modernist elevation of *choice* as a major value, many persons who claim to be Christians have assembled their own belief systems with a mixture of biblical elements along with a hodgepodge of ideas from other traditions,[13] together with a rejection of what they find "oppressive" in Christianity, such as the doctrine of the Atonement or narratives exhibiting God's wrath. Thus, pop spiritualities are not manifested only by people outside churches.

The Biblical Meta-Narrative as Eternal

Those of us who believe that the Revelation[14] of God does offer a genuine meta-narrative which is universally available and applicable and which is not

---

13. This is what sociologist Wade Clark Roof names a "pastiche spirituality," in *A Generation of Seekers: The Spiritual Journeys of the Baby Boom Generation* (New York: HarperCollins, 1993), p. 245. For a more thorough discussion of his research, see chapters 2, 5, 6, 7, and 11 of Marva J. Dawn, *Reaching Out without Dumbing Down: A Theology of Worship for the Turn-of-the-Century Culture* (Grand Rapids: Wm. B. Eerdmans Publishing Co., 1995).

14. I will follow the example of French sociologist and lay theologian Jacques Ellul in capitalizing the word *Revelation* and preceding it with the word *the* to emphasize it as the decisive gift of a gracious God and the Revelation of what cannot be discovered by human in-

violent or oppressive must especially remember that we make those claims, not because we stand outside of the biblical narrative as objective observers, but because God does. We agree with the postmodern thinkers that no one can make inflated claims about knowing the truth clearly without being influenced by our position in time and space, but we do not thereby give up all assertions of absolute truth.

Though postmodernists reject the Church's claim of the Christian meta-narrative's comprehensive inclusivity, we believe that the triune God has disclosed himself through the Revelation given to a faith community stretching all the way back to Sarah and Abraham, incarnated in the flesh in the person of Jesus Christ who lived among us, and passed on through the centuries by the guidance and empowerment of the Holy Spirit. The main theme of the Revelation, incarnated and enscriptured, is the comprehensive grace of God given freely to liberate the whole world.

The biblical narratives can be seen as universally applicable for several reasons. The Revelation knits all human beings together because they are equally created by God, because Christ died for all, and because the Spirit has been poured out upon "all flesh" and the result of that outpouring originally was that each person heard the disciples speaking in his or her own language. The Revelation of the Trinity encompasses all persons threefold.

Furthermore, the Revelation carries within it counterideological elements[15] — texts that prevent us from siding with the voices of victors, prophecies against Israel herself, oracles calling for justice building and peacemaking, narratives of suffering and oppression that call human dominion into question, accounts of the misunderstandings of the apostles and the contrasting comprehension of the "little people." Jesus himself is the most obvious element, for his submission to suffering demonstrates most graphically that God does not work through the power structures and ideologies of the world. Furthermore, on the cross he exposed and triumphed over all the principalities and powers of politics, economics, and religious institutions.[16]

---

tellect. Ellul also brilliantly observed, using linguistic tools, that the real hermeneutical gap is not between the culture/language of the first century and that of the twentieth century (for us the twenty-first), but between those who receive the Word as the Revelation of God and those who don't. See Jacques Ellul, "Innocent Notes on 'The Hermeneutic Question,'" in *Sources and Trajectories: Eight Early Articles by Jacques Ellul That Set the Stage,* trans. and ed. Marva J. Dawn (Grand Rapids: Wm. B. Eerdmans Publishing Co., 1997).

15. This phrase is from Middleton and Walsh, *Truth Is Stranger Than It Used to Be,* and elaborated with different examples on pp. 87-99 of that book.

16. See Marva J. Dawn, "The Concept of 'the Principalities and Powers' in the Works of Jacques Ellul" (Ph.D. dissertation, University of Notre Dame, 1992).

Whereas the modern world rejected Christianity's claims because they could not be scientifically proven, now postmodernity has opened people up to recognizing other kinds of knowledge and uses of reason. We can address the epistemological barriers to faith (that is, the issues of *how* we know what we know about God) by accepting the suprarational mystery of God and the community-attested Revelation and by recognizing the reasonableness of the Christian story as the best answer to the existential questions of who we are and why we exist, of what is wrong with the world and what can be done about it. As Diogenes Allen explains,

> Christian faith is not a leap *within* the order of the intellect, a leap which violates the very essence of that order. The leap of faith is a leap *from* the order of the intellect to the order of the heart. We leap because we recognize the reality of the domain of the heart, not because there is a shortage of evidence.
>
> We recognize the reality of the order of the heart when we realize that we cannot achieve the well-being we seek from possessing those goods which can be gained by power and wealth (the order of the body) and when we realize that all questions of value and self-evaluation are legitimately excluded from consideration within the order of the intellect. Faith is called a "leap" because there is a chasm between the orders of the body and the intellect and the order of the heart, which can be spanned only by a change in outlook and concerns. . . .
>
> Once we see that the intellect is not able to satisfy the concerns of the heart, and take into account the biblical teaching that God is above the power of the mind to comprehend, we recognize the appropriateness of faith. We may embrace God with all our heart, mind, soul, and strength because God is accessible to us through the good God promises to give us. At least God is accessible to those who overcome their resentment of being utterly dependent on deity for their well-being.[17]

Because the God who has disclosed himself to us is eternal, because the story of his relationship with human beings encompasses all eras, because those who believe in him already have eternal life and so share in God's freedom beyond time, and because the Revelation offers the standard by which we can assess what is of God and what is alien to his purposes, Christians can retain from each epoch what is warranted for our thinking and reject what conflicts with the Revelation of God to us. Instead of a fundamentalistic retrenchment into premodernity, I believe Christians can be at the forefront in

17. Allen, *Christian Belief in a Postmodern World*, pp. 145 and 148.

offering to the world around us a better postmodernism, not one of fragmentation and chaos, but a genuine story of community and faith.

Christianity and Premodernism

The Bible thoroughly proclaims and reveals the existence of God and the meaning of human life in relation to God. For that reason, Christians in the present age find it essential to retain from the premodern era its theocentric consciousness, its spiritual Center. Certainly our society *needs* to recover the attention to the supernatural (theme A) of cultures before the Enlightenment, for we can easily see that the massive social problems of the present world are due to human beings' prideful rejection of God as the center of and reason for existence.

Because the Bible also makes it very clear that all human beings are sinful and that human perception of God is marred by sin, we must reject premodern attitudes toward authority (theme B). Though we acknowledge that God is absolute and absolute Truth (theme C), we no longer trust that the pastor or priest is able to pass on the Truth of God absolutely truly. We acknowledge that our comprehension of God is affected by our social situation, and thus we need the whole creation, including those who do not believe the Hebrew and Christian Scriptures, to reveal more of what we can know only relatively. Thus, from the premodern age, Christians keep the focus on God and believe in his Truth, but recognize that we know it only partially and can share it with others not as authorities but as co-learners.

Christianity and Modernism

It is modernism that taught us we didn't know everything, so we can accept its turn toward relative perception, though we do not extend that relativity to God himself since God has indeed revealed himself as sovereignly knowing, caring, and saving. Moreover, the Scriptures also warn us (for example, in Ecclesiastes) against modernity's reliance on human science and technology to conquer human problems. The Revelation of God clearly exposes the myth of human progress and names as *sin* the oppressions that result from unequal distributions of "progress" and power.

Christian theology gave in too much to modernity. We allowed the rules of science to determine how we studied the Scriptures instead of retaining our sense that there are many kinds of knowledge and wisdom and that the

Bible carries within itself guides to the ways to study it — with the foundation of belief in Christ as the Revealed and Revealing One and with methods of openness to the Holy Spirit, the counsel of the community, meditation, memorization, submission to the text's formation, obedience, and trust. We allowed modernity to turn us toward entertainment in our worship and toward ministry to people's "felt needs" instead of offering them what is truly needful. In a society of choice, churches became false democracies — for example, in deciding doctrine by majority vote — rather than communities of gifted people equipped by their leadership for a corporate life formed by the biblical narratives and guided by the Holy Spirit.[18]

Theologians recognize that the tools modernity gave us — form, source, historical-critical, and redaction criticisms[19] — are inadequate, for they tend to atomize the text and leave us with nothing that forms us as a people of God. For the sake of what can be gained from them, we can retain these methods from the modern epoch, along with its sense of the relativity of our own knowledge, but the postmodernists (and, even more, the Bible) show us that we need more — for example, the people-forming results of literary, narrative, and canonical approaches to the Scriptures.[20] These tools especially help us to learn the genuine story of our faith and how it differs from the new spiritualities of our culture.

Christianity and Postmodernism

Certainly by means of critique already given in the Scriptures, Christians can agree with postmodernity's rejection of the modern world's myth of progress. We concur with the postmodern deconstruction of the technological mindset, of political ideologies, of Enlightenment hyper-rationalism. We have seen the failures of technology truly to fix our problems, the destructive use of science for evil ends, the inability of economics to bring equitable wealth to all.

---

18. These wrong turns will be explored more thoroughly in Chapter 5.

19. These methods of study look, respectively, at literary genres, at the various sources or traditions from which a text came, at historical details that enable us to understand texts in their context, and at the work of biblical editors as they put together into a narrative the traditions available to them.

20. These methods of study look closely at literary devices such as word choices or repetitions and grammatical forms, at the whole narrative of an account in order to study the broader structure and elements that give the story its form, and at the whole canon of the Scriptures, in order to see how a text fits in with what Jews and Christians have passed on as the entire Revelation of God.

From the narratives of the Revelation, we know the source of these defects in human pride, narcissism, and greed.

What we cannot accept from postmodernity is its "wholesale rejection of objectivity and the uncritical celebration of perspectival understanding,"[21] its total decentering, its reduction of life merely to a carnival, with myriads of consumerist opportunities and entertaining sideshows — including those of various spiritualities. We recognize the logical fallacy of postmodernity's rejection of meta-narratives, since its very insistence that they are violent and oppressive is itself an example of an imperious meta-narrative. Most of all, we observe the emptiness, the hopelessness, the despair, the lack of a coherent story created by postmodernity's repudiation of God.

We acknowledge, however, that there is no going back to "the good old days" of premodern absolute conviction, of infallible authorities who passed on God's truth. We readily confess that God's people throughout their history have not passed on the whole Truth of God, nor have they always passed it on in ways compatible with the character of God himself. We realize that Christendom distorted its convictions and authority with disastrous results in the violence it perpetrated, the greed of many of its leaders, the oppressions it fostered, the suffering it caused countless peoples. In past eras, for example, Christendom misconstrued the biblical formulation of "Holy War," which was actually a peace-building notion in the First Testament in that Holy War was intended to teach Israel not to fight and not to gain any booty from fighting.[22] The Crusades were an appalling manifestation of human perversion of the biblical meta-narrative.

The Biblical Meta-Narrative as Gift to the Postmodern World

Accepting the postmodernist critique of our *abuse* of the biblical meta-narrative, how can we recover the Word, the genuine story of God and his people as a crucially necessary gift for our time? First we must examine the meta-narrative itself, and then we must clarify how it forms us.

The biblical meta-narrative is the story of a faithful God, of a God who keeps his promises. When we read it in its entirety, we realize that it is different from other religious narratives because it focuses on God *in relationship*

21. Mark R. Schwehn, "Christianity and Postmodernism: Uneasy Allies," in *Christianity and Culture in the Crossfire,* ed. David A. Hoekema and Bobby Fong (Grand Rapids: Wm. B. Eerdmans Publishing Co., 1997), p. 158.

22. See Marva J. Dawn, "What the Bible *Really* Says about War," *The Other Side* 29, no. 2 (March-April 1993): 56-59.

with a specific people.[23] There are many other creation accounts in religious literature, for example, but only the Hebrew/Christian Scriptures emphasize that this Creator God is also a Covenant God. As Deuteronomy explains,

> Because the LORD your God is a [compassionate] God, he will neither abandon you nor destroy you; he will not forget the covenant with your ancestors that he swore to them.
>
> For ask now about former ages, long before your own, ever since the day that God created human beings on the earth; ask from one end of heaven to the other: has anything so great as this ever happened or has its like ever been heard of? Has any people ever heard the voice of a god speaking out of a fire, as you have heard, and lived? Or has any god ever attempted to go and take a nation for himself from the midst of another nation, by trials, by signs and wonders, by war, by a mighty hand and an outstretched arm, and by terrifying displays of great power, as the LORD your God did for you in Egypt before your very eyes? To you it was shown so that you would acknowledge that the LORD is God; there is no other besides him. From heaven he made you hear his voice to discipline you. On earth he showed you his great fire, while you heard his words coming out of the fire. And because he loved your ancestors, he chose their descendants after them. He brought you out of Egypt with his own presence, by his great power. (4:31-37)

The knowledge of God began with the LORD's intervention in the history of Israel — and from there they discovered that their covenant "I AM" was the One who had created the world.

In the same way, we offer to people in the postmodern world an introduction to the God who loves them and wants to reconcile them to himself. We tell them the story of a faithful, promising God who demonstrated his devotion by always remembering his covenant with Israel. The dependability of the Revelation is established most profoundly in the resurrection of Jesus, for in the empty tomb we see the culmination of God's work on our behalf, the fulfillment of all the prophecies concerning the Messiah, the down payment on all God's promises for the future.

The Revelation, then, offers a convincing story of hope for people in our postmodern times. It proclaims a God of compassion and gracious mercy, who gives meaning and focus to lives tossed around by postmodern randomness. It announces forgiveness and atonement and reconciliation to those torn by guilt

---

23. New possibilities for wrestling with the text because of God's *relationship* with Israel are underscored in Walter Brueggemann's *Theology of the Old Testament: Testimony, Dispute, Advocacy* (Minneapolis: Fortress Press, 1997).

and lacking skills for relationships. It describes the Trinity whom our neighbors genuinely need — a loving Creator for those who think they have to create their own identity, a perfect Model for those who have no mentors, and an empowering Spirit for those who think they have to do everything on their own.

How the Revelation Forms Us

The Revelation is not a book of rules that gives us step-by-step procedures for life. There could never be enough rules to cover all the possibilities, and usually our response to rules and regulations is to resist them. Nor is the Bible a collection of timeless truths from which we draw out basic principles or goals toward which we aim. Since the Bible contains many dialectical tensions, opposing sides can draw out contradictory timeless principles, and often people use biblical goals to justify any means. Rather, to modify a basic schema from N. T. Wright,[24] the Scriptures must be understood as a master story with multiple narratives that form us as we are immersed in them. We become part of this genuine story as we then live out of the character shaped by all of God's Revelation.

Imagine that we found an unfinished drama by William Shakespeare, that we uncovered the first five acts and the last bit of the seventh.[25] How would we produce the play? We could try to write the missing parts, but we could never be sure if we got them exactly right — and we could not check out our attempts with the author.

Instead, we would try to find actors (perhaps from the Shakespeare festival in Ashland, Oregon) who were highly experienced in the theater, who knew Shakespeare's work inside and out, who understood all his writings and his life and his personality. Then they would have to immerse themselves in the acts of the new play that had been found. With this basis, they could improvise the missing parts.

Similarly, in the Christian community we have passed on the unfinished drama of God. The first act of the play is the creation, which teaches us that

24. See N. T. Wright, *The New Testament and the People of God* (Minneapolis: Fortress, 1992), pp. 140-43. See others' use of this wonderful idea in Middleton and Walsh, *Truth Is Stranger Than It Used to Be*, pp. 182-84, and Rodney Clapp, *A Peculiar People: The Church as Culture in a Post-Christian Society* (Downers Grove, IL: InterVarsity, 1996), pp. 138-39.

25. Wright uses a five-act schema, but I find it more helpful to divide his fifth act in order to stress the differences in our lives (my Act VI) from those of biblical characters in immediate touch with Jesus (V) and to emphasize the end of time (VII) as an entirely new kind of drama.

all the people of the world are brothers and sisters, designed to live in harmony with each other and the cosmos; thus the first act prohibits the violence toward other people against which the postmodernists rightfully protest. The second act of the drama is the fall, which enables us to understand the world's brokenness and destruction. Acts III and V include the stories of Israel and of the early Christians, respectively, to offer us examples of both disobedience and trust and to demonstrate the consequences of each. Act IV is the record of the life of Jesus and manifests God's covenant action on behalf of the world as the pinnacle of all God's interventions in Act III and as the foundation for the Spirit's work through the saints in Act V. We know a little bit of the end of the drama (Act VII) from the book of Revelation, but what we know of the culmination of the world is only a sketch meant to encourage us in the struggles of the present.[26]

Act VI is where we fit in, formed by what we have learned in the preceding parts. Immersed in the meta-narrative, the grand story of the people of God — the commandments, goals, chronicles, poetry, warnings, promises, and songs of the entire Revelation — we are formed to act with the character of God's people, imitating the virtues and deeds of God himself. And we have a great advantage, for, as we improvise Act VI in keeping with the spirit of the rest of the drama, we know that the Author is still alive!

What a great gift this meta-narrative is! It offers the people of the world around us a story into which they can place themselves and find forgiveness for their past, purpose for their present, and hope for their future.

The Christian Community as Gift to the Postmodern World

The most convincing testimony to the truth of God for postmodern people will be the incarnation of God's love by, and the embodiment of his purposes in, the Christian community of those being formed by the Scriptures to be Church. Many books about "Generation X" or the "Buster Generation" (young people in their twenties and thirties) emphasize especially their need for love and compassion, their feelings of rootlessness and homelessness.[27] They are searching

---

26. See Marva J. Dawn, *Joy in Our Weakness: A Gift of Hope from the Book of Revelation* (St. Louis: Concordia, 1994).

27. See, for example, Kevin Graham Ford, *Jesus for a New Generation: Putting the Gospel in the Language of Xers* (Downers Grove: InterVarsity Press, 1995), for a Christian perspective; and see the excerpts in Chapter 3 of this book from Douglas Coupland's *Generation X: Tales for an Accelerated Culture* (New York: St. Martin's Press, 1991) and his *Life without God* (New York: Simon and Schuster, 1994) for the longing of those without God.

for genuine community, but they will not find it in the oppressive indoctrination of cults or in the kind of pop spiritualities found on the Internet. The online medium itself is "constantly faced with the evidence of its own quality as constructed, as arbitrary, and as artificial, a game played with no material stakes or consequences"; online rituals lack "the quality of physical presence."[28]

Against this artificiality and the anonymity of computer networks, Douglas Groothuis points out, "Genuine community worthy of the name is largely fashioned out of the recognition of our embodied and sometimes awkward particularities." Groothuis cites Francis Fukuyama's *Trust: The Social Virtues and the Creation of Prosperity,* which emphasizes that "trust is the expectation that arises within a community of regular, honest, and cooperative behavior, based on commonly shared norms . . . of other members of that community." Groothuis notes that such trust "is not easily established through the largely impersonal interaction of computer technologies." Consequently, those seeking to meet authentic spiritual needs in computer spiritualities will discover that developing the required behaviors and trust "when cyberspace is our primary means of interaction is difficult if not impossible."[29]

The Christian community, to be genuine gift to the postmodern world, must deliberately be an alternative society of trust and embodied faithfulness to our story and its God. Rather than becoming enculturated and entrapped by the world's values of materialistic consumerism, of narcissistic self-aggrandizement, of solitary superficiality, and of ephemeral satisfaction, members of Christ's Body must be Church by choosing his simple life of sharing, his willingness to suffer for the sake of others, his communal vulnerability, and his eternal purposes. Leaders in the Christian community must constantly equip parishioners for the mission and ministry of communicating the Christian meta-narrative, of enfolding the world around them in God's love, of deliberately choosing and living out the alternative values of the kingdom of God.

As Leszek Kolakowski stresses, what is needed in response to the kinds of "spiritualities" described at the beginning of this chapter is a people who are being trained by faithful leaders to be Church and thus to incarnate the faith. He writes,

> After centuries of the growth of the Enlightenment, we suddenly woke up in a mental and cultural disarray; we are more and more frightened in the

---

28. O'Leary, "Cyberspace as Sacred Space," p. 804.

29. Douglas Groothuis, "It Takes More Than a Virtual Village," *Books and Culture* 3, no. 3 (May/June 1997): 14. See also his book *The Soul in Cyberspace* (Grand Rapids, MI: Hourglass, 1997).

face of a world that is losing its religious legacy, and our fear is well justified. The lost myths seem to be replaced less by enlightened rationality and more by terrifying secular caricatures or substitutes. We notice with a kind of relief various symptoms of religious renaissance, and the "return of the sacred" has become a fashionable topic. And yet we — and by *we* I mean philosophers, sociologists, psychologists, anthropologists or historians — cannot contribute to this process; we can describe it — with hope or with dread — but we are not priests, and only through priesthood, prophecy, and acts of living faith can human participation in the sacred be maintained or reinforced.[30]

The community gathers in worship to hear our story in the exhortations and challenges of our priests and prophets, in the retelling of the narratives of God's word and works, in the singing of Christianity's new and old exalted hymns of faith, in the remembering of our great creeds and doctrines, and in the prayers for God's faithfulness and ours in response. The Christian community also listens together for the Holy Spirit's guidance for our improvisation of Act VI. Then we go out from our gatherings to bring the story we have learned to the world around us. In the Christian community, people left homeless by the postmodern ethos can find a home. In the community's meta-narrative, those left to wander in the postmodern condition can find true roots and a story that embraces them. Most of all, in the community and the community's meta-narrative, the godless can find the true God.

The Truth of God as Gift to the Postmodern World

Premodernism asserted that there was an objective truth that could be known by those who had the skill to see it. Modernism objected that truth was relative, that different people saw truth differently according to their own situations. Postmodernism insists that there is no truth at all, that whatever truth there might be must be created by each person, for any larger claims to truth are in reality disguised bids for power. The meta-narrative of the Christian community compassionately demonstrates that Jesus is the Truth, an objective Truth who can be known. We know him only partially, but because we know *him* we do not have to try to create truth for ourselves. Furthermore, his truth is not oppressive, for as Mark Schwehn emphasizes,

---

30. Kolakowski, *Modernity on Endless Trial*, pp. 106-7.

For Christianity, the quest for truth is bound up inextricably with disciple-ship, and therefore the shape of power is for them always cruciform. . . . So long as Christians remember that, for disciples, power is not dominion but obedience, faithfulness, and suffering servanthood, they can rightly claim an integral connection between truth and power.[31]

The Christian story we offer to our neighbors introduces them to Jesus, the Truth, who brings healing to postmodern fractured souls. He is the Way to the home for which postmodernists search. He is the Life who gives us hope for eternity — and that hope "does not disappoint us" (Romans 5:5).

I believe that this is a critical time for the world and a momentous op-portunity for the Christian community. Everyone around us is longing for a story that gives meaning to life. We have such a meta-narrative because of the God we know. I pray that, more and more, individual believers and the Chris-tian community as a whole will be formed by the biblical story so that we can improvise well — and thereby draw to the triune God the world he loves and longs to save. Particularly I pray that the essays and sermons in this book will play a small part in equipping the Christians who read them with insights and skills for deepening the contribution of the Church's worship in offering the gifts our postmodern world needs so profoundly.

31. Schwehn, "Christianity and Postmodernism," p. 163.

5

*Worship for Postmodern Times**

[Jesus prayed:] "Sanctify them in the truth; your word is truth. As you have sent me into the world, so I have sent them into the world. And for their sakes I sanctify myself, so that they also may be sanctified in truth."

John 17:17-19

F requently on airplanes I meet persons who claim to be very absorbed in "spirituality," but who have no interest in institutional churches and their worship services. "Churches don't meet my needs," they exclaim and consider the subject ended. Friendly conversation, however, often reveals that they have hidden their genuine needs even from themselves. I think particularly of a gold-bedecked professional gambler sadly departing from a visit with his son in the Midwest, of a fidgety lawyer trying to beat the plane to Anchorage, of a discourteous twenty-something with a fierce "need" to be entertained, of myself in my own frustrations over various conflicts concerning worship.

*The first version of this chapter appeared as "Worship for Postmodern Times," *Cross Accent* 5A, no. 9 (January 1997): 6-10. My thanks to editor Tom Leeseberg-Lange for permission to print this extensively adapted version here. The original article was also reprinted in *Lutheran Partners* 14, no. 3 (May/June 1998): 14-21, and was quoted in *Context: Martin E. Marty on Religion and Culture* 30, no. 14 (15 July 1998): 5-6. A small section of this chapter will also appear in a compendium of proceedings from the Institute of Liturgical Studies, 1997-1999, held at Valparaiso University in Valparaiso, Indiana. My thanks to director Dr. David Truemper for permission to use this adapted segment here.

How does the Church minister to people in postmodern times? Based on the discussion of postmodernism in the previous chapter and our recognition that the Church's meta-narrative and relationship with the One who is the Truth are supreme gifts for the society around us, what kind of thinking about worship services ought we to be doing in the third millennium? Many of the specifics will be considered in later chapters of this book, but here it is important again to paint broad brush strokes as we ponder the implications of our culture's postmodern condition for the Church's worship.

A Specific Example

Let us look at one particular case in order to frame the questions we should be asking. A few weeks before Easter two years ago, a Canadian Broadcasting producer in Montreal telephoned me. A few pastors had told her about my book *Reaching Out without Dumbing Down*, and she wondered what were the main points of my approach since she was preparing a program for Easter afternoon to focus on what congregations could do to attract Canadians to worship. One generation ago, two out of three Canadians participated in worship, but now the ratio is at most one out of three, and even less in British Columbia and Quebec. As the producer and I conversed about topics such as idolatries that invade churches, wrong turns many churches are making, confusions about what worship is, and the kinds of questions we should be asking, she kept affirming my ideas. "That is really a good point," she would say, or "I see why you say that" or "that makes a lot of sense." Consequently, I was utterly astonished when she abruptly inquired, "And what would you tell churches to do about people like me? I never go to church." She described herself as the typical middle-aged, disinterested defector from worship and asked how churches should attract her. How would you have responded?

The key question that this conversation raised is *not* what we should make worship to be in order to attract such people as this Canadian producer. The real issue — in our culture which is less and less Christian, which is post-Christian, sometimes anti-Christian — is this: What does it mean to be Church for the sake of the world when we worship and during the rest of the week?

The Answer Some Are Giving

Many leaders in churches these days simply frame their response to this Canadian producer in terms of the question of appeal. As a representative of this approach, consider these remarks from a review of my book *Reaching Out without Dumbing Down* by Rev. David Luecke, writing for *Worship Innovations*. Referring to my endorsement of Kenneth Myer's distinction between gourmet food, traditional home cooking, and fast food as examples of high, folk, or pop culture,[1] Luecke says,

> The assumption is that most people would prefer gourmet food if they could get it. That's questionable. It can be hard to digest and the cost in time or money is usually too high. . . . Home cooking in general seems to be disappearing. That leaves Burger King. The whole worship discussion could be reframed around two alternatives: If you and your congregation had to choose between being a fancy French restaurant or a Burger King, which would you prefer? . . . Most advocates of contemporary worship, including me, would opt for Burger King; in a given week it feeds a lot more people, and the food meets the needs. . . . Which kind of food service do you think Jesus and Paul would choose?

In the first place, we must note that Luecke's term, *contemporary worship,* is poorly defined at present in the various controversies over the subject. We will discuss this problem more thoroughly in Chapter 24. In addition, Luecke's comments and questions force us to raise several sets of deeper ones because his inquiries center around the issues of choice and preferences. Should these be our guidelines? The Scriptures convince me, instead, that in our response to the issues raised by the Canadian broadcaster's challenge the principal question must be, "What should the Church be?"

Luecke's review and other similar arguments raised in the worship discussions do not consider the essential, foundational biblical perspectives on the issues of who we are as God's people in community, what it means that we gather together for worship to waste time royally immersing ourselves in God's splendor to learn how to be Church, and, consequently, how we reach out to the world. Therefore, let us focus on the unbiblical notions illustrated by Luecke's review and ask the following questions regarding the responses

---

1. See pp. 183-88 of Marva J. Dawn, *Reaching Out without Dumbing Down: A Theology of Worship for the Turn-of-the-Century Culture* (Grand Rapids: Wm. B. Eerdmans Publishing Co., 1995), referring to Kenneth A. Myers, *All God's Children and Blue Suede Shoes: Christians and Popular Culture* (Westchester, IL: Crossway Books, 1989).

typified in his words. (Keep referring to the quoted paragraph above as you work through the next section.)

The Questions We Should Be Asking

1. Isn't the gospel sometimes hard to digest? Luecke complains that worship should not be like gourmet food, which "can be hard to digest" — but if worship is always easy, are we giving its participants the true God? The triune God is mysterious, infinitely beyond our imagining, eternally wiser than we — a LORD who says, "For my thoughts are not your thoughts, nor are your ways my ways" (Isaiah 55:8). Ours is a Christ who repeatedly says, "Woe to you!" (e.g., Luke 6:24-26). That can be very difficult to stomach.

2. Doesn't discipleship cost a lot in time and money? Luecke wants to avoid gourmet worship because "the cost in time and money is usually too high" — but don't we have a Christ who told a rich man to sell all he had, who warned those who wanted to turn back home that they weren't fit for the kingdom? (See Luke 18:18-27 and 9:57-62.) If our worship is not costly in terms of time, participation, and commitment, how will we teach what discipleship means? The medium must match the message.

3. Which kind of food service did Jesus choose? Since he participated faithfully in worship at the Temple and the local synagogue, in the ritualized festivals and feasts of Judaica, we could compare his choices to both home cooking and gourmet food. And what kind of "food service" does Paul signify when he urges us to "seek the things which are above"? Which kind of food service will give us "a foretaste of the feast to come"? How will our worship give its participants a vision of the heavenly kingdom? It seems we need a festival spread of gourmet cooking to be immersed in God's splendor.

4. We have to ask why the home cooking of tradition in worship is disappearing. Is the heritage that could enfold us in the language of faith practiced through the ages no longer important? Why have we lost the traditions that link us to people of faith throughout time and space? Benjamin R. Barber, director of the Walt Whitman Center for the Culture and Politics of Democracy at Rutgers University, critiques what is happening in the world in a book called *Jihad vs. McWorld*. Therein he laments the control of advertising images and an escalating world "monoculture" which is destroying social institutions and cultural folkways.[2] Should churches be

---

2. See Benjamin R. Barber, *Jihad vs. McWorld: How Globalism and Tribalism Are Reshaping the World* (New York: Ballantine Books, 1996).

contributing to this reduction of culture, this destruction of musical "home cooking"?

5. Which need does Burger King food meet besides the need for speed? If our worship is like Burger King, how will we form the habits and practices,[3] the customs and the manners of being the people of God? For example, how will we teach the royal waste of time, profound meditation, awe-full silence, reflection on meaty doctrines, musical depth, memorization of extensive texts, steadfast intimacy with the true God, the continuity of the Church, genuine community, earnest repentance, grieving lament, discipled cross-bearing, timeless truth, the beauty of holiness, and faithful goodness? Will we learn those if our worship is like Burger King food?

6. I'm not advocating only one (French) gourmet restaurant. I am advocating a plethora of them. I would hope that our worship could sometimes include Hispanic as well as soul music, songs from Madagascar as well as Norway, from South Africa and Russia, from the fourth century as well as the sixteenth, the eighteenth, or the twenty-first. Will we learn diversity at Burger King?

7. No matter which kind of food service our worship resembles, we must ask whether it meets our *genuine* needs — the needs of our lonely, decentered, hopeless, postmodern world as outlined in the previous two chapters. What is good for us and our neighbors? What will really contribute to growth in faith? As we eat, are we growing stronger or just fatter?

Of course, the food analogy breaks down and gets us in trouble if we stretch it too far. But isn't it a severe theological problem to say that our worship should be like Burger King food because other food is hard to digest and costs too much in time and money? It seems to me that then we are talking merely about marketing and entertainment, instead of discussing *worship, formation for discipleship,* and *liturgy* (which means "the work of the people").

These seven sets of questions and comments demonstrate thoroughly how wrong a question it is if churches ask only how worship can appeal to people. Various struggling congregations and denominations are not declining for lack of attractive or "contemporary" worship — remember that we will discuss this ill-defined phrase in Chapter 24 — but our churches are failing for lack of theological questioning and training, for lack of displaying a way of life worthy of being pursued. I am not an elitist about worship style; I always emphasize that many different styles can be used in truly community-building, character-forming worship — and the more diversity we can em-

3. See Dorothy C. Bass, ed., *Practicing Our Faith: A Way of Life for a Searching People* (San Francisco: Jossey-Bass, 1997).

ploy the richer our worship will be. But I am adamant that we must ask better questions about what it means to be a Christian and to be Church together, about how people are formed by the narratives of the Scriptures to follow Christ, and about pursuing the way of discipleship, which costs us all of our time and money and sometimes is very hard to digest.

Wrong Turns in the Face of Modernity and the Postmodern Condition

In the face of the ever-increasing fracturing of U.S. society, its loss of meta-narrative and negation of meaning, its despair, emptiness, and ennui, its deficit in moral consensus or commitment, its hopelessness and anomie, its rejection of authority and of any Truth claims — in sum, these destructive effects generated by the postmodern condition described in the previous chapter — what is the Church to be and do?

These are the societal illnesses for which congregations and their leaders must be concerned, rather than being concerned merely about the downward trends in worship attendance that accompanied the massive changes in U.S. society in the 1960s and have continued ever since.[4] Responding *merely to the symptoms and not to the illnesses,* many congregations have taken drastic turns in recent years without adequate thinking about the theological, ecclesiological, and missional implications of those changes. Though the following list is far too cursory, it summarizes some of the moves that should be questioned:

• In the face of the relativizing of truth, some pastors and musicians are offering less truth instead of more, becoming therapeutic instead of theological. No wonder people are bored with "church" — and the preachers themselves are bored. Don't you find yourself much more interested if you have too much to say? If we recognize that Christianity always has too much to say — as the Gospel of John concludes, "Now Jesus did many other signs . . . which are not written in this book. But these are written so that you may come to believe that Jesus is the Messiah" (20:30-31a) — then we perceive that we have to give more content and not less, especially with the biblical illiteracy that characterizes the United States. (This topic will be pursued more thoroughly in Chapter 21.)

4. See Wade Clark Roof, *A Generation of Seekers: The Spiritual Journeys of the Baby Boom Generation* (San Francisco: HarperCollins Publishers, 1993).

- With the proliferation of amusements and diversions in the U.S.–driven world monoculture, some worship leaders sacrifice content for entertaining form and confuse worship with evangelism and evangelism with marketing. As Calvin M. Johansson writes, evangelistic and worship forms should instead

  > reflect the type of life to which Christianity calls us. For example, nothing is gained by entertaining people into the kingdom, musically speaking, only to have them jolted into the reality that the Christian life is not an entertainment at all. . . . One's birthing process should be a foretaste of the lifelong faith walk toward maturity, which is God's goal for every Christian.[5]

  (This confusion of entertainment and evangelism and worship will be considered at greater length in Chapter 9.)

- As society increasingly becomes more openly pluralistic and less supportive of Christianity specifically, some congregations blur their unique identity as the people of God, instead of accentuating it with loving commitment. To say that it doesn't really matter if you are a Christian, as long as you are sincere, is to be ashamed of the gospel and the scandal of our particularity. It would make as much sense if, after my next speaking engagement, I would randomly get on any airplane and hope that I'd wind up in Portland, Oregon, as long as I'm sincere. Certainly it is true that in a pluralistic society Christians err if we are imperialistic about our particularity, coercive instead of hospitable and inviting — but our faith is in a triune God of good news, and the truth of that God's grace accomplished and demonstrated in Christ remains unique and is uniquely to be shared. (This topic will be discussed more thoroughly in Chapters 29 and 30.)
- As the culture becomes more and more rootless, some denominations and individual parishes are giving up their heritage as communities with long histories and global connections. Many people in our society are struggling to find who they are and where they belong. The description of a movie shown on a recent airplane trip provides an apt illustration. The summary in the airline magazine said that a single mother, an architect, meets an every-other-weekend dad who is a journalist, and all they have in common is the same kind of cellular phone. How will they fall in love? Think of this story from their offsprings' perspective, and realize how pervasive in our

5. Calvin M. Johansson, *Discipling Music Ministry: Twenty-first Century Directions* (Peabody, MA: Hendrickson Publishers, 1992), p. 15.

society such situations are. The children have been denied a completion to the story line of their original two parents; is a cellular phone enough to heal the rupture for them?

Children in my husband's fifth-grade classes with multiple parents demonstrate that nothing can ever totally heal the rupture. How can children without the security of completely faithful parents be able to trust who they are? In the face of such discontinuity and abandonment, to give up the roots of our faith, which goes all the way back to Sarah and Abraham, is a very harmful thing to do. We thereby give up our ties to our forebears in the Jewish and Christian heritage, our history of God's interventions, our connections to the global community of believers. (See the comments on our master narrative in Chapters 2-4.)

- In the face of the culture's loss of moral authority, some churches become tolerant to the point of ceasing to be a people formed by the narratives of Scripture. Why should we allow the relativizing of morals in our society to cause us to give up the clear instructions and moral patterns of the triune God in the Scriptures? In the name of a false compassion, genuine love is replaced with conformity to a society detached from any ethical center. (The sermon in Chapter 28 elaborates the goodness of God's commandments.)

- In response to the increasing clamor for choice, some congregations foster consumerism according to "felt needs" instead of embracing what is truly needful. Correlatively, churches are turned into a democracy in which doctrine and practice are decided by majority preferences (see Chapter 16). One result of this imagining that the Body of Christ is characterized by choice is bitter battles over taste (which will be discussed further in Chapter 15). Another result is that, in our current therapeutic society, everyone thinks he or she "needs" emotional coddling, whereas God has repeatedly taught us that Christians can *know* better. Especially in the face of suffering we learn that the will is stronger than our emotions, and that faith can trust a God who might even be momentarily hidden.[6] Ministering merely to felt needs and choices cheats worshipers of the truths and maturity they need to engage their wills over their emotions.

---

6. See Marva J. Dawn, *Joy in Our Weakness: A Gift of Hope from the Book of Revelation* (St. Louis: Concordia Publishing House, 1994).

Hear Clearly What I Am Saying

Please do not think, on the basis of the foregoing list, that I am advocating a wooden traditionalism. Jaroslav Pelikan's distinction is forever apt that *traditionalism* is the dead faith of the living, whereas *tradition* is the living faith of the dead. In the worship controversies between the "traditionalists" and the "contemporaryists," I am opposed to both polarities. I want the *best* from both sides, since the Church's treasure house is filled with both new and old. Since our congregations are linked to all God's people throughout space and time, we need both continuity with our heritage and constant reformation using faithful new forms and words and musical styles.

Also, I am not advocating biblicism or biblical idolatry. When I call for more truth and not less, I yearn for that truth to be presented without oppression or violence, with genuine care for the listeners, in vital forms, with the honest and humble recognition that we know Truth only partially.

Most of all, do not think that I am not interested in evangelism. I am, however, really worried about some misconceptions that are thriving on the lecture circuit and in the books of marketing gurus these days. I am intensely concerned for ministering to our neighbors in this postmodern world (as will be seen especially in Chapters 20 and 28-30). In fact, let us return now to the Canadian producer, introduced earlier in this chapter, who asked, "What will you tell churches to do about me? I don't go to church."

"First of all, I would like to be your friend," I replied, and she reacted with stunned silence. I told her that from our conversation I could tell that we probably had a lot in common, that we could become great friends. "We could have wonderful, probing conversations," I said.

She immediately inquired, "And would those conversations turn to the topic of faith in Christ?"

"Invariably," I acknowledged, "because Jesus Christ is the center of my life."

"And," she then broke in, "your life would show me that faith makes a difference?"

"Yes, I pray so," I responded. "And then I would hope that you might want to come with me to worship the triune God."

What We Need Is the Truth

What we need in worship is the Truth — the whole truth, nothing but the truth, so help us, God! That oath from the witness stand gives us good guidelines for the witness that takes place in our lives and in our worship services.

The Truth that the Church has to offer to people caught in the postmodern condition must be shared in all its wholeness. To those who criticize Christianity because it has been (and sometimes now is) violent and oppressive, we must respond with the repentant admission that they are right. Beyond accepting blame for Christians' failures in history, we must recognize the whole truth that we remain corrupt and fallible. The Scriptures teach us thoroughly that our nature is helplessly sinful, hopelessly lost. That truth forces us to see that we cannot know the truth entirely, that our eyes are blinded by sin, that our understanding of God is only partial. But that does not negate the Truth of God nor our recognition of Christ who is himself the Truth, the Life, and the Way.

Against the postmodern rejection of meta-narrative — that is, of the possibility that there is any universal, overarching Truth that is true for all people in all places — I believe that Christians can humbly suggest the non-oppressive, all-inclusive story, detailed more thoroughly in the previous chapter, of a triune God who creates, redeems, and unifies as manifestations of his perfect love for the whole world. The Christian meta-narrative is the account of a Promising God who always keeps his promises — a Truth clearly seen in the First Testament history of Israel and most clearly seen in the history of Jesus of Nazareth, who died and rose again in fulfillment of God's promises. We believe that this meta-narrative will reach its ultimate fulfillment when Jesus comes again to bring God's promised gracious reign to fruition — and thus the meta-narrative of God's kingdom already initiated gives us all that we most deeply need of hope, purpose, and fulfillment in this present life.

This God of eternal mystery condescends to reveal himself to us — a process to which he invites us by drawing us to worship him. That is why our worship needs to be structured as richly and deeply as possible, so that we never lose sight of the fact that God is the One who enables us to come to worship and the Infinite Center who thus receives our praise.

Furthermore, our worship must contain nothing but the truth. Music, songs, Scripture lessons, sermons, liturgical forms, architecture, and other accoutrements of art and gesture and ambience are all means by which God invites, reveals, and forms us. If we use shallow (I did not say *simple*) worship materials, they will not reveal the truth about God. Instead, these shallow materials will shape shallow theology and form us superficially. Songs with cheap or sentimental lyrics or banal music belie the coherence and integrity of God. Sermons that draw attention to the preacher's eloquence or merely to the illusory or superficial needs of the listeners deprive the congregation of the formative power of the scriptural narratives for meeting our genuine

needs for repentant insight, constant forgiveness, authentic security, uncon-
ditional love, absolute healing, faithful presence, fruitful freedom, compelling motivation and coherent guidance for daily life, and eternal hope.

Worship can never give us the whole truth, but worship must never give
us untruth or less than truth. Our finite minds cannot begin to grasp all that
there is to learn about God, but every time the community gathers we have
the opportunity to add to our total store of truth what this time of corporate
worship contributes. Only by God's grace and in the context of prayer and the
whole Christian community can worship leaders prepare services that present as much truth as possible.

Against postmodernity's rejection of the past and of authority, in the
Church we realize that we are greatly helped in our planning by the wisdom
gathered throughout the Church's existence, by history's sorting of the good
from the less-than-good in hymns and liturgies and interpretations. Now it is
our responsibility to sort through what is new in order to choose what is true —
keeping God as the Subject/Object of our worship, nurturing the truthful character of individual believers, and forming the Christian community to be outreaching with the Truth that we know.

Equipping the Saints for Ministry

If worship stays well focused on God as its Center, participants will become
better equipped to be God's witnesses to their worlds. To introduce our families and neighbors and co-workers to the Trinity and to God's gifts for them,
we need an ever-growing understanding of his promises, his character, his interventions in the world, his truth that underlies our realities. Out of a character formed by the biblical narratives, by their faithful interpretation, and by
resulting sound doctrine will flow love that responds to the love of God. Such
a character will manifest forgiveness that recognizes the potency of the Father's grace, actions that follow the model of Jesus, encouragement and compassion empowered by the Paraclete.

Of course, strong Christian character cannot be formed if the worship
hour is the only time the Church has to nurture it, but worship's subtle influence on character dare not be misdirected. If we sing only narcissistic ditties,
we will develop a faith that depends on feelings and that is inward-curved instead of outward-turned.

Worship as Truth that is thereby formative of character must be a major
issue for our churches because the immense needs of our world require persons nurtured by depth and faithfulness, rather than by what is flimsy, if not

flippant (some examples of which will be given elsewhere in this book, especially in Chapter 11). It is essential that worship carefully equip the saints with the truths of faith so that they can witness to, and serve, their neighbors. The Church needs both preachers and musicians with great faithfulness to give worship participants what they need instead of what they think they need, to offer that which is needful instead of catering to neediness. Ultimately (though probably not at first), this meat will be much more satisfying than the pabulum of a schmoozy emotionalism.

Second Timothy 3:14-17 invites us to be trained in the Holy Scriptures — to *know* them and be formed by them and not just "believe" as if that were a leap in the dark, to have habits and not selfish preferences. We need that kind of training much more than our parents did, since the society no longer supports it and since so many cultural forces alien to the gospel impinge on our lives and urge our conformity. Yet many congregations these days present only "adult forums" and sermons that merely "share opinions" on various issues rather than offering deep explication of Scripture to lay the basis for genuine Christian thinking, thorough teaching of the biblical narratives in order to form us to react as God's people with kingdom values to the problems and social issues of our everyday lives. Why does so much of the new and old music used in many congregations lack theological depth, biblical images, motivation to be about God's purposes of witnessing, justice building, and peacemaking in the world? What kind of people are our worship services forming?

A Vision

I believe that Jesus during his earthly life prayed for us — those who would believe through the witness of his disciples — that we would be sanctified in the truth and then sent out into the world to bear testimony to it (John 17:17-21). That is a wonderful description of worship: that by God's gracious invitation and Christ's intercession and the Spirit's enabling we are welcomed to learn of the Trinity through the biblical narratives passed on by faithful witnesses. Gathered in the community of saints, we are formed by the truth taught in worship's music and word to be Church so that out of our Christian character will flow the witness of our words and deeds for the sake of the world.

The postmodern world that surrounds us yearns for stability, morality, security, fidelity, faith, hope, and love. These deep needs can only be met through the One who meets our deepest need for Truth. Let us make sure that the worship services we plan and conduct present that Truth in all its clarity and beauty and goodness.

6

Why Is Setting Limits on the Media Important for Worship?

> Then Samuel said to all the house of Israel, "If you are returning
> to the LORD with all your heart, then put away the foreign gods
> and the Astartes from among you. Direct your heart to the LORD,
> and serve him only . . ."
>
> 1 Samuel 7:3

This morning on National Public Radio I heard a brief interview with a
professor from the Yale Medical School concerning his current attempt
to teach his students new skills of observation by taking them to an art museum. He emphasized that doctors these days rely so much on the results of
lab tests and imaging procedures and other technological tools that they don't
really examine their patients. He mourned that his freshmen had little experience in using their senses, so he was beginning with the visual by teaching
them to look at paintings.

Similarly, I was astonished by one evaluation of a seminary mini-
course I taught on "Music and the Arts in Christian Worship." Though I had
used all kinds of materials to engage all the senses, one student commented,
"multimedia would of [sic] enhanced the course" — deepening my concern
about the destructive effects of our screened-in culture (see also Chapter 25).
My intentions for the class periods had included utilizing a great diversity of
media to involve more of the senses, but I had separated the various elements

in order to make deeper concentration more achievable and so that involvement would be direct instead of secondhand as much as possible. For the three-day course I had played more than a dozen audio recordings of music through the ages (including Hebrew psalm singing, Gregorian chant, the Latin mass, a Bach cantata, early American music, a contemporary setting of the Lamentations of Jeremiah, Russian Orthodox music, an African-American spiritual, and a contemporary organ and brass hymn setting); passed around various kinds of tangible fabric and visual arts, including a trinitarian painting, symbols for banners, liturgical colors, historical crosses, and icons; utilized some dramatic readings of Scriptures, including one in which the entire class participated and one that imitated the style of a Greek chorus with ten readers in three different groups; led nine different short worship services all with different styles of music, especially from the world Church, which invited class members' physical movement; requested four seminary students to demonstrate liturgical dance; and lit a candle to bring fragrance and glow to the classroom. I regretted that I could not engage the sense of taste, since it was not possible to celebrate the Lord's Supper together.

Our culture, however, is so conditioned by the constant bombardment of hyped and frenzied sounds and images on television and by "virtual reality" that a few of the students found it impossible to concentrate on or to become engaged in the truly *multi* media the course was providing. For most people in our society, it seems, the term *multimedia* simply means multiple screens and a rapid rate of image/sound changes rather than the use of a diverse assortment of mixed media. I am only one of many commentators who grieve that unless something is on a screen, persons trained by our culture can no longer appreciate it.

One person who seems intent on calling our culture back to wonder at the real world is the designer of the comic strip, "Rose Is Rose." Frequently the cartoon illustrates mother Rose marveling at colors, flowers, birds, rainbows, her husband or son, or whatever. One day the strip showed Rose and her little boy Pasquale walking together at evening in the snow — Rose with a big smile on her face. Pasquale looked more serious. In the second frame he stood by himself with his eyes brightly wide open and his mouth shaped into an O. In the third frame he peered intently up into the falling snow, while Rose, several paces ahead and smaller in the drawing, glanced back at him with a questioning look. Her head leaned into the fourth frame to ask, "What happened?" and Pasquale reverently replied, "The quiet is so deep I got stuck in it!"

Why Does This Matter?

Perhaps you wonder why this topic should be made so prominent in a book about worship. Most people think that watching television or surfing the Net is at worst just a harmless waste of time or at best a great gift for gathering useful information. But this issue is critical: Are our children — are we — able to get stuck in the quiet? Are we able to waste time royally, instead of mindlessly? Are we able to concentrate, contemplate, meditate, marvel, be reverent, experience awe, cherish silence in the presence of God? Are we able to observe the wonders of God's creation in flavors and fragrances, see the beauties of the arts, hear the timbres and resonances and tones of the music of the spheres, touch the fibers of the universe and the fabrics of human ingenuity?

We are raising a generation of children who would rather look at famous paintings on a screen than see their immensity, the skill of the brush strokes, the glow of the colors in an art museum. Can it be that people actually prefer the tinny sounds of a CD-Rom with pictures on a screen to great music live in a concert hall where one can watch the melody travel from section to section of the orchestra or see the counterpoint contrasts between sides of the stage? Certainly now the sounds of a good music CD are cheaper and easier to use — and the performance has been made perfect by retakes and remasterings. What is lost to the hearer, however, is the strain and trials, the sacrifices and triumphs of human endeavor. Transferred to the Sunday worship service, the development of perfect sound tracks has caused many worshipers to be dissatisfied now with merely human musicians who make mistakes, with less than professional-sounding choirs, with preachers who stumble occasionally, with the nitty-gritty of genuine community life.

What We Can Do

Obviously we can't change the entire culture in this book. And, of course, I am not rejecting all the wonderful benefits of our CDs and films and computers and technological tools and toys. I usually stress the opposite side, however, because the destructive effects of our society's technicization are less frequently exhibited than are the advantages.

When we look seriously at what is happening in our world, how can we help but be overwhelmed? The information superhighway is entering our homes; five hundred different television channels are an imminent possibility; high resolution television sets will be readily available by the time this book comes out; our churches' children are exposed to all kinds of new opportunities for media involvement; cyberspace promises them entirely new virtual realities. It is beyond the scope of this book to discuss here how Christians can influence the television and movie industries, though that is an important subject to pursue. It is also beyond the scope of this chapter to deal with the effects of cyberspace on worship, though that is a subject I have been studying extensively; it is, however, simply too vast a topic for me to begin to consider it in this book.[1]

My main goal in this chapter is simply to urge that we in the Christian community ask better questions. In order to do that, we need, first of all, to become more aware of the hidden and harmful consequences of our culture's media bombardment. Then we must, as a community, talk together about the issues and the problems, about how we can be more supportive of each other in taking some stands for the sake of the welfare of our children — and ourselves. We and our churches must understand the stakes of our technological times and what Christians must do in the present media revolution.[2]

Let's face the question squarely: If television is causing people to be dissatisfied with the worship of our churches, should we change worship to be more like television — or should the splendor of our worship cause people to ask better questions about television?

Agents of Socialization

Let us think about the catalysts that form our children, what gives them their ideas about how to live — besides their parents and the schools. Since 98.3 percent of U.S. homes have television sets, with an average of 2.2 sets per

---

1. A few resources that I highly recommend are the following: Stanley Aronowitz, Barbara Martinsons, and Michael Menser, eds., *Technoscience and Cyberculture* (New York: Routledge, 1996); James Brook and Iain A. Boal, eds., *Resisting the Virtual Life: The Culture and Politics of Information* (San Francisco: City Lights, 1995); Tal Brooke, gen. ed., *Virtual Gods* (Eugene, OR: Harvest House Publishers, 1997); Douglas Groothuis, *The Soul in Cyberspace* (Grand Rapids: Baker Books, 1997); Stephanie Mills, ed., *Turning Away from Technology: A New Vision for the Twenty-first Century* (San Francisco: Sierra Club Books, 1997); Jeff Zaleski, *The Soul of Cyberspace: How New Technology Is Changing Our Spiritual Lives* (San Francisco: HarperSanFrancisco, 1997).

2. This topic is more thoroughly developed in chapter 10, "Amusing Ourselves to Death," in Marva J. Dawn, *Is It a Lost Cause? Having the Heart of God for the Church's Children* (Grand Rapids: Wm. B. Eerdmans Publishing Co., 1997), pp. 164-80. That chapter contains study questions that a congregational Bible study class or parents' support group could discuss together.

household,[3] we have to ask whether TV has become *the* major agent of socialization. Research reveals that in the average home the TV is turned on more than 7 hours per day; each individual watches approximately 4½ hours per day. When young people graduate from high school, they have spent more hours watching television than they have spent in school and will have viewed approximately 500,000 commercials; 80 percent of their discretionary time has been spent watching television.[4] When we remember that most investigations disclose that the amount of quality time parents spend daily with their children is usually tabulated in minutes or even seconds, we *must* consider the effects of television on their formation more seriously — or else we are seriously failing to be Church!

Bruce Forbes, a professor of religious studies and co-chair of the "Religion and Popular Culture" program unit of the American Academy of Religion, writes that these statistics cannot be dismissed with elitist scorn; when he chronicled his own behavior, he discovered that he did indeed watch at least four hours of television each day — while he dressed, ate, relaxed, and "needed" the news (a presupposition that also ought to be questioned; see below).[5] However, as an adult, Forbes was probably for the most part already formed by other agencies before the onslaught of this much television watching. We must face unflinchingly how television watching has become the new worship of our children. A dozen years ago, William Fore warned, in *Television and Religion: The Shaping of Faith, Values, and Culture,* that "religion and television are the symbols and in many ways the concrete embodiments of the powers that are contending for our very souls." Fore's thesis was that television is

> beginning to usurp a role which until recently has been the role of the church in our society, namely, to shape our system of values, embody our faith, and express our cultural essence. This shift, from a religious center to what I call a technological center, is ominous. It represents a shift from dealing with human questions to dealing instead with utilitarian questions, from asking, How will this affect people? to asking only, How will this make a profit? (11-12)

3. This information is from the U.S. Bureau of the Census, *Statistical Abstract of the United States: 1996* (Washington, DC: U.S. Government Printing Office, 1996), p. 561, cited in Bruce David Forbes, "Why Clergy Should Not Ignore Television," *Word and World* 18, no. 1 (Winter 1998): 34.

4. William F. Fore, *Television and Religion: The Shaping of Faith, Values, and Culture* (Minneapolis: Augsburg, 1987), pp. 16-17. Page references to this book in the rest of this chapter are given parenthetically in the text.

5. Forbes, p. 36.

We see that same shift, of course, in the questions that are often being asked about worship these days. Congregations are not asking about the long-term consequences for the development of Christ's disciples; they are asking about what will appeal to people and therefore make an immediate profit in the congregational numbers and finances.

Certainly TV has its blessings. It helps people escape and relax. But, as we shall see below, such escape is hardly harmless if it fosters violence and sexual immorality, greed and permanent passivity. Television also provides "*psychological compensation* for [persons'] sense of alienation or frustration born of loneliness, poverty, illness, joblessness, loss of loved ones, divorce, and similar problems" (19), but again, we must wonder if there ought not to be much more healthy ways to offer this restoration. What would happen if we could instead recover deep friendships and caring neighborhoods, if the Church could enfold the lonely and unemployed and sick and destitute in the compassion and affection which Jesus says are indeed gifts to himself? (See Matthew 25:31-46.)

Fore also notes that TV furnishes people with a sense of security and stability and belonging, with information, with a rich fantasy world, and with the means of coping — by telling us what to wear, how to speak, and how to clean our toilets (19-20). As he summarizes the present situation,

> What is happening is that the whole medium reflects and expresses the myths by which we live. These myths tell us who we are, what we have done, what power we have, who has power and who does not, what is right and what is not. It also tells us what has happened, and what has not. It takes our history and our present and interprets it to us. (21)

In sum, TV gives us our worldview and the symbol system through which we continue to interpret the world each day.[6] It is this *orientation* and this *process* that are so dangerous, for most of the values of that shaping are inimical to the message of Christ and the priorities of the kingdom of God.[7]

It is impossible for the worship of our churches (brief as it is in comparison with the 28 hours or so per week that the average person watches television) to imbue the participants completely with another worldview and symbol system for interpreting daily life. The difficulty is compounded if worship augments some of the values of TV. For that reason we need to pay closer attention to these particular dangers.

6. Forbes, p. 43.

7. See also Bruce Forbes and Jeffrey Mahan, eds., *Religion and Popular Culture in America* (Berkeley: University of California Press, 1998).

A Sampling of the Dangers to Worship[8]

In the short space of this chapter I cannot thoroughly elaborate the ideas I want to introduce or report on all the research, but let me sketch (all too briefly) for your further consideration ten dangers of media consumption and the essence of how splendorous worship is one antidote (of the many there must be) to these problems. (I will speak of these only in terms of television watching, but the same perils apply even more so to other forms of media consumption, like surfing the Net.) With greater awareness of the problems, Christians can strategize how to take advantage of media benefits without falling prey to the great perils.

1. The most obvious problem with the proliferation of media options, most clearly demonstrated by television consumption, is that involvement with them *wastes so much time.* Those of us who serve in the Church are doubtless weary of the tedious excuse, "But I don't have any time," when people are not willing to participate in various mission efforts of the congregation. Twenty years ago, in the amount of time spent watching television during one year, the average U.S. citizen could read the entire Bible at a normal pace fifteen times! What must it be now that television consumption has increased so dramatically? Reading has decreased by half since the 1960s. Other leisure activities, especially family interactions and congregational service, have declined comparably.

Certainly I recognize that there are plenty of other reasons why people don't have enough time. (I don't even own a television, and still I never have adequate time for all the projects related to God's kingdom that I would like to undertake.) My point is simply that television trains us to waste time (not in the royal sense at all). And meanwhile, subtly, it is making the most of the time to nurture in us many other character traits — many of which, as we shall see in the following points, are destructive of our skills for worship.

I am also not saying that there should be no *leisure* time in the Christian life — but I am concerned that the time-wasting not be inherently dangerous. In fact, worship that is truly immersed in the splendor of God is a *royal* waste of time (see Chapter 22), and Christians and Jews especially know the absolute necessity of a whole day set apart from our usual busy-ness. But the Sabbath day is an entire day of genuine ceasing and rest, not escapist time-wasting.[9]

---

8. This final portion of the chapter previously appeared in greatly abbreviated form as "Setting Limits on the Media," *Lutheran Libraries* 39, no. 1 (Winter 1996): 5-8. My thanks to editor Felicity Hanson for permission to expand that version extensively here.

9. See Marva J. Dawn, *Keeping the Sabbath Wholly: Ceasing, Resting, Embracing, Feasting* (Grand Rapids: Wm. B. Eerdmans Publishing Co., 1989).

2. Watching television *stifles the imagination.* I notice this especially while traveling on airplanes — people who are saturated with media in their homes cannot manage to entertain themselves. The children often don't know how to play without electronic toys, aren't ever interested in looking out the window at nature, cannot make up stories (without violence), won't read books. Adults must have the airplane movies or "short subjects"/television reruns going and get terribly grumpy when they malfunction. But the danger to worship is equally immense. If we always have to have everything presented to us visually, how can we pay attention to texts, or imagine Moses or the disciples, or contemplate the presence of God?

The increasing speed of TV is a great contributor to the loss of imagination since the mind has no time to recover from the constant bombardment. How does this affect our ability to meditate on God in the necessary silences of worship? Are we able to deal with the ambiguities of God that force our minds to go beyond what is readily apparent?

The loss of imagination is also related to some of the twaddle (Kierkegaard's word) that characterizes some churches' worship these days. As William Fore explains, "Trivialization is inevitable in the world of the technological era, with its emphasis upon utilitarian means rather than truthful ends" (32). If we simply want a God that "sells" to the masses, we will invariably reduce the truth of our multi-splendored God. If we want our faith to be developed as fast as problems are solved on sitcoms, we will not have the patience to imagine God's working in us to grow us when there are no immediate, visible results.

Worship that is filled with splendor, in contrast, will greatly stimulate the imagination — with symbols and other works of art, with a wide variety of musical sounds, with texts and preaching full of images and thought-provoking challenges, with silences that give inspiration free rein.

3. Much more critical, Jane Healy's research demonstrates thoroughly that children who watch television extensively develop *smaller brains.* Without output, constant input fails to bridge the hemispheres of the brain, and lack of involvement with the environment decreases the proliferation of dendrites. Only in conversation and by manipulating things — toys, a musical instrument, one's legs in running — does the brain build new pathways and the information received actually get learned. Thus, Healy emphasizes that the media's bombardment not only causes our children to be unable to think; it also prevents them from actually developing the brain space to think in.[10]

---

10. See Jane Healy, *Endangered Minds: Why Our Children Don't Think* (New York: Simon and Schuster, 1990). A fuller description of her work is offered in the first chapter

This point is especially critical if we want to train our children to worship (for it is, indeed, a learned skill that will not happen automatically). Their ability to pay attention for longer periods of time depends on having the brain space to do so. I cannot urge parents strongly enough to avoid exposing their children to much television when they are young and their minds are in the formative stages.

The inverse is also true: if in worship we engage the children in singing, holding hymnbooks and finding pages in them, sitting and rising for various parts of the worship service, repeating memorized creeds and prayers and liturgical elements, putting their offerings in the basket and passing the peace of God, and other elements of the worship service, we contribute to the development of their intellectual capacities.

4. Neil Postman's *Amusing Ourselves to Death* accentuates also that television makes us *less motivated to think* — and this is true even of the supposedly "good" programs. Those who created "Sesame Street," for example, invented it to help children love school, but they learned instead to love school only if it is like Sesame Street — with nonsequential learning, fast-paced entertainment, and no consequences. The very medium itself emphasizes feeling and amusement rather than linear, rational thought.[11] This is especially destructive for a faith that is based on what we *know* about the God who transforms us through the renewal of our minds (see Romans 12:2).

All of the elements of worship listed above with regard to the imagination certainly are possible motivators for better thinking. However, the major reason why the splendor of worship ignites thought is that it is *God's* splendor with which we are concerned — and that gives us a radically different perspective from which to think, a slant on the world and on our life from outside ourselves.

5. Very apparent to all of us are the effects of television viewing on the *violence* and *sexual immorality* in our culture.[12] Various watch groups have made it clear that the amount, vividness, blatancy, and constant bombardment of television brutality and eroticism are escalating at an incredible rate — and that much of the rape, aggressiveness, destructiveness, and crime on our streets is directly related. Even programming that is not sexually explicit or violent indirectly contributes to sexual problems and incivility because the very medium of

---

of my *Reaching Out without Dumbing Down: A Theology of Worship for the Turn-of-the-Century Culture* (Grand Rapids: Wm. B. Eerdmans Publishing Co., 1995).

11. See Neil Postman, *Amusing Ourselves to Death* (New York: Viking Penguin, 1985).

12. See, for example, Patrick D. Miller's comments on the latter in his editorial "Good-bye Seinfeld," *Theology Today* 55, no. 2 (July 1998): 147-51.

television trains us in, and increases our demand for, instant gratification. One might wonder why this should be important for us to note in a book about worship, but if the Subject/Object of our worship is the God of peace and faithfulness, then too much formation by violence-saturated media and sultry advertisements or lustful programs will make it much more difficult for us to understand the radical (that is, getting to the roots of things) alternatives of the way of life we follow to be God's people, to be Church. Furthermore, the demand for instant gratification is, of course, one of the driving forces in many of the conflicts over worship.

Worship that immerses us in the splendor of God's *shalom* and creation design, in contrast, will give us a vision of much better practices for living than those espoused by the media. Songs and texts and preaching and prayers will help to form us to be peacemakers and justice builders, chaste friends and faithful lovers. Worship that resists the cry for instant gratification, moreover, contributes to the building of these virtues.

6. Much of the violence in our culture is perpetrated, of course, by persons who lack loving and supportive communities — but that, too, is indirectly related to media consumption. And television's perpetration of our culture's lack of social intimacy and tenderness in affectionate communities also contributes to the society's mad enslavement to genital intimacy outside of God's design for it within the protective framework of a covenantally committed marriage.[13] Jacques Ellul, a prophetic French sociologist and Christian witness, made it clear in many of his books that the rise of the technological milieu is paralleled by a corresponding *decrease in skills (and time!) for intimacy.* According to a report by Fortino & Associates, U.S. citizens daily spend an average of only about four or five minutes conversing with their spouse and about thirty seconds talking with their children! Frequently in conversations with young people at their convocations and in discussions after my lectures at colleges, I hear from them both their awareness that televisions and other technological toys and tools (like Walkmans) hinder their development of skills for intimacy and also their pain that they have been deprived of family communication.

One of the reasons why this danger is important for worship is that people often want the wrong kinds of intimacy in worship — the coziness of a God small enough to be merely cuddly, the subjective comfort of sentimentalized songs (that in an elitist way leave out those who don't "feel" close to God), the affectionate intimacy of friends in the congregation that ignores

13. See Marva J. Dawn, *Sexual Character: Beyond Technique to Intimacy* (Grand Rapids: Wm. B. Eerdmans Publishing Co., 1993).

the stranger, or a form of private devotion that neglects to create public ritual into which anyone can enter.

Worship that immerses us in the splendor of our triune God, in contrast, will welcome us into the communion of saints, the community of those formed in the image of this relational God. God's is a genuine intimacy — open to the stranger and nourishing the virtues of compassionate caring. His Revelation is full of instructions for building intimacy and of models that invite us to take the necessary time to do so.[14]

7. No one can doubt that television fosters *greed,* and not only in its advertisements.[15] Shouldn't it be "strange, unreal" to us — as it is to old Jack, the main character of one of Wendell Berry's stories — "That a whole roomful of people should sit with their mouths open like a nest of young birds, peering into a picture box the invariable message of which is the desirability of Something Else or Someplace Else"?[16]

Certainly we all know that much of children's programming is driven by the toy and treats manufacturers whose products are flagrantly pushed. Because I do not own a television and rarely watch one, I'm very aware of content as I watch. I am astonished at the increasing number of advertisements, the acceleration of their hype, the psychological subtlety of their appeal, and yet — paradoxically — their inanity. Nevertheless, people find themselves humming the jingles, and the name recognition in their subconscious influences their purchasing decisions. Meanwhile, the values inculcated about what we should own and how we should dress have pulled us further from the way of life of the One who had no place to lay his head. (Don't worry: I'm *very* aware that I'm equally pulled away and tempted by other forms of indoctrination. Probably I'm in greater danger because other methods are not so blatantly inane.)

The greed nurtured by endless commercials takes unhealthy shapes in connection with worship. We become greedy for what makes us feel good, instead of for what will transform us. We become possessive about our particular ways of doing things, our own tastes in musical style, our special place to sit, our cozy coterie of friends.

14. See Marva J. Dawn, *Truly the Community: Romans 12 and How to Be the Church* (Grand Rapids: Wm. B. Eerdmans Publishing Co., 1992; reissued 1997), for a consideration of this loss of intimacy in our culture and for instructions and discussion questions on how we can build genuine community in our churches.

15. See a deeper discussion of this danger in Chapter 7 of this book and in chapter 9, "Santa Claus Is Coming to Town," of *Is It a Lost Cause?,* pp. 145-63.

16. Wendell Berry, *The Memory of Old Jack* (New York: Harcourt Brace Jovanovich, 1974), p. 188.

Royally wasting time through immersion in the splendor of God, in contrast, generates generosity. We learn that we operate not out of scarcity (which makes us grab for ourselves) but out of abundance — which allows us to enjoy more thoroughly the richness of God's presence in all its flavors and forms and which frees us to share the gifts of the Church's heritage with the world.

8. The greed fostered by media is just one aspect of the larger problem that television produces a *muddled perception of reality.* Sitcoms pretend that major life problems can be solved in half an hour; advertisements stir us emotionally into feeling that the right purchases are the ticket to those quick solutions. Playing particularly on our fears and desires, commercials don't really give us many facts about a product so that we can make logical, cognitive decisions. Rather, they give us cozy scenes and appeal to our hunger for intimacy — a hunger caused, in part, by the very medium that is offering such scenes. Jacques Ellul warned us forty years ago that one of the dangers of escalating technology and decreasing skills of intimacy is that we reverse the poles and technologize our intimacy (parents saying goodnight over the intercom instead of tucking children in, as one student reported) and intimize our technology (as exemplified in such ads).

One other major distortion of reality that we must consider here is the muddled perceptions created by television "news." Why has the wide availability of news programs made us think that we have to know every little thing reported? How much does it affect what we do about world situations for us to see the superficial reports about them offered in small bites every evening on "the tube"? Ellul frequently pointed out that daily news on the media fosters a catastrophic, fragmentary, and inadequate view of the world. One evening in a small city hotel I turned on the television news and heard a reporter describe half a dozen rapes and several resultant deaths in a row, after which this beautifully dressed, carefully coifed, lovely young woman smiled beguilingly at me and said sweetly, "See you tomorrow." Why should I tune in tomorrow? I had just listened to enough murder and mayhem to last me the rest of my life! I certainly didn't "need" that news, although I did pray for the victims' families and those victims still living — but the news did make me much more nervous about sleeping there that night.

William Fore summarizes the distortions of reality by the media as follows:

> Thus the mass-media worldview tells us that we are basically good, that happiness is the chief end of life, and that happiness consists in obtaining material goods. The media transform the value of sexuality into sex appeal,

the value of self-respect into pride, the value of will-to-live into will-to-power. They exacerbate acquisitiveness into greed; they deal with insecurity by generating more insecurity, and anxiety by generating more anxiety. They change the value of recreation into competition and the value of rest into escape. And perhaps worst of all, the media constrict our experience and substitute media world for real world so that we become less and less able to make the fine value-judgments that living in such a complex world requires. (67)

All of this affects our worship in many ways, most prominently in the inability of many participants to listen to more than sound bites. Some people who come to worship expect that God should solve their problems immediately, that they should be able to have a quick spiritual fix. One of the greatest dangers is that the intimidating number of calamities and crises makes it difficult to believe that the One we worship is still Lord of the cosmos.

These muddled perceptions generated by television must be offset by a broad vision of the reality — the character and interventions — of our God, who is cosmically sovereign and compassionately saving.[17] Worship that continually adds to our perceptions of God's splendors and our awareness of his commitment to us equips us with a worldview to resist the catastrophic notions and quick-fix techniques of our culture and with the prayerful concern and caring patience necessary to be of genuine service to those harmed by social and natural forces.

9. Television is particularly dangerous to the worship of the triune God because *its view of religion is usually superficial and often prejudiced.* Contemplate how religion is portrayed — or, as was primarily the case in the past, was not portrayed — in the media. Religion's absence from general programming until recently delivered the subliminal message that religion is marginal.[18] Religious characters that did appear were usually weird, lightweight, arrogant, or pretentious. The excerpts of Princess Diana's funeral that were replayed on the news did not include any of the traditional elements from the rites of the Church of England; the funeral of Mother Teresa was hardly covered.

On the other hand, the medium itself has replaced religion in giving people their sense of ultimate meaning and in justifying their behaviors and

17. See especially chapters 10-12, 15-17, and 21-26 of Marva J. Dawn, *To Walk and Not Faint: A Month of Meditations on Isaiah 40,* 2nd ed. (Grand Rapids: Wm. B. Eerdmans Publishing Co., 1997).

18. Forbes, p. 39.

way of life.[19] These implicitly theological themes have been presented differently by television; that is, ultimate meaning has come from a source of redemption unrelated to God,[20] and behaviors have been justified by morés arising from the rebellions of the sixties rather than from God's purposes for human beings revealed in the biblical commandments. Religion has often been depicted as the legalistic spoiler of everyone's fun, rather than the conveyor of a way of life that is the most satisfying because it conforms to the created nature of our true humanity.

Moreover, by means of various factors listed in this chapter, television has robbed "genuine religious vocabularies of their power. The symbols, rites, images, and references of religion no longer move people" (28). As William Fore asserts, the solution is not "to make worship just like television — with its constant hype and glitz — but to invite people to recognize the phoniness of that medium, to cherish instead reflection and genuine thought instead of brainwashing" (29).

Worship of our triune God in all his splendor contradicts television's false notions of both God and his people by enfolding us in the ultimate meaning of loving him and enjoying him forever in that royal waste of time. We discover the beauty of the Creator's designs and moral foundations, the freedom of Christ's thorough redemption, the Joy of the Spirit's empowerment to live an obedient life.

10. The problem with the media revolution that bothers me most is what Neil Postman calls the *"Low Information-Action Ratio"* (note the acronym). Television offers its viewers enormous amounts of data about which they cannot do a thing; consequently, it trains them to receive and discard information without acting on it. Television makes us L.I.A.R.s because we do not do what we could with the truths we learn. We watch news reports about poverty, but we don't lessen our consumption in order to give more away to feed the hungry and to build economic possibilities for others. We learn about wars and crime, but we contribute to violence ourselves because we don't have enough time to listen to our children or to help provide post-incarceration guidance to a former prisoner. Think what this L.I.A.R. training does to sermons and Christian education, as it turns us into L.I.A.R.s who know God's will but don't live according to his purposes, who know the needs of the world but don't change our lifestyles to ameliorate them.

19. William Fore (p. 62) suggests that this new religion has its own "liturgical year," including the Rose Bowl parade, Super Sunday baseball, the U.S. Open in tennis, and the Super Bowl.

20. Forbes, pp. 40-41.

The severity of the low information-action ratio will escalate rapidly as more and more people get hooked into the Internet. Already scores of people have told me that they waste too much time surfing and chatting. I always ask them what they do with the information they gain — and, with the exception of some scholars gathering specific information for research, very few achieve anything with it. This is the theological problem with which I wrestle most: How will we train worshipers to act on their Christian beliefs if they have been trained by television not to act on what they know and, consequently, view the narratives of the faith as simply more information?

Immersion in the full splendor of God is one antidote to this L.I.A.R. syndrome, for the nature of God is to engage us in response. Praying "Thy will be done" commissions us as agents for the fulfillment of God's purposes. Hearing the instructions of the New Testament letters challenges us to be Church in practical, tangible ways. Singing together knits us into a community of activists, supporting each other and finding strength in the larger whole of the Church.

This list of media hazards is lamentably brief, but I hope that its highlighting of ten infectious dangers will lead to further conversation and study (preferably together with members of your Christian community). I pray that this brief sketch is enough to make us deeply concerned — and that we won't be L.I.A.R.s in response! I believe this is a key time for churches and individual Christians to be at the forefront in setting limits to media consumption, in deepening family bonds and faith roots for children so that they have moral values by which to weigh the media they observe, and in offering to the world both prophetic wisdom and workable solutions to the problems that the media inherently engender.

Who Will Hold the Media Responsible?

It should be horrifying to us to realize that though television is a (if not *the*) major source of socialization in our culture, it has absolutely no controls on its content. Our society elects school board members and invests in national programs of testing and standardization in order to hold schools accountable for their processes of socializing our children — with mixed results, of course. But what means do we have in our culture for holding television responsible for its socialization of the violence, immorality, incivility, and greed noted above?[21] As William Fore summarizes the problem, the media

21. I am indebted to my brother, Glen Gersmehl, for pointing out to me that of the

reflect the values in the culture, and they legitimate, circulate, and amplify them and thus, in reality, "create" them as potent values, through the process of resonance. By choosing to repeat and amplify some of the myriad of possible values, attitudes, and worldviews, and not to repeat or amplify others, the media become a powerful process that helps to create, maintain, and change our culture, and those who become expert at finding and amplifying these messages feel no moral responsibility for *what* is resonated, but only that it is done well. (44)

My concern in this chapter is not to fight for some means of restricting television's promulgation of values destructive to society (though that would be a worthy use of Christians' time and abilities). Instead, my purpose is to urge those of you who are concerned enough about worship to read this book to take decisive steps in your home and churches to limit the influence of the media. Let me name some of those steps and urge you to consider with other people how we can implement them for the sake of enabling members of our families and Christian communities to worship.[22]

1. *We can and must set limits* on our families' use of media. Quentin Schultze suggests a three to one ratio of family interaction/relational activities and media consumption. Without imposing such limits, he warns, we reverse the worldwide, ageless habit of parents teaching their children the wisdom of their faith and heritage, and we allow the children instead to float aimlessly — without a sense of who they are or what life is really for.[23]

Bill McKibben urges us to participate in the "TV Free America" campaign held every year, sponsored by the American Medical Association, the Children's Defense Fund, the Natural Resources Defense Council, the Congress of National Black Churches, the National Religious Partnership for the Environment, and the Family Research Council. Similarly, the pope has called for a TV-free Lent. In these disciplines, McKibben insists, the emphasis is not "on renunciation," but

---

three major sources of socialization in our society — schools, parents, and television — the latter is the only one with virtually no societal controls. As national coordinator for the Lutheran Peace Fellowship, Glen is especially concerned for the socialization of children by television into passivity, greed, and violence. For more information, contact LPF at 1710 11th Ave., Seattle, WA 98122, phone (206) 720-0313, or lpf@ecunet.org.

22. My book *Is It a Lost Cause?* elaborates these points and offers discussion questions (for parents, church leaders, and congregations) in terms of raising children.

23. See Quentin J. Schultze, *Winning Your Kids Back from the Media* (Downers Grove, IL: InterVarsity Press, 1994), for an excellent tool for better familial thinking about the issues.

on the great pleasure that comes when you turn off the television and re-join the living world, and on the opportunity to reflect, to think, in the still-ness of the unplugged world. Solitude and silence and darkness have always been key parts of the religious life, but they have been banished by televi-sion. We need to reclaim them, and in so doing to break the materialist en-chantment that now holds us in its thrall, to shrug off some of the witch-craft that makes us long constantly for things that will not satisfy us.[24]

2. *We can and must root ourselves and our children in the Christian worldview, its morals and values,* so that we are more able to assess the media we explore. We certainly cannot be totally without the media, since our schools and offices and peers engage in their use, but we must maintain a crit-ical distance, become equipped with skills for making wise choices about their use, and keep our consciences finely honed to reject what is inimical to God's way of life and his purposes and meaning for us.

3. *We can and must continue to learn the dangers of media* as well as the benefits and *take the lead in helping others to see these dangers,* which are usu-ally hidden. Our faith communities can work together to develop workable limits for families and authentic solutions to the generational clashes that arise when parents care enough to limit their children's involvement. Many nonbelievers genuinely want to join Christians in preventing the emotional, social, intellectual, and spiritual damage their children are exposed to in the proliferation of hazardous media materials.

4. *We can and must stop letting television divert a major portion of Chris-tians' interests, motivations, satisfactions, and energies away from our religious center in the triune God.*[25] I don't think I overstate the case. Worship is not of interest to our unchurched neighbors, not so much because of its style or substance, but because they don't see that those who regularly participate in it are any different from anybody else. Television, of course, is not the only source of that problem, but through the dangers listed above and others it certainly contributes voluminously to our lack of Christian character and conduct.

Though I have met dozens of families throughout the country who have chosen not to use TV, none of them has ever regretted it. Instead they re-port — or I have witnessed — that their children were more filled with won-der and imagination, more often involved in the arts and physical activities,

---

24. Bill McKibben, "Returning God to the Center: Consumerism and the Environ-mental Threat," in *The Consuming Passion: Christianity and the Consumer Culture,* ed. Rodney Clapp (Downers Grove, IL: InterVarsity Press, 1998), p. 48.

25. This sentence includes some modified phrases from Fore, p. 28.

more occupied in reading, more engaged in conversations, more interested in other people, and more concerned about spiritual matters. Though I have never in my adult life owned a television set, and neither has my husband, we have never regretted that choice either. We didn't want to train our minds and souls in violence, sexual immorality, greed, and a low information-action ratio. I am NOT saying that all Christians should make the same choice. I AM saying that I hope and pray all Christian single adults and families will seriously consider the dangers listed above and think prayerfully about their own choices.

7

The Church as a Colony of the Kingdom in a Consumer Culture

> "If then you have not been faithful with the dishonest wealth, who will entrust to you the true riches? . . . No slave can serve two masters; for a slave will either hate the one and love the other, or be devoted to the one and despise the other. You cannot serve God and wealth."
>
> Luke 16:11, 13

If the Christ we follow sent out his disciples with no extra possessions (Luke 9:1-6 and 10:1-12) and warned would-be devotees that he had nowhere to lay his head (see Luke 9:57-62), then we must recognize that it is extremely difficult to live in a Christian way in a consumer culture.[1] Furthermore, we have to ask if it is really possible to have genuinely *Christian* worship in such a culture — characterized as our society is by individualism (rather than biblical community), consumption (as opposed to generosity and sharing), manipulative advertising (instead of truth), and intentional fomenting of desires

---

1. Two excellent collections of essays that wrestle with the issues are *The Consuming Passion: Christianity and the Consumer Culture*, ed. Rodney Clapp (Downers Grove, IL: InterVarsity Press, 1998), and *Rethinking Materialism: Perspectives on the Spiritual Dimension of Economic Behavior*, ed. Robert Wuthnow (Grand Rapids: Wm. B. Eerdmans Publishing Co., 1995).

(in contrast to the scriptural recognition that human desires often derive from our sinful nature and must, therefore, be frequently held in check).

Perhaps this all seems too strongly put — but my purpose in this chapter is to sound a wake-up call and wrestle with some questions. Are we aware, in thinking about worship, of how necessary our materialistic society makes it for Christians to be constantly vigilant against the inroads of the shopper mentality? As God's people we want to think with an orientation entirely different from the world's emphases on taste and choice, opinion and self-fulfillment. We want to be formed instead to ask questions about God's call and will and purposes — and about our faithfulness, obedience, and service in response.

This brief essay, of course, cannot present a full description of the whole range of issues or offer much practical advice since that would require several books and/or long symposia. My purpose is only to introduce a few of the questions by sketching some of the roots of the present state of affairs in our society and by posing select implications for churches' decisions about worship. Before that, however, it would be good to get a glimpse of the seriousness of the problem from a non-Christian perspective.

David Myers reports that charts of research revealed by the Higher Education Research Institute at the Graduate School of Education at UCLA demonstrated that intensifying materialism corresponded to less possibility of developing a meaningful philosophy of life. Similarly, Cornell University research disclosed that economics professors were partly responsible for their students' materialism.

> Their nationwide survey of college professors revealed that economists, despite having relatively high salaries, were more than twice as likely as those in other disciplines to contribute no money to private charities. In responding to public television appeals, their median (and most common) gift was nothing. In laboratory monetary games, students behave more selfishly after taking economics courses.[2]

Do our worship services offer the same training? Let us face the issue squarely: it won't matter what we preach or teach, if what the people primarily learn from — namely, the *culture* of worship — immerses them in consumerism.

---

2. David Myers, "Money and Misery," in Clapp, ed., *The Consuming Passion*, p. 53.

The Roots in Religion and Other Sources
of Our Culture's Materialism

It was a great surprise to me, in reading about our society's consumerism, to discover that religion is one of its sources — but my astonishment arose because I have always thought about religion in terms of its objective content (for example, Jesus warning against the dangers of Mammon) rather than its emotional responses. Colin Campbell, in *The Romantic Ethic and the Spirit of Modern Consumerism*, annotates how genuine Christian piety devolved over time into a substitute religiosity that stirred in people a hunger for equally strong sentiments for their own sake and not as a response to spiritual truths. He suggests that the Puritans had "developed a 'taste' for the strong meat of powerful religious emotion, and when their convictions waned, [found themselves] seeking alternative fare with which to satisfy their appetite."[3]

Campbell demonstrates that this change came about because of a tension between two sides of the early Protestant ethic. One side displayed the traits for which the Puritans are famous — rationality, instrumentality, industry and achievement, and greater suspicion of pleasure than of comfort. The second stream, arising from the Arminian revolt against predestination and its greater optimism about human potential, exhibited fervent feeling, introspection, and an abiding stress on self-fulfillment. This led first to "the cults of benevolence and melancholy, and then into a fully fledged Sentimentalism" (136-37).

Campbell summarizes his thesis as follows:

> It is now possible to state the general nature of the conclusion reached concerning the relationship between the romantic ethic and the spirit of modern consumerism. The latter, labelled self-illusory hedonism, is characterized by a longing to experience in reality those pleasures created and enjoyed in imagination, a longing which results in the ceaseless consumption of novelty. Such an outlook, with its characteristic dissatisfaction with real life and an eagerness for new experiences, lies at the heart of much conduct that is most typical of modern life, and underpins such central institutions as fashion and romantic love. The romantic ethic can be seen to possess a basic congruence, or 'elective affinity', with this spirit, and to have given rise to a character type and ethic highly conducive to the adoption of such attitudes. In particular, romantic teachings concerning the good, the

---

3. Colin Campbell, *The Romantic Ethic and the Spirit of Modern Consumerism* (Oxford: Basil Blackwell, 1987), p. 134. Page references to this book in the following paragraphs are given parenthetically in the text.

true and the beautiful, provide both the legitimation and the motivation necessary for modern consumer behaviour to become prevalent throughout the contemporary industrial world.

The thesis advanced in this book is not merely that the Romantic Movement assisted crucially at the birth of modern consumerism; it is also maintained that romanticism has continued in the two centuries or so since that time to work in such a way as to overcome the forces of traditionalism and provide a renewed impetus to the dynamic of consumerism. (205-6)

This thesis does not, however, explain why Protestantism became so secularized in the first place, as Craig Gay points out in "Sensualists without Heart: Contemporary Consumerism in Light of the Modern Project." How did it come about that "the object of Christian belief had been eclipsed by interest in the subjective act of believing"? And why did "modern consumer behavior [become] so narrowly confined to the consumption of *material* products and services"?[4] Gay points to "the impact of the scientific method on the modern imagination" as insisted upon by such Christians as C. S. Lewis in *The Abolition of Man*.[5] Leszek Kolakowski modifies this perspective by saying that it is not so much the logic of science that has led to the loss of a truly religious focus, but, as Gay summarizes his work, "our decision to submit ourselves to the logic of science for the sake of trying to achieve more effective control over our circumstances."[6] Kolakowski grieves that we have "abandoned the religious quest for truth and meaning for the sake of comfort and convenience."[7]

Gay insists that consumerism represents the highest ideals of modernity. He encourages us to see these two things:

4. Craig M. Gay, "Sensualists without Heart: Contemporary Consumerism in Light of the Modern Project," in Clapp, ed., *The Consuming Passion*, p. 38.

5. Gay, "Sensualists without Heart," p. 30. I highly recommend Lewis's *The Abolition of Man* (New York: Simon and Schuster, 1996). See also the works on technology by Jacques Ellul cited in the bibliography and Neil Postman's *Technopoly: The Surrender of Culture to Technology* (New York: Alfred A. Knopf, 1992).

6. Gay, "Sensualists without Heart," p. 31. Leszek Kolakowski's book, *Modernity on Endless Trial* (Chicago: University of Chicago Press, 1990), is an excellent set of essays dealing with this fundamental question of our postmodern times: "Why is the malaise associated with the experience of modernity so widely felt, and where are the sources of those aspects of modernity that make this malaise particularly painful?" (p. 6). His essays deal with such topics as the loss of taboos, the task of intellectuals, the role of philosophy, the importance of the sacred (see Chapter 19 of this book), and whether there is a genuine "crisis" in Christianity.

7. This is from Kolakowski's essay, "The Illusion of Demythologization," in *Modernity on Endless Trial*, p. 99.

first, that our culture invites us to locate the sum total of human happiness here and now and in the consumption of the fruits of the technological economy; and second, that we have not been tricked into this, but that we actually chose this path several hundred years ago and continue to choose it on a more-or-less daily basis.

Furthermore, this thesis involves the following two commitments:

The first is the commitment to self-creation and autonomous self-definition. We are told today that we are, or at least ought to be, entirely free to make whatever we would of ourselves; and so long as our projects of self-construction do not obviously interfere with anyone else's, we must not be hindered by tradition, custom, laws or outmoded notions of "human nature" as we fashion our own identities. This commitment amounts finally to a repudiation of the belief in moral order. The second commitment entails shrinking the range of possible human aspirations to those circumscribed by secular existence.[8]

We must respond to both of these commitments — and our first reaction must be to expose our society's illusion that the selves we create without any hindrance from heritage or mores have any substance. Ferenc Maté comments on the way consumption-driven lives are constructed by ads — "We put on our slogan-blaring T-shirt and figure we have made a declaration of Self" — and then describes Ashley Bickerton's sobering *Tormented Self Portrait,* exhibited in the Whitney Museum's Biennial in 1989. This was

no traditional portrait. It was a large featureless black box hanging on the wall. Made of black plastic. The lid was plexiglass. The only colors were in the forest of decals attached to the lid; Marlboro, Tylenol, Blue Rock water, TV Guide, Nike, Citibank, US Sprint, Trojan. Down the sides were two long decals declaring "Season 87/88," suggesting that next year there would be new labels. Through the plexiglass lid you could see inside the box. It was empty.[9]

The selves we create are so empty because of the second commitment Gay exposes — the limiting of human desires to those encompassed in secular existence. After his famous visit to America in the mid-1800s Alexis de Tocqueville warned that such circumscription would take place. Disturbed by

8. Gay, "Sensualists without Heart," p. 20.
9. Ferenc Maté, *A Reasonable Life: Toward a Simpler, Secure, More Humane Existence* (New York: Albatross Publishing House, 1993), pp. 177-78.

the extreme love of money that he saw at the root of everything in the United States, he worried that its citizens might "finally become so engrossed in a cowardly love of immediate pleasures that their interest in their own future and in that of their descendants may vanish, and that they will prefer tamely to follow the course of their destiny rather than make a sudden energetic effort necessary to set things right."[10]

I must add that Tocqueville's predictions are among my strongest reasons for thinking that this book on worship needs this chapter on consumerism, for *two of the symptoms he named concerning society are now manifested in churches in conflicts over worship* — namely, (1) *lack of concern about the future,* for many churches throwing out their heritage do not recognize that deep discipleship for the long haul cannot be built on worship not rooted in the deeper wisdom of the larger Church as it has been immersed in the splendor of God; and (2) *a tame following of the present course* in that congregations are not willing to expend the "sudden energetic effort necessary to set things right" by building genuine community and working on the worship issues in a way that asks the right questions.

A century earlier than Tocqueville, John Wesley had seen the inevitable problem that riches could become one's religion, and he raised the question of whether such a loss of spirit could be avoided. He wrote:

> I fear, wherever riches have increased, the essence of religion has decreased in the same proportion. Therefore I do not see how it is possible, in the nature of things, for any revival of true religion to continue long. For religion must necessarily produce both industry and frugality, and these cannot but produce riches. But as riches increase, so will pride, anger, and love of the world in all its branches. How then is it possible that Methodism, that is, a religion of the heart, though it flourishes now as a greenly tree, should continue in this state? For the Methodists in every place grow diligent and frugal; consequently they increase in goods. Hence they proportionately increase in pride, in anger, in the desire of the flesh, the desire of the eyes, and the pride of life. So, although the form of religion remains, the spirit is swiftly vanishing away. Is there no way to prevent this — this continual decay of pure religion? We ought not to prevent people from being diligent and frugal; *we must exhort all Christians to gain all they can, and to save all they can; that is, in effect, to grow rich.*[11]

10. Alexis de Tocqueville, *Democracy in America,* trans. George Lawrence (Garden City, NY: Doubleday/Anchor, 1969), p. 645.

11. From Southey's *Life of Wesley,* quoted in Max Weber, *The Protestant Ethic and the Spirit of Capitalism,* trans. Talcott Parsons (New York: Charles Scribner's Sons, 1958), p. 175.

After elaborating on the fulfillment of Wesley's warning, Max Weber lamented that this destruction of the highest spiritual and cultural values would lead to the end of any attempt to justify economic compulsions, and the pursuit of wealth would "become associated with purely mundane passions" only.

Weber wondered what would happen at the end of this progression of modern rationalistic society — "whether at the end of this tremendous development entirely new prophets will arise, or there will be a great rebirth of old ideas and ideals, or, if neither, mechanized petrification, embellished with a sort of convulsive self-importance."[12] Would he be surprised that the modern "enlightened" society is being profusely questioned by postmodern philosophers, cynics, and nihilists, but that its economic compulsions and purely mundane passions rage on without much disapproval? Would he have expected the way the United States has taken the lead in spreading consumerism throughout the world — with its destruction of local cultures, its enhancement of passivity, its nurturing of selfish devotion to the satisfaction of an individual's endlessly multiplying wants — as documented by Benjamin R. Barber, in his book *Jihad vs. McWorld?*[13] In such a society, *can worship escape these monocultural influences? And what happens if our worship itself fosters consumerism concerning worship?*

Certainly revivalistic worship did that, as Jackson Lears observed. "By popularizing a pattern of self-transformation that would prove easily adaptable to advertisers' rhetorical strategies, evangelical revivalists . . . played a powerful if unwitting part in creating a congenial cultural climate for the rise of national advertising."[14] Now that pattern seems to have come full circle with the present church-growth strategies to market our churches.

Two other perspectives need to be added for better understanding of the roots of our society's excessive consumerism — the first of which is Philip Rieff's insights into "the triumph of the therapeutic" in our culture.[15] He summarizes the significance of the turn in his well-known aphorism, "Reli-

12. Weber, *The Protestant Ethic and the Spirit of Capitalism,* p. 182.

13. Benjamin R. Barber, *Jihad vs. McWorld: How Globalism and Tribalism Are Reshaping the World* (New York: Ballantine Books, 1996).

14. Jackson Lears, *Fables of Abundance* (New York: BasicBooks, 1994), p. 47, as quoted in Rodney Clapp, "The Theology of Consumption and the Consumption of Theology: Toward a Christian Response to Consumerism," in Clapp, ed., *The Consuming Passion,* p. 181.

15. I am indebted to Craig M. Gay's "Sensualists without Heart" for prompting me to read many of the resources in this section — Campbell, Kolakowski, Weber, and Rieff — and for reminding me of Tocqueville and Lewis.

gious man was born to be saved, [modern] psychological man is born to be pleased."[16] If we want those who come to worship to be religious people rather than people primarily needing to be pleased, we must understand the process by which the therapeutic has triumphed. It will be necessary to include long quotations from Rieff's own summary of his thesis in order to give a proper synopsis of his insights.

Initially, Rieff explains as follows the two main functions of every culture:

> (1) to organize the moral demands men make upon themselves into a system of symbols that make men intelligible and trustworthy to each other, thus rendering also the world intelligible and trustworthy; (2) to organize the expressive remissions by which men release themselves, in some degree, from the strain of conforming to the controlling symbolic, internalized variant readings of culture that constitute individual character. The process by which a culture changes at its profoundest level may be traced in the shifting balance of controls and releases which constitute a system of moral demands.

> Those who transmit the moral demand system are a cultural elite, exemplifying those demands in their character and behavior. But an elite cannot merely teach or write of the moral demand system without acting out some part of it. However the labor of exemplary enactment is divided, no culture survives long without its elite, those cadres which demonstrate the particular balance of control and remission in the culture itself.

> No culture of which we are aware has yet escaped the tension between the modalities of control and release by which every culture constitutes itself. (232-33)

Next, Rieff explains that "A cultural revolution occurs when the releasing or remissive symbolic grows more compelling than the controlling one; then it is that the inherent tensions reach a breaking point" (233-34). He suggests that Roman culture might have been on the verge of such a breaking point when Christianity arose and offered "a new symbolic order of controls and remissions" (234).

---

16. Philip Rieff, *The Triumph of the Therapeutic: Uses of Faith after Freud* (London: Chatto & Windus, 1966), pp. 24-25. Page references to this book in the following pages are given parenthetically in the text. Obviously Rieff wrote before the advent of inclusive language. I apologize that it became too cumbersome to change all his uses of the term *man*, but we can certainly be sure that he intended them in the sense of *anthropos* or "human being."

Rieff's ensuing description of the breaking point is powerfully insightful. He alerts us to these changes:

> At the breaking point, a culture can no longer maintain itself as an established span of moral demands. Its jurisdiction contracts; it demands less, permits more. Bread and circuses become confused with right and duty. Spectacle becomes a functional substitute for sacrament. Massive regressions occur, with large sections of the population returning to levels of destructive aggression historically accessible to it. At times of impending transition to a new moral order, symbolic forms and their institutional objectifications change their relative weights in that order. Competing symbolisms gather support in competing elites; they jostle each other for priority of place as the organizers of the next phase in the psychohistorical process. (234)

The problem of the modern world was that its competing symbols no longer provided a sense of oracle or vision. Rieff explains that

> In all cultures before our own, the competing symbols took the form of languages of faith. A language of faith is always revelatory, communicating through some mouthpiece of the god-term a system of interdicts — a pattern of "thou shalt nots," or "taboos." The language of science is not revelatory but analytic; for this reason, the scientist can never claim that his own terms have a prophetic function. His work is non-moral, that is, without interdictory purpose. (234)

Since the clinical attitude of science strives for neutrality (which, of course, the postmodernists have now questioned), its therapeutic effect was "culturally dubious" (235).

In answer to the question "What, then, should churchmen do?" Rieff reports that the answer was clear: "become, avowedly, therapists, administrating a therapeutic institution — under the justificatory mandate that Jesus himself was the first therapeutic" (251). He quotes an article by John Wren-Lewis that insists that church leaders could become professional therapeutics "'only if they break away radically from almost all, if not all, of their traditional religious pursuits'" — which obviously appalls Rieff, who wonders that Wren-Lewis could be so "calmly confident that community life no longer needs . . . doctrinal integrations of self into communal purposes." The result, he objects, is that

> Both East and West are now committed, culturally as well as economically, to the gospel of self-fulfillment. Yet neither the American nor the Russian

translations of the gospel can be transformed into a spiritual perception. (252)

This has given rise to a people "emancipated from an ethic of hard work," who have

> grown morally less self-demanding. They have been released from the old system of self-demands by a convergence of doctrines that do not resort to new restrictions but rather propose jointly the superiority of all that money can buy, technology can make, and science can conceive.[17]
>
> Certain naïve ascetic doctrines, which once did contain spiritual perceptions of great depth, such as that of holy poverty, now embarrass the churches, competing as they do for pride of place in a culture of affluence. Such perceptions are practically taboo subjects, specially among Americans. (253)

Rieff makes it glaringly clear *why churches must understand themselves as an alternative society if they are to be Church in a consumer world* of money, technology, and science and offer to it instead the superior splendor of all that God gives, God makes, and God conceives.

The other perspective we need to add for understanding the extreme danger consumerism is to being Church comes from Rodney Clapp's insights on discontentment in "The Theology of Consumption and the Consumption of Theology: Toward a Christian Response to Consumerism." Here Clapp notes that though insatiability has existed since the fall of humanity, it is uniquely in modern capitalism and consumerism that we find "the idealization and constant encouragement of insatiability — the deification of dissatisfaction." Certainly this sacralized "consumption has devoured classical Christian theology, and with it much of classical Christian practice."[18]

Clapp insists that this idolatry must be examined and challenged in our churches specifically in terms of the character of the consumer. How do the key character traits of shoppers compare to the principles and purposes of the Christian way of being and living?

Since consumers are "schooled in insatiability" (190), they can never be satisfied. Since their makeup consists "basically of unmet needs that can be

---

17. Readers here might remember from Chapter 4 the Tower of Babel of science, technology, and economics constructed in the modern world and now questioned appropriately by the postmodernists.

18. Clapp, "The Theology of Consumption and the Consumption of Theology," p. 188. Page references to this article in the following paragraphs are given parenthetically in the text.

requited by commodified goods and experiences," they "should think first and foremost of [themselves] and meeting [their] felt needs." They are taught that the highest value is "freedom, defined as a vast array of choices." Consequently, "One of the most striking ways we are trained and reinforced in the consumptive way of life is exactly through a flood of ever-proliferating choices" (191).

This is exactly why I believe unremittingly that it is *utterly dangerous for churches to offer choices of worship styles.* By doing so we reinforce the idolatrous way of life that worship is intended to expose, disarm, and conquer (see this threefold work of Christ against the powers in Colossians 2:14-15).

Models of Faith above Consumerism

Many Christian writers offer examples of ways in which we can be Church and resist our society's materialistic consumption. Rodney Clapp introduces Lendol and Kathy Knight Calder, who counteract the consumer culture's mediation of "reality" by thoroughly enjoying their natural surroundings in New Hampshire and encouraging their children to share their wonder in creation. Once as they walked by the nearby lake, which was unusually still and serene, three-year-old Abigail exclaimed that the lake "was not talking or laughing." The family had discussed how "different parts of creation 'speak' to God." Kathy and Lendol also perceive that the consumer culture masters us if we let it define time for us. To resist this, they labor to follow natural and liturgical rhythms — the church year instead of consumer holidays (197). Other aspects of their opposition to the consumer mentality include their cultivation of gratitude, their stress on generosity, and their recognition that they are in this struggle for the long haul (198).

All of the Calders' insights give tremendous wisdom for our thinking about worship. How can we more thoroughly immerse worship participants in the splendor of God's creation, in the Sabbath and liturgical rhythms, in gratitude, generosity, and courage for the long haul, so that what we do when we are gathered equips us to resist the consumerist ideologies and idolatries of our culture?

Clapp also cites the example of elder Christoph Arnold, who, when asked about consumer technology that the Bruderhof Christian communities had tried and then quit, quickly answered

> "VCRs. We had VCRs for a while, but then we noticed the children weren't singing. They weren't playing and running and making up songs. They

wanted to put in a tape and sit in front of the TV. So we locked up the VCRs. Now the children are singing again." (199-200)[19]

I often wonder how much better congregational singing would be if we were able to encourage more families to lock up their TVs and VCRs and then we offered them the delights of "singing schools."

Bill McKibben, in "Returning God to the Center: Consumerism and the Environmental Threat," describes how numerous people thanked him for restoring Christmas the way they wanted to celebrate it when he suggested that they limit spending to $100. He summarizes,

> This taught me some useful lessons: that the effect of consumerism on the planet is mirrored precisely in its effect on the soul, that finding true joy means passing up momentary pleasure, and that joy, deep bubbling joy, is the only really subversive force felt in our society. The only way to make people doubt, even for a minute, the inevitability of their course in life is to show them they are being cheated of the truest happiness.[20]

That is why our worship must be immersed in the splendor of God — to help people discover that anything less is to be robbed of true Joy.

McKibben also emphasizes that television is the essential anchor of the "growth culture" (which is why the preceding chapter in this book was on media limitation). He gathered 2,400 hours of videotape — all the programs offered on TV during one day — and after spending a year to study them asked, *"What would the world look like if this was your main source of information?"* (emphasis his). His distillation of "all those thousands of game shows and talk shows and sitcoms and commercials" was the single notion, "'You are the most important thing on the face of the earth. Your immediate desires are all that count. Do It Your Way. This Bud's for You.'" Consequently, he concludes, "We are led daily, hourly, into temptation."[21] Can worship expose those temptations if it becomes more like television?

---

19. See also my report of an article on this subject in the Bruderhof's publication, *The Plough,* in Marva J. Dawn, *Is It a Lost Cause? Having the Heart of God for the Church's Children* (Grand Rapids: Wm. B. Eerdmans Publishing Co., 1997), pp. 172-73.

20. Bill McKibben, "Returning God to the Center: Consumerism and the Environmental Threat," in Clapp, ed., *The Consuming Passion,* pp. 46-47.

21. McKibben, "Returning God to the Center," p. 47.

Worship That Transforms

Since we are reflecting upon ways to resist the consumerism of our culture especially because we are concerned about its effects on worship, let us consider an example of worship that nurtures a change in attitude about one aspect of consumption. Tsvi Blanchard describes a ritual developed under the leadership of the National Jewish Center for Learning and Leadership, which wondered how driving — probably the most important event in the life of high school students — could be made holy and more distinctly Jewish. How could participation in a ceremony imbue students' posture toward the car with the community's ethical concerns?[22]

Blanchard describes the ceremony at a centrally located parking lot as follows:

> Together with their families (as on Passover), the students would stand next to their cars. They would then celebrate by reciting the blessing over wine (as at the sanctification of the Sabbath). They would, however, use "bubbly" grape juice, which feels as special as champagne and expresses their responsible commitment to avoid drinking and driving. After this, they would read personal statements of their views on "sacred driving." These statements would explain how they connected their being Jewish with the meaning that freedom, responsibility and adulthood had for them. Finally, they would enter their cars, circle the lot seven times (a symbol from the traditional Jewish marriage ceremony, which for them expressed the covenantal nature of driving), and having taken responsibility for the serious implications of being a driver, they would drive off (symbolizing their increased adult independence from their families as well as their joy at driving the car).
>
> The students' sanctification of using a car has all the features we derived from our rabbinic text. Inherited symbols of holiness are employed in a new context. Appropriate boundaries are acknowledged and connected to personal as well as communal identity. Jewish values (freedom, power, responsibility, conscious awareness of the meaning of actions) are expressed by the way in which consumption occurs. (Holiness is more often in how we act rather than in what we do.) We have even found a good definition of one important aspect of Jewish stewardship: sacred consumption is an act of joyful responsibility. (96)

22. Tsvi Blanchard, "After Eden: The Search for the Holy in a Consumer Society," in Clapp, ed., *The Consuming Passion*, pp. 91-106. Specific page references to this article in the following paragraphs are given parenthetically in the text.

This ceremony — and the conversation with the young people that produced it — seemed to me an exceptional idea for helping the youth rethink their involvement not only in driving but in other aspects of life as well. However, Blanchard recognizes that many other "important questions went unaddressed," such as these:

> Were they aware of the social cost of the automobile? Of the cost to those poor who must spend money they do not have to buy cars in order to get to work? Did they attend to the ecological and health cost of auto-centered transport? Of the social inequalities of auto-centered transport? How might they integrate paying the real social cost of a car, rather than merely its price, into their understanding of the responsibilities that come with a driver's license?

Blanchard raises these questions because otherwise "the students merely celebrate their own advantages without taking any responsibility for the cost to others." He reminds us that in the Passover Seder drops of wine are removed from the cup for each of the ten plagues suffered by the Egyptians as those are recited in order to acknowledge with regret the pain suffered by others in the redemption of the Jews. Thus Blanchard suggests that we still need "the kind of ritual symbolization that, by the very way in which we consume resources, acknowledges the pain and deprivation of others" (101).

Christians seem in general to have lost this sense of worship which the rituals of our forebears, the Jews, teach us: how to symbolize a unique way of life filled with conscious awareness of the meaning of actions, compassion for others, concern for the world, communal identity and responsibility, and corporate celebration of God's gifts that are to be carefully stewarded.

Worship in Antithesis to a Consumer Culture

What kinds of questions must we ask so that we do not hinder or destroy — by consumerist behavior — the possibility of genuinely Christian lives? Craig Gay reminds us that the original meaning of the word *consume* is "to burn, to exhaust, or to destroy completely," and he encourages us "to try to prevent our neighbor from being destroyed by such behavior as well."[23] Everyone must be alert, as Wendell Berry reminds us, to "resist the language, the ideas, and the categories of this ubiquitous sales talk, no matter from whose mouth it issues." Berry continues, "Nobody who is awake accepts the favors of these

23. Gay, "Sensibility without Heart," p. 38.

hawkers of guaranteed satisfactions, these escape artists, these institutional and commercial fanatics."[24] Many church leaders, however, seem not to be awake, for sales talk seems to be invading and conquering churches — guaranteed satisfactions in church growth are proliferating, and escape from the difficult work of creating genuine community and spreading the reign of God is offered in simplistic techniques of changes in worship style. What kinds of provocative questions must we ask lest such consumerism continue to ravage Christian worship?

Most important, our churches must give up the superstitious belief that quick techniques can offer solutions to the intractable problems of being Church in a non-Christian society. Wendell Berry offers a good example, out of his concern for being Christian about farming, that provides an analogy to my disquietude about the damage of consumerism to being Church. He emphasizes that soil loss is a problem embarrassing to those who think technology can fix everything. Since soil isn't lost "in a huge slab," no one can "engineer a glamorous, large, and speedy solution" (and certainly many new problems would be caused in doing so). Berry insists that soil "is lost a little at a time over millions of acres by the careless acts of millions of people." Consequently, "It cannot be saved by heroic feats of gigantic technology but only by millions of small acts and restraints, conditioned by small fidelities, skills, and desires. Soil loss is ultimately a cultural problem; it will be corrected only by cultural solutions."[25]

In the same way, restoration of worship that does not fall prey to consumerist glamour — because it is set in genuine Christian community and a way of life that offers alternatives and tangible witness to the world — will require great skill and fidelity issuing in "millions of small acts and restraints." At root, once again, we see that the fundamental need is for our churches to be colonies of the kingdom of God, an alternative society — not possessed by possessions, not consumed by consumerism, but alive to the gospel and generous in sharing it by being Church.

Philip Yancey calls for the same kind of alternativity in this excerpt from *What's So Amazing about Grace?*

> Early on, Stalin built a village in Poland called Nowa Huta, or "New Town," to demonstrate the promise of communism. He could not change the entire country at once, he said, but he could construct one new town with a

24. Wendell Berry, "Preface: The Joy of Sales Resistance," in *Sex, Economy, Freedom and Community: Eight Essays* (New York: Pantheon Books, 1993), p. xi.

25. Berry, "Conservation and the Local Economy," in *Sex, Economy, Freedom and Community*, pp. 13-14.

shiny steel factory, spacious apartments, plentiful parks, and broad streets as a token of what would follow. Later, Nowa Huta became one of the hotbeds of Solidarity, demonstrating instead the failure of communism to make just one town work.

What if Christians used that same approach in secular society and succeeded? In the world the Christians should work harder toward establishing colonies of the kingdom that point to our true home. All too often the church holds up a mirror reflecting back the society around it, rather than a window revealing a different way.[26]

Our worship, especially, must be such a window — but not a plain one. Truly, if our worship immerses us in the splendor of God and forms us to be Church as a community practicing God's way of life, we will be a glorious stained-glass window, proclaiming the beauty of Christ's salvation.

It is crucial at this time that our churches ask fundamental questions about who we are as Church and how we practice being Church in our worship life. Above all, we must resist any inroads of the consumer culture into our life as a colony of the kingdom offering alternatives. We dare not let worship be just another consumer item for which people shop.

---

26. Philip Yancey, *What's So Amazing about Grace?* (Grand Rapids: Zondervan Publishing House, 1997), p. 262.

PART II

Worshiping God: The Splendor of Our Infinite Center

Ascribe to the LORD the glory of his name;
   worship the LORD in holy splendor.

Psalm 29:2

Ascribe to the LORD the glory due his name;
   worship the LORD in the splendor of his holiness.

Psalm 29:2 (NASV)

Worship is for God! Everything is *due* him. His holiness, or set-apartness, is so infinitely full of splendor that we shall never — in all eternity — run out of new dimensions of worship. Consequently, we want our worship to be full of splendor, totally prodigal in luxuriant praise, a royal waste of time!

We come in the holiness of God's grace through us, for only because the LORD has invited us to come into his presence and has set us apart as his holy saints through the work of Christ can we possibly enter to worship him. Glory! How can we do anything but worship God as fully as possible with all the best gifts at our command? Glory! How can we respond in any way but with the utter, wasteful (in the world's terms) devotion of our lives? Glory!

How can we help but want to be Church? How can we not seek eagerly to welcome our neighbors into the holy splendor?

Starting with this section of the book, each part will begin with a sample sermon. These sermons display the theme of the section and are included to offer a model of that section's focus in thoroughly scriptural preaching. I pray the sermons will also nourish the spiritual life of the readers. The sermon initiating this section invites us to be newly astonished at the transfiguration of Christ and filled with hope as a result.

Each sermon will list all the texts for the day, and I encourage you to keep them before you as you read — since I usually refer to the texts as the listeners had them in their worship folders. All the remaining discussions in this book invite you into the opportunity for us continually to practice together the uniqueness of the Church — that we who are part of it are formed by what we believe is the Revelation of God. We might often disagree on specifics of interpretation, but we must never stop being immersed in the Bible, for it is the primary source for us to learn the language of faith.

Many of the troubles concerning worship in our churches arise because of a great confusion between worship and evangelism — to the detriment of both. Therefore, Chapter 9, immediately following the initial sermon, specifically addresses that confusion and why — and to what degree — the two should be separated in our thinking and lives. When the two are confused, worship is turned away from the God who is to be the Center and focuses instead on the people who are there — which, of course, the Church must do, but not to the detriment of genuine praise to God. The confusion causes worship to be utilitarian, rather than a royal waste of time!

Chapter 10 is an essay on preaching inspired by a concerto performance by famed violinist Nadja Salerno-Sonnenberg, and Chapter 12 concludes the section with another sample sermon to underscore the imperative of rooting everything in Christ and his resurrection. Chapter 11, on the opposite side, gives some examples of what happens when we don't keep God as the Infinite Center of our worship.

8

"Why Are We Not Astonished?":
A Sermon*

Texts for the Last Sunday after the Epiphany, Series C —
Exodus 34:29-35; Psalm 99; 2 Corinthians 3:12–4:2; Luke 9:28-43

When I was with the youth group just before this worship service, I asked
the teenagers why in our worship we say, "The Lord be with you — and
also with you," and one of the young women answered, "Because it's tradition."
But why is it the tradition? Perhaps we all need to understand why we say these
lines, so that we can say them more meaningfully to each other.

We repeat these phrases at several places in the worship of the Church
to remember that we are a community in this place — that all who lead worship here cannot fulfill their callings unless you are supporting them. Similarly, I cannot preach well unless you participate with me. Please assure me of
your willingness to work hard with me to explore today's texts by responding
attentively when you answer my blessing with "And also with you."

The Lord be with you. [Response: And also with you!]

Let us pray: Luminous Christ, resplendent in your glory now, give us a
glimpse of your radiant brilliance — not simply to dazzle, but to transfigure

*This is an edited transcript of a sermon presented at First Lutheran Church in
Ellensburg, Washington, on February 22, 1998, as the beginning of the Larry Danton Lecture Series on the topic "The Most Important Thing Christians Do: Worship."

us, to change us from our dullness into light, so that in the world we might reflect your splendor. Amen.

This week millions throughout the world have been watching the Olympics. Many commentators have done horrible things to the participants, like pushing microphones into their faces just after they suffered a loss or failed to make the top three. How terribly we treat those who are struggling with their fading glory. On the other hand, how much we want to create famous people — and then we have to wonder how their lives will go on after we have done that to them. For example, think of fifteen-year-old Tara Lipinski, who won the gold medal in women's figure skating. Now that she has reached the top of the world at the age of fifteen, what *on earth* will she do for encores?

I raise that issue today to help us all think about our human hunger for fame, our human longing for glory. Perhaps you don't want to be an Olympic gold medalist, but I would guess that each of us sitting in this sanctuary longs to be important, needs to matter in the world. I'm sure this is true of more of you than just myself — because I know I'm not the only sinner in this crowd.

Why is it that we have a deep dissatisfaction in our lives? Why does each person here want to be more valuable, more important to people? Why do we need so profoundly to make our mark in the world?

Our texts for this Sunday give us powerful answers to those questions, so let us look closely at each of them in turn to see how God would change us today. How does God want to take us out of this never-ending scramble for glory and help us to learn instead who we are as the people of God — especially a people who, as the apostle Paul says, are being changed from one degree of glory to another?

Perhaps one problem that some of us might have with these texts for today is that we know the stories too well, and as a result they have ceased to astonish us. In this age of super psychedelia, of hyperlink hopping from one Web site to another, in an age of increasingly dazzling special effects in movies and television, when many of us can inhabit cyberspace and become part of a virtual reality that is so virtual that it is a reality that is an unreality — in such a world, how can we find meaning in these old stories? How can you and I know who we are as God's people and what we have to offer the world? There is too much of the grandiose around us — so we are not very intrigued by a man with a shining face, another man with shining clothes, and the sudden appearance out of time of Moses and Elijah. But these accounts of faith that form us are much more astonishing than we realize; we need to hear them afresh and let them fill us with wonder.

I hope you are as thrilled as I am to be in worship this morning. Right now, worship is the most important thing we need, and especially what we need is to adore the God revealed in these texts and to be transformed ourselves by these texts. I believe that Moses and the Psalmist and Paul and Jesus have enormously significant insights to teach us for making sense of our lives in the midst of our supercharged but transient world.

So let us look back at Moses. As he wakens us up to think about a glory that will not last, we will notice especially some key points in the text. There are several *wondrous* things in this account. First of all, this event in Exodus 34:29-35 takes place after the Israelites' idolatrous worship of the golden calf. At that time Moses had smashed the tablets on which God had written the commandments. It is indeed a *wonder* that once again Moses has been up on the mountain speaking with the LORD. How astonishing it is that God in his mercy renewed the covenant with his people!

The second *wonder* is that Moses, a human being, could talk with God and not be destroyed. This is *GOD* we're speaking about. We have so domesticated God in the twentieth/twenty-first century that we easily forget that God is a blaze who singes, a consuming fire. How amazing it is that Moses could talk with him face to face.

And look! That had a powerful effect on him. Moses became filled with the glory of God, but — it is a *wonder* — he didn't even know that his face was shining.

Notice what happens when the Israelites discover this. When they see him with his shining face, they are afraid. Sometimes I think we don't have enough fear of God. I don't mean terror, but indeed we scarcely remember that he is *GOD*. We have so relativized everything that we have turned God into a buddy-buddy. We forget that all those who ever encountered God in the Bible fell on their faces. Isaiah, for example, said, "Woe is me! I am lost, for I am a man of unclean lips . . . yet my eyes have seen the King, the LORD of hosts" (6:5). Martin Luther translated "I am lost" as "I am annihilated!" If you ever faced God, it would kill you. His holiness could not tolerate your sinfulness.

Yes, indeed, the people of Israel were fearful; they were filled with *wonder* at the splendor they beheld as a sign of Moses' encounter with God. So Moses spoke with the leaders of the people until the rest of the assembly could return, and then he tells them what the LORD had said. He passes on to them all the *wonder* of the true God, the LORD, in relationship with them.

After telling them, however, he puts a veil over his face, for he recognizes that the glory is going to fade. Does he simply want to keep his prestige among the people, as Paul suggests in 2 Corinthians 3?

Notice that whenever Moses entered again into the presence of the LORD the shine came back. Every time he was *with* God, he came out glorious again. Truly it was *wonder*-full to see the renewed shining and hear a new word from the LORD!

This account is a delightful challenge for us. It invites us to think about all the *wonders* of God, the absolutely astonishing truth that God in all his unfathomable immensity condescends to tell us who he is and helps us to know him, so that we have the opportunity, the privilege, to do his will.

Let us turn now to the reading from Luke 9:28-43 — truly one of the most extraordinary texts in the whole Gospel narrative. We have been listening to Luke since the beginning of Advent, and there are certain stylistic devices in Luke that we may have noticed.

One of the marks of Luke that is no longer rendered in our newest translations is his frequent use of the Greek word *egeneto*. It seems to be one of his favorite words. The King James Version translated this word in the Christmas story as "and it came to pass." Do you remember that lovely phrase?[1] I'm disappointed that modern translations leave it out, for the phrase reminds us that God is in charge. "It came to pass" because God planned it. If we pay attention to this word, we start to see the transcendent splendor, the infinite wisdom, the eternal wonder of a sovereign God who wills his perfect purposes and they come to pass. The New Revised Standard Version uses the translation "now" for Luke's *egeneto,* but let us begin this account in our minds with "and it came to pass."

The setting of this event is especially important. Luke tells us that the scene we are about to consider happened eight days after Jesus had spoken certain things. As we look back in the Gospel account, we discover that what he had said to his disciples was a foretelling of his death and his resurrection. The disciples, of course, hadn't wanted to hear that, but Jesus softened his proclamation by promising that some who were present would not die until they had seen the kingdom of God.

What a magnificent promise! Some would have the chance to envision the fullness of God's kingdom before it is fulfilled. Some would see the true

---

1. At this point in the aural sermon I asked the worship participants to raise their hands if they remembered that phrase and afterward said, "That was just to wake you up," which made them laugh. I am increasingly troubled by the passivity of people in U.S. culture, caused primarily by television's numbing effects, and I constantly try to find ways to engage people in physical actions and verbal responses that involve them more directly in the texts. One of the most important is that I always ask them (since my sermons are primarily biblical) to follow along with the texts as they are printed in their worship folder or bulletin insert or pew Bible. I was thrilled to be told by one mother after this sermon that her son, in his early teens, commented, "How can she talk like that? I listened to every word she said." I think the interest lies in the details, the close reading of the texts (see Chapter 21).

glory that faded from Moses as an anticipation of the final glory that Jesus would make possible.

What a privilege that we can peek in, too, and catch a glimpse of God's splendor. Let us watch closely as Jesus takes his best friends, Peter and James and John, and goes with them to a mountain to pray. Verse 29 informs us that while he was praying his appearance radically changed.

Pause just a minute with me and consider the invitation and challenge of this transformation. When was the last time that during your prayers your whole life changed? After this worship service, continue to reflect on the monumental possibilities of prayer. How might God want to refashion us through our conversation with him? Might we leave our devotional times or corporate worship services resplendent like Moses with the glory of God? Are we open to God turning us around, sending us off on a new course, or confirming us in a path we were questioning?

Recently such a transformation happened to me. I was working on some writing projects, but not making much progress — and not listening very well to God in prayer either. I kept bumping into walls — writer's block, frustrations piled high, interruptions and confusions. After six weeks of writing that accomplished only a chapter or two, I was urged by a friend to take a personal retreat and pray about my writing, but she questioned whether I would be willing to give up the projects on which I was working. My retreat turned out to be God hitting me over the head with a two-by-four; suddenly it jumped out at me that the reason I was making so little progress in my writing was that I was working on the wrong book. Just like that — in the midst of prayer — God set me on a different course for that aspect of my life. God opened me up to what had been truly burning in my awareness, to what my true passion really was — but I had been too dense to listen all along. I had not been giving God any space in my prayers.

I use that example only to invite you into the wonder of our God. What might happen if your prayers gave more space to God? What could develop if we really learned to listen to God and let God change us? What would come to pass if we stopped getting in the way and let God be God in us and for us and through us? How astonishing it will be when God more fully has his way with us!

Let's return now to verse 29. As Jesus was praying, his face changed and his clothes became dazzling white. What words could we use to describe this shining, this brilliance, the wonder of his glory? Think about words like *glistening, radiant,* or — my favorite — *effulgent.* Don't you use that word all the time?

The closest I can come to imagining it is by remembering the first time I saw the Mendenhall glacier, which is just a short walk from where I was staying on the outskirts of Juneau, Alaska. All the ice crystals of that glacier catch the sun and reflect it in skillions of glimmerings refracted again in thousands of directions. Since I am visually handicapped, all those sparklings scattered again because of the clutter of my lenses and unloosed a brilliance inside my eye that was totally overpowering.

The Juneau glacier is an image, inviting us to wonder at the shimmering radiance of Jesus on the mountain of transfiguration. Why are you and I not more astonished? How can we read these texts with such a humdrum attitude? This account is describing for us the event of Peter, James, and John seeing *GOD!* On that mountain *all heaven* broke loose.

Verse 30 tells us that next Moses and Elijah appeared in glorious splendor and that they were conversing with Jesus. Luke introduces it with "and behold!" He wants to shake us out of our lethargy, to grab us by the shirt collar and say, "Look at this. Isn't this astonishing?"

Even as a little girl, I used to wonder how Peter and the others knew that those people were Moses and Elijah. The text doesn't tell us, but somehow they knew, in spite of a lack of photographs and videos. And why was it that Moses and Elijah appeared? Scholars have debated about that through time. Maybe Moses was there to represent the Law of the First Testament, and Elijah represented the Prophets. Perhaps it was because both of those men had not ended their life on earth in the usual way — Moses being "buried by God" and Elijah being taken up in the fiery chariot. I like to think they were there because they were such good friends of God, and they came to comfort Jesus before the agonies he was about to endure.

There is no need for us to figure out why those two were there. What is important is that, as Luke alone tells us, they were speaking about Jesus' *departure*.[2] The Greek word is *exodus*. The word hints that it was more than just his death (and then the resurrection) which was about to be fulfilled in Jerusalem. The word *departure* suggests to us the ascension of Jesus — which fits in with a particular mark of Luke that we must observe.[3]

---

2. Again, in the aural version of this sermon, I tried to engage the congregation more actively and told them, "This is a very important word to Luke, so underline it on your bulletin insert. If you haven't got a pen, underline it in your head."

3. In the aural version I added a joke here to engage the congregants a bit more. "Don't you think we should have a major church festival to celebrate the Ascension? Since our society has totally ruined Christmas and Easter for us, Ascension could become an important holiday that the world couldn't steal. When I was a youth, my hometown flew Santa Claus in by helicopter for the Christmas parade. Later they added flying in the Easter bunny. But Ascension they couldn't ruin because our world doesn't have the foggiest notion what to do with someone flying out."

For Luke the ascension is the key. He ends his Gospel with an account of it; he begins the book of Acts with another narrative of it. In verse 51 of this ninth chapter we are studying today, Luke refers to the ascension at the turning point of the whole Gospel. He writes, "And *it came to pass,* when the time was come that he should *be received up,* he steadfastly *set his face* to go to Jerusalem" (Luke 9:51, KJV; emphasis added). The ascension is so important because that is when Jesus received his glory again. That is when all the work of Christ on our behalf was affirmed as sufficient and perfect. At that point Jesus took up again the divine powers which he had voluntarily laid aside in his immense humbling of himself to become a servant for us. In the ascension Jesus again became the resplendent Lord of the kingdom and made all its joys available to us. If he had not ascended, we would all have to go over to Galilee to find him. If Jesus had not ascended, his eternal glory could not be ours.

When those three on the mountain were talking about Jesus' departure, perhaps they were discussing all the things that Jesus would do to make it possible for you and me to be welcomed into the glory of the people of God.

Peter, James, and John experienced it only partially. As a result, Peter did a silly thing. Before we get to that, though, we have to notice the description of their situation. The original Greek tells us that they were weighed down, burdened by sleep — but now they have been thoroughly awakened. It is not that they stayed awake, but that in their drowsiness God *alarmed* them with his glory [pun intended], so that now they were exceptionally alert. Have you ever experienced that? — when you are nodding over a book or something else, and suddenly a sound rouses you and you become intensely responsive to whatever is going on. Your hearing becomes phenomenally acute; your eyes catch the slightest movement — even if it is just a bush scratching the wall in the wind and not the burglar you had feared.

Just as Peter, James, and John became exceptionally alert and were realizing what was happening, they saw the full glory of Jesus and the two men with him, but soon thereafter Moses and Elijah seemed to be leaving. As they were going, Peter does his silly thing. Out of an attempt to grab on to the experience, Peter falls into a temptation common to all of us who worship.[4] This text introduces the problem of trying to control worship. Peter wants to control Jesus. "Oh, God, it is good to be here," we say, too. "I like this splendor, this glory, so let's try to prolong it." Peter said, "Let's pitch a few tents and

4. Keep in mind for the following remarks that this sermon began a three-day lecture series on the subject of worship.

hang around for a while." Perhaps we say, "Let's hang on to these emotions. Let's package a way to produce them. Let's stick to just what we know" — or to a certain style, or to whatever is comfortable, or to human glory and fame. We try to be in charge, and then God is prevented from doing what he wants to do in us because we have put ourselves in the way.[5] Why do we try to control God — this God who showers upon us the abundance of his graces, who condescends to reveal himself to us in these texts?

Just as Peter said this, a cloud came. Have you noticed throughout the Bible that a cloud means God is there? In the wilderness Israel was led by the pillar of cloud. Remember the cloud of God's glory that descended on the tabernacle, that filled the temple. Don't forget the promise that at the end of time those who are alive and those who are already dead will be caught up together into the clouds — so that we shall ever be with the LORD (1 Thessalonians 4:17). All those clouds signify the presence of *GOD*. That is why, when the cloud covered the disciples on the mountain of transfiguration, they were terrified. Once again, notice! You and I cannot stand in the presence of God. This is a wonder-full occurrence — that Peter, James, and John survived this appearing of *GOD*.

However, this cloud in Luke 9 teaches us that God's presence — even though God is infinitely and eternally beyond us — is a presence of grace! God speaks from the cloud and declares, "This is my Son, my chosen one." The Greek word that Luke uses reminds us that Jesus remains the chosen one throughout all of time. Consequently, when God commands, "Listen to him," Luke records that with a continuing imperative. "Keep on listening."

This is an urgent invitation to us. Keep on listening to God. Come every week to worship because God will always have new things to tell you. Read your Bible every day, because God's Revelation always gives words to change our lives. Keep on listening in your prayers, for God always wants to surprise us.

When the voice had finished speaking, Jesus was found alone. The stunning experience was over — and the disciples were so awed by its mystery that they kept silent. That must have been a major accomplishment for Peter, who is frequently pictured in the Scriptures as having a severe case of foot-in-mouth disease. Luke underscores their silence by stating literally that they told no one nothing. We can't use such double negatives in English, but the

---

5. At this point in the aural sermon I made several comments about the choir anthem for the day as it pertained to the Scripture texts, but since I don't have the anthem's text before me I won't include that here. I simply want to note the value of commenting on other aspects of the worship service in our sermons in order to tie things together.

text stresses that at first the disciples revealed nothing of this astonishing event to no one, nowhere, no how. They had to ponder its significance for a long time. Not until the second letter of Peter is there an explanation of what this transfiguration meant (see 2 Peter 1:16-19).

We won't spend time now considering the rest of the Gospel text concerning the healing of a worried father's son, except to note one point in order to catch another quick glimpse of this Jesus who causes us such wonder. At the end of the story of the healing Jesus performed after coming down from the mountain, we notice the dialectical character of God as revealed in Christ. Verse 42 declares that Jesus rebuked the spirit and thus, by his power, healed the boy. Then, as an act of deep compassion, he gave him back to his father, for, as we were told in verse 38, this was the man's only child. When I read the Gospel text before this sermon, I accentuated the pathos of the father's plea. "Your disciples couldn't heal him," he cried. "It is my only son; can't you do something?" The connections are momentous. God the Father had said, "This is my Son, my chosen one. Keep listening to him," and this father cries, "This is my son, my only child, but the evil spirit torments him and throws him into convulsions and is destroying him." God's Son rescued the other son, though he himself would not be rescued from what would destroy him.

Because he would not be rescued, he triumphed over all the oppressing powers. Thus, the grace of God hears our begging, too; the sovereignty of God sets us free also from the spirits that torment us. In all the sadnesses of our lives, this Jesus, whom we have seen in all his glory, also brings us both sides of the dialectic — always he brings both the power to do what is truly needed and the compassion to do it for us.

Notice the response of the people to this immense generosity and grace of Jesus when he gave the boy back to his father. Luke says they were all amazed at the greatness of God.

This is so astonishing — what Jesus has been in the glorification depicted in this account, who Jesus is and how he acts, and how he reveals to the disciples the immensity of the kingdom of God and its goodness toward those who suffer. We have to ask who we are in response to this vision of the kingdom. How do we respond to this wonder? Who are we because Christ was transfigured — that is, who are we as his people because we have seen him today in new ways?

Paul gives us good insights in today's text from 2 Corinthians 3 and 4. We can't help but notice that Paul reminds us in chapter 3 verse 12 of our confident hope. He connects this hope to the previous verses with a "therefore" or "since, then." In earlier verses Paul had contrasted a God of judgment with a God of righteousness. In the kingdom that Jesus has brought, he has covered us with God's own righteousness. What a hope that gives us — not to be dependent upon ourselves any longer, but to be able simply to trust in the righteousness that God confers out of his immense grace and mercy.

What Joy it constantly brings to our lives if we always know that through Christ we are deeply loved by God.[6] We *always* know we are the beloved of God because we look at the cross. We cannot know that he loves us simply because we feel good about him, because we have "nice vibes" about God. We *know* Jesus loves us because he died, and he rose, and he ascended.

Consequently, Paul can say, "since we have such a hope, we have great boldness." Many of the commentators at the Olympics talked about how terrifying it must be to wait just before beginning an event for which one had trained and strained for four years. Those who win, they noted, are the ones who can most successfully cope with that tension and channel it constructively. Isn't it wonderful that in our Christian life we never have to labor under a pressure to win? We already know that we have won the gold! Knowing that the first prize is ours, we are set free! Knowing that we have won the gold, we have enormous boldness, Paul says.

We are not like Moses. We do not have to put a veil over our faces and cover them up — because the glory isn't fading. The glory is always ours; it is in our baptism. It is in that relationship with God to which *GOD* will always be faithful.

Paul understands this profoundly. He is one who can say, "when[ever] they hear the reading of the old covenant, that same veil is still there" (3:14), because Paul himself had previously had the veil on. He had thought the old covenant meant legalism. He thought it meant obeying the Law by his own efforts. He forgot that the commandments began with "I am *YHWH* your God, who brought you out of the land of Egypt, out of the house of slavery" (Exodus 20:2). Judaica, properly understood, is not legalism; it begins with gospel, with the grace of a covenant God who liberated his people. Paul had

---

6. The comments of this paragraph referred specifically to my conversation with the congregation's youth group in the hour preceding the worship service. I always try in my sermons to make some connection in particular ways with young people in the congregation — using their concerns as examples or referring to my conversations with them or especially asking them to notice something — so that they become more involved and so that the whole congregation becomes more aware of each other across any lines of separation like age and thereby becomes more knit together as a community.

not understood that, he had lost sight of *YHWH*'s grace — and you and I lose sight of it, too, don't we?

How many of you sometimes say, "I *should* be a better Christian"? There isn't such a thing in the vocabulary of our Christian faith. You *are* a Christian; you *belong* to the kingdom revealed in Christ's transfiguration. The delightful truth is that the more we concentrate on the saints that we *are* by the mercy of God through Christ, the more we will *act* like the saints that we are. God already set you free. You already have the gold — so now you get to skate the exhibition. Now you skate simply for the Joy of it. You don't have to worry about winning any more.

That is why Paul can say in verse 16, "when one turns to the Lord, the veil is removed." We can see the *wonder* of the kingdom. Furthermore, in verse 17, "the Lord is the Spirit, and where the Spirit of the Lord is, there is freedom." We obey God's commands, not because we have to, but because we want to. We who are God's people are the ones who are free to be glorious.

Only by God's grace are we set free never to have to justify our existence; we never have to prove to others that we are wonderful. We are declared important, beautiful, saints! — by God's forgiveness and reconciliation. And therefore you and I can go out from this place this morning and change the world.

That is what Paul says in verse 18. The more we look at the transfigured Christ — the more we look at his glory with unveiled faces (because we are not bound into that legalism of trying to prove ourselves or justify ourselves or win by our own efforts) — the more we are changed. We do see the Lord's glory as though reflected in a mirror, though, because we are not on that mountain of transfiguration. Instead, we see Christ's transfiguration reflected in God's Word, and therefore we see it even more deeply than those who were there, for we know the entire narrative of Jesus' *departure*. We can see the transfigured Christ also reflected in the mirror of the Christian community, in our worship together. We see the glory of the kingdom in the way God intervenes in the world. And because we see the Lord's glory reflected in those three mirrors — Word, world, community — you and I are changed.

This is one of my favorite verses in the whole Bible, this promise in verse 18: the more we look at God, the more we become like God. We are transformed into the same image, Paul says, from one degree of glory to another. Oh, the *wonder* of it all!

It is very much like marriage or deep friendship. People who are together a lot pick up each other's mannerisms, their language habits, their likes and dislikes.[7] Isn't it astonishing that this happens between us and God? What an overwhelming Joy this is: the more we look at Jesus, the more we become like him! The more you dwell in God's presence, the more you shine.[8] Let us take this seriously in the days to come: Jesus shines through you — in the world and for it.

This is the greatest wonder of all: we are transformed from one degree of glory to another. As we grow in faith, God's community becomes more and more reflective of God's splendor. The more we worship together, the more we pray together, the more we study together, the more we can be the people that God has called us to be.

That is why Paul begins chapter 4 with the word *therefore*. (One of my professors in college insisted that if we saw a "therefore," we should always ask what it was there for.) Therefore, Paul proclaims, since you are free, since you are changed from one degree of glory to another, since Jesus has been transfigured before us so that we have seen the glory of his kingdom, since we have been mercied (as chapter 4 verse 1 declares) — *therefore* we engage in our ministries, whatever they might be.[9] We engage in all our ministries without losing heart.

A friend who is a peace activist once told me that he liked to hang around with me because he needed my hope. Because of Christ's *departure* and all that it involved, we never lose heart. We have seen his glory, and so we have all the hope of the kingdom of God.

Therefore, we don't use any underhanded schemes, Paul says. We don't use gimmicks in our worship services. We reject shameful tactics or hidden wiles. We do not use cunning, nor do we falsify God's Word. All we do is openly state the truth. Our methods are pure; we do not try to be anything but faithful to reveal the glory of God.

I dare you. I invite you. Let us go to the mountain, behold the glory of the kingdom, and then live the truth of the kingdom. I dare you to be the

---

7. Here again, in the aural sermon, I asked the people specifically to nod if they had experienced becoming in certain ways like someone else with whom they spent a lot of time. I was especially glad that a few young children nodded, that they discovered that this sermon was about their lives, too.

8. At this point I referred to the worship service's closing song, "Shine, Jesus, Shine," by Graham Kendrick of England, from *With One Voice*. It is important that our sermons reveal how everything else in the worship service is connected; certainly we plan, as outlined in Chapter 26, for music, texts, and sermon to be cohesive.

9. Here the aural sermon named several specific occupations and vocations of congregation members — college professor, rancher, retired activist, public school superintendent.

truth, speak the truth, act the truth, delight in the truth of God's grace through Jesus Christ.

Then notice what will happen. Paul says we will commend ourselves to the conscience of the world around us. Oh, the wonder of it: when we are transformed, our lives give our neighbors a warrant for belief!

Our world is desperate for that, for a reason to believe. Our society needs *you*. Our neighbors need to see the glory of the transfigured Christ. Because Jesus is transfigured before us today, and you and I have observed it, we are being changed from one degree of glory to another, and therefore, having our ministries, we do not — never, nowhere, no how — lose heart. Isn't it astonishing?

Let us pray: Compassionate Lord, many in our world are troubled. Radiant and glorious Christ, all of us need a vision of your beauty and grace. Use us to show forth your glory. Set us apart in these days, resplendent Jesus, for the ministries to which you have called us, a ministry from our unveiled faces to those who cannot see your beauty because of the veil that blinds them. Help us not to lose heart when our neighbors seem more attracted to the dazzles of the world, when their own inner darknesses keep them from even wanting your light. Instead, God of splendor, keep calling us out of our darknesses and keep changing us from one degree of glory to another. Set us free by your Holy Spirit to have the boldness of your mercy so that in your world we can live and speak the truth, to your honor and glory and praise into the ages of the ages — and for the sake of your world. Amen.

[Hymn of Response: "I Want to Walk as a Child of the Light; I Want to Follow Jesus"]

9

Don't Let the People
Cop Out of Witnessing

I call upon the LORD, who is worthy to be praised . . .

Psalm 18:3

Exalt the LORD our God,
   and worship at his holy mountain;
   for the LORD our God is holy.

Psalm 99:9, NIV

Only those who believe in God can *worship* God! Since the term *worship* has to do with the *worthiness* of the One who is worshiped, certainly only those who know and acknowledge that worth can genuinely ascribe it and proclaim it. That is why the misunderstanding concerning the difference between worship and evangelism that is so prevalent in present-day conflicts concerning worship is so dangerous.

My earlier book about worship, *Reaching Out without Dumbing Down*, has been criticized for not saying enough about evangelism, and yet its basic thesis is that the reaching out of witness and caring is the result of the formation of the believers' and the community's character. Worship is, of course, only one of the formative agents, but its importance is so subtle that it is often missed unless we separate the issues carefully and read the instructions of the Scriptures faithfully and devotedly.

The ultimate well-being of the Church is gravely sabotaged by the fact that throughout the United States and in other countries controversies over worship rage as pastors and other leaders ask such questions as "How can worship be made more exciting for people in these postmodern times?" or "What style of music should we use to make our worship appealing to the 'unchurched'?" Perhaps you think I am overstating the case by calling it sabotage, but I encourage you to read this chapter prayerfully and with diligent reflection to ask with me — in the midst of our postmodern, post-Christian (sometimes anti-Christian) society — what it means to be the Church, what corporate worship is and how God's people conduct it, and what it means for followers of Christ to reach out to our neighbors in caring and evangelism if we are truly being Church. It is crucial for us to comprehend that arguments about appealing to unbelievers by means of a particular style of worship betray a serious confusion between worship and evangelism, to the severe detriment of both. Therefore, let us investigate carefully here the necessary distinctions so that we can be more faithful in our Churchbeing.

Churchbeing

Let us use this new word, *Churchbeing*, because words like *community* and *church* are misused, overused, abused, and confused. Churches think they're a "community" because that is what the word *church* suggests, without realizing how much the technological milieu hinders us from really caring for each other with the gutsy, sacrificial love of genuine community. Moreover, when we find out how much effort it takes truly to be the kind of community the Bible describes, we are often not willing to involve ourselves in that much struggle and suffering.[1] In our overly entertained and blatantly consumerism-oriented culture (see Chapter 7 again), with little concern for serving the common good, many "churches" have become, in George Hunsberger's masterful phrases, "vendors of religious services and goods," instead of "a body of people sent on a mission."[2]

1. See Marva J. Dawn, *Truly the Community: Romans 12 and How to Be the Church* (Grand Rapids: Wm. B. Eerdmans Publishing Co., 1992; reissued 1997).
2. See George R. Hunsberger, "Sizing Up the Shape of the Church," in *The Church Between Gospel and Culture: The Emerging Mission in North America*, ed. George R. Hunsberger and Craig Van Gelder (Grand Rapids: Wm. B. Eerdmans Publishing Co., 1996), pp. 333-46.

To be truly the Church instead of merely a collection of religious shoppers means, primarily, for every single member of a genuine community to realize that the triune God has loved us first and called us to be his own — and to be his instruments. Freed by the gospel, each of us responds to God with lives that glorify him, and we exercise our gifts to upbuild and extend the Christian community. Corporate worship by us is possible only because God has first summoned us to it and gives us himself in it. We respond with praise and thanksgiving, openness to be transformed and to grow spiritually, and renewed commitment to serve him in the world. Such worship in which we encounter God and are changed by his presence both comes out of Churchbeing and deepens it; it forms the Christian community to be an alternative society, living in the image of Christ according to the values of God's kingdom.

The description in the preceding paragraph is extremely important, for only if we truly understand such Churchbeing do we have the personal and corporate resources to resist, and not be incapacitated by, our idolatrous and consumerist culture. Then we Christians can really rediscover again and again the profound Joy of being God's people, and we will participate with rich gladness in the rhythm of being nurtured by worship and then sharing our faith and love with our neighbors.

Let us keep that rhythm in mind lest we confuse worship and evangelism. Put simply, we must remember that worship is *for God,* in contrast to evangelism, which is *for the unbeliever.*

Typical Results of the Confusion

Many churches have been torn apart because of conflicts generated by this serious confusion between worship and evangelism: that worship ought to be designed to appeal to the unbeliever or "unchurched" and therefore should make use of a certain kind of accessible "style." Deep at the root, the disagreements arise because declining numbers have put congregations and denominations in a great panic over how to attract new members. Many pastors, lay leaders, and national church officers seem to be thoroughly disdaining God's own instructions when they accept the false advice of marketing gurus to "throw out the traditions" of their churches in order to "appeal" to the world around them and thereby "grow." Speaking about the way television distorts the meaning of worship, William Fore reminds us of John Kenneth Galbraith's insistence that

the basic purpose of advertising is to get people to buy something they don't need. Apparently, the purveyors of the electronic church think the values of the gospel are so obscure that only the hard sell can move them off the shelf. Slogans, pop songs, glad names, bad names, stacking the cards, the bandwagon — every technique basic to advertising is part of the stock-in-trade of the electronic church, which is, indeed, selling something people *don't* need — a superficial, magical God.[3]

The result of this hard sell on television and also in many churches is often a push for a worship style that lacks theological substance, invites passivity, and fosters an easy-listening consumerism that provides neither music nor words that will help worship participants remember deep truths.[4] One dire consequence of adopting this quick-fix technique is that *the real problems* — namely, *failure to educate* concerning the meaning and practice of worship, *failure to understand* the real idolatries that keep people from participating in the Church, and *failure to equip* the priesthood of all believers for outreach to the world — *remain unaddressed.*

As you read these pages, keep in mind that I am convinced that we *should* be using new music and new worship forms; however, we use them not to attract people, but because they are faithful in praising God and forming us to be his people. If we choose a certain musical style or other elements simply to appeal to those outside our walls, then we are forcing worship to bear the brunt of evangelism, which is instead the task of all believers. Don't misunderstand: good worship *will be* evangelistic, but that is not its primary purpose, for it is directed toward God, not toward the neighbor. No passage in the Scriptures says, "Worship the Lord to attract the unbeliever." Rather, in countless texts we are commanded, invited, urged, wooed to worship the Trinity because God is worthy of our praise. As stated at the beginning of this chapter, *worship* can actually be done only by those who recognize that worthiness.

Furthermore, the worship service is part of the entire educational process of the Christian community by which God's people are equipped to introduce others to his worthiness. Evangelism or sharing is done by all of us who realize that everyone around us needs God's grace. Out of our love for

---

3. William F. Fore, *Television and Religion: The Shaping of Faith, Values, and Culture* (Minneapolis: Augsburg, 1987), p. 88.

4. It is essential that church leaders ask better questions of the church marketers, rather than merely accepting advice from the gurus that might not be biblically faithful. Let me direct your attention to an extraordinarily helpful book by Philip Kenneson and James Street called *Selling Out the Church: The Dangers of Church Marketing* (Nashville: Abingdon Press, 1997), an excellent exposé of the problems with church marketers and the false notions that they are propagating in churches.

God and our love for those neighbors, we are eager to serve them and pass on the witness of faith. Evangelism happens in our daily lives, our regular encounters, our simple conversations and carings — or at evangelistic events, which have a focus different from that of worship — in order that we can bring others with us to worship God. Evangelism is the means; worship is the end.

The Difference between Worship and Evangelism

The difference can be illustrated easily. When leading worship seminars, I usually hold up an 8″ × 10″ school picture of my husband, to whom I've been joyfully married for 110 months and 21 days today (as I write this). I tell the audience all about Myron — what a wonderful elementary school teacher he is, how magnificently beautiful are the gardens he grows, how gently he cares for me in my plethora of physical handicaps — all this to introduce him to the listeners, as in evangelism. But is that how I will talk to him when I arrive home after several days away teaching? No, then I will speak to him words of adoration and love, listen to what he tells me about his work (how he has intervened in the world), talk with him about my own work (how might I have been more faithful?), sort out problems with him, and so forth — as in worship. Our conversations will be in the language of mutual intimacy and growth for the purpose of strengthening our relationship, rather than in the idiom of introduction.

Worship is the language of love and growth between believers and God; evangelism is the language of introduction between those who believe and those who don't. To confuse the two and put on worship the burden of evangelism robs the people of God of their responsibility to care about the neighbor, defrauds the believers of transforming depth, and steals from God the profound praise of which he is worthy.

Of course, the distinction is not total, for if believers worship with gladness and passion, anyone not yet a part of the community certainly will be attracted to the One who is the object of their worship. But to focus the worship on evangelistic introduction deprives believers of deeper nurturing toward Churchbeing and deprives God of the intimate and involved worship due him from the Church.

Practicing Christly Gestures

Usually persons who object to the kinds of distinctions I am trying to make for the sake of deeper Churchbeing do so by pointing to Willow Creek in Barrington, Illinois, and the enormous numbers of people it attracts to its Sunday morning events. Let us be very clear about what precisely Willow Creek is doing, for Bill Hybels, its founding pastor, himself emphatically declares that their programs on Sunday mornings are not the congregation's *worship* services (which are held on Wednesday evenings for the seriously committed believers).

What Willow Creek does on Sunday mornings it does extremely well. Its dramas and music are professionally performed; the sermons provide good teaching. The auditorium is perfectly well appointed; the acoustics and instruments are superb. Certainly I would not criticize Willow Creek's sense that they are doing what God has given them to do.

The problem is that many congregations try to imitate them by turning their Sunday morning worship services into such evangelistic events — without adequately understanding the difficulty of moving people from the passivity of those events into the activity of Churchbeing, from the surface into the life itself. How will they encourage those who have been spectators of fine performances to become involved in the *liturgy,* the "work of the people"? I am told by critics that such performances are necessary for people in our television and cyberspace culture, but the very problems of that culture are thus transferred to the churches — for faith is not merely intellectual assent to doctrinal positions or an expression of emotions, as we will see more deeply in Chapter 29. Faith is a lived language, and it cannot be learned unless one participates in it and practices it. If one's introduction to Christ comes from a polished performance, how will that person have the courage to live his or her own awkward, stumbling version of the Christ-life?

Brett Webb-Mitchell offers the felicitous image of "Christly gestures" and emphasizes that people cannot learn them if they do not engage in them. In the *New Oxford Review,* Webb-Mitchell told three stories about handicapped persons participating in worship and about learning the meaning of church rites, such as infant baptism. He stressed that these gestures unite us — able and disabled, male and female, young and old — and then concluded as follows:

> What these three stories have in common is the practice of particular gestures that not only enable us to communicate with one another, but, even more powerfully, shape and nurture our perspective on God in Christ. Ges-

tures are learned and become part of our nature as we grow into the Christian community. . . . We might want to consider the gestures being acted out by the members of Christ's body as God's way of crafting us into the ways of God.[5]

In a chapter for a book on *Human Disability and the Service of God,* Webb-Mitchell elaborates further his image of gestures to remind us all of the importance of learning in a community of believers the art of Churchbeing. He explains that "Teaching the gestures of the body of Christ is like initiating someone into the practices of a craft." This designation "craft" could be applied to various occupations such as furniture making, the visual arts, boat building, and teaching and/or performing with musical instruments. "In medieval Europe, the term was even used to characterize intellectual enquiry, as in the liberal arts; this was considered the craft of the free person."

In the craft tradition, an apprentice must first learn from a mentor. Since the apprentice is not a "tabula rasa,"

the apprentice may hold certain interpretations or judgments, some of which will need to be eradicated or transformed. Or, there may exist certain desires which must be drawn out of the person and into the good that is known only in the practice of the gestures of the body of Christ. The mentor needs to understand that the apprentice has both a potential and need for learning these virtuous gestures as a member of Christian community.[6]

If all Christians understood that they themselves and those to whom our churches reach out need such mentoring, such practiced learning of the craft of Churchbeing, they would not settle for mere entertainment and passivity.[7]

As Webb-Mitchell's emphasis on learning the Christly gestures underscores, churches' "seekers' services" do not address the root problems of our times because they *remove the responsibility of witness and nurturing from all the people of God.* Since statistics show that most people come to believe in Christ through friendship with someone committed to him and since growing in faith requires deep mentoring both to eradicate false under-

---

5. Brett Webb-Mitchell, "A Protestant View of Physical Gestures in Church Life," *New Oxford Review* 62, no. 8 (October 1995): 20-21.

6. Brett Webb-Mitchell, "Crafting Christians into the Gestures of the Body of Christ," in *Human Disability and the Service of God: Reassessing Religious Practice,* ed. Nancy Eiesland and Don Saliers (Nashville: Abingdon, 1998), p. 276. See also Brett Webb-Mitchell, *Christly Gestures: The End of Christian Education* (New York: Crossroad Publishing Company, forthcoming).

7. See the emphasis on a need for new catechumenal processes in Chapter 20 below.

standings and to develop truly Christian perspectives, it is essential that the gospel be specifically incarnated in caring individuals rather than only proclaimed in performances, no matter how polished they might be. The gospel has always been incarnated — as in Christ, so in human beings who have died to themselves and risen again to life engaged in by the power of the Holy Spirit.

To be the sort of people who will gladly fulfill our responsibility for witness and mentoring and nurturing care we need meaty worship — worship that engages us deeply in an encounter with the God whose splendor is illimitably beyond our understanding, worship that shakes us out of our narcissism and consumerism, worship that disciplines us and thereby equips us for the work of the kingdom in witness and vocation and suffering.

Why Is Our Witness So Weak?

Once in a seminary class, after I had emphasized that evangelism was the work of all the people and not of the worship service, one class member protested, "But the people don't do it."

"That doesn't prove that the biblical model is wrong," I responded. It merely points out again how much our churches are failing in Churchbeing.

The pervasive and powerful confusion in our society between evangelism and worship has severely hampered the necessary paradigm shifts of Churchbeing. When and how will our congregations begin to equip the people for both worship and witness? It will require great catechumenal training, intensive mentoring, for our churches are in severe trouble. Many congregations and denominations have failed for decades or perhaps even centuries to teach people what worship is and to educate members to be witnesses, to care for their neighbors, and to minister to the world around them as active parts of the Body of Christ.

Why don't Christians talk about their faith with their neighbors? Charts in sociological studies as well as personal conversations and class discussions all convince me of the same thing: each person has one or several of certain common reasons or rationalizations for not doing so. Different studies highlight alternate excuses, and the reasons vary according to an individual's personality, so the following list of explanations is not in any particular order by proportion. Here, however, are some of the most common hindrances to the witness aspect of Churchbeing and some beginning responses (of course, these are too brief and noncontextualized) of how truly being the Church would solve the problem:

■ "I don't know enough. My neighbors ask tough questions that I can't answer." In genuine Churchbeing we are all continuing to grow, so you will learn more answers as you go. Also, you are part of an entire community that can help you with the tough questions.

■ "I'm not skilled enough. Evangelism should be done by a professional." To tell others how God has changed your life does not require skill, for God has promised that the Holy Spirit will give us wisdom and words for witness. What is most required is genuine love for your neighbor — and God gives you that love, too.

■ "I don't have enough time. It takes all my efforts just to get by." Giving witness to your faith is not an added-on job. The original Greek version of Matthew 28:19 literally says, "while you are going, be making disciples." Helping others to know how Christ has changed your life happens while you are at work, when you chat with your neighbors, whenever you assist someone else in a crisis, all the time. (And maybe we should also ask if you are needing too much to get by — as discussed in Chapter 7.)

■ "I'm not brave enough. I'm afraid of rejection." That's good — then you won't trample on people's feelings, and you'll be very sensitive to their concerns and fears. But some of your fear will be taken away when you think about the perfect love of God for you and pass that love on to the persons with whom you converse.

■ "I'm not bold enough. I am a very timid and shy person." Are you afraid to talk with people you know well about whatever makes you most excited? God is not necessarily asking you to talk with complete strangers — though he might ask that of persons less shy — but simply to let your Churchbeing affect your daily conversations.

■ "I'm not sure enough. It is very difficult for me to share my faith." It is actually very helpful to those who do not yet know God to discover that no one knows God perfectly and that no one's faith is completely mature. Share your wrestlings, your confusions — and in the process invite your neighbor to discover with you all the intricacies of the basic truth you know, which is that God has manifested his love for you in the death and resurrection of Christ on your behalf.

■ "I'm not strong enough. I'm afraid of how people might respond." What is the worst thing that someone could do to you? We don't even live in a country where people could kill us for our faith, so what other responses might we get and how could they really hurt us? Whatever responses we might receive won't change in the slightest the fact that we have been faithful in trying to introduce the person to God.

■ "I don't have any non-Christian friends or neighbors." This is a serious problem shared by many Christians. Genuine Churchbeing will open us up to look for those who need our love and care and friendship. However, we don't become their friends in order to make them a target for our evangelism practice. We love them for God's sake and see what happens in our friendship.

■ "I don't have a friendly church. Where would I take guests to worship?" This is another serious problem shared by many Christians. Let us keep asking what we ourselves can do to become more welcoming in our daily lives and to make our congregations more hospitable[8] — and especially how we can involve our young people in this vital ministry.[9]

■ "TV preachers have given evangelism a bad name." This is true — all the more reason that our neighbors need to see in you a Christian who is not consumed by greed or sexual passions, a Christian who is trustworthy and faithful, a Christian who speaks of God with integrity and gentleness.

■ "We can't talk about faith anymore in our culture. This is a pluralistic society." By God's grace, faith talk is being welcomed back these days into the public square, as evidenced by more openness in television programs and movies. Moreover, pluralism does not mean that we back down on what we believe, but that we offer it as a gift, with respect and gentleness, with openness to hear the truth claims of our partner in conversation (see Chapter 30).

Some of the other reasons why Christians are not willing to talk about their faith are not usually admitted and verbalized. Perhaps the most prominent of these is that Christians, too, are enfolded in our culture's passivity, its "Low Information-Action Ratio." Television and the Internet overload us

8. I've suggested many ideas to practice and questions to consider in *Truly the Community.*
9. On the importance of involving our children in Churchbeing, see Marva J. Dawn, *Is It a Lost Cause? Having the Heart of God for the Church's Children* (Grand Rapids: Wm. B. Eerdmans Publishing Co., 1997).

with tons of information that we cannot or will not act on because its immensity paralyzes us and too much entertainment lulls us. It takes genuine Churchbeing to shake us out of this societal sloth.

Similarly, perhaps we don't talk about our faith because it hasn't really grabbed hold of all of our lives. Perhaps we are merely religious consumers ourselves. Then may God evangelize us! Let us pray that we will become astonished afresh by the immensity of the Father's grace and mercy toward us. Let us pray that Christ will give us a new vision of himself, a previously unknown and invigorating sense of his overwhelming love, and deepened commitment to participating in his marvelous purposes in and for the world. Oh, that the Holy Spirit will fill us with such renewing Joy that we can say with the apostles, "we cannot keep from speaking about what we have seen and heard" (Acts 4:20)!

The Example of the Early Church

We can see the interrelationships of worship and witness most clearly in Acts 2. A very important progression takes place in that chapter, which we can summarize in the following points:

1. The believers were gathered (for worship?) when the amazing gift of the Holy Spirit was poured out (Acts 2:1-4).
2. The coming of the Spirit caused such a sound that crowds gathered and wondered what was happening when they heard their native languages (vv. 5-12).
3. The crowd was divided between those who wanted to know more about what was happening and those who merely sneered (vv. 12-13).
4. Peter gave an evangelistic address that thoroughly recounted the history of Israel and God's grafting on of the Gentiles into the covenant promises (vv. 14-36).
5. The result of his address was conviction and a desire for change (v. 37).
6. Peter gave further instruction about first steps of repentance and baptism, urged those who were interested to receive God's promises and gifts, including forgiveness and the Holy Spirit, and added other "arguments and exhortations" so that the people could be saved from "this corrupt generation" in which they lived (vv. 38-40).
7. Three thousand responded to his invitation and were added to the Christian community through their baptism (v. 41).
8. The new believers, along with the more mature, became deeply devoted

in all the aspects of Churchbeing (vv. 42-47). The Greek phrase translated "devoted themselves" accentuates that they *continually* were devoted to these seven things: careful instruction in the Scriptures, committed and caring community life, participation in the Lord's Supper, persevering and communal prayer, the experience of signs and wonders, selling their possessions and sharing the proceeds with any who had need, and regular worship in the temple and in their homes.

9. The result was that God was glorified, they experienced great gladness, and they were formed to be generous (vv. 46-47a).

10. Because the believers became such Churchbeing people, they had favor with all the people. The result in the world was that their neighbors who observed them and how they lived were also, by the Lord's grace, added to the community (vv. 47b-c).

In a culture just as pagan and anti-Christian as ours (both Romans/ Greeks and Jews were opposed to this new "Jesus movement"), the early Christians did not try to figure out how to attract their neighbors. They did not try to control the process. Instead, they simply practiced Churchbeing, so that the Lord could do his work of adding new believers.

The more I study this text, the more I am convinced that the reason churches ultimately lose members is that our community life does not offer enough warrant for belief. I worry about congregations that focus on having "exciting" worship services because this merely fosters our society's self-gratification and does not welcome believers into the disciplines of the alternative lifestyle of Churchbeing. We might attract lots of consumers if our worship services are merely entertaining, but, unless we continually increase the emotional hype, we cannot expect consumers not to turn away to other diversions when the difficulties of being a Christian surface — or else we merely continue contributing to their shallowness.

Evangelism is not the task of the corporate worship service, but it is not the sole task of individual believers either. It is the result of our community life, of the evidence given by our thorough Churchbeing that life in relationship with God and with each other is much more grace-filled and fulfilling and true than any other possibility.

As George Lindbeck insightfully notes, pagan converts in the first centuries of the Church did not first understand the faith and then decide to become Christian converts; rather, they first decided and then came to understand (see Chapter 20 concerning the Church's catechumenal processes). Lindbeck comments, "More precisely, they were first attracted by the Christian community and form of life." In contrast, today "the churches primarily accommodate to the prevailing culture rather than shape it."[10] The confusion of evangelism and worship this chapter criticizes is ultimately dangerous to the kind of Churchbeing that will truly benefit our neighbors.

An Example of an Evangelistic Event

Though I work diligently to erase the prevailing confusion of evangelism and worship that has led many congregations to reduce worship to whatever is appealing, I am not opposed to evangelistic events — provided there is excellent follow-up with personal incarnations of the gospel. One good example of the kind of event that can serve Churchbeing well is presently being offered by the Mennonite congregation to which I belonged during the years that I was working on my doctorate in South Bend. Periodically this church sponsors an eight-week series of evening events called "Soup for the Soul." These evenings begin with a light supper of soup, bread, and fruit. After the meal there is a short devotional, fellowship and sharing, and particular activities for adults and children. These programs not only give time for informal fellowship, among the members of the congregation, but also provide the opportunity to invite friends, neighbors, and co-workers who might enter into the congregational life in this informal way before participating in the more formal Sunday morning worship context. Furthermore, the "main event" of the evening gives the Mennonite members and their visitors the opportunity to consider how their faith connects with their work, their travel, their interests and hobbies, and so forth.

Other possibilities for sharing the life of the congregation with the watching world include small groups, elder groups, prayer meetings, Bible study gatherings, and other such neighborhood or office events. But the most important entry point into the congregation is *you*. How can we equip congregation members to understand that the biblical picture of church growth is through the Spirit-empowered and grace-filled witness of believing saints?

Hospitality for Those Interested

When churches offer a course for new members, we usually give classes on our congregation's vision and plans for the future, on the history and theol-

---

10. George A. Lindbeck, *The Nature of Doctrine: Religion and Theology in a Postliberal Age* (Philadelphia: Westminster Press, 1984), p. 132.

ogy of our denomination, on our church's structure and ties to the larger Church, on our congregation's purpose and belief statements, on our parish's history and present outreach and ministry, on stewardship in all of life, on the requirements and possibilities of membership — but I rarely see on the outlines of such courses a specific session devoted to the meaning and practice of worship. We have failed for years to teach people what worship is all about.

Let's begin with our children — teaching them the gestures of worship in our homes,[11] in our worship services,[12] and in our congregation's educational opportunities by means of such programs as "Logos"[13] and "Children in Worship."[14] Meanwhile, we can use Sunday morning adult forums, explained-liturgy services, evening classes, and new member mentoring to help their parents learn the purposes and practices of worship.[15]

Worshiping is indeed a trained skill, especially in a culture that is consumer oriented. To move people away from the worship of themselves and various idolatries pervading our society requires a deliberate educative practice. What a gift it would be to our neighbors if every person in our congregations were skilled in the gestures of worship and prepared to be hospitable to strangers who might join us in exercising them! In my twenty years of being a

11. See especially chapter 5, "The Heart of God Revealed in Worship," in Dawn, *Is It a Lost Cause?*, pp. 64-88.

12. For example, see Chapter 22 of this book and the appendix of Marva J. Dawn, *Reaching Out without Dumbing Down: A Theology of Worship for the Turn-of-the-Century Culture* (Grand Rapids: Wm. B. Eerdmans Publishing Co., 1995), for ideas concerning children's sermons and worship.

13. "Logos" is a midweek school program involving worship skills along with Bible teaching, games and sports, and common meals. For information contact the Logos System Associates, 1405 Frey Road, Pittsburgh, PA 15235.

14. "Children in Worship" is a Sunday morning "children's church" program for children up to fourth grade that actually engages them in worship practices and in learning about the Church year. For information contact Professor Sonja Stewart, Western Theological Seminary, 86 E. 12th St., Holland, MI 49423, telephone (616) 392-8555. See also *Young Children and Worship* by Sonja M. Stewart and Jerome W. Berryman (Louisville: Westminster/John Knox Press, 1989).

15. Several congregations have reported to me that they are using *Reaching Out without Dumbing Down* for classes concerning worship. Audio cassettes of several of my lectures on worship (for lay people and for clergy) and explained-liturgy worship services are available from Dottie Davis, tape ministry coordinator, Christians Equipped for Ministry, 10918 NE 152nd Ave., Vancouver, WA 98682, telephone (360) 892-3618. These tapes don't have to be purchased; they can be simply borrowed and returned. Videotapes of my course on "Worship for Postmodern Times" will be available from the Regent College bookstore (1-800-663-8664) in Vancouver, B.C., after the summer session, 1999.

worship guest more than half the weeks each year when I'm on the road for speaking engagements, *only once* has the person sitting next to me leaned over and said, "Let me show you how our worship goes so that you can participate." This elderly gentleman in New Orleans now always sits next to me in my mind and reminds me to make sure that those around me are enabled in every imaginable way to participate as fully as possible.

Part of our congregation's training for Churchbeing must be to nurture in all the members a spirit of hospitality. May the infinitely welcoming triune God teach us all to embrace our neighbors with the fullness of his love through our care and witness. Then, if they are drawn to worship the Trinity, may we each greet them warmly with graceful assistance and gentle mentoring and kindred ardor for all the ways in which God will teach us about himself through our corporate praise.

10

Ah, Nadja! — Passion in Preaching

I have told the glad news of deliverance
   in the great congregation;
see, I have not restrained my lips,
   as you know, O LORD.
I have not hidden your saving help within my heart;
   I have spoken of your faithfulness and your salvation;
I have not concealed your steadfast love and your faithfulness
   from the great congregation.

Psalm 40:9-10

At first this chapter was entitled "Passionate about Preaching," but then I realized that the preaching itself is not what those who do it ought to be passionate about — it is the text that must kindle their ardor. More accurately, it is the LORD of the text who makes us fervent, and his presence is conveyed to us by the text. But it was Nadja who gave me this chapter.

Last night my husband and I savored our monthly date to hear the Oregon Symphony. We have really good seats in the front row of the upper balcony of the symphony's concert hall, so that we get a good view of the soloist through my husband's binoculars. (Being visually handicapped, I hardly see anything of the stage without them.) I watched intently as the symphony's music director, James DePreist, conducted and Nadja Salerno-Sonnenberg played Felix Mendelssohn's Violin Concerto in E Minor. Actually, Nadja doesn't *play* the violin. She dances, dreams, and discourses with it; makes it sing and cry and laugh; exults, romances, and grows angry through it; soars, leaps, flits, and floats with it; smiles, frowns, marvels, and sighs over it; paints, tints, and sculpts with it; aches, rejoices, laments, yearns, lambastes, jokes, and frolics through it. Her feet never stand still; her fingers scamper; her face is constantly in motion. With eyes closed in supreme concentration, she appears usually to be overwhelmed by the immense beauty she is creating.

When the concerto was finished, all of us in the capacity crowd bolted to our feet in thunderous applause and bravo calls. After the second half of the concert, in which the orchestra performed Hindemith's symphony *Mathis der Maler,* ten times more people than usual hurried to the main floor for the Sunday-only post-concert discussion with the soloist. Nadja's devotion to the music is echoed in the ardor of her audience.

I was haunted all the way home — at first by wondering about the difference between her and other performers. Then I realized that I was even more haunted by wishing the gospel could have such an impact, since its music is even more of a gift. Mendelssohn's concerto is called "the jewel" of the repertoire, but the gospel is the best news in the world and the splendor of God is better than life! If Nadja can be such a force for music that she stirs people of all ages, why can't we inspire the saints as powerfully when we preach?

She gives herself exhaustively to the service of the world's best music. Those who preach have the privilege of entrusting themselves entirely into the hands of the supreme Composer, so that his praise resounds with the melodies and harmonies of the cosmos.

Passion Is the Key

Nadja breathes in the music and becomes so engrossed in it that she sings it forth, constantly finding new nuances, new colors to carol. We, too, can bring "out of [our] treasure what is new and what is old," for we are "scribe[s] who [have] been trained for the kingdom of heaven" (Matthew 13:52). We have the possibility of becoming so enraptured by the text, so passionate about the Lord of the text, that we can hardly wait to speak it forth to the congregation.

I know that I am not a great preacher, but I can certainly tell the difference when the text takes over, as opposed to when I try to "convince the crowd" out of my own capacities. When Spirit-passion takes over, when the text speaks for itself, then both we and the listeners are transported into another world, into the dominion of God. What an immense privilege it is to display the kingdom and invite the Christian community to participate more fully in it.

Nadja welcomes everyone into the music because she is passionate. Her autobiography begins, "This is something I know for a fact: You have to work hardest for the thing you love most. And when it's music that you love, you're in for the fight of your life."[1] She is not afraid to let her devotion be seen — and the result is that others can envision and hear what they have not understood before.

Of course, we can't all be as fiery as Nadja. Our passion will come out differently in distinct personalities; it will be expressed in diverse ways. Six months ago, sixteen-year-old Sarah Chang played the Sibelius violin concerto with the Oregon Symphony. She is reserved, gentle, and graceful, in contrast to Nadja's robustness and aggressiveness, but her music is equally compelling. By her body's turns and tilts she displayed the tangled movement of Sibelius's musical line and enabled me to follow his progressions with a new comprehension I've never experienced before.

Similarly, every preacher, by his or her particular passionate involvement with the text, might help us to see meanings we've never noticed before.[2] Each might be a vehicle for wholly new ways to think about texts, how they welcome us into God's presence and form us to be God's people.

Our passion is kindled by absorption into the texts, by diligent study and prayer, by eagerness to work hard at listening to them so that they can reveal new insights into, and intimacies with, God. Sometimes the texts force us to probe them again and again, to bow before them in humility and obedience, to let the "three-personed" God "batter" our hearts, as John Donne wrote. This is especially crucial when the texts assigned for the day are difficult, dissonant, dark, or devastating. Engaged in the texts for the sake of their Lord, we are set free to let their mysteries stay suspended, to allow their questions to linger unanswered, to challenge those who hear to tarry devoutly in the presence of divine, impenetrable Truth.

There is safety there. In our postmodern world, people are desperate for a place where the inscrutable can be queried and quarried. In the assurance that God is the absolute Truth even if we can't know it absolutely, what is confusing can be sorted out and what is baffling can be made less threatening. In

---

1. Nadja Salerno-Sonnenberg, *Nadja: On My Way* (New York: Crown Publishers, 1989), p. 1.

2. See, for example, Charles L. Campbell, *Preaching Jesus: New Directions for Homiletics in Hans Frei's Postliberal Theology* (Grand Rapids: Wm. B. Eerdmans Publishing Co., 1997).

the security of the constancy of God's love, what is beyond comprehension can be accepted.

This happens more fully if the preacher is confident that God can be trusted and if the Christian community incarnates God's love. Both the preacher's certainty and the possibility of genuine community are matters of spiritual intimacy.

Intimacy with God and the Community

Before the Mendelssohn concerto began, Nadja and James DePreist amused us all by engaging in a bit of "shtick" — DePreist pulling back his crutch[3] when Nadja reached for it in front of the associate concertmaster, who had stood up to take it and set it on the floor as usual. Nadja responded by jabbing Jimmy with her bow.

During the post-concert discussion one attendee asked about this rapport between the two. Nadja responded that the number one factor in any performance is always one's relationship with the conductor. Second is one's relationship with the orchestra, which is amplified if the conductor is the musical director himself and if he has good rapport with the orchestra.

The parallels are obvious. Any sermon depends on our relationship with God. That is such a truism as to seem almost trite, and yet it is profoundly difficult for those who constantly speak of God to keep speaking with God. A while ago, a month of depression because I was making no progress on writing knocked me to my knees to learn that my failure to listen to God had led to weeks of working on the wrong track. I realized the need for much greater intentionality in setting aside daily times for Scripture meditation and prayer, monthly retreats for deeper reflection, Sabbath days of resting in God's grace in order to learn to listen more attentively.

Second most important for sermons is our partnership with the congregation, which is integrally related to their intimacy with God. You have probably noticed by now that my sermons always begin with the liturgical refrain, "The Lord be with you" "And also with you." I need the connection — and need to explain why it is important — to build a relationship that often has begun only a day or two before. Since most of my preaching is as a guest in a congregation, I do not have the privilege of those of you who live among

---

3. DePreist contracted polio while on a State Department tour in Bangkok in 1962, but recovered sufficiently to win a first prize in the 1964 Dimitri Mitropoulos International Conducting Competition.

a people and serve that people all the time — and the result is sermons that are not so directly relevant, not so intimately upbuilding. Sometimes that makes possible more admonition or observations that cannot be revealed by the resident pastor. Often a guest preacher can be a voice from outside to underscore the theology of the community's leaders. But always there is less of a relationship, and thus my sermons can only be second best. They are monstrous if God does not inhabit them.

Nadja said that the third most important factor in her performance is the acoustics of the concert hall. That might cause us to think about the setting in which we preach, the ambience of our worship spaces. We do not need to be very interested at this point in acoustics and architecture and adornments, though those are significant concerns, but the true atmosphere of our worship abode depends primarily on whether we have created genuine community[4] and on the cohesiveness of the worship service in which the sermon finds its place (see Chapter 16).

As one example, during the discussion time Nadja was asked about the fact that she is attracting young people to concert halls, and she responded that she considers it a great responsibility about which she is very glad.[5] Similarly, in our preaching we pay attention to accessible word choices and add specific examples so that the youth of the community feel welcomed and a part of the congregation's kingdom life. Most important, good rapport with all the people outside of the worship service invites them more thoroughly into the sermon's dance with God.

On Being a Wordsmith

Someone in the post-concert discussion commented on how quietly Nadja had played certain portions of the concerto. She responded somewhat like this: "I'm very big on colors. Every time I play I try to create as many colors as possible — as many as I have the control to produce."

Those remarks also offer stimulating parallels for our thinking about preaching. If we are painting the kingdom of God so that listeners can enter it more fully, then we have enormous possibilities for hues and shades and tints and nuances.

4. See Chapters 12-17 of this book and also Marva J. Dawn, *Truly the Community: Romans 12 and How to Be the Church* (Grand Rapids: Wm. B. Eerdmans Publishing Co., 1992; reissued 1997).

5. She wrote her book, *Nadja: On My Way,* in order to encourage children in their playing and to tell them about developing a career.

It is wondrous to me that I had written the first three words of the previous sentence's series just because I liked how they sounded together to describe assorted colors, but then, upon reading it, my husband informed me that in the art world the word *hue* especially signifies a specific color; the word *shade* technically means a darkening of a color by the addition of black; and the word *tint* particularly indicates the lightening of a color by the addition of white. To shade the hues of God to darken them more profoundly is to deepen our humility before his mystery and hiddenness; to tint God's colors more brightly is to heighten our Joy at all the splendors and excellences of his glory. Then the final word *nuances* in the series above inserts the possibility of indicating these slight differences in pigments so that others can notice and appreciate them. To make careful theological nuances is an important task of the preacher.

We carefully craft our words, for example, to indicate the difference between God bringing good out of the sufferings that we endure and God being the cause of our pain and sorrow. Even as the Jews went beyond their earliest emphasis on monotheism, which included "the satan" or "the accusing one" among the counsel of God,[6] and learned in the Babylonian captivity to name a power of evil without deifying that power,[7] so we can distinguish between God sending and God remaining sovereign over the troubles that we encounter.

One of the great advantages of the Revised Common Lectionary is that over the course of three years, with four different readings each Sunday and festival day (from the First Testament, Psalms, Epistles, and Gospels), the preacher possesses the resources of multitudes of narratives that disclose an abundance of attributes and interventions of God to evoke in the listener myriads of insights and affections and motivations and transformations. The immense possibilities create a significant reason for congregation members to be present at every worship service. There is much too much to learn about God, far too many ways to encounter God, enormously too deep of an eternity to explore for anyone to miss any of the gatherings of the community.

Nadja's final qualification concerning her attempts to produce colors in

---

6. See Job 1:6-12 and 2:1 to see how the Hebrew *ha-satan*, "the accuser," functions somewhat as an *agent provocateur*.

7. Thus, we distinguish between the absolute monotheism of the early Hebrews, the dualistic Zoroastrianism of the Babylonians (which had a god of evil and a god of good who were equally powerful), and the monotheism of later Judaica, which could recognize a power of evil without compromising God's ultimate sovereignty. In the First Testament the word *Satan* first functions as a proper name, without the article *ha* ("the"), only in post-Babylonian 1 Chronicles 21:1 — compare 2 Samuel 24:1, written six hundred years earlier.

her playing — that she creates the colors she has the control to produce — warns us, too. Our paintbrushes are words, and we work hard to use them skillfully in order "to present [ourselves] to God as one approved by him, a worker who has no need to be ashamed, rightly explaining the word of truth" (2 Timothy 2:15). We are wordsmiths, artisans, caretakers of words in a society that renders them inflated and hypocritical, deceptive and meaningless.[8]

The Word exercises control over our words. We need disciplines of attentiveness and study, habits of preparation and organization, practices of prayer and fellowship, and a life of obedience so that our hues are accurate, our shades and tints faithful, our nuances clear. Then we picture as much of God as possible; we sketch the kingdom and flesh it out in myriads of colors.

The Word We Preach

Nadja was asked about the violin she played, and she exulted that it was a Guarnerius and that with only one more payment she would own it completely.[9] A superior instrument enables a performer to produce stellar sound.

How we can rejoice that the Word we preach is premier — we proclaim the Trinity, the only true God, disclosed to us in the words of Scripture, a faithful narrative, God's Revelation.[10] Even as a violin improves with age, so God's Word becomes more precious to us as we live with it; in addition, the Revelation is becoming increasingly valuable as our society veers more and more into a postmodern despair that increases persons' desperation for a sure reference point. As we saw in Chapter 4, the biblical meta-narrative is a great gift for the postmodern world. With such a good instrument upon which to sing, we can voice sermons of scintillating color.

---

8. See Jacques Ellul, *The Humiliation of the Word,* trans. Joyce Main Hanks (Grand Rapids: Wm. B. Eerdmans Publishing Co., 1985).

9. I'm not sure, but I think Nadja said her violin was made in 1731, which means it was probably made by Giuseppe Antonio Guarneri (1687?-1745), one of the world's premier violin makers. Of course, such a precious work of art would be enormously expensive, but older violins, and especially those made by the Guarneri family in the seventeenth to eighteenth centuries, produce a much richer sound and are well worth the fortune they cost.

10. In capitalizing the word *Revelation* I follow the practice of Jacques Ellul, whose "Innocent Notes on 'The Hermeneutic Question'" makes clear the trustworthiness of Scripture and the importance of a presupposition of faith in reading it. See *Sources and Trajectories: Eight Early Articles by Jacques Ellul That Set the Stage,* trans. and ed. Marva J. Dawn (Grand Rapids: Wm. B. Eerdmans Publishing Co., 1997), pp. 184-203.

Consider, for example, the images of the Word and some of the results when we preach it in this American Bible Society hymn:

God's word alive and active, proclaimed throughout the years,
still comforts us when hurting and calms our hidden fears.
God's word of truth and justice sets weary captives free
and joins God's holy people in new community.

God's word alive and active, declared the whole world round
in tongues of many peoples and signed without a sound —
This word of hope and freedom speaks deeply to the soul
of those who long for oneness and yearn to be made whole.

God's word alive and active is offered free to all,
in ev'ry tribe and nation so all will hear God's call
to feed the hungry children, give drink to those who thirst,
and serve the human fam'ly by putting God's will first.

God's word alive and active is Jesus Christ our Lord,
God's gift of love incarnate that all might be restored.
The whole creation longs for the day when we're set free
to live as God intended with sacred dignity.

God's word alive and active our song of songs will be;
its message we will follow throughout eternity.
And when the saints are gathered and death has ceased to be,
we'll praise our wondrous Maker in songs of victory.[11]

Our present preaching is a foretaste of those future songs. Those who hear can catch visions of the eternal kingdom in order to inhabit it now.

Battling the Demons

After her stunning performance of the Mendelssohn concerto, Nadja found it impossible to sit still. During the post-concert discussion she sat on the stool next to James DePreist and fidgeted. She answered with great animation, just as she plays with constant motion of her entire body. It would, obviously, take

11. This hymn by Gladys G. Moore is sung to the tune "Aurelia" by Samuel Sebastian Wesley (1864). I have modified the punctuation given in the *Moravian Book of Worship* for grammatical correctness.

her a long time to come down from the intense euphoria, the "rush" of the evening.

Because the final piece of the concert had been the Hindemith symphony's third movement, "The Temptation of Saint Anthony," I wanted to ask Nadja if she ever fought the demons. Hindemith's composition is based on Matthias Grünewald's *Isenheim Altarpiece,* painted in 1519 for the chapel in a hospital dedicated to treating victims of skin diseases. The 17′ by 11′ altarpiece, composed of a series of ten separate scenes painted on three folding panels, concludes with a shocking and lurid scene of a grotesque and deformed St. Anthony beset by demons and monsters invented from actual and imagined creatures thrown together hodgepodge. (The symphony program featured a photograph of this portion of the altarpiece on the cover.) Those of us who "get high" while doing our work of preaching then usually suffer a corresponding low time afterward.

If we are passionate about the texts and the Lord of the texts when we preach, it will cost us. We are painting a vision of the kingdom of God in opposition to the reign in this world of other powers, so it is a spiritual battle we are fighting, which will also physically exhaust us. We will have to allow ourselves plenty of time to recover, a Sabbath of rest. Nadja and James DePreist went to supper after the concert; preachers, too, need Sabbath feasting to wind down and stoke up.[12]

We might also have to fight the darknesses of doubts, the fiends of seeming failure in society's terms, the monsters of our personal hang-ups, the demons of misunderstanding on the part of those who hear or refuse to hear. More and more I am helped by regular reading of the Psalms. Meditate on these words, with my annotations, from Psalm 138 — the psalm used in worship yesterday, the fifth Sunday after the Epiphany:

Of David

This canonical title, part of verse one in the Hebrew text, gives us a believer's orientation, a model of one who triumphed over doubts, failures, hang-ups, and misunderstandings through trust in his LORD.

> I give you thanks, O LORD, with my whole heart;
> before the gods I sing your praise;
> I bow down toward your holy temple
> and give thanks to your name for your steadfast love

---

12. See Marva J. Dawn, *Keeping the Sabbath Wholly: Ceasing, Resting, Embracing, Feasting* (Grand Rapids: Wm. B. Eerdmans Publishing Co., 1989).

> and your faithfulness;
>   for you have exalted your name and your word
>   above everything.
> On the day I called, you answered me,
>   you increased my strength of soul.

Giving thanks with our whole *heart,* which in Hebrew means our deliberate intentionality more than feelings, is a good discipline for fighting the demons. We sing God's praises before those gods, and they have to flee in terror. Notice also the disciplines of corporate worship (in the temple) and focus on God's character (the Hebrew significance of *name*), especially his attributes of *chesedh* (constantly enfolding love) and faithfulness in hearing the prayers of his people and in strengthening their whole being.[13]

> All the kings of the earth shall praise you, O Lord,
>   for they have heard the words of your mouth.
> They shall sing of the ways of the Lord,
>   for great is the glory of the Lord.
> For though the Lord is high, he regards the lowly;
>   but the haughty he perceives from far away.

When we are humbled before the Lord, the faithful I AM of the eternal covenant, we are able to put our own work in proper perspective. Someday the whole world will know the truth of the Lord; in the meanwhile, we have the privilege of bearing the Word, of singing God's ways, of honoring his glory out of our confidence that he watches over our concerns.

> Though I walk in the midst of trouble,
>   you preserve me against the wrath of my enemies;
> you stretch out your hand,
>   and your right hand delivers me.
> The Lord will fulfill his purpose for me;
>   your steadfast love, O Lord, endures forever.
>   Do not forsake the work of your hands.

The second to last line of this hymn is creedal, a poetic assurance reiterated constantly in the Psalms and elsewhere. The Lord can be trusted,

---

13. For more thorough explication of these attributes of the Lord, see Marva J. Dawn, *I'm Lonely, Lord — How Long? Meditations on the Psalms,* 2nd ed. (Grand Rapids: Wm. B. Eerdmans Publishing Co., 1998).

for *chesedh* is absolute and perpetual, pervasive and abundant — and, therefore, we can know that he will fulfill his purposes in and through and for us. But we do have doubts and fears, so once again we cry for God not to abandon us — all the while remembering that he has created us and creates us still.

Similarly, contemplate Psalm 28, assigned for the week focusing on "The Cost of Ministry" in *A Guide to Prayer,* as it speaks these words of comfort and hope into our struggles:

> To you, O LORD, I call;
> my rock, do not refuse to hear me,
> for if you are silent to me,
> I shall be like those who go down to the Pit.
> Hear the voice of my supplication,
> as I cry to you for help,
> as I lift up my hands
> toward your most holy sanctuary. . . .
> Blessed be the LORD,
> for he has heard the sound of my pleadings.
> The LORD is my strength and my shield;
> in him my heart trusts;
> so I am helped, and my heart exults,
> and with my song I give thanks to him.
> The LORD is the strength of his people;
> he is the saving refuge of his anointed.
> O save your people, and bless your heritage;
> be their shepherd, and carry them forever.   Psalm 28:1-2, 6-9

The verses I left out describe the workings of the wicked — many of the phrases of which, I keep realizing, apply to me. But the LORD is the one who carries us, who shepherds us, who is our strength. In our fights with the forces of evil, we can be sure that he is not silent, that he never refuses to hear us. The very Word, the preaching of which ushers us into the battles, is our best sword for defeating the demons. I wonder what Nadja uses.

Restoring the Passion

Our best protection against the foes, of course, is a constant nourishing of our spiritual life. This is not the place for an extended discussion of means by which church leaders can be sustained and edified,[14] but one comment must be made.

In the post-concert discussion Nadja was asked what she would say to parents and teachers of young musicians. She responded that concerned adults must see if the young person loves to play. It doesn't matter, she insisted, if they have all the technique and lots of talent. What matters is if they love to play.

Those who preach need gifts for their faith that free them to love to preach. When preaching becomes a burden or merely a duty to us, then we need to take time to reignite our sacred fire. I pray that those reading this book have a community that will support them in taking time for devotions, solitude, meditation, Sabbath, retreat, prayer, refreshment, silence, contemplation, reflection, study, renewal — whatever words we use, whatever forms are useful — for "rooting and establishing" our faith and fostering its growth, for kindling our love and stoking its flames.

When to Be Hard on Ourselves

Finally, someone in the post-concert discussion asked Nadja if she is hard on herself before performing. She answered somewhat like this: "No, not before performing. That is the time for confidence and staying loose; you shouldn't knock yourself when you are nervous. But I am very hard on myself when I practice."

My devotional readings in A Guide to Prayer for this week included a quotation by Urban T. Holmes III stressing that fear of failure lies at the root of a lack of passion on the part of clergy.[15] Any anxiety about failure is accentuated if we are hard on ourselves just before preaching, instead of letting ourselves rest in the sure knowledge that we are the beloved of God and privileged to be servants of his Word and words. In contrast, our passion is propelled if we present ourselves "with eyes wide open to the mercies of God" (as J. B. Phillips paraphrases Romans 12:1) — as those who are already chosen, holy, and dearly loved (Colossians 3:12).

But we, like Nadja, need to be very hard on ourselves when we practice. We carefully schedule daily periods to nurture our own spiritual growth. We

14. Eugene H. Peterson's books are excellent sources for that. See, for example, *The Contemplative Pastor* and *Five Smooth Stones for Pastoral Work,* both in second editions published by Wm. B. Eerdmans Publishing Co. in 1997.

15. Rueben P. Job and Norman Shawchuck, eds., *A Guide to Prayer: For Ministers and Other Servants* (Nashville: The Upper Room, 1983), p. 82.

allow plenty of time to engage in and absorb the texts about which we preach; we meditate upon them and sit before them with open minds and lives. We spend all week preparing our sermons. Then those disciplines set us free to preach out of the sheer beauty of the music.

I first learned this from my friend, Diana Schmück, a brilliant chamber musician and accompanist. Having taught myself to play the piano (with a resulting lack of good technique), I couldn't understand why someone so good needed to review scales when she practiced. Diana filled me with awe when she drilled one phrase over and over countless times to make the fingering seamless, when she and her twin sister rehearsed sets of phrases moving backwards through a duet to strengthen their memory, when she pored over scores to learn structure and notice nuances. The results of these disciplines are evident when she performs in concerts — with absolute freedom and abandonment to the delights and passions of the beauty her skill creates.

Similarly, we read phrases over and over to make seamless theological connections. We study texts in Hebrew and Greek and various translations to strengthen our understanding. We pore over the structures of biblical books and notice nuances in semantic domains to learn why authors might have chosen a particular word to convey specific meanings. The result is freedom to "play" with texts.[16]

One other reason for the fear of failure that leads to lack of passion must be mentioned here. Our times are characterized by so much competition between churches to attract members. Pastors feel that their sermons need to be great in order for their congregations to grow, and that is usually understood in terms of growing in numbers but not necessarily in depth — fatter, but not stronger. That is put crassly, but it fiercely distresses me that the work of proclaiming the gospel is being reduced these days to consumerist and competitive marketing terms (see, in contrast, Luke 22:24-27).[17]

Nadja Salerno-Sonnenberg is one of the world's greatest violinists, not because she plays to be the greatest, but because she plays for the love of it. During a radio interview the final day of her performances in Portland, she said that a near-tragic accident, which she had described in the post-concert discussion, caused her to realize that she couldn't live without playing the vi-

---

16. For excellent suggestions for preparation and a superb emphasis on the importance of preaching out of love and out of "playing" with the texts, see Robert Farrar Capon, *The Foolishness of Preaching: Proclaiming the Gospel against the Wisdom of the World* (Grand Rapids: Wm. B. Eerdmans Publishing Co., 1998) — truly one of the best new books on preaching I've found lately.

17. See also Philip D. Kenneson and James L. Street, *Selling Out the Church: The Dangers of Church Marketing* (Nashville: Abingdon Press, 1997).

olin. Slicing a finger severely, but having it restored by a skillful physician (and, I would add, the grace of God), Nadja experienced deep renewal in her art and life.

We don't preach to attract crowds; we preach because we are overwhelmed by the splendor of God's love and overflowing with eagerness to proclaim his mercy. That takes us full circle back to where this chapter began. It was the wrong question to ask how the gospel could have more impact, how our preaching could influence as many people as Nadja's violin playing. The question is how preachers could more Joy-fully play with texts out of passion for God. As good stewards of the multifaceted grace of God, then, we who preach speak the very oracles of God (1 Peter 4:10-11). If we serve the gospel well, its influence will shine forth in a diamond's array of God's colors.

11

Keeping God as the Infinite
Center of Our Worship

You shall not make for yourself an idol, whether in the form of anything that is in heaven above, or that is on the earth beneath, or that is in the water under the earth. You shall not bow down to them or worship them, for I the LORD your God am a jealous God . . .

Exodus 20:4-5a

One of the most frequent accusations in response to my book *Reaching Out without Dumbing Down* is that I spoke for balance between contemporary and traditional music and forms in worship and yet seem to side with the mainline traditionalists as opposed to those advocating a "seeker-targeted perspective." Let me reply to that accusation more thoroughly as an introduction to this chapter's subject, which is a further elaboration of what I mean by the necessity of keeping God as the Infinite Center of our worship.

There are five main reasons why I seem to be advocating traditionalism, but actually am not — and they all connect directly to the problem of keeping God as the Center. The first reason is that I speak strongly against those who throw out the traditions without understanding them. But I am equally opposed to those who cling to the traditions without understanding them. The issue is not the traditions themselves, but the problem that many don't bother to learn why the Church has worshiped with certain forms for hundreds of years. And the major value of those forms is that they are enormously God-centered. The liturgy of the Catholic mass is composed throughout of direct quotations from the Scriptures, which is why Martin Luther maintained most of it and dispensed only with accretions that were unbiblical.

The second cause for my seeming to be a traditionalist is that I urgently warn churches not to sacrifice substance for style — but that does not mean that I am opposed to contemporary forms and styles of music. The question is not which style is better, since both new and old genres can contain faithful words. The issue is whether we are choosing a particular piece of music for its content or simply because we want a certain style. Many congregations are jumping too easily to the fad of "contemporary" services simply because that is what sells these days without serious questioning of why a church should do so.

The problem here is one of sorting. By and large, denominational hymnbooks have sorted the music of the past, so that most (but not all) of what some might call "traditional" is quite good theologically and musically. Far too many churches are not doing a good job of sorting what they use from "contemporary" music because they choose it primarily for its style, and the result is worship filled with stuff that trivializes God and forms narcissistic people. Personally I use a wide variety of music, from all epochs and using a diversity of instruments — but I insist that it must be appropriate to God's character and to the formation of genuine disciples and a genuine community. Criteria for such sorting will be offered in Chapter 26 of this book.

Third, I might seem to side with the traditionalists because much of the push for "contemporary" worship arises from a serious confusion between evangelism and worship, to the great detriment of both (as explicated in Chapter 9 above). I think "seeker-sensitive" events or evangelistic rallies can be wonderful (if there is good follow-up), but we ought not to confuse them with worship, which is *for God* and directed to God. Worship is the work of the people who know God and practice the language of faith. If worship is too much like the culture around us, how will we form people centered on God instead and knowing the culture and language and habits and behaviors of discipleship?

Evangelism is the work of all the saints, not of the worship service. *We* are the witnesses who reach out to our neighbors and speak to them of the gospel. In our post-Christian society, we need to take lessons from the earliest Christians, whose surrounding culture was much like ours in the present. By their community life, they offered alternatives to the world that attracted people to this milieu, to this life in union with Christ. Then they brought interested people into a long catechumenal process that culminated in their participation with the believers in worship. If we want to follow Christ's command, every member of the Christian community will always be "making disciples" as we are "going" about our daily life; then the new believers will be brought into the Church for "baptizing in the name" of the Trinity and a continued life of worship and growth in faith.

The fourth source of my seeming traditionalism is, I am told, that *Reaching Out without Dumbing Down* does not offer enough positive models of good contemporary music. I thought it was better not to offer too many suggestions — because if I did some people might simply use my suggestions instead of doing the necessary sorting themselves. I did mention far more "traditional" hymns because I thought most of the readers of the book by and large would recognize them and understand why they illustrated my points. Moreover, the problem here goes beyond labels to the nature of music and the epochs from which it comes. Metrical hymns with several stanzas inherently allow the possibility for more substance than a short chorus, but that doesn't mean that hymns are better than choruses — it simply means that we have to look harder for choruses with substance. Also, songs written in the 1800s, when the United States was far more Christian, come from an ethos conducive to writing faithful texts. In our times, poets and musicians have to be enormously resistant to our consumerist, noncommunal, narcissistic, quick-fix oriented culture to write texts faithful to the Scriptures. But there are many good examples of good new songs — though they can be harder to find because they are newer and therefore not universally known.

Finally, as explained in this book's Introduction, *Reaching Out without Dumbing Down* was very much affected by a great grief — a grief that arose because, as a freelance theologian and therefore a guest in other churches almost every other week, I was horrified by all the "dumbing down" I experienced in congregations' worship. On the other side, I was dismayed that so many "traditionalists" are stuck in ruts and frequently inhospitable and therefore not "reaching out." What I adamantly resist is the mindless rejection or adoption of either old or new music without recognizing that both have to be clearly taught and hospitably employed. With both there is an immense need to teach people what worship is and how to engage in it. The keys to using any style of music or form are education and hospitality.

Along with Carol Doran and Thomas Troeger, I am urging churches to find a way between "the distortions of antiquarianism and faddishness." After critiquing some of the defects of traditionalistic worship, they write,

> On the other hand, we have observed the disillusionment of people who were originally attracted by the idea of completely innovative worship.

What starts with a burst of enthusiasm begins to wear thin because people cannot come up with an endless supply of new ideas and because ritual by nature is repetitive. Innovators who get rid of one tradition usually settle into their own, which often fails to stand the test of time. The new songs that were so appealing upon their introduction grow tiresome for lack of musical substance. They may not hold the same meaning for the new members as they did for the founders. The absence of prayers, words, and music inherited from ancient tradition gives the service a flimsy feeling, as if faith and worship were simply one more passing fashion among the myriad fads that come and go.[1]

I think our churches need to do much deeper thinking about what it means to worship God, what it means to nurture and to live the life of faith, what it means to be a Christian community that offers alternatives to the world, and how we can best reach out to our neighbors with the gospel and in service to them. In order to do all that we have to stop asking which style of music to use and ask instead what will help us keep God at the center.[2]

The Infinite Center[3]

During the months that I was struggling to find a title for this book, I settled for awhile on "The Infinite Center," which is a line from a hymn text by Susan Palo Cherwien, superb poet and grace-full friend and deep thinker. Though her phrase did not eventually become this book's title, I am deeply grateful for Susan's ability to capture my primary concern for worship. As chapter five of *Reaching Out without Dumbing Down* elaborates, everything we plan for our corporate gatherings must be consistent with who God is and what it means to worship him. Nothing that we do should ever let us forget that worship is for God.

God is the Subject of our worship, for he is the one who makes it possi-

1. Carol Doran and Thomas H. Troeger, *Trouble at the Table: Gathering the Tribes for Worship* (Nashville: Abingdon Press, 1992), p. 117.

2. For a more theologically responsible effort to bring "traditional" and "contemporary" music together, see Barry Liesch, *The New Worship: Straight Talk on Music and the Church* (Grand Rapids: Baker Book House, 1996).

3. Several of the paragraphs in this section also appear in my chapter, "Reaching Out without Dumbing Down: A Theology of Worship for Postmodern Times," in *Confident Witness, Changing World*, ed. Craig Van Gelder (Grand Rapids: Wm. B. Eerdmans Publishing Co., forthcoming). My thanks to Craig and to Judy Bos, administrator for the Gospel and Our Culture Network, for permission to use this modified version here.

ble for us to enter into his presence; God is the one who gives us himself in the Word, the water, the supper. How we conduct worship must teach all the participants that and enfold them in that reality. Worship is not the pastor inviting us into his or her living room, but God welcoming us into a holy place set apart to honor him.

Keeping God the Center does not narrow our options, though it gives us our primary criterion for sorting through them. That sentence might seem like a contradiction, except that God is infinitely beyond our imagining. Therefore, we need all kinds of sounds, spirit, styles, and shapes to evoke the Trinity's splendor. They must all be consistent, however, with what God has revealed about himself.

This truth leads to many questions that we who plan worship and the worship space must ask. Does the order of worship clearly reflect that God is the Subject? Is there too much focus on the pastor or musicians that would detract from participants' awareness that God is the inviter? Does the worship space reveal God's special presence? Do the participants' attitudes, the leaders' demeanors and gestures, the worship ambience keep God as the Subject?

Is the God portrayed by our worship the biblical God of Abraham and Sarah, Jesus and Mary? Does our worship focus one-sidedly on comfortable aspects of God's character, such as his mercy and love, without the dialectical balancing of his holiness and wrath? Is Jesus reduced to an immanent "buddy" or "brother" without the accompanying transcendence of God's infinite majesty? Is the Trinity diminished to merely rigid doctrines without the unsettling winds of the Spirit? (Indeed, the Church needs more doctrine these days, not less, but not rigidly so.) All these questions ask whether our worship really keeps the God of the Bible as its Subject.

God is, of course, also the Object of our worship, so indeed we do properly ask "for whom is worship?" too. We respond to the Trinity's wooing, give thanks for the Creator's grace, praise Christ's name, ask for the Spirit's empowerment. Unless we see God first as Subject, however, we cannot really answer with true adoration. Sadly, many "contemporary" worship leaders confuse genuine praise with "happy songs" and thus cater to personal fun or comfort or well-being as the object instead of naming the attributes and actions of God. Older hymns sometimes made the same mistake (such songs as "I Come to the Garden Alone"), but such narcissism was less likely in earlier eras that were more communally directed and more theologically substantive.

Two aspects of worship contribute especially to the loss of God as the Subject and Object. One is the architecture. Older sanctuaries, by their cross shape and lofty height and their visual focus on the altar, could keep worship participants' gaze on God. The placement of the organist and the choir in the balcony permitted them to be servants of worship instead of performers. However, long naves looking toward elevated pulpits share modern church architecture's problem of putting the preacher (and usually now the musicians) "on stage." Worship attenders in contemporary and traditional spaces must all be reminded that they are — each one — the actors in worship, that the leaders are not there to perform but to direct the action, that God is the audience (object) of the "work of the people" (the Greek *leitourgia* or liturgy). Conversely, we can only be actors in worship because God acted first as Subject and because God continues to speak to us, his audience, through texts, sermons, hymns, and liturgy.

The second aspect that especially dethrones God in worship is the reduction of the gifts of the people to merely the financial offering.[4] We have for many years failed to train believers in the meaning of worship, so that now attenders frequently say, "I didn't get much out of that service," without realizing that the problem is their failure to put much into it. Furthermore, the lack of heartfelt participation by parents is the chief contributor to their children's rejection of all that worship means.

I once asked my seventh- and eighth-grade confirmation students how many of them liked the liturgy, and their answers matched one for one. Every youth who hated it was the child of a father who didn't sing it. (Research confirms that the influence of fathers' worship practices on the retention of their children in faith far outweighs the influence of mothers. Most desirable, of course, is the active participation in the Christian community and worship of both parents.)

I hear frequently from youth directors that the kids with whom they work reject the worship style of their parents. I think it goes deeper than that. I am convinced that very often the youth reject instead the phoniness of their parents who go through the motions of worship, but whose daily lives are not transformed by it. Similarly, it is not usually the liturgy that alienates worshipers; it is the lack of Joy[5] with which it is conducted. Everywhere as I travel throughout the world in my freelancing work I see people who love worship because they know what it means and Who invites them into its holiness.

In all of this I am not rejecting new styles and forms for worship. I am

4. See especially C. Welton Gaddy, *The Gift of Worship* (Nashville: Broadman Press, 1992), on the subject of offerings in worship.

5. I purposely capitalize this word, for I do not mean simple exuberance, happiness, or excitement. I use the word to signify that deep, abiding confidence and gratitude and trust that are ours when we keep God as the Subject, when our lives are transformed by the truth of the Resurrection, when we genuinely worship God and not ourselves.

only rejecting the false questions. Style is not the issue. The genuine worship of GOD is.

When God Is Not the Center

In previous eras, when what was done in mainline churches was dictated by the heritage of the denominations and the culture was more foundationally Christian, there was less possibility of moving away from God as the Infinite Center. In our times of famous celebrities in the media, less structured worship, and less support for the identity of Christianity in the culture, such a move is far more likely. As a result, too much of what is happening these days in worship pulls us away from centering on God — or does not have enough substance to hint at the infinity of God's splendor. Let me give actual examples from two worship services at which I was present in the last year — one a summer congregational service at which I was the guest preacher and the other an evening worship service (for which I was not a leader) at a denominational regional convention for which I was the keynote speaker. After such experiences I usually ask questions of as many people as I can to make sure my responses are not idiosyncratic. Let me also add that I do not doubt the sincerity of the faith of the two leaders described; I am, however, convinced that such leadership is harmful to worship participants, for it prevents them from moving beyond milk to solid food, and as a result they remain unskilled in the practice of faith (see Hebrews 5:11-14).

1. In the congregational service I had no idea at what point the worship began, because the leader was chattering away and gave no specific sense that God had called us here. The reason that worship in the Christian heritage always begins with the invocation, "In the name of the Father and of the Son and of the Holy Spirit," is so that we remember we are part of the whole company of believers since the time of the Gospels who have been baptized into that triune name, who believe in that triune God, and who are gathered together across space and time to worship him. Patter that depends on the worship leader for its content can hardly convey so clearly the presence of God and such a mighty cloud of witnesses.

The first song of the service, printed in the worship order as "He Is Exulted" (the worship planners probably meant "He Is Exalted"), did not give any reasons why, or any further images to elaborate that one idea. Merely to sing over and over that God is exalted does not teach anyone, especially those who might be visitors at worship, who God is and why who he is matters.

When the worship leader and I had discussed the service, I had asked that a common confession of sins from the hymnal be included, but when he introduced it, the leader chattered on and on explaining that I was the one who had chosen it. My very reason for selecting it was to get us away from making up everything ourselves and into the common liturgy of the Church, but his patter prevented that commonality and turned the attention to me — probably because he didn't want to be blamed for choosing such a "formal" confession. It seemed that he was embarrassed to use something out of the hymnbook. Never did he say anything about the fact that we need confession; never was there an announcement of forgiveness. We were so distracted from the presence of God before whom we need to confess that to do so was nearly impossible — and then I was glad I hadn't been immersed too deeply in awareness of my sin because it would have been very painful for me to hear no responding word of grace. One of the reasons why the liturgy of the tradition has always meant so much to me is that the absolution is clearly pronounced — I can almost "taste and see that the Lord is good" (Psalm 34:8) — and it does not come from one leader, but from the entire Church as commanded by Christ himself.

This was followed by the song "I Believe" as a statement of faith, but the song was only about Jesus, so the Trinity was fractured.

Three Scripture lessons were read without any statement of where in the Bible they were from and no acknowledgment that this was the Word of the Lord. When I went forward to give the sermon, I wanted to hold up the Bible and say "Thanks be to God!" for this Word, this Revelation by which God wants to form us to be his people. Because I believe that the sermon should be coherent with the rest of the worship service, I found it extremely difficult to preach since I had no sense that we'd been given much of God in what had preceded.

"Family Prayer Time," as the bulletin named it, began with patter from the leader about how good it felt to be in worship — "It just makes my heart shine to see all you families" — and a long story about what he had done for a young teenager who had been at camp that week. This was followed by two songs, the first of which repeated over and over and over, "you are my strength, my life, my hope." Those are indeed great words, but never did the song do any more fleshing out of why it matters that God is those three things for us, how we know he is, or what difference it makes in our lives. How would anyone who is not presently experiencing hope find any? The final song, "As for Me and My House," took that text from Joshua 24 entirely out of the context of Joshua's rebuke of the children of Israel and turned his admonition into a sentimentalized coziness.

At the end of the "worship" service I was asked to give a benediction, but once again I found that very hard to do since the entire event seemed more like a talk show, with all the focus on its host. How could I suddenly ask God to come to send us out?

2. At the large regional church gathering, none of the melodies were ever introduced and no music was printed, so people could participate only if they already knew the songs. None of the people around me was singing by the middle of the service; those who had tried at first to participate gave up after the first few songs.

The same peppy chorus was used as in example 1, so now I will write out the complete text:

> "My life is in You, Lord,
> My strength is in You, Lord,
> My hope is in You, Lord,
> in You, It's in You.
> "My life is in You, Lord,
> My strength is in You, Lord,
> My hope is in You, Lord,
> in You, It's in You."

We had to sing it twice. Another song was this:

> "Celebrate, Jesus, celebrate!
> Celebrate, Jesus, celebrate!
> Celebrate, Jesus, celebrate!
> Celebrate, Jesus, celebrate!"

Again, we have to ask, Why? How? For what? What difference will it make? Tell me something important about this Jesus whom we are celebrating! The models of true praise in the Scriptures never merely say to God, "we exalt you," "we love you." Rather, praising God always includes the naming of his attributes and interventions.

After this the pastor bragged that this was the kind of worship they had every Sunday morning and that more people came to this than to their "traditional" service. That seemed almost like bragging that he is keeping the congregation studying a first-grade reading book! (See Chapter 29 and George Lindbeck's insights into the language of faith.)

Then the pastor had to introduce himself — even though "worship" had supposedly already begun and even though his name was printed in the worship folder. Thus our attention was pulled toward him, rather than the God we were wanting to worship.

As he read the litanies, everything was done in a tone of voice which suggested that only through his hype could this be made interesting. It continually reminded me (and others) of a game show host trying to rev up the audience. Held a few weeks after Easter, the service seemed to include no genuine wonder that Christ is risen! Instead, every section of the liturgy printed in the worship folder was prefaced by some personal patter.

During a time of silent prayer, music was played that seemed to many to be manipulative (and totally distracted me from thinking about God). Several of the worship attendees commented to me that this background music sounded like mall Muzak designed to get a person to buy something.

A solo was sung — of the type designed to arouse sentimental emotions — and afterward the congregation remained respectfully silent. After a short pause, however, the leading pastor walked to the microphone and initiated applause through the amplification system. If our attention had been on God, it was immediately slammed back to focus on the performer of the solo.

I realize that I may get some criticism about this chapter — that some might say that it reveals my prejudices for the traditional, that it sounds elitist, that it is unduly critical. However, I must emphasize that I tried my utmost to keep God at the center of what was happening in these two worship services (and I have an arduously developed ability to remain focused), but the comments or actions of the leaders kept pulling me away. The value of the liturgies established by the Church over time (in new settings and old) is that they do not depend on any leader's personality; instead they keep the focus on the God who is the Subject of our worship.

Keeping God the Center

Style is not the issue. What matters is that whatever songs or forms we use keep us aware that God has invited us into worship, that God is present, that God is eminently worthy to receive our praise, that there is so much to learn about God that we will never get done. The question is whether our worship services immerse us in God's splendor.

Our world is desperate for God. In the face of growing postmodern despair and chaos, the escalating gap between rich and poor, the intensifying violence and global political and economic confusions, our world desperately needs worship services where God is encountered in as much of his fullness as possible.

12

"Everything Depends on the Resurrection": A Sermon*

Texts for the Sixth Sunday after the Epiphany, Series C:
Jeremiah 17:5-10; Psalm 1; 1 Corinthians 15:12-20; Luke 6:17-26

L et us remember that we are a community gathered together here to see
how God's Word would form us to be his people: The Lord be with you.
[Response: And also with you!]

Let us pray. Compassionate Christ, in your gracious honesty give us a
true understanding of ourselves, and then in your tender mercy and by the
power of your resurrection, raise us up to new life. Amen.[1]

You probably all noticed that I ended the reading of our Gospel text today by

---

*This is an edited transcript of a sermon given at Beautiful Savior Lutheran Church
in Vancouver, Washington, on February 15, 1998. Several of the examples in this sermon
apply specifically to the Beautiful Savior congregation, but I left them in that way so that
the specificity would be preserved. Please substitute your own congregation's name as you
read and put in your own similar examples so that the power of these texts will be apparent for the death and resurrection that every congregation needs.

1. This prayer was followed by my usual invitation for all the worshipers to take out
their bulletin insert so that they would be prepared to follow along with the texts. As noted
in previous chapters, this is one device intended to help overcome the cultural passivity
that prevents engagement with the texts and consequent formation.

saying, "This is the Word of the Lord," instead of the usual "This is the Gospel of the Lord." Jesus' attacks certainly are more prophetic denunciation at first than words of hope and good news. Later we will discover that they are richly both.

Let's look carefully, then, at this passage from Luke 6 — the first portion of a more extended "Sermon on the Plain." Our reading begins just after Jesus had chosen the twelve in whom he would invest the most time. As they come down together from the mountain a *large crowd* of disciples and a *large number* of people are gathered from the whole area — from all over Judea, Jerusalem, and the coastal cities of Tyre and Sidon. This is a mammoth crowd, and they have come expecting something good. They know Jesus' reputation. They want to hear him; they want to be healed; perhaps they want a bit of spectacle to liven up their boring lives; and — as they begin to see others set free from evil spirits — they want to touch him. Power was going out, and they wanted to be part of it. "You've got a good thing going, Jesus," his agent might say. "Keep it up."

But Jesus doesn't. Instead he disrupts the party. He looks straight at the disciples, not the crowd, and says, "Blessed, you poor." We like to make that comfortable for ourselves. We mentally add, "poor in spirit" from Matthew's Gospel, but Luke won't let us off the hook. Jesus said "poor," and none of us in this room is! The disciples weren't either. They had been successful fishermen — we saw the great catch in last Sunday's Gospel reading (Luke 5:4-9). One had been a tax collector, who probably gave himself a tidy profit. Those disciples weren't really poor — yet. Nor are we — so if one has to be poor to possess the kingdom of God, we don't have it.

Ooooo, Jesus won't let us go. He says "Blessed, the ones hungry now; blessed the ones weeping now; blessed are you when people hate you, reject you, humiliate you, slander and vilify you. Ah, yes! Leap for joy when that happens, for then you are just like the prophets." Do any of us qualify? Do any of us want to?

Put yourself in the crowd on that plain. We came for a good time, and the day started that way, with the healings and all. But now Jesus seems to be deliberately alienating us, forcing us to recognize that the power going out from him can singe us, too.

Indeed, it engulfs us in deadly flames, for Jesus warns us, "Woe to you if you have plenty; woe if you are satisfied; woe if you are laughing; woe if you are flattered and acclaimed. Woe if you don't understand that what the kingdom is about is your death."

Jesus won't let us go. He is here in his Word today to demolish our pretensions, to make it *very clear* that we have it all wrong if we think Christianity is about trying to be good enough. We have it all wrong if we think Beautiful Savior is a great congregation because we give away lots of money, build houses, and undertake numerous other good projects for the needy of our community and world. "Woe to you," Jesus says, and it is a death sentence.

But that is never God's only word to us, though it is an absolutely necessary one. Today the gospel — the good news — comes in the Epistle lesson, and it is about our resurrection from the dead.

One has to wonder what was going on in the Corinthian congregation that made the apostle Paul slog through the circling argument we heard in our Epistle reading this morning. It seems that he was dealing in this letter with the opposite problem from what we have today. The Corinthians believed that Christ had been raised from the dead, but they couldn't quite believe that this meant that they, too, would be raised. Our problem is that we think we are raised without needing Christ to die and be raised. We keep wanting to get away from the death sentence of today's text from Luke.

However, the reason Beautiful Savior is a powerful congregation is not that we do great things, but that great things happen here because GOD does them. Forgiveness has been declared this morning to every one of us, no matter how rich we are. We will eat and drink grace in a few minutes, no matter how much we need the warnings of Jesus' words of woe. *In spite of* our good reputations, we will leave this place raised again by the immense mystery of our baptism — that we die with Christ and are resurrected again because Jesus Christ has been raised from the dead.

However, even Paul has to give us a bit of a scare this morning first — to make sure that we really recognize that *everything* hinges on the resurrection. If there is no resurrection, we might as well pack up and go home; there is truly no reason to be here. But if there is a resurrection from the dead, then all heaven breaks loose. Then what we find in this place is the best good news to be had in the world.

Let us look carefully at the progression of Paul's argument, so that its good news can surprise us again with the wonder of it all.

In a more literal rendering of the original Greek, verse 12 begins, "But if Christ is being preached as having been raised from the dead, how can certain ones among you say that there is no resurrection from the dead?" Do people understand the implications? Last week in the first verses from 1 Corinthians 15 we heard the list of all those who saw Jesus after his resurrection, and Paul noted that many who saw the Christ were still alive and could testify to the accuracy of Paul's list. This is the preaching of the disciples, Paul insists, passed on to you Corinthians. How, then, can you doubt your own resurrection?

Now Paul embarks on a spiraling progression: "and if there is no resurrection from the dead, neither has Christ been raised." If you don't believe God is capable of raising the dead, then do you doubt that he raised Jesus?

Furthermore, "if Christ has not been raised, then also our preaching [is] foolish" — without result, without purpose, untrue, vain. If we doubt that Christ has been raised, then our preaching makes no sense — it is ludicrous, pointless, meaningless, worthless, downright false.

Moreover, "foolish [is] your faith." It, too, is without result, without purpose, untrue, vain. Why be deceived? Why believe illusions? Why bother? Why come mess with this Christianity stuff if Christ has not been raised?

In addition, "we are [then] found also [to be] testifying falsely of God, for we testified of God that he raised the Christ, whom he did not raise if it is [true] that the dead are not raised." This is getting even worse: we are caught lying about God! Everything we understand about God hinges on his fulfillment of the promise to raise Jesus — all of God's promises to his covenant people culminate in this one.

Again, "if the dead are not raised, neither has Christ been raised." Paul repeats this phrase, with a slight variation, to lead us into the next round of the spiral.

"And if Christ has not been raised, your faith — groundless, fallacious; you are yet in your sins." The absence of a verb in the description of our faith stresses that not only is your faith without foundation, not only is it false — but if Christ has not been raised, you are stuck with yourself, with your inability to be who you want to be, with your not being able to say, do, or think what you wish you could. If Christ is not raised, you cannot be delivered from yourself.

"Consequently also the ones having fallen asleep in Christ have perished. They are utterly destroyed." The repercussions are getting more and more dire. Think about the implications if those who have died are not with God, as we have thought.

All these phrases Paul has stacked up, all these spiraling ramifications, culminate in this last remark of the case: "If for this life only we have been brought to hope, we are of all human beings most to be pitied." If we hope only for what good we can experience in this life, then how wretched and miserable we are, for this life is full of inconveniences, frustrations, bad experiences, blatant evil, undeserved suffering, profound tragedies. Does our faith invite us only to those? Is there no greater hope?

By this time we are as full of anguish and grief as we were listening to the sermon of Jesus. Are we left only with the warnings and exploded promises? The pictures Jesus and Paul have painted are realistic, true to our lives. Is there no good news?

"BUT NOW," Paul says. Those are two of his best words in the biblical vocabulary; they signal a dramatic change. After this extensive case, after all the implications of vanity and meaninglessness, Paul exclaims, "BUT NOW, Christ *has* been raised from the dead, the first fruits of the ones having fallen asleep." This "BUT NOW" explodes with ecstasy! Better than winning an Olympic gold medal, better than being cleared of all scandal, better than having perfect weather, plenty of money, the best job or spouse in the world — this is the best news in the cosmos: *Christ has been raised from the dead!* That changes EVERYTHING! Christ is risen

so we do know that we, too, shall be raised;

we do know that our preaching is not meaningless;

we do know that our faith is not in vain;

we do know that what we have learned about God can be trusted;

we do know that those who have died are alive in Christ;

we do know that suffering and sorrow are not the last word;

we do know that there is a solid foundation to our faith;

we do know that there is a joyous reason to be here to celebrate our resurrection;

we do know that we are not wretched or pitiable, but instead we have the best news to share, the best news in all the world: we are home free;

we do know that, no matter who or what we are, God welcomes us into this story, this hope, this love, this forgiveness, this new life, this resurrection, this Joy!

Contrary to those who say that Christ was not raised from the dead, Paul insists, "But in fact Christ has been raised."[2] Let us glory in the implications! Jesus, in his resurrection, is the first fruits of God's great harvest — not simply of people, but also of what we do and give and love into being because we are set free by Christ's resurrection.

Now we can circle back to discover that even Jesus' sermon in Luke becomes gospel for us now, for it is pure grace that Jesus warns us not to trust

2. I wanted at this point to put in a few theological jabs against those who want to turn the resurrection into a nice idea, but not a historical fact — especially because a member of the Jesus Seminar had spoken at an event nearby only a few weeks before this sermon. But to do so would have been to muddle the sermon — to turn it into a battleground instead of a proclamation, good argument instead of good news. I am shocked at how often I forget what I should be about and let sermons degenerate into my own theological or ecclesiological agendas. Perhaps you, too, need Paul's reminder, "For I decided to know nothing among you except Jesus Christ, and him crucified" (1 Cor. 2:2).

ourselves. It is grace that he invites us into the life of the kingdom — with whatever poverty, hunger, or mourning that might involve. Out of the resurrection we are set free to participate in the needs of the world as the blessed ones of God. The resurrection reassembles us as blessed.

Now we can also look at today's Jeremiah text and see the fruitfulness made possible by God's deliverance.

Turn with me to Jeremiah 17, and rejoice with me in the possibilities. In verse 5 Jeremiah reminds us of what we have come from, the curse of trusting in ourselves and other human beings. Just as the Jews to whom Jeremiah spoke had turned away from their deliverer, the covenant God, the "I AM" who had rescued them from bondage in Egypt, so we regularly veer away from letting the God who liberated us from our bondages be everything in our lives. The result is dryness, a salt desert, wilderness, no true good.

But, oh, how blessed we are because we have given up on ourselves this morning; we have submitted to the death sentence. Only thus could we be resurrected. And now we are the ones in verse 7 planted by the river; our roots soak in God's water of life, and even in the driest times we suffer no anxiety. We can still produce houses with Habitat for Humanity, create support for those with AIDS, gather gifts for the families of prisoners, establish education programs to anchor the faith of our children, and do all the other wonderful things that happen corporately here at Beautiful Savior and in our homes and individual lives. We are not worried about what we do; we simply soak in the baptismal water and continue to produce fruit.

Oh, such good news it is — this resurrection! But we must not forget Jeremiah's closing warning: the heart is deceitful above all things, and it is incurable. We cannot know the heart. The only thing we can do with it is die. Then *YHWH,* who searches the heart, will raise us up and make us fruitful.

How blessed we are, we who are the children of God. Reading the law of the Scriptures sets us free from ourselves — for the impossibility of our being what God requires helps us *know* that we can do nothing but die to our own efforts. Then reading the gospel sets us free — to be true to our new resurrected selves and become all that God creates us to be. BUT NOW, Christ has been raised from the dead — and so are we. Let's eat and drink to that! Let's celebrate at the table today our death and resurrection, our new life as the blessed ones. We continue toward that celebration as we sing out our Joy, with hymn #764 from *With One Voice,*[3] "Blest Are They."

---

3. *With One Voice: A Lutheran Resource for Worship* (Minneapolis: Augsburg Fortress, 1997).

Blest are they, the poor in spirit; theirs is the kingdom of God.
Blest are they, full of sorrow; they shall be consoled.

Refrain: Rejoice and be glad!
Blessèd are you, holy are you.
Rejoice and be glad!
Yours is the kingdom of God!

Blest are they, the lowly ones; they shall inherit the earth.
Blest are they who hunger and thirst; they shall have their fill.
   Refrain

Blest are they who show mercy, mercy shall be theirs.
Blest are they, the pure of heart; they shall see God.
   Refrain

Blest are they who seek peace; they are the children of God.
Blest are they who suffer in faith; the glory of God is theirs.
   Refrain

Blest are you who suffer hate, all because of me.
Rejoice; be glad, yours is the kingdom; shine for all to see.
   Refrain.

David Haas, b. 1957

PART III

Being Church: Building Community

Ascribe to the LORD the glory of his name;
worship the LORD in holy splendor.

Psalm 29:2

The verbs in this verse, the theme verse for this book, are all plural. We are always called to ascribe glory to the LORD *together* and to worship in the holy splendor of God's community. Do the people in our churches realize that almost all of the verbs that instruct God's people in the Bible are plural, with the exception of those in Timothy, Titus, and Philemon — letters written specifically to those three men? How much difference it would make in our conversations about worship and in our being Church if we really understood that we are in this together!

However, we live in a society bereft of genuine community. Yes, I know that we all participate in lots of groups and activities — soccer or baseball parents, the exercise club, neighborhood block parties, various associations related to our work and our children's schools, Internet groups and chat rooms, craft guilds and trade unions, societies for our hobbies, and our churches. But would the members of any of these organizations die for one another? Do we really live our lives in common? Lack of time and too much space between us prevent us from actually investing our lives in each other.

The problems of community spiral with struggles over worship. The less our church is truly a community, the more we will have what Carol

Doran and Thomas Troeger call *Trouble at the Table*[1] — and, unless there is an intentional effort to counteract the anti-communal temptations of our times, worship will contribute to the decline of the church as Body by fostering destructive battles over taste or narcissistic private comfort.

The chapters in Part III are intended to raise questions, to point out elements of the controversies that are destructive to community, and to give models of community building. Truly to build community in our churches will take a lot of "time wasting." The kind of prodigal love that genuine community requires is not efficient, not apparently productive, not at all economical, not very useful in our culture's terms — but it imitates the extravagance of the LORD whose name forms our communal life.

This section's initial sermon arose from the apostle Paul's delightful joking in 1 Corinthians 12 about noncommunal behavior. The essay in Chapter 14 was first written for an Advent issue of the denominational journal *Reformed Worship,* but its suggestions for building community can apply to churches of any affiliation and in other seasons of the church year.

The final three chapters in this section give different perspectives on this same issue: what or who is responsible for worship planning. Chapter 15 elaborates the dangers to community when worship is allowed to become a matter of taste. Chapter 16 deals with the proper use of one's position as pastor or musician for making the kinds of decisions for worship that will upbuild the community, whereas Chapter 17 is composed of letters written to those who are grieving because some in authority have abused their power and caused deep wounds to others and consequently to the community in conflicts over worship.

In all of our worship decisions, we must never lose sight of the Body as a source of wisdom and as the recipient of our decisions' effects. As Wendell Berry remarks, "The Amish question 'What will this do to our community?' tends toward the right answer for the world"[2] — and for the Church we desire to be.

---

1. This book gives excellent suggestions and resources for drawing the congregation into a community of worship. See Carol Doran and Thomas H. Troeger, *Trouble at the Table: Gathering the Tribes for Worship* (Nashville: Abingdon Press, 1992).

2. Wendell Berry, "Out of Your Car, Off Your Horse," in *Sex, Economy, Freedom and Community: Eight Essays* (New York: Pantheon Books, 1993), p. 20.

13

"What If We All Were an Eye?": A Sermon*

Texts for the Second Sunday after the Epiphany, Series C: Nehemiah 8:1-3,
5-6, 8-12; Psalm 19; 1 Corinthians 12:12-27; Luke 4:14-21

Because our topic today is the unity of the Christian Body, let us begin by
remembering that we are community together in this act of worship, in
this time of listening to the Word of the Lord. As I extend to you the presence
of God with the words, "The Lord be with you," please support me in our
work of hearing his voice by sounding like you mean it when you answer
back, "And also with you."

The Lord be with you. [Response: And also with you!]

Let us pray: Triune God, as your people in this place we hear the stir-
ring challenge of your Word today. As your Scriptures come into our lives
at this time, may they change us. We believe that whenever we gather together for worship we are transformed by your Word to be your people, to
carry your kingdom into the world. In your grace open our hearts and
minds and lives to be renewed by the power of your Spirit, to your honor

*This is an edited transcript of a sermon given at West Side Presbyterian Church,
Ridgewood, New Jersey, on January 25, 1998, as the culmination of a weekend of study-
ing issues of worship in connection with the building up of the community of the
Church.

and glory and praise into the ages of the ages — and for the sake of the world. Amen.

There are many times when it seems to me that God changes the bookmarks in the common lectionary. I value the privilege of preaching on texts chosen by the larger Church, the texts of the Revised Common Lectionary shared across many denominational lines — but we hadn't looked at the assigned texts for today when we chose this weekend for the congregational leadership retreat on the subject of worship as it leads to community and ministry. Yet look at the wonderful correspondence between the Church's texts and that weekend theme.

Each one of today's texts can be exceptionally formative of every one of us here. As we look at these texts, therefore, let me encourage each one of you to keep asking, "What does this Word say to my life in the rest of the week?" and, even more important, "What does it say to us as a community in this place?"

Whenever we come to worship, we can ask these questions. How do the texts that we hear make us different? In what ways do the Scriptures call us as God's people to be unusual in the world? We carry the kingdom of God wherever we go, and every text that we hear on Sundays and at other worship times teaches us in some way about that carrying. How is each one of you a very important part of the Body of Christ? How do we all together reflect God's grace and mercy?

First, let's look at the First Testament text from Nehemiah. This passage gives us the foundation for our theme today, for it reminds us that all of our worship comes out of the Word. Notice carefully in this account that the people of Israel, newly returned to Jerusalem, were gathered together to hear the Scriptures, and, as the Torah was read, they wept — both for the grief of it and for the joy of it.

This is a good place to start our explorations today; it is indeed a stunning story. Nehemiah had just completed building the wall around Jerusalem — something that everyone had said could never be done and that had been forbidden by an edict of the conquering monarch. Nehemiah, nevertheless, had persuaded Artaxerxes, the present king, to allow him to reconstruct the wall and support him in the endeavor (Nehemiah 2:1-8), and after his return to Jerusalem from Susa, the capitol of Babylon, he had finished the job in just fifty-two days (6:15). The nations surrounding the Israelites, Nehemiah wrote, "were afraid and fell greatly in their own esteem; for they perceived that this work had been accomplished with the help of our God" (6:16).

What good is a wall, however, if the people inside it are rotten?

Nehemiah next sought to reconstruct the people, so chapter 8 begins with Ezra the scribe reading the law. We Gentiles who are people grafted on to our Jewish roots must understand clearly what is meant here by the word *law*. This is not the abuse of the law that the apostle Paul condemns in the New Testament. Rather, the law, *Torah* in Hebrew, was the means by which the Jews could be led by God, how they knew God's will; it might correspond to our receiving the Holy Spirit ever since the Pentecost outpouring upon everyone. Thus, *Torah* might be better understood as instruction, God's directions for their lives as his people. That is why the people were so attentive to the long reading (8:3).

That is also why the prophet Nehemiah and the priest Ezra encouraged the people to celebrate. The cause for their festival, for their great rejoicing, was that they had understood the Word, that they knew the LORD was their strength (8:10-12). That is our delight, too, for when we gather for worship, we, too, comprehend more of the Word and learn more about our God who is the source of our energy. Every time we listen to the Scriptures we notice again the foundation of our lives together in the power of our LORD.

Let us also all be aware of this wonderful element in the Bible: God's Word includes an *abundance* of parties. Jews and Christians in the Scriptures are frequently encouraged to revel in the Joy of being the people of God. We in the present day also receive from the *Torah* this invitation to celebrate: the great gift of the Sabbath day. That is one whole day of partying per week! And we, too, have the same enormous reason to celebrate — the great privilege it is to gather for worship and then to be God's people in the world.

Why is that such a privilege? We hear an answer to that question in today's Gospel reading from Luke 4, in which Jesus comes back to his hometown of Nazareth. Now it is always hard for the hometown boy to go back and preach, but because of the way the common lectionary is set up we did not hear today the end of this account, in which his former neighbors try to throw him over the cliff. (That gives us another very important reason to be here next week when we'll hear the rest of the story.) Instead, our reading ends on a very positive note, with the people still being stunned by Jesus. "Who is this man?" they murmur. "We thought he was just the carpenter's son."

In the synagogue Jesus reads the assigned text for the day, a phenomenal passage from Isaiah. As he verbalizes the text, I can't help but quiver with elation and ecstasy and exhilaration, for we have learned that Jesus is its fulfillment. This man, Jesus of Nazareth, is indeed the One who brings good news to the poor, who proclaims release to the captives and recovery of sight to the blind, who sets the oppressed free.

Perhaps this text means more to me because I have been almost blind. For seven months I could barely see because of a retinal hemorrhage in my good eye. After half a year I underwent a surgery that had previously failed twice on my other eye and left it severely damaged. Then for a month I had to wait to see if the surgery had worked this time, for my vision remained blurry as my eye healed. I'll never forget the Sunday morning, the first Sunday of a new year, when I sat down for a worship service, opened my bulletin, prepared to get out a double set of magnifiers, and suddenly realized I could read that bulletin without them! I understood with a great leap of Joy what this text means: how glorious is the recovery of sight to the blind!

But this text is indeed true for all of us, though maybe not so dramatically in our physical being. The Word is alive among us, and it is true for all of us that Christ coming into our lives *changes everything!* "Today," Jesus said to the shocked residents of Nazareth, "*today* this Scripture is fulfilled in your hearing! I am here. The kingdom of God has arrived!"

Christ's words were shocking to his neighbors; perhaps they should be more startling to us. Why do we let this Word become so ordinary, so non-mysterious, so non-threatening? Truly it is amazing — such a gift! — that Jesus has brought God's kingdom to us and invites us to be part of it. The people in Nehemiah's day wept because the Word exposed them for who they were, and it reveals the same to us. The Word discloses our desperation — but then it also brings us the kingdom!

An interesting sidelight is that when the Gospel writers recorded that sentence — that the kingdom of God has come — they preserved it with a Greek verb tense which underscores its permanence, which indicates that once the kingdom has arrived it continues to remain. No matter what might be going on in our circumstances, no matter the griefs that you and I bear,[1] no matter the struggles of our economic or political or personal lives, the kingdom of God is here! And when we come to worship, we celebrate that kingdom with a grand *Jubilate Deo.*[2] What a great "glory to God" we always

---

1. This sentence was very important in the aural sermon, because the beloved bell choir director for this congregation had died suddenly and unexpectedly a few days before and her funeral was to be held on that Sunday afternoon. Reflecting on larger issues of the Word as it is spoken in our congregations, I wonder how often we are reminded in our worship that the presence of the kingdom of God can *always* be making a difference in whatever we are encountering.

2. This was the title and some of the text of the choir anthem sung by a very large choir just prior to this sermon. I try always to include some mention of choir anthems, other special music, or the hymns in a sermon to tie together the worship components into a cohesive whole and thereby to deepen the teaching of both music and sermon.

want to be singing! We rejoice in the opportunity to verbalize and harmonize what we know — that we have been ushered into the kingdom of God by the person of Jesus Christ and that we spend our lives carrying that kingdom wherever we go.

That is why the text from First Corinthians is hilariously important for us today. I hope you caught the text's humor as it was read; sometimes we are simply too dry about the Scriptures. We don't realize that some passages are intended to be outrageously funny, in order that when we are laughing our heads off we suddenly realize that the text is about us.

Just look at what the apostle Paul does. He sets up a double-sided argument — we will call the two perspectives A and B — and he develops both angles with delightful humor. Motif A is that the Body of Christ has lots of members; theme B is that there is only one Body. Most congregations have problems with one or the other. Some parishes have many members, lots of variety, but little unity. Other churches have the problem of great unity, but hardly any diversity, no sharing of various gifts. Paul knew that if the people at Corinth were going to hear his plea for both unity and diversity — since, you might remember, the church of Corinth was utterly torn apart by petty arguments — the only way to go about it was to make them laugh, so that they could then realize that they were laughing at themselves. It is a healthful practice.[3]

Paul begins in 1 Corinthians 12:12 with a basic summary: "Just as in your body there are many members, and yet it is just one body, so it is with Christ." Then he underscores the basis for this unity: "we have all been baptized in the one Spirit into this body; we all eat and drink of that same Spirit" — this is the Body of Christ. Here is our foundation again, that kingdom stuff. You and I by our baptism were all brought into the kingdom, and you and I, when we celebrate the Lord's Supper as the highlight of our worship, eat and drink the kingdom's feast so that we are strengthened to serve it — and we participate in these gifts together, as one Body, with no barriers between us. At the same time our feasting uses bread made from multiple grains of wheat scattered in the field; we drink wine pressed from thousands of grapes growing on the hillside — a diversity gathered into one.

Then Paul develops the A side of the illustration. There are many members, and you need all of them. The foot can't say, "Oh, dear, give me a hand here; I guess I don't fit in since I'm only a foot." Let's try to imagine this body

---

3. I was astonished in the aural sermon that the congregation really laughed at this point. It is impossible to convey on paper the immense humor that the Spirit brought to our community that day through this Word.

composed only of assorted hands. It would be very difficult to get around, wouldn't it? Or again, what if the ear said, "I hear that I'm not an eye; perhaps I don't belong." How ridiculous — and yet don't we do it often, thinking such things as "I can't play the violin like she can" or "I wish I could play the cello."[4]

"If the whole body were an eye," Paul probes, "where would the hearing be?" What a ludicrous picture! Can you just envision this great big eyeball rolling down the street?

Having laughed at that, can we better remember that in the Body of Christ there is no such thing as jealousy? I don't have to be jealous of these fine string players, because we are in the kingdom together, so I don't have to be able to play those instruments. I don't have to be jealous of the bell ringers and organist who have played today; I can simply celebrate their gifts, thank God for them, and rejoice in the praise into which they lead me.

Wouldn't it be amazing if we, the Church, could model in the world the complete absence of jealousy? — if we could instead be entirely grateful that we are here together and that each of us has gifts to offer the whole? Paul summarizes this first motif of his discourse in verses 18 and 19 when he insists that God has arranged all the members, placing each one of them precisely as he desired. We all have gifts to contribute to the community and to the community's worship — and none is more important than any other. In concluding the motif he inquires, "where would the body be" if all were a single member, without all our differing gifts?

I learned this secret years ago from a deep friend of mine who requires kidney dialysis three times a week. When we lived in the same town, we regularly had long telephone conversations while he was on a dialysis run; he was an "attached" audience. One day I came back from leading a retreat and was telling him quite excitedly all about it — this and that and another thing, on and on. The poor dear listened to it all and then said, with genuine warmth and gratitude, "I am so glad we are parts of the body together." I asked why, and he responded, "Because all those things you described — I own them, too."

There he was, fastened to a machine with large needles in his arm, and yet exhibiting no jealousy — only gratitude and humble partnership. This is what we can be when the kingdom of God sets us free to rejoice in each

4. These musicians were sitting close beside me after having played in a string quartet with the choir anthem, *"Jubilate Deo."* This comment in the aural sermon gave rise to several remarks about not taking the congregation's fine musicians for granted and a humorous sentence concerning where they ought to be exiled if they don't properly appreciate such skilled players.

other's role in the Body, when we live by grace and gratitude. This morning let me challenge each one of you to discover this anew or afresh: that in this Body in this place we can celebrate each other's gifts.

Now Paul goes on to side B of his case: there is one body, and every part of the body is necessary to make it whole. Perhaps I especially value this side of his discussion because so many parts of my body don't work very well. I recognize daily how much is missing. Today it is essential that each one of you here realizes how important it is that *you* not be missing.

Does everyone in this congregation know that if he or she is not here for worship the Body suffers? Does each person here know that if you are not contributing your gifts for the well-being of the Church, this Body is hurt? Do we all experience the great thrill that we are absolutely essential for the Body of Christ in this place?

Paul tells us that by poking fun again: "the eye can't say to the hand, I don't need you; or the head to the feet . . ." He even concludes that those parts which don't seem very honorable are the very ones whom God and the community clothe with greater honor. We in the Church are the ones who can welcome everyone, who can never forget that each person has ways to contribute to our carrying and passing on of the kingdom. Especially in our worship we help each other learn the language of faith. We learn each other's songs; we share with each other our respective maturities of belief.

Paul goes on in the text to emphasize how this is reinforced in the Church. There is no schism in the Body because we know we are many members unified in the person of Christ, because in that one Body we must all have the same care for each other. Consequently, I expect that your congregational meeting today will be quite delightful because we will respectfully honor each other's contributions, because we will work for consensus on controversial issues.[5]

Moreover, Paul writes, we are willing to suffer for each other and with each other. Our society can hardly understand suffering love, since it is a cul-

---

5. What would happen in our congregational meetings if we would remind each other of these words from Paul before we begin the business and whenever conflict is on the edge of erupting? People have called me a "hopeless idealist," but I think a more accurate title is "hopeful realist." It is my responsibility in sermons to paint a picture of what the kingdom of God is like so that we can all aim for it. See Jacques Ellul's clarification of the term *realism* in chapter 4, "On Christian Pessimism," in *Sources and Trajectories: Eight Early Articles by Jacques Ellul That Set the Stage,* trans. and ed. Marva J. Dawn (Grand Rapids: Wm. B. Eerdmans Publishing Co., 1997), pp. 92-112. See also Marva J. Dawn, *Truly the Community: Romans 12 and How to Be the Church* (Grand Rapids: Wm. B. Eerdmans Publishing Co., 1992; reissued 1997), especially pp. 76-176.

ture of indifference,[6] so this gives us a possibility for modeling extremely well to the world an alternative way of living. Paul's original Greek is stronger than we usually make this text in English, for the preposition is smashed on to the front of the verb. Thus, it is not the verb *suffer;* it is a more tenacious *suffer-with.*

The same is true of the second verb in verse 27; it is *rejoice-with.* We are so intimately knitted together as the Body of Christ in this place that we share in each other's concerns and burdens, pleasures and passions. Let me give a silly example. Once when I was about to speak for a large youth convention and had a monstrous headache because of my visual handicaps, one of the members of my own youth group said to me, "How are you, Marva? You look terrible." I thanked her, told her of the splitting headache, and wondered aloud how to go on stage and lead the Bible study for these thousands of youth, and then she promised to pray for me. She was the sort who really would — so I went on stage more hopefully, began the Bible study, became engrossed in the text and enjoyed myself, and suddenly realized that my head no longer ached. When I left the stage, this young woman asked again how I was feeling, and after I gleefully told her that the headache had gone, she responded, "I know. I've got it."

Are we willing to carry each other's headaches? each other's financial burdens? each other's sorrows and griefs? Are we willing to demonstrate to the world that we deliberately accept each other's pain because we share the kingdom, because we are part of the same Body? And can we gladly celebrate with each other one another's rejoicings, without any jealousy, as we considered earlier?

Paul summarizes in verse 27 by writing, "Now you are the body of Christ [a unity] and individually members of it [with particular gifts]." I wish I could go to each person sitting here today and speak this verse to your face. Television has trained people in our culture to be passive, to get lots of information that we can't or don't act upon. How will we overcome that in the Church — or will we simply hear these words today, say "That was interesting," and walk out the door without wanting to change? If I could I would jump out of this pulpit, grab you each by the hand, and say, "Is this just information or do you think it could transform your life?"

Christ has already changed us. He has already set us free, healed our blind spirits, opened our ears. And now Paul reminds us, "This is what we are: we *are* this body!" *Today this Scripture is being fulfilled in your hearing.* May

---

6. At the congregational leaders' retreat the previous two days I had stressed that the opposite of love is not hate, but indifference.

God keep fulfilling it through you in the days to come — that each of you will remember that you are absolutely essential to this body, that you together will celebrate the kingdom in your worship here and carry it out from this place into the world. In the name of the Father, and of the Son, and of the Holy Spirit. Amen.

Let us pray: Gracious God, we realize that the Christian community is a splendid gift. We don't live as your people because we have to, ought to, should, or must. We live because the Scriptures are fulfilled in Jesus Christ. As a result, we are eager this morning to live the way you have described us, as a people unified and diverse. We yearn to make this biblical account our life story. May this Word be fulfilled in our lives, so that we, no matter what our gifts might be, may be part of the mission of your Church. As we gather for worship each week, may we be strengthened and encouraged and empowered and motivated to carry your kingdom into the world. We ask this confidently because we know it is your will and we know that your Holy Spirit has been poured out upon us. Send us out knowing that the Scriptures will continue to be fulfilled in and through us for the sake of your world and to your honor and glory and praise into the ages of the ages. Amen.

14

*Building Community in Worship**

> Like good stewards of the manifold grace of God, serve one an-
> other with whatever gift each of you has received.
>
> 1 Peter 4:10

In our fragmented and alienated, individualistic and competitive society, many people wonder if the Christian Church is any different. Congregations and denominations seem constantly to be fighting within or against each other; strangers who visit a worship service often are not welcomed or even acknowledged by anyone. Sometimes churches designate particular individuals to be the "greeters" in order to be hospitable, but that practice often militates against a genuine hospitality on the part of all the members of the parish.

In the season of Advent, as we prepare to welcome the Christ Child into our hearts and homes, we would do well to reflect upon the question of how to build genuine and welcoming community in our congregations. The nurturing of the unity of the Body is an important aspect of every small group and particular ministry in a parish, but in this brief space we will limit our focus especially to the building of community by means of our specific worship

*This essay first appeared as "Worship That Develops Strong Community," in the Advent issue of *Reformed Worship* 45 (September 1997): 26-29. My thanks to editor Emily Brink for permission to reprint this expanded version here.

practices. What elements in the corporate service can contribute to the nurturing of our common life together? How can a sense of the Christian community be established and reinforced while we are meeting together to praise God and grow in faith? How can we display in our gatherings in the "Temple" the "one accord" of the early Christians, whose "singleness of heart" led to having great favor with their neighbors? (These phrases are from the King James Version of Acts 2:46-47.)

Dangers to Community in Worship

We must ask our questions carefully, for too often the concept of community is perceived merely in terms of a feeling of coziness with God or compatibility with other members of the congregation. To reduce the importance of genuine community on the part of God's people to such emotions or sentiments is terribly destructive. Often the result is the formation of an elitist "in" group or a narcissism that takes the focus off God. In *Christian Ethics Today* (June 1996), Molly T. Marshall wrote about the dangers of thinking about the church as a family — for that can inhibit our ability to welcome strangers or cause us to squeeze out people with whom we cannot attain intimacy.

Similarly, Darrell Guder and his team from the Gospel and Our Culture Network critique contemporary images of community that exhibit what Parker Palmer calls an "ideology of intimacy."[1] Such images emphasize

> sameness, closeness, warmth, and comfort. Difference, distance, conflict, and sacrifice are alien to this approach and therefore are to be avoided at all costs. Modern communities maintain a facade of unity and harmony by eliminating the strange and cultivating the familiar, by suppressing dissimilarity and emphasizing agreement. The traumatic and tragic events of human life are glossed over, ignored, or explained away. Those who are strange — other than we are — are either excluded or quickly made like us.

The results are "homogeneous communities of retreat where persons must be protected from one another as well as from outsiders, and where reality is suppressed and denied due to fear and anxiety."[2]

Community in the biblical sense is more open to the realities of differ-

---

1. See Parker Palmer's very helpful book, *The Company of Strangers: Christians and the Renewal of America's Public Life* (New York: Crossroad, 1986), p. 108.
2. Darrell L. Guder, ed., *Missional Church: A Vision for the Sending of the Church in North America* (Grand Rapids: Wm. B. Eerdmans Publishing Co., 1998), p. 179.

ences, more openly gracious to all, more deliberate, an act of will. It does not depend upon feelings of affection. In fact, sometimes (perhaps always?) God seems to put us in a community together with people whom we don't like so that we learn the real meaning of *agapē* — that intelligent, purposeful love directed toward another's need which comes first from God and then flows through us to our neighbor. To develop a community that practices biblical principles is very difficult in this technologically efficient society. It takes a lot of work and time, sacrifice and commitment.

The Triune God

Before we consider some practical ways to build community, we must note this obvious, but often overlooked, truth: the triune God wants our churches to be genuine communities. The night before his crucifixion Jesus prayed that we would all be one, even as he is one with the Father. Furthermore, as the apostle Paul stresses by means of a series of repetitive phrases in 1 Corinthians 12, "one and the same Spirit" gives us all our various gifts, puts us as particular members into the Body just as he wills, and makes all those members *one* Body of Christ.

Since we know that God is at work to make us all one, we are set free to enjoy the process — knowing that it does not depend upon us. What we do to build community is a response to the grace of a unifying God; who we are as the *people* of God is an image of the relationship within the Godhead. When we have struggles in our communities, we can have confidence that God is at work to bring to completion the good work he has begun in establishing his Church.

Developing Hospitality

Genuine community in worship is made more possible by some of the mechanical things that we do before the service begins. In order for the worship to be open to everyone, we must remove any barriers to public, common life. Though many congregations these days use overhead projections, those are often difficult to see — impossible for elderly persons who have cataracts. We want to be sure that there are plenty of songbooks and bulletins or whatever else we use, large-print worship materials for the visually impaired or partially sighted, perhaps interpreters or earphones for the hearing impaired, no impediments to wheelchairs.

The alternative Christian community must be an inclusive one. Are our churches being formed to be inclusive of the great mix of ages, social classes, races, and gifts among God's people? I belong to a black, inner-city congregation that gives me, a white person, the opportunity to learn from my African-American sisters and brothers; it is a congregation devoted to its neighborhood, offering room in its building for scouts, African dance classes, economic development groups, and local black history month celebrations. These services provide enormous opportunities for genuine hospitality to our neighbors.

To counteract our culture's wariness, members of the congregation need to be trained specifically to be hospitable to strangers (and to each other). Do our worship practices form us to welcome outsiders, to invite newcomers, to tell others about our faith, to care for members of the community who are missing from corporate gatherings?[3] We can each welcome those who sit beside us, make sure they know how to follow our order of service, point them to pages or instructions, and, with specific education, explain to them why we do what we do.

Many contemporary critics of worship maintain that building community requires us to jettison the habits of the past and use new materials that are in the idiom of the culture. This notion is dangerous in that Christianity is not simply an intellectual assent to a set of doctrinal propositions, nor is it merely having certain emotional/spiritual experiences. Rather, it is a way of life, a language, a set of habits, an entire culture. If we conform worship too much to the prevailing culture, it is difficult for participants to learn the unique "language" of faith, to be formed by the community and the Word to be followers of Christ.

I have found, contrarily, that any kind of music or style of worship, including both new and old, can be hospitable if the persons who participate in it welcome the strangers, if the customary rituals do not become empty performance, if the leaders give gentle and invitational explanations of what we do and why, if melodies for singing are clearly played or perhaps led by a cantor, if the printed music is available to everyone, if *corporate* worship is kept open as a "public space" into which every person can enter rather than becoming the private coziness of individuals in their devotional relationship to God. Most of the rest of the comments in this chapter are further extensions of this principle of hospitality for the sake of building genuine community.

---

3. See the excellent evangelism questionnaire from St. John Lutheran Church, Northumberland, PA, in Jim Petersen, "Join the Crowd," *The Lutheran*, October 1995, p. 40.

Music

The Christian community, as the New Testament emphasizes repeatedly, is a unity of diversity. We capture that best musically when we learn to sing each other's songs, when members of the Body help each other learn why their faith is nurtured and strengthened by particular sets of words and music, when different persons in the community contribute their gifts of playing musical instruments or singing, arranging and composing.

These contributions, however, must not take the place of *everyone* in the Body participating in the work of worship. Memorized liturgical refrains, repeated each week, enable small children to participate in singing them; children's choirs can teach new songs to the adults; "Children in Worship" programs enable youngsters to learn about, and then participate in, worship practices; teen and adult choirs can practice the hymns for worship in order to lead them from within the congregation; songs for worship can be taught in a preceding Sunday school hour or played the previous week by organists or instrumentalists during the offering or as preludes/postludes — these are just a few of the ways in which we can build community by making it possible for each person to join in the singing of the worship service.

Music is also an important means by which we can gain a sense of the entire Christian community throughout space and time. By singing songs from other Christian ethnic groups and from all epochs of our faith — going all the way back to our roots in Judaica and forward to the angels' songs in heaven recorded in the Revelation — we learn the global and timeless dimensions of the people of God. One of the best developments of recent years is that the new hymnbooks of most major denominations contain more music from around the world. In my home congregation, located in an inner-city African-American neighborhood, we sing a great blend of musical styles each week, including soul music, chorales from our Lutheran heritage, songs from South Africa or Taizé, and contemporary choruses.

We must be careful in choosing new music from our era (as opposed to the music in hymnbooks, which has already for the most part been sorted by history so that the best usually remains). Since we live in an increasingly narcissistic culture, we must guard against new songs that are self-centered, that fail to convey the we-ness (and wee-ness) of the Church. We want to avoid music that focuses only on our personal feelings of happiness, instead of equipping us to be a missional community that reaches out beyond ourselves with the good news of grace in Christ and cares for the world around us with peacemaking and justice building.

Highlighting Gifts of the Community

Already we have considered building community in worship by utilizing the gifts of musicians in the congregation. It seems to me that applause for particular musical contributions should be discouraged because it highlights some gifts more than others and hinders all the members of the Body from knowing that their presence and singing are equally important and that their gifts are also vital for the well-being of the whole.

Our worship needs the offerings of those who make banners, grow flowers, write or perform chancel dramas, choreograph or present liturgical dances, weave vestments or altar cloths, carve furniture, make pottery vessels, or bake bread for the Lord's Supper. Other members of the Body devote their energies and skills to ushering, designing the worship folders, serving at the Lord's Table, reading Scripture lessons, or leading prayers. Correlatively, the art in the worship space can reflect the occupations of community members; for example, a beautiful stained-glass window in a sanctuary in a Pacific Northwest seacoast town centers around Jesus calling the disciples away from their nets and spreads out to picture contemporary fishermen and loggers.

It is especially important that we highlight the gifts of the children and teenagers in the community. In one church in upstate New York, the elementary school children play their bells and chant to lead the congregation every Sunday in singing a psalm. In another congregation, entire families do the ushering for the week, so that young children participate with their parents in passing out the bulletins and taking the offering. Other churches feature their children's art work as bulletin covers or use their prayers in the worship service. In my home congregation, the young people serve as greeters, Scripture readers, drama participants, acolytes, ushers, and providers of refreshments for the fellowship hour following worship.

Communal Prayers

One particularly important aspect of worship for building community is the corporate prayers. Many congregations pray through the whole list of members by mentioning a few names and their concerns each Sunday. By praying for the members' ministries and occupations out in the world, we increase the sense that we are gathered in worship to strengthen us all together for our outreach to others when we are dispersed — and by conscious verbalizing of this truth we enable congregation members to continue to support each other's work in daily life.

It is essential that we train members of the congregation to comprehend that prayers are more than the words we speak about others. Prayer also involves placing ourselves into God's hands for the effecting of his answers. Thus, when we pray "Thy will be done," we are seeking God's wisdom for how we can be agents for actuating his will. If we pray in the corporate Body for someone who is ill, for example, then as members all of us look for ways to "put legs on our prayers" by sending cards or taking flowers, preparing meals or doing housework, caring for children or in some other way easing the strain, helping to defray medical expenses or offering rides to the doctor. Thus, prayer is the chief way in which the sense of community established and nurtured in the worship service is widened into other aspects of congregational life.

Prayer also can encourage our concern for the larger community of the global Church. Many congregations pray each week for a sister congregation elsewhere in the world, for missionaries of the denomination (especially particular ones supported by the congregation), for churches of other denominations in the neighborhood, for parishes in areas hit by natural disasters, for persecuted Christians such as the South Sudanese refugees and Palestinians being deprived of their homes near Jerusalem and Bethlehem.

Building Community by Preaching

As the primary educational vehicle of the worship service, the pastor's sermon plays a critical role in building the community. Simple language choices are vital, for the constant use of the plural *we* to describe faith pulls the congregation away from the individualism so rife in our culture. It is also essential for the pastor continually to emphasize that faith is not something we construct by ourselves for our personal use, but rather a gift, into which we are invited, that has been passed on through the community of believers since Sarah and Abraham. (Saying the historic creeds of the Church with the plural pronoun, *we*, and looking at each other while we say them also reinforces this sense of communal faith.)

We build community through our preaching, furthermore, by instructing parishioners in the foundational doctrines that form the Church. What we believe about creation, for example, reminds us that all people are created in the image of God and therefore are vitally important for the whole Body. God's commissions to human beings in Genesis 1 command us to care for each other and for the interrelationships of all the earth.

Similarly, the doctrine of incarnation teaches us to embody God's grace for each other in practical, tangible ways. Likewise, our beliefs about spiritual gifts, poured out upon us by God's sending of the Holy Spirit, free our communities to value the diversity of *charisma* we each possess even as we work for unity in our use of those gifts. Comparable examples could be given of many other doctrines of the Church that lay essential principles for our churches' growth in communal life. Well-rounded preaching (the common lectionary is a great help) will cultivate both virtues and insights from the Scriptures and the Church's teachings that will contribute to strengthening the community.

The sermon also builds community with specific instructions — for being hospitable, for carrying the corporate prayers into daily life, for each adult to participate more in the spiritual nurturing of the congregation's children, for more outreach to the neighbors. Short messages specifically for the youngest children help them to feel a part of the community; sermon illustrations concerning the youth's schools or activities enable them to know that they are valued. To demonstrate how the Scriptures form us, the pastor can include familiar situations from the members' lives and occupations (excluding those that would break confidences or cause embarrassment), and thereby the people learn afresh that worship trains us together in the habits and practices of faith.

God Is the Source; We Are the Agents

My purpose in this chapter has been merely to begin a conversation in each congregation concerning ways in which our particular worship services can build community. I pray that these ideas stir you to new thinking and creativity — but not to quick-fix techniques or gimmicks. We do not manipulate community; it is God's initiative to make us one. But we can foster community, work to prevent anything from hindering or disrupting it, and celebrate it.

Advent is a good time to focus on the issues, for, as we anticipate the Christ Child's coming, our worship can equip us to be a community to receive him. Then, may this season of the Church year unite us in responding to the Father's gift of the Child with Spirit-empowered and community-supported witness and outreach to the world.

15

Worship Is Not a Matter of Taste

. . . [L]ead a life worthy of the calling to which you have been called, with all humility and gentleness, with patience, bearing with one another in love, making every effort to maintain the unity of the Spirit in the bond of peace.

Ephesians 4:1b-3

A cartoon by Rob Suggs[1] illustrates a problem that plagues many churches trying to respond to the dwindling of congregations in postmodern times. In an effort to appeal to religious consumers, these churches become like "Saint Happy's: The Worship Place," where the slogan is "Have It Thy Way." While selecting from the overhead menu their preferences for "Liturgy Lite" or "Kiddy Kristianity," shoppers can also order "feelgood filet" or "happy homily" among other choices for sermons, sing "jingles for Jesus" or "boomer beat" or other happy tunes, pick their favorite kinds of bread and juice or wine from the communion bar, and sample side orders of "12-step groups" or "12-holes golf." Down on the service counter between the male and female pastors waiting to take orders is the cash register, plastered with the ad, "Hey Kids! Collect . . . *Pastors* of the *Universe* Action Figures."

What does it take to attract the baby boomers or busters or X-ers or the blank generation to our churches for worship? That question, which is being

---

1. Unfortunately, I'm unable to mention the source of this cartoon since it was clipped for me by someone else.

186

asked by more and more mainline and evangelical churches, reveals again the terrible confusion between evangelism and worship that we considered in Chapter 9, invites many of the culture's idolatries into our sanctuaries, and leads to the "dumbing down" illustrated by Rob Suggs's cartoon. My goal is to help churches ask better questions about the meaning and purposes of worship, to develop a theological approach to worship in postmodern times.

Musical Taste Is Not the Entry Point

I have been a co-speaker at a few conferences with a person who says, "Every congregation must have at least two styles of worship, two points of entry into the congregation." Wrong! As we saw in Chapter 9, worship is not the entry point; *you are!* I want 490 points of entry into the congregation if there are 490 members. If we confuse this, not every person in the pews recognizes that he or she is a vital part of the Christian community and its outreach to the world around us. Not only is the idea of taste as an entry point wrong biblically, but also it is extremely destructive of genuine community, fosters an independent view of the local congregation, and reduces worship simply to a matter of preferences instead of an entering into God's presence in the company of the Church throughout space and time.

The idea of worship style as the point of entry is also wrong statistically. According to a 1995 study in the Evangelical Lutheran Church of America dealing with effective ministry and membership growth, a mere 1 percent joined a congregation because of its musical style. The largest proportion, 28 percent, joined because of faith and beliefs, 22 percent because of family and friends, 5 percent because of the hospitality ("atmosphere"), and 19 percent because of the location of the facilities.[2]

Reasons for the "Point of Entry" Theory

Many churches have bought into the notion that they must have at least two "styles" of worship services in order to attract new members. The major reason for the popularity of this notion is that it gives a quick-fix answer to the problem of declining numbers in churches, thereby confusing worship with evangelism, as delineated in Chapter 9. It is much easier to change the kind of

2. Carolyn J. Lewis, "Invitational Evangelism Makes Churches Grow," *The Lutheran* 9, no. 5 (May 1996): 46.

music offered than to change the hearts of members to make them more hospitable in worship and daily life, more willing to witness, more loving toward their neighbors.

Certainly the desperation of churches to get the society interested in them also arises because Christianity is not supported by the culture as it once was. The media pokes fun at us or ignores us. Biblical images are no longer taught in literature studies, and the faith roots of our nation's history are overlooked in history courses. Sunday sports interfere with the possibility of worship for our youth. Even the churches' own rites (the chief example of which is weddings) have been taken over by cultural values of consumerism and glamour, competition and glitter. So much is desacralized that there no longer seems to be a need in our society for churches.

Churches, too, have made many wrong turns in the face of modernism and postmodernism — and once these turns are made, it is hard to go back. (Many of these wrong choices are delineated in Chapter 5.) Finally, the advance of the theory that every congregation must have at least two styles of worship is directly related to many of our culture's idolatries that have invaded the churches. (Several of these are noted in Chapter 19.)

Historical Roots

It is important that we understand the historical roots of this push for taste so that we can see how destructive of genuine community it is. The United States, as William Fore observes, was founded with a tension between communal concern for the well-being of others and the independent spirit of those fleeing religious or political persecution or pursuing their pioneering autonomy. During the last quarter century, Fore explains, Robert Bellah and his colleagues have analyzed the current national values and beliefs and have found them "moving away from the republican ideal of the public welfare and toward the liberal ideal of individual self-interest."

Recognizing that shift is crucial, for

> just as it was the function of religion in the early days of the republic to provide the moral vision which gave the nation its cohesion and impetus, so *now that role is increasingly being assumed by television.* The difference is ominous. One is rooted in the lives of individuals in the context of the worshiping community; the other is rooted in an economic system interested only in profits, with a technology interested only in results. The one is committed to community and the ideal of self-sacrifice for the greater good of

the commonweal; the other is committed to utilitarianism and to the development of technology for the purpose of instantly gratifying the needs of the individual.[3]

As Fore points out, when self-gratification controls worship, it corrupts the two sides of the nation's founding balance by pretending to be for the good of the community while simultaneously promoting individuality.

Those who advocate more than one style of worship as good for a congregation are deceiving us, for in truth such a development is injurious (often fatally) to genuine community. Let's look more closely at how dangerous it is to turn churches into a battlefield over taste.

The Conflict of "Traditional" vs. "Contemporary" Taste

Sometimes those who want "traditional" or "contemporary" styles of worship fight a war of control in a congregation; then frequently the war splits the Body into two more or less vitriolic camps that each have their own worship service. In other places the leadership of a church decides to split worship into two services with different "styles" for the sake of attracting the neighbors; this choice is almost as destructive of community as the bitter war. Readers might think that I overstate the case, but let me point out several very harmful effects of such splitting. All of these are very destructive of the Churchbeing we defined in Chapter 9.

1. If we set up different kinds of worship at different times, this fosters the "vendors/consumers" disposition and promotes the notion of marketing religion. It is difficult enough, as we saw in Chapter 7, to avoid the consumerism of our culture. Causing people to shop for the musical style they prefer makes it even less possible to wean them from this mentality.

2. The division into a "traditional" and a "contemporary" service is destructive to community because these terms are so poorly defined and the result is a narrowing of the community's appreciation. Which tradition do we mean? The historic mass, for example, is often denigrated as the work of white Europeans — when in actuality it was composed in the early centuries of the Church from biblical roots in Judaica, Africa, and Asia Minor. Similarly, what is meant by contemporary? (This will be discussed further in Chapter 24.) Do we mean choruses from Taizé, pop songs, or the esoteric mu-

---

3. William F. Fore, *Television and Religion: The Shaping of Faith, Values, and Culture* (Minneapolis: Augsburg, 1987), p. 198.

sic of contemporary composer Krzysztof Penderecki? In *Reaching Out without Dumbing Down* I cited Thomas Gieschen's list of ten kinds of new sacred choral styles. Their names aren't important here; what matters is that congregations are limiting themselves to two kinds of sounds instead of recognizing that there are hundreds — and that almost all of them could be helpful in revealing the splendor of God.

3. The division into "traditional" and "contemporary" seems to match the tension of truth and love in the Scriptures. For example, Ephesus in Revelation 2 has lost its love, whereas Pergamum is rebuked for having false teaching. Older music, written in eras that were more objective in orientation, most often stresses content, whereas new music is frequently more directed to loving God. Both are needed, so they ought not to be separated.

4. Furthermore, of all the various tastes in music that there are, why should we limit ourselves simply to traditional and contemporary?[4] How will a community decide which taste to follow? Research shows that people in the United States are quite evenly divided among those who prefer hard rock, soft rock, classical, jazz, blues, country and western, contemporary easy listening, and several other kinds. Which idiom should we choose? Since Christianity is a different language altogether (see Chapter 29), what language should we use to capture its grammar?

5. When congregations divide the Body into a "traditional" and a "contemporary" service, this often separates the old from the young according to their preference for what they know. The result is that young families no longer worship next to those more experienced in the faith who could be mentors to them — and the old are bereft of the vitality of the young.

6. Moreover, what the old know comes from a culture that was much more Christian than contemporary culture. We must face the fact that the surrounding ethos has much more effect on contemporary musical composition than most people realize — although there certainly are numerous examples of contemporary composers who have thoroughly resisted the influence of their milieu.

7. To split a congregation into traditional and contemporary worship services deprives the "traditionalists" of new expressions of faith. They do not learn anything fresh and lack the nourishment of reformation and renewal.

8. Similarly, splitting the congregation robs the "contemporaryists" of continuity with the Church throughout time. It steals from them their roots

---

4. For "an illustrated guide to all the major traditions of music in worship," see Andrew Wilson-Dickson, *The Story of Christian Music: From Gregorian Chant to Black Gospel* (Minneapolis: Fortress Press, 1996).

in Judaica and the early Church and takes from them the wisdom of all the ages of the developing Church.

9. Furthermore, different styles of worship often split the loyalists from the returnees, to the detriment of both in much the same ways as the splitting of old from young. People who have rebelled against the Church for a while and then come back need the mentoring of those who have never left.

10. Such a division also usually separates the organists from the guitarists, and it is most often the former who have been trained in what worship means and how to bring cohesion to a service. As a result, worship services are often under the direction of leaders who do not really know what they are doing.

11. Peter Marty adds another reason — that if people come to worship expecting only one certain style of music, then we lose the possibility of "authentic surprise." As an artist told Bill Moyers, "If you know what you are looking for, you will never see what you do not expect to find." The worship wars, Marty writes, "are dulling the brilliance of the grace and beauty that color the church's praise."[5]

12. A flyer that arrived at my home to advertise an evangelism conference offered a model of a "spirited praise and worship service." If that is the only kind of worship a community has, how will the people learn to lament? Are praise choruses enough for a community's faith? They certainly aren't enough for a funeral, for example.

13. Furthermore, those who advocate some kinds of worship services that tend to reduce participants to an audience usually do not take into significant consideration the relation between style and content, "particularly of the degree to which adopting an entertainment style baptizes the content of a culture of diversion."[6]

14. Similarly, certain styles of worship services almost inevitably entail the problem of a star clergy and cult of personality, which are inimical to the biblical picture of Christian community in which all gifts are equally important for the Body. The last place in which anybody ought to be famous is in the Church.

15. It is important to learn to sing songs I might not like for the sake of the community. Notice that I did not say "songs that are of questionable theology" or "songs with little musical merit." But if tunes are interesting and

5. Peter W. Marty, "Beyond the Polarization: Grace and Surprise in Worship," *Christian Century* 115, no. 9 (March 18-25, 1998): 285.

6. This comes from Frederick J. Gaiser's review of Walt Kallestad's book, *Entertainment Evangelism: Taking the Church Public* (Nashville: Abingdon Press, 1996), in *Word and World* 18, no. 1 (Winter 1998): 104.

singable and if the words are theologically sound, then a Christian should be willing to sing it for the sake of brothers and sisters for whom it might be especially useful spiritually. (Criteria for choosing music will be offered in Chapter 26.) By such willingness the whole community learns to appreciate a wider diversity of musical styles for the sake of caring for each other in the Body.

16. The worst result of turning worship into a matter of taste is that to do so is to lose sight of the fact that it is *God* we are worshiping — not ourselves. And God, I hear, has widely eclectic tastes!

All of the dangers above contribute to narcissism, to preferring ourselves, which in turn prevents witness, concern, and outreach to the neighbor. Could Christians instead use the common criteria given in Chapter 26 to assess what we do in order to bring together opposing sides of various arguments and an intermingling of styles in worship? Can we learn better what it means to be Church as we talk together about worship practices? Can we make sure that old and young worship together for the sake of wisdom and vitality for all? Most of all, can we be theologically faithful about worship instead of being beguiled by the unbiblical advice of church marketers?

Why All of This Matters

In *Postmodern Theory and Biblical Theology: Vanquishing God's Shadow,* Brian D. Ingraffia shows why it is so dangerous to turn worship into a matter of taste: it becomes an idolatry of power instead of faithfulness to God. Friedrich Nietzsche described as follows how he could bring about a change in intellectual "taste":

> What changes the general taste? The fact that some individuals who are powerful and influential announce without any shame, *hoc est ridiculum, hoc est absurdum,* in short, the judgement of their taste and nausea; and then they enforce it tyrannically.[7]

Decisions about worship need to be grounded in the Revelation, in the wisdom of the Church through time and space, in tradition and community, and in the new winds of the Spirit in order to form faithful judgment. The

---

7. Friedrich Nietzsche, *The Gay Science,* quoted in Brian D. Ingraffia, *Postmodern Theory and Biblical Theology: Vanquishing God's Shadow* (Cambridge: Cambridge University Press, 1996), p. 19.

path that will lead us to truth about worship is not that of power and influence, but of humility and obedience before God.

Most recently I talked about these issues in a clergy conference on Saint Michael and All Angels day (September 29). This important feast day is often neglected in our churches, but it is very momentous because it reminds us of where our attentions should be fixed for the sake of the right conflicts. I read for the conference participants a bit of Revelation 12, beginning with verse 7, which tells of St. Michael and his angels warring against the dragon and his forces and casting them out of heaven. Subsequently, Revelation 13 and 14 show how the dragon and the two beasts parody the Trinity.[8] The issue, then, is the cosmic battle to preserve the Lordship of the true GOD against the idolatries that imitate him. Let us not fight against each other over minor matters of taste, which become idolatrous and divisive. Instead, let us concentrate our energies on the war against all that leads us away from God, against the beasts and dragons that pretend to satisfy our deepest longings for the one true God.

On the positive side, the most important reason why all of this matters is that Jesus himself wants his Church to be united, instead of divided according to anything, including taste. In the "high priestly prayer" of John 17, we hear that the unity of our community enables us to participate in the greatest of all unities — that of Father, Son, and Holy Spirit. By such unity the world will know that Jesus is the Christ, sent by God for the salvation of the world.

How can we want to divide our church community according to taste if we meditate on words such as these?

> "I ask not only on behalf of these [disciples], but also on behalf of those who will believe in me through their word [Jesus prayed for us!], that they may all be one. As you, Father, are in me and I am in you, may they also be in us, so that the world may believe that you have sent me. The glory that you have given me I have given them, so that they may be one, as we are one, I in them and you in me, that they may become completely one, so that the world may know that you have sent me and have loved them even as you have loved me." (John 17:20-23)

---

8. See chapters 23 and 24 of Marva J. Dawn, *Joy in Our Weakness: A Gift of Hope from the Book of Revelation* (St. Louis: Concordia Publishing House, 1994).

16

The Art of the Chef or Conducting the Symphony: In Praise of Authority

> The gifts that he gave were that some would be . . . pastors and teachers, to equip the saints for the work of ministry, for building up the body of Christ.
>
> Ephesians 4:11-12

My friend David Hendricksen told me about a restaurant in Greeneville, Tennessee, called Diedra's. Its chef prepares only three choices for the main dinner entré each evening, and the restaurant is open only three nights each week for dinner. Since she has spent careful time designing and developing the feast, she will not rush around to make extra when what she has made is gone. As soon as guests have savored all of the day's creations, no more will be offered — until the next time the place is open, for which the chef will craft three other possibilities. Everyone knows that to go there is to experience the finest skill. The chef's work is superb — the food is artfully conceived, tastefully prepared, exquisite in presentation.

Contrast that with a large chain restaurant. No one cares what you choose. Everything will be the same tomorrow as it was today. As soon as one dish is emptied, another large tray of the same will be dumped into the heating or chilling bins. Ultimately, when there are too many choices, nothing matters.

Analogies are always inadequate — and this one certainly is because some people might interpret it to mean that congregations should offer three entrés or choices of worship style (the danger of which we discussed in the previous chapter). My point with this metaphor is the need for crafting, for carefulness, for the authority of the chef to choose how best to serve her customers. In the same way, pastors and musicians employ their finest artistry to create worship that nurtures the people of God with the splendor of God.

Certainly I am not saying (and have never said) that there is only one way to do worship well. I believe instead that there could be an unlimited multitude of excellent forms and structures and tools for God's people to worship him (since God's splendor is too great for us ever to capture it); but to choose what we do by means of an attempt to please the people is to lose carefulness. We can enrich everyone's understanding of God with a wide variety of resources and careful planning, but to attempt to cater to everyone's tastes is to wind up with hodgepodge.

I do indeed speak positively of the heritage of the Church in the catholic mass — primarily because so many worship or church-growth gurus are bashing it these days. The result of that bashing has been an almost knee-jerk reaction on the part of numerous pastors and congregations simply to discard the tradition without ever understanding why it has stood so well the test of time. I believe that our forebears in the Church were very wise to construct the historic liturgy as they did. It is thoroughly biblical, entirely God-centered, upbuilding to the community, nurturing of genuine discipleship — and it follows a brilliantly logical progression of thought that guides the worshiper from repentance and forgiveness into exaltation and then instruction and empowerment for ministry.

With the guidance of the Church's tradition, congregational leaders can construct many ways to worship well. Several clarifications are necessary in this chapter if we want to understand the kind of leadership that worship needs in order for its participants to be Church.

Conducting the Symphony

The last thing churches should do if they want to worship well is conduct a survey asking members what they *want* for worship. What the people want might not be good for them, and our churches are in the business of forming Christians, not catering to consumerist choices.

This is certainly a countercultural stance, for everyone (it seems) thinks that the Church should be a democracy. However, the true Church has never been — and ought never to be — a democracy. It is, primarily, a Spiritocracy, a Body with Christ as the Head, a *charismacracy* (my coined word to signify leadership by those exercising Spirit-endowed gifts, *charisma* in Greek). What an odd thing to be in the era of the World Wide Web.

The great gift of the World Wide Web, everyone (it seems) declares, is that it democratizes the world. There is no such thing as authority, because everyone can participate equally. Cyberspace is a world of no footnotes, no hierarchies, constant destabilization of anyone's input. Those who write about cyberspace recognize that the Internet will be hard on religions that emphasize authority and hierarchy. Now we live in the milieu of freedom and individualism.

However, critics also are beginning to recognize that the claims of the cyberspace world for equality and democracy are deceptive. It is not necessarily a world of freedom of access, but one controlled by the hierarchy of those with wealth and power. Furthermore, the lack of any authority amplifies the postmodern inability to know how to weight information — and so a person's life becomes increasingly "virtual," with more and more stacks of data without ordering or significance, with more superficiality and less of an attention span, more hype and less real experience, less humanity, less meaning.[1] In addition, with the proliferation of web sites there is also a proliferation of garbage, so there is great need for some means of discernment, some test by which information can be evaluated.

In contrast, when we are being Church, our churches are not controlled by a hierarchy of wealth and power; rather, they function as a *charismacracy* with the authority of Spirit-given gifts in a Christ-centered Body to weigh, to order, to discern, to test according to God's standards revealed in the Scriptures interpreted by the whole community. Since more and more people are finding it impossible to resist the lures of cyberspace, it seems to me to be a critical time for the Church to be very clear about our identity and not to be ashamed of offering our gifts of genuine authority, unfailing stability, trustworthy security, and true freedom. Perhaps worship is the most important realm in which the Church is significantly countercultural, for worship is under authority — first that of God and then that of the *charismacracy*.

Paul Dahlstrom and his seminary students in a course on "Worship: Traditions and Practices" explored the analogy of leading worship to conducting a symphony.[2] Dahlstrom and the class participants discovered that

1. By far the strongest and most broadly ranged of the books listed in Chapter 6 above that expose the illusions of cyberspace is *Resisting the Virtual Life: The Culture and Politics of Information*, ed. James Brook and Iain A. Boal (San Francisco: City Lights, 1995).

2. The class sessions, the students' discoveries, and Dahlstrom's analyses are recorded in Paul T. Dahlstrom, *Worshiping: Present and Future Hope* (Lima, OH: Fairway Press, 1996). Page references to this book in the following paragraphs are given parenthetically in the text.

church musicians often seemed to have a very good sense of the meaning of worship and carefulness in leading it (59). One student wondered if that might be because musicians have a score (that is, the printed music that gives them exact notes and markings for volume level, speed, mood, and so forth) which guides many of the particulars of their performance (60). The class ascertained that the leading of worship needed "a metaphor that somehow captured the purpose, organized the activity, and inspired dedication" (61).

The value of their metaphor of conducting a symphony is that it emphasizes the following aspects:[3]

1. *Unity.* Even though a symphonic piece often has three or four differing movements (usually one or two relatively faster segments and one or two slower ones), these parts relate to each other. The same is true of any kind of art; the elements of a painting, similarly, must work together — with enough variety for interest but not enough to make the piece incoherent. Even so the components of worship must be congruent with each other.

2. *Movements.* A symphonic piece varies widely in mood or tone or tempo between the individual segments or portions of the piece. Similarly, the timbre of confession and absolution is vastly different from the spirit in hymns of praise.

3. *Progression.* There is a flow as the symphony progresses to its climax and ending. So worship finds its high points in the Gospel reading and the Lord's Supper, but the liturgy that surrounds them makes a progression from the entrance into worship to the dismissal into ministry.

4. *The musical score.* There are specific notes to be played. So worship has a theme, usually generated by the texts assigned for the day or chosen by the pastor. There are numerous possibilities for the score — thousands of symphonies to choose from, a wide range of texts. However, the performers must be faithful to the musical score, even as pastors must be true to the text. (Obviously the analogy can't be stretched too far here because a musical score demands note accuracy far beyond the requirements of worship. Perhaps we can avoid this problem by seeing the composer of the score as the Church, with its arranger being a particular congregation's worship committee.)

5. *Diversity.* Different symphonies require vastly different instrumenta-

---

3. Though various points are fleshed out in the rest of Dahlstrom's book, I have chosen to create my own list here.

tion. Even so, worship calls for a variety of musical sounds to display the rich splendor of God.

6. *Numerous styles.* Symphonic music encompasses a wide diversity of sounds and flavors from all eras and areas — from spare to lush harmonies, from romantic poignancy to marching brassiness, from jazz to Latin or African rhythms, from European to Asian melodies. Even so, the music of the Church entails gifts from all the people of God throughout time and space.

7. *Relationships.* The conductor's highest loyalty is to the spirit of the music (for which the written score and the composer are valuable guides) — just as the worship leader's superior authority is God (to whom the community and the Scriptures are reliable escorts). Other relationships are also essential in order for the symphony to be played well. A conductor works together closely with the instrumentalists, just as the pastor and musician in worship work with each other as teammates, and both work with the worship committee to plan and carry out the best worship they can craft for the sake of the particular congregation they serve.

8. *Authority.* The conductor exercises the authority that is necessary for the performance — otherwise each musician could go his or her own way — and the conductor is chosen for that position because of his or her understanding of the composers, their music, and how that music should be interpreted. Similarly, the pastor and musician are mentors to the rest of the congregation in the art of worship, and out of their expertise they exercise the authority of choosing and leading the elements of worship.

The Kind of Authority the Church Needs

This is not authoritarianism. It is the authority expressed by the centurion who had people over him and under him (see the accounts in Matthew 8:5-10 and Luke 7:1-10). It is never a unilateral authority, but always that of a grace-filled community. We could have plenty of disagreements about some of the particulars of how this authority is played out, but what is essential is that it be the process of the *Spiritocracy* and the *charismacracy*.

It is the authority of the pastor who has daily devotions and a regular Sabbath to keep his or her spiritual life strong, who diligently explores and submits to God's Revelation in the Scriptures and to the Word himself, who has studied the meaning of worship and its practice throughout the Church, who works together with the congregation's musicians and worship committee to plan the best, most cohesive way to immerse the congregation in the splendor of God revealed in the texts for the day.

It is the authority of the musicians (be they guitarists or organists, flute players, singers, choir directors, or whatever) who have studied church music, who practice diligently to hone their skills, who study on their own and work with the pastor to understand the scriptural foundation for each worship service, who attend training seminars and research new resources in order to find the best music to immerse the congregation in the splendor of God revealed in melodies and hymn texts, choral anthems and instrumental pieces.

It is the authority of the worship committee composed of a diversity of people (of all ages, races, social classes, levels of expertise) who are all spiritually diligent people, engaging regularly in Bible study and worship practices, attending worship conferences or other educational possibilities, who are committed to working together as a team with the pastor and musicians, open to comments and suggestions from the rest of the congregation, eager to craft worship that immerses the congregation in the splendor of God through every element that the service contains.

In other words, this is the authority of the gifted community, under the Holy Spirit's directions, talking together to create worship services that keep the focus on God, unite the members of the congregation into a genuine community, and form the believers to be faithful followers of Christ.

Under such authority the congregation cannot engage in battles over taste that make worship like the large chain restaurant, where nothing is prepared well and no one cares whether the customers eat anything good for them. Rather, worship will be like home cooking — only done by the chef at Diedra's — so that the food is nutritious as well as a delight to the eye and the soul. It will be the Bread of Life that worshipers receive.

Every Church Is Liturgical

Lest the reader think that the principles enunciated here apply only to what are called "liturgical" churches, which make use of previous centuries of church ordering, let me add a few other clarifications. The continued bashing of "liturgical" churches by church marketers who say that "liturgy doesn't appeal to contemporary people" is based on a misunderstanding of what liturgy is. The name *leitourgia* simply means "the work of the people." Since most churches involve worship participants in singing songs and in silently or vocally joining in the prayers, all are liturgical, according to the original meaning of the word.

In our time, the word *liturgy* usually signifies a church's ordering of its worship, and in fact all worship services have some sort of ordering. The pattern might not follow that of the traditional catholic mass, but most congregations usually develop customs over time that are generally adhered to week after week. Whether acknowledged or not, most worship services follow the habits of a liturgy.

Since the Scriptures repeatedly invite us all to join in the praise of the assembly, to sing to the LORD with thankful hearts, to pray and listen and heed, our question must be whether a particular congregation's practices or liturgy invites participation by the entire assembly. Our goal must be to create the possibility for every person present to become actively engaged in the encounter with God. Never should only pastors or musicians be the performers.

Some denominations have more formal liturgy and use elements dating from the earliest centuries of the Church, thus sharing worship materials with other Christian communities throughout space and time. These traditional liturgies are not boring in themselves, but they can be made so when they are led without carefulness. While there is no absolute standard of how things should be done, the Scriptures call us frequently to faithfulness, to decency and order, to attentiveness. Pastors and musicians and congregation members all need to follow the score of the symphony (to reemploy the analogy above) with more of a sense of the art of engaging in the "music-making" of every aspect in worship. Whatever forms and styles are used, they must be appropriate and be employed appropriately.

A good example of this sense of liturgy occurred one fall day in chapel at Gordon College in Massachusetts when the ordering included different kinds of involvement by all the people and drew on a wide range of resources new and old. A student ensemble led two contemporary songs — one a reminder of God's presence and the other a setting of Lamentations 3:22-23. Since I was unfamiliar with one of the songs and wondered if others might be, too, I had asked the music team to make sure that before singing everyone present heard the words and the melody clearly; the students did a great job of introducing both so that all could participate. Others offered a call to worship and prayers that cultivated Churchbeing. Even the announcements, which were about service projects, tied in well with my sermon theme of the challenge to be a genuine Christian community in this postmodern world. We closed with the hymn "God of Grace and God of Glory." Everything and everyone in the worship service — new music and old, prayers and message, students and faculty — worked together to receive from God "wisdom . . . courage for the living of these days!"

Godly Authority in an Age of Opinion[4]

In a postmodern world, where few people believe that there is any absolute or objective Truth and most people want to reject any configuration of authority, theologians are easily accused of foisting their own opinions on others if we try to suggest that some things have been discerned by the continually tested consensus of the Church to be normative for Christian life and worship. I learned the importance of making clear distinctions concerning the nature of the authority church leaders exercise as opposed to mere opinion when at a youth convocation a charming high school student asked me to comment on a moral issue. After I had carefully described some of the moral dimensions involved in the subject, she turned away saying, "I just wanted to know your opinion."

"That was not my opinion," I responded. "If I had given you my opinion, I would have said the opposite. But I am under the authority of God's Word, and I can't escape the scriptural moral directives as the larger Church has discerned them."

Of course, it would be easier to excuse all behaviors and let everyone choose whatever they want — but do we really love others if we allow them to rebel against God's designs for his human creation? Rather, God's immense love and mercy for us compel us to seek to be faithful to his Word. If our desire is to be formed by the narratives of the Scriptures to be God's people, then we must use our best tools to study the Bible and be submissive to what is learned by the whole Church in its *Spiritocracy*. This does not make God's Word oppressive, for the biblical narratives convince us that God commands what is good out of his grace and transforms his people into believers who want to live his best.

Similarly, I am convinced that we can draw some criteria from God's Word by which to assess what we do in worship; by which to learn better how the gifts of God can be employed; by which to choose carefully the best forms and materials for biblically faithful worship; by which to defuse the conflicts between advocates of certain "styles" of worship, between the clergy and the musicians, between the professionals and the laypersons. Worship is a moral issue (that is, some choices are better or worse than others), for how it is conducted can form participants to be anything from narcissistically inward-

4. This section contains part of my chapter, "Reaching Out without Dumbing Down: A Theology of Worship for Postmodern Times," in *Confident Witness, Changing World*, ed. Craig Van Gelder (Grand Rapids: Wm. B. Eerdmans Publishing Co., forthcoming). My thanks to Craig and to Judy Bos, administrator for the Gospel and Our Culture Network, for permission to use this modified version here.

turned to faithful in following Jesus in crucifying servanthood. What questions does the Word give us to help us, as the *charismacracy* of the Church, to think more theologically, biblically, and faithfully about worship? Throughout all my work on issues of worship I especially emphasize three fundamental criteria that I believe the biblical canon gives us for assessing what we do in worship and why — that God be the Infinite Center, that worship upbuild the Body, and that believers be nurtured in faith and life. These may lead to myriads of different choices in different parts of the world, but they never mean catering to everyone's tastes. Instead, if these are our primary guidelines, we will discover God's authority, under which we then will engage with all the Body in the process of exercising our authority to craft and lead worship according to the gifts given us to be pastors and teachers (and musicians) as gifts to the churches — until the day prophesied in Philippians 2:9-11, when the dominion of Christ is complete, and the medium and the message are finally perfectly one.

17

For Those Who Grieve

"Blessed are those who mourn, for they will be comforted. . . .
"Blessed are those who hunger and thirst for righteousness, for
they will be filled. . . .
"Blessed are the pure in heart, for they will see God.
"Blessed are the peacemakers, for they will be called
children of God.
"Blessed are those who are persecuted for righteousness' sake,
for theirs is the kingdom of heaven."

Matthew 5:4, 6, 8-10

Today I received in the mail an invitation to attend the closing celebration of the Holy Spirit Centre in Hamilton, Ontario, Canada. I led a retreat there many years ago for lay participants and for the Sisters of Social Service who ministered at the Centre. I am grieving with the sisters as they bring to a close more than fifty-two years of service at their lovely Mount Cenacle facility; I remember clearly their beautiful chapels and ten-acre grounds. I recall the buildings so well because it was there that I stayed for the first time ever in a "retreat master's" room, complete with a confessional. When I told the directing sister that I had thought only priests could stay in such a room, she informed me that the pope had once slept in the bed I was using. During the course of the weekend retreat, she also heightened my awareness (first implanted by a Benedictine spiritual directee and friends at Notre Dame) of the crisis many Catholic orders are enduring as aged sisters retire with no younger postulants to take their place. After serving selflessly for long years, many nuns have to wonder if the order will have adequate income to care for them in their old age.

The problem is a culture that trains its young to discard such old-fashioned notions as sacrifice, commitment, and service to God and fellow human beings.

The invasion into our churches of our culture's rejection of biblical virtues has led to deep woundedness in many of you reading this book. For that reason I felt it necessary to include the following four letters — for pastors, for musicians, for congregation members, and for congregational council/presbytery/board of elders members. (Even if you are not presently suffering because of some sort of conflict over worship, you might want to read this chapter to heighten your awareness of the pain others are experiencing.) These letters were not written for any one person in particular; rather, they respond to the many specific situations and injuries that have been reported to me by numerous persons at theological conferences and gatherings for church musicians, synod assemblies, presbyteries, councils, and denominational conventions.[1]

The sum of my message to each of you is this: You are the beloved of God — and that is costing you fiercely. Know that your tears are recorded by God.[2] Someday you will know for sure that all of this struggle has been worth it, just as the poet of Psalm 42–43 believed that whatever was preventing him from leading worship would someday end so that his hope to return would not be in vain. In the interim, please believe that *many* of us are enormously encouraged that you are willing to pay the price of pain to stand up for a better way than the easy road of popularity and success. We are immensely grateful that you keep persevering faithfully, trying to serve to the best of your abilities in your situation. There is no quick remedy; there is no technique to win over the opposition; there is no immediate fix. There is only the long haul and the meanwhile as we wait for Christ to come again and for that heaven when we will perfectly worship in all the splendor of God's tabernacle presence.

I purposely wrote "heaven when" in the preceding paragraph, for the

---

1. A counseling book that gives helpful suggestions for finding peaceful solutions in situations of woundedness is Kirk E. Farnsworth's *Wounded Workers: Recovering from Heartache in the Workplace and the Church* (Mukilteo, WA: WinePress Publishing, 1998).

2. See Psalm 56 and chapter 10, "Our God Records Our Tears," in Marva J. Dawn, *I'm Lonely, LORD — How Long? Meditations on the Psalms*, 2nd ed. (Grand Rapids: Wm. B. Eerdmans Publishing Co., 1998), pp. 65-72.

confinement of heaven in people's imaginations to a *place* rather than a *time* prevents us from experiencing the depth of comfort heaven can be to us now. These are extremely difficult times for those who want to take the Christian life seriously. "But the hour is coming," Jesus said, "and *is now here* [because of his presence], when the true worshipers will worship the Father in spirit and truth, for the Father seeks such as these to worship him" (John 4:23). It is because the Father is seeking us and calling forth the worship we are trying to offer, because Jesus is here with us and the Spirit empowering us, that we can continue against the odds to work for genuinely spiritual and truthful worship.

How ironic! As I write these words, the New York Philharmonic is playing on the radio a recording of the symphonic dances from Leonard Bernstein's "West Side Story" under his direction, and right this moment the song is "There's a Place for Us — Somewhere." The searching of the two lovers from opposite sides of the gang wars for a place to be together reminds us that people throughout time have yearned to be able to live their dreams of harmony — between two clashing races or families, between organists and pastors, congregational committees and professional leaders. There is not only a time but also a place where heaven exists now — and that is in the heart of God. I pray that you, wounded servant, may find strength and rest in that place, for you *are* God's beloved. Hang in there!

To Struggling Pastors

Dear Shepherd of Souls,

I know it is deathly hard for you these days to fulfill your call from God to be truly a *pastor*. You want what is good for the people; they want to be amused and entertained. You want to draw them away from their idolatries, and they want to bring those very idolatries into the congregation's worship.

You are probably also getting flak from other clergy — maybe even from your bishop. THE major crusades these days are to turn our worship services into evangelistic rallies (which have their own place), to sacrifice the Church's identity to be appealing to the masses and grow in numbers, to mistake our very particularity (which Jesus told us would be a stumbling block) for an inconsequential matter, to turn the office of pastoral ministry into the position of CEO.

BLESS YOU! Bless you a thousand times that you are resisting these pressures, for indeed they would mean the death of the Church if God were not always watching over his Bride and preserving a remnant. I used the term *crusades* above deliberately, for many people are getting brutalized with swords and spears in the process.

Certainly it helps us in these difficult days to keep remembering that the truth lies in the middle between two extremes. (Don't we wish we could KNOW the truth for sure and not have to wonder all the time whether we're wrong after all? How I wish I could KNOW God's presence more tangibly and more confidently hope that we can survive all this mess.) Anyway, here are the poles I see, between which we must find a faithful path:

worship has been too stuffy in the past	—	loss of form usually displaces content
churches have not been concerned for the unchurched	—	mass appeal sacrifices identity and integrity
our particularity has been oppressively proclaimed	—	it is eliminated completely
pastors were not "professional" enough	—	professionalism kills the pastoral spirit

I know that you are trying to find a positive middle between these extreme poles, and I commend you for enduring the tensions. I know that you make worship "accessible," but you have not allowed your personality to invade. You recognize that the Church's forms were developed to make rituals and words public (those of the whole Church) and open to any stranger. But congregation members probably still criticize you, saying that worship is not welcoming enough, when really the problem lies with them and their lack of hospitality. Thanks for your genuine leadership as you keep trying to equip the members for their ministries of outreach.

I know that you have done a good job of instructing people, so that they can understand what the Church is and why what we do is important as well as different from the world — and in all your instruction you have not changed what your congregation is as a community of those who follow Jesus. But you are being lambasted, aren't you, because when you attempt to pry people loose from their idolatries of success the shoe fits a bit too closely. Thanks for your continued graciousness in struggling to help people see that the best way to attract our neighbors is by being a people who have an alternative way of life that offers gifts of freedom and true love and generosity. Keep educating (that job has to be done so much more these days!). Probably on their deathbeds (hopefully sooner) the people will be glad that you wouldn't settle for easy coziness with no content, for affability instead of instruction, or for anything else that would have kept them from learning the deep truths of faith.

Some members certainly didn't like it when you insisted on preserving Advent and Lent, did they? Of course, the real problem is that some members want to eliminate all talk of sin or to get rid entirely of doctrines like the Atonement. You have always remembered that what we believe matters, that we need our doctrinal bones to keep the proper shape of the Church. Thanks for being so good at helping set people free from guilt by enabling them to face up to their sin. No, you are not being a pessimist if you don't let people escape the fact of the source of human brokenness; the Church certainly does not need mindless optimism. You keep a good balance of realism buoyed by genuine hope in the fullness of God's salvation. Well done, good and faithful servant! You are steadfastly proclaiming the gospel and not just happy twaddle.

And BRAVO that you insist on having your devotional time each day and your Sabbath day each week! Others can do the administrivia — but what your congregation truly needs is for you to be a *spiritual* leader. I am so grateful that you are actually *pastoral,* that you have such a shepherding heart for the souls in your care. Certainly some people object that you are more concerned for souls than for numbers, but some day the multiplication will be obvious to them. All those whom you are feeding so nutritiously will, in turn, feed other lambs. In my more angry moments, I sometimes think that pastors who don't care enough to give their congregants deeper worship are like the "hired hands" in John 10:1-18, who care nothing for the sheep, but only for their own fame. Thank you for your fidelity to the Word and prayer (Acts 6) and to the people you equip.

Oh, yes, one more thing: thank you that when you lead worship and preach you constantly point the congregants to God and not to yourself. I do indeed become immersed in God's splendor when I participate under your leadership. You haven't resorted to gimmicks or showiness, but you lead with genuine Joy. I know that such strength isn't appreciated as it should be these days, but you are following the footsteps of the great prophets and apostles — and often suffering the same fate.

I keep thinking about a remark you made when we were sitting together before that worship service at the conference last summer. You said something to the effect that you weren't getting as thrilled about the good worship at the conference as you had in former times. I was actually relieved to hear you say that, because sometimes I wonder why I don't experience the surging Joy that I often did in the past. But I know it is because I am so weighed down by concerns for the Church, so burdened by all the needs in the world around me, so tired from too much work and too fast a pace, etc., etc. It is often hard to let go of all that to let God come in all God's mystery and surprise. Anyway, it reminds me that I dare not depend on feelings to judge what God is doing with me as I worship him. Probably you are so overwhelmed by how much you are being hassled about worship that you are having trouble right now letting go when you are not in charge to simply let others lead you into the encounter with God.

There is nothing I can say to make your cross easier to bear, but know that in these dangerous times the Church is very blessed to have your leadership. You often seem to be alone, but throughout the kingdom of God there are many others going through the same tribulations as you. Everywhere I go there are pockets of resistance to the sales pitches and numbers games; please continue to be one of the models of faithfulness and countercultural integrity. And remember: there is a great cloud of witnesses cheering you on as you run this lonely race, as you fight this good fight of faith with weapons of love and grace and truth. *Shalom!*

I wish you peace and then Joy in your ministry and life.

To Wounded and Bruised Musicians

Dear Gifted Servant of Our God,

I know you are being accused of being elitist because you want to use the best music of all the ages as you play for worship. Your pastor even told you that you had no concern for the nonbeliever — although you told her about that fellow who came in off the street, listened to you practice, and insisted it was the most beautiful music he'd ever heard! Somehow it doesn't seem "blessed," does it, "when people revile you and persecute you and utter all kinds of evil against you falsely on [Christ's] account" (Matthew 5:11).

Let me thank you for your continued devotion to God's truth as you sort through new music to find the finest. Often you are being more theological than your pastor when you keep questioning some of the suggestions you are given for songs to use.

But it is terribly painful, isn't it, when you are told that all your training in church music and in organ technique won't be needed in the future. Why can't people see the difference between the rich splendor of great music (old and new!) and the flimsy monotony of the same three guitar chords over and over? You have done well in working hard to find better songs for the guitarists to play. And I know you have spent a lot of time arranging music so that the youth who play instruments in their high school bands can play for worship. You have helped many people to understand that it is not so much a question of style, but of what sounds capture specific texts best — that a wide variety of instruments (and the huge diversity of timbres and tones on the organ) show us more of the attributes of God.

What amazes me so much is that you have continued to be patient in teaching about music, even though you have been made the scapegoat for the whole congregation's failure to be outreaching. You are to be commended for your heroic efforts to make the worship of God as filled with beauty and awe as possible.

I call it heroic because you are not simply fighting the ignorance and narrow-mindedness of congregation members or the pastor; you are dealing with the entire anti-cultural direction of our society. The world monoculture produced by promotion and packaging is destroying genuine culture. And this push for everything to sound the same that has also invaded the churches is throwing out twenty centuries of church music development throughout the globe. Bravo for you that you are trying to give the people whom you serve a sense of the Church's praise throughout time and space!

You told me once that you would just die if you couldn't play the organ. I understand that: it is your gift to play it, and we are inwardly compelled to use our gifts to serve God — that is who we are! I know that this makes it especially hard right now because you feel that more and more your integrity is threatened. How far can you go along with what the pastor demands when you believe firmly that it is destructive to the spiritual life of the congregation? How can you talk with the pastor about your theological concerns when she seems to believe all the unbiblical advice of the church marketers?

I think two biblical texts give us some parameters. One is Paul's exhortation in Romans 12:18: "If it is possible, so far as it depends on you, live peaceably with all." And the opposite is this instruction from Jesus in Luke 10:10-11: "But whenever you enter a town and they do not welcome you, go out into its streets and say, 'Even the dust of your town that clings to our feet, we wipe off in protest against you. Yet know this: the kingdom of God has come near.'" Both texts call us to account.

We are commanded by the first to do absolutely everything we can to build up the community. We can never give up trying to talk with pastors who are not being theological, with church councils who are asking the wrong questions, with congregation members who have no training in being Church. We must swallow our pride, listen to just criticism, learn from our mistakes, and never stop trying to communicate the biblical/theological/ecclesiological bases for our musical concerns.

The second text is not an easy recipe for quitting, for it urges us to make sure first that our efforts have genuinely brought the kingdom of God. We don't work hard for good music merely to demonstrate our dexterity on the organ bench (or in conducting a choir or playing the guitar). But when we have done our best to serve God and his people well, there might come a time when we have to leave — not only for our own sake, but also for the sake of the community (rather than split a church by a fight between the musician and pastor or council). I pray that God will give you the wisdom to know when your efforts are no longer making any headway.

But in the meanwhile, know that I thank God every time I think of you, always making my prayer with Joy because of the way you bring the splendor of his presence to people through your exquisite music. I am lifted to the "seventh heaven" when I hear you play; it is indeed a foretaste of the feast to come. May God always give you your heart's desire, since your deepest love is to serve him in song. My love and prayers are with you.

To a Congregation Member

Dear Worshiper Who Wonders What Happened,

I know you are shell-shocked. The new pastor came in and threw out everything that had been meaningful to you in worship for the past several years since you joined the congregation. What can you do? After all, he's the pastor.

Yes, I know that many people thought the former pastor was too stiff in worship. But nobody expected that the new pastor's reaction to that would be to go to the opposite extreme and undo all the reverence and formality. I'm sure that you wonder why there can't be some point in the middle between these two extremes. You probably feel quite alone trying to create that point, since many of the congregation members are either mad or gloating, on the attack or on the defensive. As you have heard me say many times, the root problem is that the congregation members — and the pastor, too — need to learn to be a genuine community.

It seems hopeless, doesn't it? You have tried talking with the pastor, and he keeps insisting that you are both after the same goals. Deep inside you know that this is only partially true. Of course, you both are very concerned about all the people in the neighborhood who don't seem to care about God at all — at least they don't belong to any church. But you know that the way to give them God is not to reduce worship to a one-man show, with the addition of a few mindless songs repeated over and over *ad nauseum*. You feel that if something isn't done soon, all the good habits of worship the congregation formerly knew will be lost.

It seems to me that you have three choices. The first is the hardest, but the most worthwhile in the long run — and that would be to continue working on the process of conversing with the pastor until he can see the wisdom of the balance you are suggesting. I hesitate to urge you to undertake this, for I know it will be a grueling and, no doubt, very long process, and in the meanwhile you will find yourself starved for substantive worship. A great part of the process will be demonstrating your concern for the neighbors by your willingness to make endless calls on them, assist in follow-up with visitors, mentor new believers, and train them in the meaning and practice of worship. Perhaps you and the pastor can attend conferences on evangelism together; better yet, urge him to participate with you in a conference on worship sponsored by your denominational musicians' organization.

To sustain you for this arduous loyalty, be sure to keep your own spiritual life strong by means of devotional habits and good worship however you can get it. The process will be especially helped if you are seriously committed to the congregation as your primary community. Then you will endure the hard work out of love for them, as well as love for God and the stranger. There will be lots of pain — you're in the process of setting the broken bones of the Body, and there's pain in the rebreaking (because the bones are crooked now), the resetting, and the healing. But the whole Body will be very much stronger because you have persisted for its sake and helped it to survive more spiritually.

When I said you had three choices, I wasn't quite serious because the second would be simply to grin and bear what's happening. Fortunately I know you won't do that because you care too much about your faith and the Church. But I know you'll be tempted simply to let things go. That's exactly why churches are in so much trouble these days — because most people would rather not bother about it all when the leadership chooses directions that are harmful to the faith. We've been trained by our culture to be passive, and when too many congregation members remain dormant rather than trouble the waters, the result is catastrophic. I keep remembering Martin Niemoeller, a "confessing" Lutheran at the time of Hitler, saying that when the Nazis came for the infirm he didn't protest because he wasn't infirm — and the same for several other categories of people, including the Jews. But then, he said, "when they came for me," there was no one left to protest.

I'm certainly not saying, of course, that your situation is like the Nazi era. I'm simply wanting to alert Christians to the immensity of the problem in churches that so many members sit back idly and don't protest when the leadership makes decisions destructive of being Church. So thank you for your willingness to go the many extra miles and to bear many other people's share of the conversation and work. (I'm referring, of course, to Matthew 5:41

and the law that Roman soldiers could order Jewish peasants to carry their packs for one mile.)

The third choice is the last resort. If you find yourself still hitting your head against the wall after much effort, you might find it necessary to go elsewhere. You have heard me speak strongly against "church shopping," but that is a critique of those who simply change churches to be more entertained or to avoid being held accountable. Your situation is very much different from those who leave whenever they aren't being coddled. You would be leaving because you had done all you could and any further efforts would be destructive to the community and to your future service.

I know you won't make this choice too soon because of your commitment to the people of the community. And I know it will be a source of great grief to you if you have to make this choice — because you have said, "These are the people I want to grow old with." So I commend you to God and pray that the new pastor will recognize the wisdom of what you are urging long before such a step could become necessary.

Meanwhile, know that many of us are grateful for your heroic efforts to call your congregation to worship immersed in the splendor of our God. Know that many others throughout the denominations and the country are taking the same lonely stand; you are part of a great company of witnesses! My prayers are with you, too.

To the Congregational Leader

Dear Member of the Congregational Council/Presbytery/Board of Elders,

I know you are shell-shocked. The new pastor came in and immediately insisted that the congregation's worship be split into two kinds of services — one traditional and one contemporary — and you are already feeling a growing gap between people as some folks start arguing that one kind is better than the other.

I know the immense pain this is causing you! That young couple you had been mentoring in the faith is choosing to go to the "contemporary" service, and you are worried that their children are not learning the deep hymns of the faith. And — knowing you — I would expect that you miss the fine intermingling your congregation used to have, in which you learned new music, too.

Probably the pastor does not see how much this split is dividing the congregation and how destructive it is to both sides of the divide. I would guess that your congregational leadership council (or presbytery or whatever) is quite torn, too.

Though the obvious reason for this kind of worship service splitting is that the marketing gurus are telling pastors that this is what they should do, the deeper reasons for such decisions are desperate fears — fear on the part of the pastor or leaders that we are not keeping up in numbers with other congregations, panic over the decline in attendance, anxiety about complaints received, worry that the church will decline to nothing. Many pastors don't really understand the worship of the Church throughout time — they have not received much training in the subject — and they are not confident that it is what the world needs. Consequently, they don't lead it with much enthusiasm and don't train the people in the habits and skills of worship.

There are two very important things you can do in your present situation. One is to try to minister to the pastor and set him free from his fears. Help him to recognize that numbers are not the way to measure his success; urge him to remember that the call of Christians is to "make disciples." Remind him that attendance is more a matter of personal invitation and hospitality on the part of the whole congregation than it is of worship style. Assure him that you will do all you can to diffuse complaints and to lead conversations to resolve difficulties. Help him realize that what is especially needed in the congregation is the building of genuine community so that complaints can be discussed together.

The other important thing you can do is to help the council and the pastor learn more about worship — perhaps through a monthly discussion of a book (I can give you suggestions) or through attendance together at a worship conference sponsored by your denomination. If they refuse to do either of those, you can continue to bring short pieces — articles from church music journals, for example — to raise the issues.

I'm not so idealistic as to think either of these processes will be easy, for fears are deep and ignorance is stubborn. But if we "do not fear their fear" (as the Greek of 1 Peter 3:14 reads), our compassion and encouragement can often be vehicles for setting others free from their anxieties. Above all, "perfect love casts out fear" (1 John 4:18), so we must keep remembering that Christ is Lord of his Church and ultimately we are not responsible for its numbers and attendance and community life. We are accountable only for our faithfulness in serving God's purposes to the best of our abilities.

On the matter of educating the clergy on the subject of worship, I have discovered that usually they are glad to learn if they can be taught in a way that doesn't humiliate them. Pastors often see the errors of their decisions when they can be led gently to recognize how destructive of community life and true worship those decisions were.

But this takes a long time — and then it will be even longer before the two kinds of services can be gradually melded back into one composite of all kinds of music. All the hard work it will take, however, is worth it for the sake of restoring the community. And in the process the whole congregation will learn important habits of worship and compelling insights into the meaning of being Church.

If the pastor is completely impervious to your efforts, then follow the procedure of Matthew 18:15-20, always remembering that this is a pattern for winning back your brother. Find other members of the council or congregation to work together with you (I should have been saying this all along, so that you don't work on the fear-deliverance and educational processes alone). Most important, keep praying together with other members of the congregation who are concerned. Do all that you can in the meanwhile to sustain the church's community life.

My main purpose in this letter is not so much to give you instruction on what to do — because you are already working hard to teach people about worship. My chief desire is to help you know that you are not alone in your passion to hold the congregation together in worship. Many leaders in churches throughout the country and in every denomination are suffering from the results of this bad advice to have two kinds of worship in order to appeal to the world. I hear that advice so often that I frequently wonder if I'm wrong in opposing it.

But whenever I return to the Scriptures, I discover again why the advice is misguided. It is based on wrong definitions of worship, an inability to sustain the hard work of community in the face of the world's divisiveness and emphasis on choice, and ungodly fears about numbers and success. If we concentrated instead on creating worship filled with the splendor of God and the gifts of the community, on building genuine community life that reaches out to the world with generous hospitality, and on living the alternative way of life of Christ's disciples, then the world would be pounding on our doors wanting the gifts that the Church offers. Our model must be the early Church in its great alternativity, its eager proclamation of the Resurrection, its immense care for the neighbors, its careful catechumenal processes.

You have heard me say this many times: the root problem of most of the churches' woes is that all of us — congregations and pastors alike — need to learn what it means to be the community that is the Church. That is why the last thing we ought to do is divide the community along the lines of worship taste. The issue is more important than that immediate problem, so all your investment of energy in trying to end the division is well worth it. May God keep giving you the wisdom, gentleness, patience, and hope that you need to continue serving your congregation and your pastor in this critical work. Let me know how I can support you as you bear this burden by abiding in Christ.

Being Church: Forming Character

Ascribe to the LORD the glory of his name;
worship the LORD in holy splendor.

Psalm 29:2

If we truly acclaim the glory of the LORD's name — that is, his character — then we will be gradually formed into his likeness. As Paul declares, "all of us, with unveiled faces, seeing the glory of the Lord as though reflected in a mirror, are being transformed into the same image from one degree of glory to another; for this comes from the Lord, the Spirit" (2 Corinthians 3:18).

We worship God because God is so worthy. One of the results of our worship will be that we shall be changed. The more we embrace all that God is as we royally waste our time in his presence, the more his holy splendor will nurture our character. That is the thesis of the initial sermon in this section. "One Hundred *B'rakhot*" is a Jewish custom of acknowledging that God is behind everything; it leads to more thorough thanksgiving.

Many conflicts in churches over worship polarize into two sides, one of which is accused of wanting banality and the other of being elitist. Chapter 19 attempts to dig into the deeper yearnings and failures that lead to certain worship choices.

Because our society is increasingly unfamiliar with what a church is, what God's people believe, and how they live, we find ourselves in the same position as the earliest Christians who already near the beginning of their history began to develop catechumenal processes whereby those coming to faith from a pagan environment were mentored by experienced believers. Chapter 20 is a modified version of my chapter in a three-booklet series developed by the Evangelical Lutheran Church in America concerning the present-day catechumenate. My article for that collection ponders the idolatries and searchings that represent people's attempts to satisfy or repress by other means their profound need for God; then it shows how our mentoring can form them to know and experience how God alone quenches their thirst.

Chapter 21 emphasizes that in this age of excess subjectivity and abstraction or unframed overloads of information, children (and adults, too) need the interest of details and the comprehensiveness of a master narrative by which to understand them. Chapter 22 then gives two examples of children's sermons that underscore the importance of the Bible in our worship practices and character development.

To become God's people is, indeed, a royal waste of time; it won't really get us ahead in the world to be so different, to be suffering servants in the image of Jesus. However, what greater Joy can there be than to enter into the extravagant splendor of God, to live with the kind of character that ascribes to our LORD the glory due his name?

18

"One Hundred B'rakhot": A Sermon*

Texts for Thanksgiving Day: 1 Chronicles 29:10-13;
Philippians 4:4-7; Matthew 6:25-33

One of the best habits that we have had in the Church for hundreds of years is the set of phrases, "The Lord be with you. And also with you." Remember that we say these phrases in our worship services to keep in mind that we are gathered here as a community together. I can't preach well if you don't listen well, so as we say those phrases, please join in that commitment to participate with me and support me as we work together in this sermon.

The Lord be with you. [Response: And also with you!]

Let us pray. [Singing] *Baruch atah Adonai Elohenu melek ha-olam.* Blessed art thou, O LORD our God, King of the universe, that you have created this day in which to praise you, that you have brought us here to this house of worship — this place where we gather as your people to remember the kind of God that you are. *Baruch atah Adonai Elohenu melek ha-olam.* Amen.

You might have been shocked to hear a Hebrew prayer in this Lutheran worship service, but I think it is important to remember on this Thanksgiving Day that thanksgiving for us didn't start with the Puritans. Our roots as God's people go back to the Hebrew people. Let us together look very closely at our

---

*This is an edited transcript of a sermon given on Thanksgiving Day, November 27, 1997, at Bethel Lutheran Church in Cupertino, California.

Scripture lessons for today to consider one way in which we might live out our Jewish roots. Especially I would like to teach you the Jewish custom of the 100 *B'rakhot.* If you would please turn to today's first Bible reading from 1 Chronicles 29, beginning with verse 10, you will notice that David blessed the LORD in the presence of all the people gathered together. What he said begins with a form that the Jews call a *B'rakha,* from the Hebrew word *"Baruch,"* which means "blessed." "Blessed are you, O LORD, the God of our ancestor Israel forever and ever."

Observe carefully how this sentence is printed in the text; do you notice that the word LORD appears in capital letters? I encourage you to develop the habit of looking for the word printed this way whenever you are reading in the First Testament, for it tells us something very important. When the name LORD is written with all the letters capitalized in English, the word in the Hebrew text is the four-consonant name that we enunciate *Yahweh,* the name of the God who is, who called himself "I am," the God who always keeps his covenants with his people. That name signifies, among other things, that because God is, everything else falls into place. What I want you to notice in 1 Chronicles is that most of David's prayer in verses 10-13 is composed of recounting what that "I am" is like.

The Hebrew line I sang began with *"Baruch,"* which means "blessed," *"atah,"* (you), and then *"Adonai,"* which is *not* the Hebrew word for the name "I am." The Jews were so worried about blaspheming God's name, *YHWH,* that they never spoke it, but said the name *Adonai* or "Master" (Lord) instead. Don't you wish such respect still existed today? In fact, among Orthodox Jews it does. They will not say the name *God* because they do not want to mis-speak it. This morning as we think about Thanksgiving we could benefit from a bit more of their awe and reverence, their concern that we not mis-speak what God is like.

Notice the description David gives us of this God in the next few verses. This is a God who has all the greatness, the power, the glory, the victory, the majesty. All that is in heaven and earth is his. His is the kingdom. He is exalted as head above all. All strength comes from him. Indeed, if we have a God like that, is there anything to worry about?

Have you noticed how often in the Bible the great saints pray like this: "Blessed are you, O LORD our God, that you are like such and so; you are like this and that, and you have done everything and anything, and you have taken care of whomever and whenever" — and therefore it becomes really easy to ask for whatever is needed. You and I often reverse the proportions, don't we? We spend all our time asking for things or worrying about situations. My point this morning is that if we thought more about the character of our God, we wouldn't have to worry about what we ask.

My favorite example of this practice is Daniel. When Daniel was in a terrible predicament, for the king was about to say "Off with your head" because he was observing his ritual practices of worshiping the God of Israel — at such a time Daniel prayed by naming all sorts of things about God, and then he said, "Well, God, since that's what you're like, everything will be fine." That is a rough paraphrase of Daniel, of course, but its point is clear.

You can notice the same practice in Moses, in David, in Elijah, and in all the great Jewish prophets, in Mary, in Deborah, in Hannah, and in all the great Jewish women. All of them focus on the character of God — and then, because this is what God is like, they trust that everything else will ultimately fall into place.

The habit that I want us to consider this morning is the Jewish practice of trying to say at least 100 *B'rakhot* a day. That word *B'rakhot* is the plural form of the noun *B'rakha;* as I mentioned earlier, it comes from the verb at the beginning of the Hebrew prayer, "Blessed are you" or *"Baruch atah."* Can you imagine what it would be like if you tried at least 100 times a day to say sentences like these: "Blessed are you, O LORD our God, King of the universe, that you have created men and women with intelligent minds who have invented alarm clocks so that I woke up on time this morning"; "Blessed are you, O LORD our God, King of the universe, that you have caused the sun to shine and the rain to fall so that the fruits of the harvest could be made into this breakfast cereal"? How might this change our attitudes?

What the Jews sought — and still seek — to accomplish by saying 100 *B'rakhot* a day was to find Joy in every aspect of life because of their sense that God is behind it all. Since we eat packaged food, and live in packaged houses, and have plenty of appliances and conveniences, it's quite easy to forget that God is the source of everything. The value of saying a *B'rakha* is that we keep remembering that God is King of the universe after all, and therefore he's in control of all that happens. And because he is, everything will be quite all right.

Yet, of course, it's *not* quite all right. So how do we deal with the fact that life doesn't go very well? You and I worry and get anxious and don't know quite what to do sometimes about all the things that go wrong, all the messes in our lives. Just think how it might change our perspectives if we would respond to those negative things, those twists in our plans, those subversions and corruptions and sins against us with "Blessed are you, O LORD our God, King of the universe, that you have created us with spirits to trust you, that you have undergirded us throughout our lives, that you have throughout our history demonstrated your faithfulness."

If I asked you all today to tell me about your ethnic heritage, most of you would probably answer that you are German, or Norwegian, or Swedish. I wonder if any of you would say "Jewish" — for all of us have our faith roots in Hebrew beliefs. What a blessing it is that we Gentiles have been "grafted on" to the Jewish stock, as the Scriptures say. Because this is the source of much of our knowledge of God, let me invite you to enter into this particular habit of our forebears — to know this thankfulness and praise — so that in all of our lives we can put everything into the right perspective. Think how saying 100 *B'rakhot* would change our disposition, our way of life, our behavior because the practice would keep us more mindful of God's gracious gifting.

Now I have to confess: I'm the chief of sinners. I had already planned this sermon more than a week ago, and yet, this Tuesday when I got hung up in airports and had a terribly bumpy ride flying into San Francisco because of the violent rainstorms, missed the bus to San Jose, got soaking wet waiting at the bus stop with myriads of cars going by and splashing me with all the water that was pouring down, I was *not* thankful. I got to Cupertino about 2 a.m., and when my nephew greeted me and asked how I was, the first thing I answered was "Grumpy!" I don't practice very well what I preach, which is why I need this sermon probably more than you. (But I'm sure you need it too.)

Perhaps some of us came to worship this morning hoping for a nice little sentimentalized pat on the back so that we could go home and overeat and feel good about ourselves. But I don't intend to give you a nice sermon. I intend to open the way for God to change our lives. I intend to challenge us all by asking, "Is this our life pattern: to remember that God is at the root of all good gifts and gracious unfoldings?"

Let's observe the practice of Jesus, who was a faithful Jew. Look at today's Gospel lesson from Matthew 6:25-33. The first thing that always strikes me in this passage is how hilariously funny it is. Certainly it is good Jewish humor from Jesus — and we are reminded that sometimes the only way to take the Bible seriously is to let its whimsy tickle us and point out our ludicrousness. Jesus says, "And can any of you by worrying add a single hour to your span of life?" The original Greek actually says, "add a cubit." A cubit is the length from the tip of your forefinger to your elbow. Isn't that splendidly comic? Could we by worrying add this much to our height, or add so much to the length of our days? Certainly all of us in the United States today know that worry is the very thing that subtracts years from our lives!

Jesus pokes fun at us and says, "Aha, your worry doesn't get you anywhere, does it?" In fact, psychologists estimate that 95 percent of the things we worry about never happen. What a stupid waste of time!

Jesus then continues to tell us what we could do instead. "Look at the birds. Look at the lilies. Look at the grass. Look at the way your Father takes care of these." I can imagine Jesus, in his faithfulness, saying, *"Baruch atah Adonai"* — "Blessed are you, O LORD our God, King of the universe, that you have caused the sun and the rain to produce for us the lilies and the lilacs, the roses and the rhododendrons, the daffodils and the daisies and the dahlias." "Blessed are you, O LORD our God, King of the universe, that you provide seed for the birds to eat and grapes from the grapevine." "Blessed are you, O LORD our God, King of the universe, that everything is under your control and I need not worry about it."

Notice the model that Jesus gives us — and then he asks us, "Why do you have such little faith? Are you like the Gentiles? Do you not know how to do 100 *B'rakhot?* Are you just like the pagans?"

You and I have been grafted on to the Jewish roots of Christ's first disciples. We get to share in the understandings of the people of God who know Who our God is, the great "I am," the LORD, the King of the Universe. Therefore, why do we have such little faith that we would sit around worrying?

Jesus tells us in verses 32-33 what to do instead: remember that your Father knows. He is, after all, the King of the universe. Seek his kingdom. (And we seek his kingdom by knowing the King.) Seek his righteousness by saying a *B'rakha* so that you'll keep remembering what God is like. Thereby you can become like that God and live that God's way in the world — knowing that everything you need will be added to you.

This morning's reading from the apostle Paul likewise teaches us this lesson well. Look at the Epistle lesson from Philippians 4:4-7, and remember that Paul was also a faithful Jew, who probably practiced the *B'rakhot*. Notice verse 6, which we can paraphrase, "But when you are giving your requests to God in prayers and supplications, do that with thanksgiving." If, when we implore God, we always remember, "Blessed are you, O LORD our God, King of the universe, that you are continually faithful to hear and answer our prayers," then we will surround our petitions with gratitude and know that God will answer them in a way that is best for us. We can trust that.

The great blessing of the *B'rakhot* is that they teach us to trust. We realize that if this is the sort of God we have, then we certainly have nothing to fear. That is why Paul can say at the beginning of this Epistle lesson, "Rejoice in the LORD always; again I will say, Rejoice."

Some of you might be thinking, "I just can't rejoice all the time." But let me remind you that this practice is not one you have to do all by yourself — though when you yourself are able to rejoice, it will be enormously beneficial. It would be better for us this morning if we would express the original Greek in the colloquial, "Rejoice y'all." We don't usually read it that way because our

English language doesn't convey the plurality of the verb. God is not commanding, "Rejoice as an individual"; God is urging, "Rejoice as a people." We rejoice together. One of the reasons we need to gather here for worship on Thanksgiving Day is because our own expressions of thanks are too shallow, too flimsy. We need the whole Body of the people of God. If I'm ill and can't remember what the Joy of the gospel is, you can remember for me; you can stand next to me and sing these wonderful hymns of the faith and remind me of what our God is like.

We do the *B'rakhot* together. Because we are the people of God, we gather in this worship service together to listen attentively to the words of Scripture and hear this magnificent choir, to sing hymns of faith and rejoice together in God's bounty.

We gather together, and we are helped by each other to do this rejoicing, to do this thanksgiving, because we are part of a people. One severe problem with churches in the United States is that we have lost our Jewish sense that we are God's *people,* not persons — that we are part of a whole Body of people who remember together who God is.

Since we know this God, our lives are changed. That's why Paul can say in verse 5, "your gentleness [can] be known to everyone." When you are doing 100 *B'rakhot,* it gives you much more patience. All of this is possible, Paul declares, because God is so near. Every time we say, "Blessed are you, O LORD our God, King of the universe," we realize what a magnificent gift it is that this God who is Monarch of the entire cosmos could care to be with us.

"The Lord is near." Blessed are you, O LORD our God, King of the universe, that you have condescended to come to be among us as our Messiah and to be like us, to give us your Spirit, to inhabit us. Therefore we rejoice. Therefore we need not worry. Therefore we can bring all of our concerns to God with thanksgiving — trusting God, knowing that God, in all God's grace and mercy, cares for us as we need.

That is why in verse 7 Paul writes, "And the peace of God, which surpasses all understanding, will guard your hearts and your minds in Christ Jesus." Our translations say "surpasses," but it seems to me that often God's peace simply "bypasses" our understanding. We might not comprehend everything, but we don't have to, because God does. With our finite brains we get so upset or anxious or worried about things because we can't figure out how they will turn out. Let us instead remember, "Blessed are you, O LORD our God, King of the universe. You are in charge; and because you are — with love as well as power — I can know that everything will ultimately be well." Thus we experience the *Shalom* of God — not because we understand, but because we trust.

"One Hundred B'rakhot": A Sermon

What will happen the rest of today? And what will happen the rest of your life? I hope we don't go from this place and simply say, "Well, that was nice." This sermon will have failed if it is only nice — or only interesting. Rather, may it challenge you to become a practitioner of the 100 B'rakhot. This is a sermon asking you — and asking me — after we leave this worship service and when we are tempted to complain to say instead, "Blessed are you, O LORD our God, King of the universe, that, even in this mess I see, you are still LORD." It is asking us to go from this place and not take for granted the plethora of blessings we have, the overabundance of good gifts we have been given. Saying the 100 B'rakhot will remind us of the source of our great wealth, so that we bless that God and join that God in caring for those who don't have such bounty. (It is a good start that this morning this congregation has gathered the wonderful cornucopia of gifts for others that is here at the front of the sanctuary. May we multiply that exceedingly in the days and years to come!)

May we go from this place so eager to bless the LORD our God, the King of the universe, that we become like him and share his goodness with the world. I'm inviting each of us into a change of perspective, into a change of heart, of mind, of body, of life.

Let us pray: [singing] *Baruch atah Adonai Elohenu melek ha-olam.* Blessed are you, O LORD our God, King of the universe, that you have in your grace and mercy created us to be your people, a people of thanksgiving all of our lives. May we never forget that you are the source of all our gifts, so that we are set free from our worries to share our wealth eagerly with the world in need. Amen.

19

Do They Really Want *Such Banality?*
or Are We Really *Hearing the Yearnings?*

I solemnly urge you: proclaim the message; be persistent whether
the time is favorable or unfavorable; convince, rebuke, and encourage, with the utmost patience in teaching. For the time is
coming when people will not put up with sound doctrine, but
having itching ears, they will accumulate for themselves teachers
to suit their own desires, and will turn away from listening to the
truth and wander away to myths.

2 Timothy 4:1b-4

Recently a very gifted organist, who has devoted his life to learning about
church music and to playing it with excellence for the people he serves,
asked me sadly, "Do the people really want this banality they are getting when
they turn away from our churches where worship is rich and deep?"

I am not concerned in this chapter with debating whether or not what
people turn to is indeed banal — for such discussion could easily degenerate
into elitism or argue merely for what is a matter of taste. Rather, I am concerned about the reasons why people turn away from churches where musicians work hard to serve them. Too often the musicians get blamed, and that
seems to me to be scapegoating.

What I want most to consider in this chapter is the issue of how we
might really care about the people in our world — and specifically, to hear

better the yearnings that cause people to turn away from worship that could nourish faith and develop Christian character in them. First, however, it is necessary for us to recognize what idolatries lead to the problems at issue in this chapter.

What Idolatries Invade the Church?

In 1996, the Gospel and Our Culture Network sponsored a conference called "Confident Witness — Changing World," which studied the progression from culture to gospel by means of the Church. In order to discern the various aspects of our society that influence worship, my workshop focused on the way certain values in the culture become idolatrous as they invade our congregations. In the two workshop sessions, participants named and described various idolatries — and I urged them to see that many of those sacralizations lead to polarizations with an opposing idolatry. Thus, in relation to the question at the beginning of this chapter, an assumption that people are turning to what is banal might lead to an idolatry of the opposite kind of music, elitism about taste, smugness about knowing better. Recognizing our own temptations, then, not only helps us to sympathize with nonbelievers or other believers, but also reveals some of the forces that deflect our worship services from their biblical purposes. In my two workshop sessions, the following idolatries were named:[1]

materialism	spiritualism
busy-ness, efficiency	
bigger	smaller
the new	the old
traditionalism	contemporaryism
the 90's/2000's sound	favorite old hymns
organs	guitars
musical elite/classical	combos/contemporary
musical style, particular liturgical form	

---

1. This list and the following paragraph of summation also appear in my chapter, "Reaching Out without Dumbing Down: A Theology of Worship for Postmodern Times," in *Confident Witness, Changing World*, ed. Craig Van Gelder (Grand Rapids: Wm. B. Eerdmans Publishing Co., forthcoming). My thanks to Craig and to Judy Bos, administrator for the Gospel and Our Culture Network, for permission to use this material here.

entertainment, feeling good,
    comfort
anonymity   the inner circle
vicarious subjectivity, famous
    people, performance
self-esteem
the Word
charismatic personality (pastor or
    worship leader or musician)
expectations for what one will get
    out of the worship service
expectations for a certain style —
    for example, from blacks, women, etc.
passivity
boredom
order   chaos
technique, gimmicks
the congregation or leaders as
    vendors of religious goods
looks, show, makeup, clothes
haughty ritual   no ritual
power
money
instant gratification
competition, success, numbers
keeping up with the Joneses of
    other churches
program
building, furnishings, art, musical
    instruments
quiet   no silence
homogeneity   diversity for its own sake
forced inclusivity
clericalism
choice, consumer mentality,
    church shopping
knowledge   feeling
television
leisure
sports

```
mountains, beaches — glories
    of the Pacific NW that beckon
    on Sundays
lay ministry                              elite, professionalism
optimism                                  pessimism
democracy
nationalism                               hatred of our country
identity
"expansionism instead
    of mission,"2 sheep stealing
frivolity, fun, amusement
```

I have refrained from imposing any order on the list. Recognition of various idolatries by the two groups was random, though obviously sometimes one insight touched off several others. Sometimes the way the idolatry affects worship is not immediately apparent. Rather than duplicate the discussion here, I will leave the list to generate the reader's own reflection on how these cultural/ religious idolatries might be infiltrating your congregation and its worship. Some of the idolatries on the list were immediately paired as the participants began to realize that two values might be dialectical opposites, both of which are necessary in worship and both of which can be taken to an unhealthy or unbiblical extreme. Many of the items on the list can be very good attributes in the character of a congregation until they are excessively pursued or understood rigidly. All of us who plan or lead and/or participate in worship must be wary lest personal tastes or ideologies determine our choices and reactions. We must ask better questions about the meaning of worship.

Character Formation as a Goal

As noted above, my major consideration in response to the question that began this chapter is to ask how we might really care about the people in our world — and specifically, how we could better hear the yearnings that drive people to leave worship that could nourish more substantive faith and develop Christian character in them. A brief sketch of my background might explain a bit why these are my interests.

---

2. Douglas John Hall used this phrase in his plenary address for the Gospel and Our Culture Network conference. See his essay "Metamorphosis: From Christendom to Diaspora," in *Confident Witness, Changing World.*

I grew up in the Lutheran Church, with a strong biblical background from Lutheran elementary school and from devout parents who taught there and with a strong worship background because my father was an organist, choir director, and superb composer. Consequently, I address worship issues out of lifelong participation in music making and out of lifelong training in Scriptures and ethics — so I ask questions out of a desire for churches' worship to be biblically faithful and for that worship to form its participants to be biblically faithful.

Furthermore, I was a gung-ho evangelist as a child. Starting in the fourth grade, I had a newspaper route, and I used to ask my customers if they knew Christ. (I know now that this wasn't very tactful, but at least I wasn't pushy and they knew that my question was genuinely sincere.) I was always inviting people to worship, making up new songs as I pedaled around my route, and leading my friends in Bible studies. Evangelism, worship, music, nurturing faith — those were the big things in my life (along with sports). My favorite subjects in school were religion and memory work and singing/band (I was put in the high school band at the end of sixth grade).

My first teaching job was in the English department at the University of Idaho, and I wound up teaching Literature of the Bible. Because there was a deep spiritual ferment on the campus at the time, many students came to talk to me about faith — and some of them started coming to the Lutheran church near campus. I spent countless hours teaching students about Christ and about worship.

After that I went into campus ministry at the same school and at nearby Washington State University by being based at a Lutheran church near the latter. There I directed an adult and a youth choir and helped with a high school/college student singing team. I also led the music for the Sunday school openings and wrote/directed folk services and Christmas programs. Meanwhile, I was working with hundreds of college students at all stages of faith and worship participation. Evangelism, worship, music, nurturing faith — those remained the principal foci of my life. I don't think that has changed very much in all the years since then, through different church jobs, four more graduate degrees, twenty years of freelancing as a theologian, and worldwide training of seminarians and church leaders.

I list all this because some people charge that I am too idealistic in trying to duplicate my own childhood biblical and musical training in an age that is too different for that to happen. I have plenty of experience in teaching people about worship and training young people in choirs (and I have numerous friends who do the same), so I know that it can be done. (I am not an academic ivory towerite, as some critics like to say, but a teacher and musician who has been in the trenches working with believers and nonbelievers for more than thirty years.)

Moreover, one can't read passages like Deuteronomy 6:4-9 ("Recite [these words] to your children and talk about them when you are at home and when you are away . . . ," v. 7) or 2 Timothy 1:3-14 ("I am reminded of your sincere faith, a faith that lived first in your grandmother Lois and your mother Eunice and now, I am sure, lives in you . . . ," v. 5) without realizing that the nurturing families of those texts existed in times and places as unfaithful as ours. If we all give in to despair and give up trying to encourage deeper nurturing of faith and character in our churches, especially in our worship, then what will happen?

In an age "when people will not put up with sound doctrine, but having itching ears . . . will accumulate for themselves teachers to suit their own desires," who will call them back to listening to the truth and away from the myths (2 Timothy 4:3-4)? The writer to Timothy responds to the situation by urging him to "preach the word; be ready in season and out of season, reprove, rebuke, exhort, with great patience and instruction. . . . be sober in all things, endure hardship, do the work of an evangelist, fulfill your ministry" (4:2 and 5, NASV).

All of this is to say that when we wonder why so many people are leaving churches of deeper nurturing for others that offer what might seem banal, our response must be to ask deeper questions, to try to understand what concerns might underlie their leaving, to see how we are failing, and to work for positive change so that all can be nurtured — recognizing all the while that this will require of us serious hard work, the courage to "hang in there" when what we do is "out of season," great patience and lots of instruction, the ability to endure hardship and suffering, fervent evangelism, and zeal to carry out our ministries fully.

Concerns and Responses

Lest this essay get too long, let me sketch only briefly some of the reasons why people leave our churches' worship, what seem to me to be inadequate — or even harmful — responses, and what efforts we might expend instead. I am convinced that people leave for real reasons, so we cannot respond without going beyond what might seem to be a choice for the banal.

1. It seems to me that a large proportion of people leave more traditionally oriented churches because *they are searching for intimacy and think it can't be found in "liturgy."* Our culture is one of immediacy — and especially

immediacy of intimacy, even though the result is a false one. What I mean by that is that talk show intimacy, cyberspace intimacy (unless the relationship is founded in other ways that include genuine vulnerability and more total knowledge of the other person), casual genital intimacy, and other similar deceptions have generated the impression that all feelings of closeness should be directly and instantly available.

Many churches respond to this genuine yearning by dumping everything from worship that seems more remote and joining the rush to instantly available feelings of coziness. I believe that this is, in the long run, harmful to worshipers, for it doesn't deal with the needs for deep consciousness of God's presence, deep relationship with God, and deep intimacy with others — needs all aggravated by the profound loss of true intimacy in the technicization of our cultural milieu.[3] There is not space in this book for me to outline all the research, but it is important for us to realize that certain styles of music actually generate "feelings" of intimacy by the way the sound vibrations affect us physically (see Chapter 26 for a brief sketch). It is crucial that the intimacy with God we offer in worship be based on God's character as a God of relationship and not on musical manipulation.

What we must do, therefore, is surround and fill our worship with genuine intimacy — true friendship on the part of congregational members, genuine care for the person sitting next to us, the truest intimacy with God, which is based not merely on feelings but on how God reveals himself to us. The pastor of my hometown congregation calls every person by name when he or she comes to the Lord's Supper and as everyone leaves the sanctuary. He gets to know visitors before worship begins and names them also. In contradiction of the marketing gurus' predictions, the church has liturgical worship (using a wide variety of new and old music) and is yet growing at an astonishing rate. One of the reasons for this growth is the phenomenal pastoral care of this man who offers the genuine intimacy of knowing our names and the even deeper love of God revealed in the splendor of worship. (I warned you that all the points in this discussion are going to take serious hard work! But I am convinced that the extra teaching and care are worth it, for God is worthy of our deepest love and best praise.)

2. We must expand point #1 to add that *people are searching for genuine*

---

3. For more on the influence of technicization on intimacy, see Jacques Ellul, *The New Demons*, trans. C. Edward Hopkin (New York: Seabury Press, 1975), pp. 70-80; see also Marva J. Dawn, *Sexual Character: Beyond Technique to Intimacy* (Grand Rapids: Wm. B. Eerdmans Publishing Co., 1993), and Marva J. Dawn, *Truly the Community: Romans 12 and How to Be the Church* (Grand Rapids: Wm. B. Eerdmans Publishing Co., 1992; reissued 1997).

community. We must face this fact: churches stuck in traditionalistic ruts are not known to be very hospitable.

I think enough has been said in Chapters 13-17 of this book to merit no further dwelling on this issue here. However, many churches respond to the need for community by turning the worship service into "communal gush." This is harmful for two reasons: (1) good feelings radiating in a worship setting often do not translate into a relationship that lasts in tough times; and (2) often these good feelings take the place of communal formation by God's Revelation.

Having said that, however, I must urge congregations such as the one represented by the organist who asked the question at the beginning of this chapter to learn to be more hospitable. This organist was serving the people well with his musical gifts; members of the congregation, however, were failing to be hospitable. Genuine community is much more than good feelings generated by cozy music, but people can hardly discover what that true relationship entails if they are alienated from the beginning by coldness or total neglect.

3. People often leave churches that nurture deeper faith and Christian character because *they long for the emotional high of "praise" worship.* Since ours is an age in which "exciting," "thrilling," "sensational," and "dynamic" are the key words (my husband is sick of every year's "new and exciting" programs for elementary school teachers), we must recognize that the whole cultural ethos militates against our attempts to offer worship with more substance. We must also realize that people need these emotional highs because so much in life is scary, chaotic, shifting, or anxiety-ridden. When much of life is a "downer," can we blame people for wanting worship to give them an "upper"?

If churches respond to this need merely by turning their worship services into an emotional lift, however, they will have to increase the hype constantly in order for that to remain effective. Like drugs or alcohol, emotional highs need intensifying escalation to be sufficient.

Our churches instead must help worship participants to learn that objective truths about God give a more lasting high. To learn deeper truth might not seem to be so wonderful at first, but it is a Joy that stays. To become a person of more profoundly Christian character might not seem to give the immediate emotional boost that is sought, but it provides the spiritual resources necessary for dealing with the chaotic and tension-causing situations of daily life in the long haul.

4. *Many people are searching for greater freedom of self-expression* — the freedom to move or clap, to be enthusiastic or more exuberant. It is certainly

true that many traditionalistic (note that adjective carefully) worship services seem to put people in a straitjacket.

However, as many churches turn their worship services completely into self-expression, three negative results must be noted. The first is that worship becomes *private* devotional praise instead of *corporate* worship. The second is that the freedom becomes libertinism if there is no disciplining boundary. And the third is that self-expression itself can become what is worshiped, and the idolatrous focus can become not God, but how much fun it is to be jiving. That last comment might seem too harsh to some readers, but it arises from the admissions of countless young people at their convocations, in small group or dinner table conversations, in Sunday school classes, and in camp staff training sessions.

Because this particular yearning in people reveals the dialectical dangers of extremes, it is important for churches to realize that the solution lies at neither pole. Traditionalistic worship with excess sternness has been replaced with the opposite side of an oversupply of hype. The issue quickly becomes one of taste. If instead worship planners choose elements according to criteria that go beyond taste (some suggestions are offered in Chapter 26), then a wide variety of styles can be used in worship that allow greater freedom of expression by a larger diversity of people. However, those choices are made according to theological and character-forming criteria so that it is not *self-expression* but worshipful response to God. It is a self formed by God, rather than a selfish one; it is true freedom because it arises from discipline; it is Joy-full participation because it is an investment of the total self.

5. On the opposite side, *in an entertainment culture, some people would prefer to remain passive in worship.* These people do not want more enthusiastic involvement in worship; they want only to sit back and watch.

Many churches decide to cater to this "couch potato" lifestyle by reducing worship to easy listening with not much involvement, with everything done by the pastor and worship band. This is detrimental to character formation because faith must be *practiced*, because to worship God requires investment of ourselves.

How can we help people see that relationship with God requires work, but that the work is vastly fulfilling? I really mean that adverb *vastly* because to invest ourselves in God not only will be gratifying to ourselves but will also be beneficial to the cosmos.

If people leave our churches for worship that requires less of them, we have to realize that it is the whole passive culture we are opposing — but also if they leave for a place that looks like more fun, we have to ask ourselves if we are displaying adequately the Joy that it is to worship God with effort. Maybe people leave because they don't see in us that the work of worship is worth it.

6. Closely related to all of the points above is our culture's *idolatry of the new.* Many people leave churches that could be nurturing of faith and character for those which offer what is new (and thus is thought to be more exciting), or the people simply change churches to give themselves something new. Much of this arises because we live in an age that rejects authority, tradition, hierarchy, anything that seems too outdated to be relevant.

Some churches respond by throwing out the old traditions and plunging into the new without adequate theological thought, or preparation, or sorting of the new, or recognition of the weaknesses associated with some things new. Other churches respond in the opposite way by clinging so tightly to the old that the traditional is worshiped instead of God. Both extremes wind up with less than the whole Church.

What we must do instead is use new music and new forms responsibly — without sacrificing content simply to be new, with careful attention to theological and musical questions in choosing the new (see Chapter 26), with adequate teaching so that the congregation welcomes the new, and without losing the great gifts from the past. By doing so we will help people see the value of the larger narrative, of being part of the whole Church throughout space and time, of biblical authority, of roots in tradition, of constant reformation and renewal, of anchored wisdom with fresh vitality, of all that we can learn from every epoch.

7. One more hidden reason why people leave churches with worship more rooted in the traditions of the Church for those with more culturally appealing worship forms is our society's *rejection of the sacred.* I use this strong description because it is important for us to see the source of our culture's need to uproot itself from all tradition.

Many churches respond to this impulse by rejecting all the forms by which the Church has understood worship during its long history. At its foundation, this is not so much a veto of the forms as a denial of the Church as the carrier of God's revelation, of the Spirit's guidance as these forms were developed, of the authority of the Body, of the sacred inspiration of the biblical texts that were the core of those worship practices.[4] Sometimes the rejection of the sacred is more obvious in the elimination of all awe and reverence from worship, in reducing God to his immanence without any sense of transcendence.

---

4. An excellent resource concerning the Church's development of its worship practices is Gordon W. Lathrop's *Holy Things: A Liturgical Theology* (Minneapolis: Augsburg Fortress, 1993).

I am sure that some readers will think that previous paragraph too strong, but hear me clearly. I am not saying that all the traditions are sacred. I am saying that God has been behind their development (even though human error is also part of the process), so we cannot throw them all out willy-nilly without more careful discernment of what is of God and what might be human idolatries.

It is urgently necessary that we state the case overly rigorously so that we can see the danger when churches think that by themselves they can devise something better than the whole Church (though both are under God). As we learned from Leszek Kolakowski in Chapter 4, "To reject the sacred is to reject our own limits."[5] Of course, Kolakowski is talking about the total rejection of the sacred by modernity in its worst forms, and I'm certainly not accusing churches of doing that. But Kolakowski has caused me to think more seriously about the immense danger when churches think they can free themselves from all tradition and be totally autonomous from the whole Church as the bearer of the sacred.

The opposite side is equally dangerous — when churches think that God hasn't done anything new for the last one hundred years or even in the last ten years. The traditionalist side can be almost equally reductionistic of the sacred — although in general the tradition itself is rooted in a greater sense of God's transcendence and a larger sense of the Church because it arose in a culture that had not yet so thoroughly rejected the sacred.

What churches must do, in the face of our culture's rejection of the sacred, is offer worship that gives the largest vision possible of the full splendor of God. This requires careful attention to what the Church has learned over time about how worship can do that, and it requires the best use of all the tools — new and old — for displaying God's splendor and immersing worshipers in it.

8. Many people leave churches that intend to offer deeper nurturing because *they do not understand why we do what we do when the Church worships.*

What many churches do in response is eliminate anything that is different from the surrounding culture and reduce their worship services to a few songs that are simple to sing, a band that always plays in ways that sound familiar, and a preacher who does everything else. The misconception frequently touted is that worship should be user-friendly. I am certainly not advocating worship that alienates or is totally inaccessible, nor do I think people ought to need a great amount of education before worship can be meaningful

---

5. Leszek Kolakowski, *Modernity on Endless Trial* (Chicago: University of Chicago Press, 1990), p. 73. See the context of the larger quotation in Chapter 4, pp. 40-41 above.

to them, but I am warning against the constant reduction of anything that stretches people, of anything that makes them uneasy. The Scriptures make it clear that being confronted by God is not always comfortable or comforting. Reductionistic worship is extremely harmful because it sacrifices the identity of the Church (which people in our unchristian culture of course don't understand yet) and of God, for God is not easily understandable. We must be careful that it is not God's earthly servants who offend, but the Lord of the gospel himself is a stone of stumbling and a rock of offense. User-friendly worship seems to me to sacrifice an awe-full lot of God. Moreover, believers must learn that faith is not always going to be comfortably understandable as we live it out in daily life, nor is it always cozy to be a disciple.

Let's think about this problem in another way. If children join the Boy Scouts and don't understand how to tie knots, the troop won't eliminate knot-tying so that the kids will stay; instead, the Scouts do all they can to help the children learn it. Our model must be the early Church, which existed in a pagan (I use that term loosely) environment very much like ours. The Church was very careful to invite, welcome, teach, and instruct, so that nonbelievers were eager to learn and then be admitted to worship. If people are leaving churches because they don't understand everything, then perhaps we have made them feel like they *should* understand everything right off or we have embarrassed them in their lack of understanding. Our churches must make a far greater effort to help worship participants know that it is good to be a learner still, to relieve their embarrassment, to make worship such a delight that everyone knows it is *worth* learning more as we participate in this splendor.

Moreover, what we must do instead of reducing worship is continually teach people more and more of the meaning of what we do in worship and immerse them in the beauty of its practices. We can educate through Sunday morning adult classes, new member classes, a yearly explained-liturgy worship service, conversations with people well versed in worship, children's sermons, and written instructions. We could develop a "singing school" program for children and a catechumenal program for adults by which they gradually learn more and more of the great gifts of worship (see the following chapter). We could invest in establishing a Christian school that educates the young and also involves the parents. We could spend five minutes at the beginning of every worship service helping everyone to learn more of why we do what we do. Most of all, however, we should not reduce the splendor of worship; instead, we must make sure that we have found a balance of both accessibility and richness, mystery and instruction.

9. Closely related to the previous point, a few people have told me that

they have left churches of more substance for those that are more emotionally oriented or geared to entertainment because *they get too much information in daily life and they want simply to enjoy worship.* Certainly it is true that
people in our culture suffer from a glut of information.

Churches often respond to this problem by sacrificing content for form.
This is dangerous (as we will see more thoroughly in Chapter 21) because ultimately long-term interest and memory and formation lie in the details.
Moreover, it is essential for us to remember Marshall McLuhan's famous dic-
tum that "the medium is the message." It is impossible to separate content totally from the form in which it is conveyed.

The solution in an information-burdened society is not to create worship that omits information about God, but instead to give people a better
framework for dealing with all the data that inundate them in daily life. We
need to give people a richer view of God and of the way of life of God's people
so that they have an Infinite Center for their existence and a structure for
dealing with what they hear and see, for what they learn and the situations
they encounter.

This has to be carefully considered when we construct worship, for the
service must have a sense to its progression, display coherence between all the
parts, and provide a pattern for encountering God. This will also affect how
we plan and present our sermons, for we will want to offer an awareness of
how what we teach fits together with previous sermons and with the rest of
worship. This need for providing the master narrative in which information
can be understood will also influence the ways in which we instruct about
worship, for we will reveal worship's relevance for daily life and the perspective with which we live it.

10. Some people are overwhelmed by suffering and are attracted to worship services that offer emotional highs because *they think that these will help
them cope with suffering better.* This point is related to many others; for example, the lack of genuine hospitality in many churches (perhaps more true of
"traditional" than of "contemporary" churches) leaves many sufferers alone
instead of supported by the community. Similarly, there is great confusion
over what kinds of music are the most truly healing.

Many churches respond to suffering in their worship services by gloss-
ing it over with "happy songs." Of course, this is injurious to those who suffer
because sooner or later the "warm fuzzy" feelings fade away, and the sorrow
or pain must be faced. Questions inevitably arise about where God is in all
the troubles. Unless persons have more evidence of God's care beyond their
feelings, their doubts will have no response.

The reason why many hymns passed down through the ages have stood the test of time is that they give a full picture of who God is and how God is there for us in our suffering. Churches need to offer in their worship services genuine lament, the opportunity for thorough repentance and a clear statement of forgiveness, the truth of God's character and interventions in the world, and earnest prayers for the concerns of members and guests and the world in order to be faithful in the face of so much suffering.

Once again, I don't speak as a mere observer. I have struggled with health complications ever since the measles virus destroyed my pancreas when I was a teenager. This has led to blindness in one eye from retinal bleeding (I was totally blind for seven months); kidney disease (mine function less than 20 percent); nerve dysfunction in my legs and digestive processes. I also seem to be a magnet for collecting rare disorders and other maladies — a dentist pulled the wrong tooth (complicating my jaw breakdown); sudden deafness syndrome impaired one ear; an intussusception strangled fifteen inches of my intestine, which turned gangrenous, and its removal led to problematic scar tissue; breast cancer led to a mastectomy and extremely deleterious chemotherapy; arthritis afflicts my hands; demineralizing of the upper torso bones leads to severe pain. Also a doctor's misdiagnosis of a foot problem led to a shattered foot, a rebuilding after a year in casts, then a broken leg that healed crooked, so now I wear a leg brace. Frequently I get wounds inside that brace, so I spend plenty of time on crutches or in a wheelchair. And those are just the most noticeable physical afflictions.

Part of the great grief I feel about so many churches these days is that their worship seems to trivialize the suffering of God and to provide meager resources for dealing with the pain of people present and the pain of the physically and spiritually hungry world. Also, many congregations seem to value only success in the world's terms, whereas the Bible expounds instead a theology of weakness.[6]

Suffering has also made me realize how much our churches fail to be genuine, caring communities that are different from our technicized, consumerist, narcissistic world. Of course, I am guilty, too — which is why I need the deep discipleship of others in the community to hold me accountable. I need worship that brings me into an encounter with the holy God, who wants to transform our lives into the character of his suffering Son.

6. This theology of weakness is elaborated more fully in Marva J. Dawn, *Joy in Our Weakness: A Gift of Hope from the Book of Revelation* (St. Louis: Concordia Publishing House, 1994).

What Would Happen If We All Were Artists?

In answer to the question at the beginning of this chapter, I am sure that no one intentionally chooses banality for worship. Other reasons lead to people's turning to churches whose worship seems to some to be banal. How might all churches address those deeper needs without resorting to the harmful choices sketched in the ten points above? How might all churches help worship participants know that in response to God we all are called to the "work" of worshiping God and of being Church for the sake of the world?

In other words, how might our churches help worship participants know that in response to the splendor of God we are all artists? Wendell Berry's words inviting people to understand their work in a new way (he sees no difference between his being a farmer and a poet) might be applied to how we view our participation in worship.

> If . . . we believe that we are living souls, God's dust and God's breath, acting our parts among other creatures all made of the same dust and breath as ourselves; and if we understand that we are free, within the obvious limits of mortal human life, to do evil or good to ourselves and to the other creatures — then all our acts have a supreme significance. If it is true that we are living souls and morally free, then all of us are artists. All of us are makers, within mortal terms and limits, of our lives, of one another's lives, of things we need and use.
>
> This, Ananda Coomaraswamy wrote, is "the normal view," which "assumes . . . not that the artist is a special kind of man, but that every man who is not a mere idler or parasite is necessarily some special kind of artist." But since even mere idlers and parasites may be said to work inescapably, by proxy or influence, it might be better to say that everybody is an artist — either good or bad, responsible or irresponsible. Any life, by working or not working, by working well or poorly, inescapably changes other lives and so changes the world. This is why our division of the "fine arts" from "craftsmanship" and "craftsmanship" from "labor," is so arbitrary, meaningless, and destructive. As Walter Shewring rightly said, both "the plowman and the potter have a cosmic function." And bad art in any trade dishonors and damages Creation.
>
> If we think of ourselves as living souls, immortal creatures, living in the midst of a Creation that is mostly mysterious, and if we see that everything we make or do cannot help but have an everlasting significance for ourselves, for others, and for the world, then we see why some religious teachers have understood work as a form of prayer.[7]

7. Wendell Berry, "Christianity and the Survival of Creation," in *Sex, Economy, Freedom and Community: Eight Essays* (New York: Pantheon Books, 1993), pp. 110-11.

Wouldn't it be wonderful if all who worship would realize that what they do in worship — the music they make, their attention to the sermon and prayers, and the way they live in response to the God they have encountered in worship — has cosmic significance?

Furthermore, if we all recognize that what we do in worship is art, then we would recognize that all musical forms and styles must be chosen carefully for their musical and textual and spiritual merit, that they must be sung or played as excellently as possible, and that they must be offered to God as the best we can craft. Moreover,

> We must see that no art begins in itself; it begins in other arts, in attitudes and ideas antecedent to any art, in nature, and in inspiration. . . . Traditionally, the arts have been ways of making that have placed a just value on their materials or subjects, on the uses and the users of the things made by art, and on the artists themselves. They have, that is, been ways of giving honor to the works of God. The great artistic traditions have had nothing to do with what we call "self-expression." . . . The arts, traditionally, belong to the neighborhood. They are the means by which the neighborhood lives, works, remembers, worships, and enjoys itself.[8]

The art of worship belongs to the Church. It is the means by which the people of God live, work, remember, learn to be Church, and enjoy being God's.

Healthy churches will worship God deeply and will be formed by their practices and education to have God's character, to be a people set apart by God to live as artists in community, as sentinels on the wall to warn of dangers, as ambassadors of the kingdom of God to share its Joys, as friends reaching out with genuine intimacy to their neighbors. They will not fall prey to the idolatries of numbers or success, spectacle or power, emotional highs or simply what is new, but will instead be the servants and cross-bearers and witnesses Christ called us to be.

---

8. Berry, "Christianity and the Survival of Creation," p. 112.

20

Why Is a Catechumenal Process Needed
in Contemporary Culture?*

My soul thirsts for God,
  for the living God.
When shall I come and behold
  the face of God?

Psalm 42:2

Everyone has deep within himself or herself a profound, unquenchable yearning — which is at root a yearning for God — and we all try various methods to deal with it. Around forty years ago, C. S. Lewis used the fitting German term *Sehnsucht* to name this pressing, restless longing for fulfillment that nothing can satisfy more than temporarily.

Lewis observed that human beings try to handle this hunger in three different ways. The "fool" thinks that if she can reach a particular goal, she will be satisfied. After dedicating herself to achieving it, she discovers in the

*This essay first appeared as "How Does Contemporary Culture Yearn for God?" in *Welcome to Christ: A Lutheran Introduction to the Catechumenate,* ed. Samuel Torvend and Lani Willis (Minneapolis: Augsburg Fortress, 1997), pp. 35-47. This booklet is the first of a three-part series, which also includes *Welcome to Christ: A Lutheran Catechetical Guide* and *Welcome to Christ: Lutheran Rites for the Catechumenate,* also published by Augsburg Fortress in 1997. My thanks to the editors and to Carolyn Road of Augsburg Fortress for permission to reprint this revised version here.

end that it doesn't satisfy her for long. Consequently, she spends her life jumping from one inadequate goal to another.

The "sensible" person, in contrast, recognizes that the yearning cannot be stilled, so he tries instead to push it under. This isn't successful either, for the longing keeps surfacing, and his attempts to repress it must constantly be renewed.

Lewis proposed a third way, which truly deals with *Sehnsucht* and the roots of the longing itself. He says that if we heed this intense yearning and (#1) nothing in the world satisfies it, and (#2) nothing in the world can push it under, then (#3) we must realize that we are made for another world.

Lewis was not the first to recognize this potent human hunger. The early church father St. Augustine wrote, "Oh, Lord, Thou hast made us for Thyself, and our hearts are restless until they rest in Thee." Long before St. Augustine, the book of Ecclesiastes illustrated the vanity of trying to satisfy or repress one's *Sehnsucht*. Now, at the beginning of the new millennium in the United States, several elements of our society aggravate the yearning and accentuate the despair of its unquenchableness — and call for fresh insight, new compassion, and a return to a catechumenal formational process on the part of the Church.[1]

As Christians we know that the other world for which we are made is God's presence in God's kingdom, which will be fully experienced only at the end of time. To some extent that world can be tasted now in the Christian community, which incarnates God's truth in its rites and life together. However, the post-Christian society of the United States (and other nations) leaves many people bereft of the basic Christian understandings and formative processes that once could be assumed in our culture. Therefore, if we want to help people in these times to enter the new creation, the alternative society of the Christian community, we must understand their attempts to appease or push under the *Sehnsucht*. Then by a deep process of catechumenal formation, we can incorporate them into the Body that will truly satisfy their desire by nourishing their relationship with God.

Because of this deep yearning, it is not sufficient merely to appeal to people to participate in a worship service that might be immediately gratifying but does not expose their false goals and ineffective measures of repression. Rather, it is important that each Christian be concerned for the neigh-

---

1. Ever since the early church, the catechumenate has been the discipline of offering an open-ended period of time during which candidates for baptism explore the Christian faith more deeply through study of the Scriptures, prayer, worship, and careful mentoring by Christians experienced in the practices and ministries of daily life.

bor who is caught in these endless attempts to appease or restrain the yearning — and give witness to the alternativity of life in God. Then it is crucially necessary for churches to welcome such seekers into the training of carefully nurturing mentors, to equip them with a new way of life and to invite them into the rich practices of God's people, which will continue to immerse them in God's splendor.

Goals That Do Not Satisfy

By which goals do persons in our culture try to appease their spiritual hunger? Actually these inadequate goals are idolatries, for anything that takes the place of the one true God is an idol — whether or not the worshipers consciously claim it as god and whether or not they recognize that they are worshiping it. Some of our idolatries begin with genuine care for things that are important, but we let that devotion get out of hand. In fact, some of the controversies over worship in churches are caused by none other than idolatrous esteem for certain forms or styles.[2]

What makes idolatries so intense in the present age is that so much of life is becoming ambiguous, chaotic, fearsome, unmoored. As a result, people cling more desperately to whatever they think might be capable of freeing them from pain, confusion, emptiness, or meaninglessness. Their ultimate concerns are often trite, violent, enslaving, or flimsy. Never do they ultimately satisfy. Never do they form contentment.

The Idolatry of Ease

Certainly one of the ringing cries of contemporary U.S. culture is for ease, comfort, the total absence of any kind of suffering. Consequently, many of our major social controversies — such as the issues of abortion, euthanasia, or the convenient availability of divorce — are argued on the basis of a false compassion that "eases suffering" in the short run, but causes long-term consequences that are only beginning to be recognized. Social analysts perceive, for example, that fatherlessness in the home is the root of many social problems besides violence and crime.

---

2. To pursue this issue more deeply, see chapter 3 on idolatries in Marva J. Dawn, *Reaching Out without Dumbing Down: A Theology of Worship for the Turn-of-the-Century Culture* (Grand Rapids: Wm. B. Eerdmans Publishing Co., 1995).

To make one's own comfort the goal of existence can never result in ful-fillment of one's spiritual yearning, for suffering is inevitable since we live in a broken, corrupt world. We often undergo tribulations as the natural conse-quences of our bad choices. Many of our afflictions are undeserved, due to the evils of others. Some arise from the simple fact of bodily aging, the pres-ence in the world of disease — all because our sin brought death. Since the death ratio has always been the same — one per person — we can never es-cape suffering on earth, but people go to great lengths to try.

In the midst of anguish, those who suffer often look to the Church — and what shall we give them? We ought not to respond to their yearning with easy answers or the guarantee of ease. We certainly do not want to respond to this searching with worship services that avoid the problems of evil and suf-fering or merely attempt to cover them up with an "upbeat" happiness. The Christian community does not promise an end to all suffering in this life; rather, it trains its members in the truths of faith, which enable us to recog-nize suffering's source in sinfulness and its meaning in the grace of God. God's people can even "boast" in our suffering, for we know that it produces perseverance, then character, and then a hope that will not disappoint us (Romans 5:3-5). What people need is not the illusion that they can escape from suffering, but purpose to endure it and hope that it can be redeemed. Rather than chasing after an endlessly elusive comfort, we all need to be im-mersed in a faithful community that supports us in our suffering, that works to alleviate what can be eased, that embodies the presence of the God who genuinely comforts the afflicted and also afflicts the comfortable.

Materialistic Consumerism

Some of the suffering experienced in our culture is brought on by the perpet-ual pursuit of material possessions — even as those treasures are sought as an escape from suffering. The interminable spiral discloses the impossibility of extinguishing *Sehnsucht* in human solaces or stuff.

The idolatry of possessions has plagued us since the beginning of hu-man existence, as reflected biblically in the stories of Adam and Eve, who wanted to possess wisdom; Jacob and Esau, who struggled over the birthright; and Jacob's wives, who longed for sons and the status sons would give them. The impossibility that acquiring possessions could ever quench our hunger for more possessions is recorded in Isaiah 55, where the LORD asks why we continually waste our money on what is not bread and our labor for what will not satisfy.

Our present culture, however, specializes in inflaming the endless lust for possessions with advertisements that constantly convince us we need more (especially to create the ease we have never found). The marketers don't tell us much about their products, but they spend a great deal of energy (and enormous amounts of money) appealing to our fears and dreams. Thus, the idolatry of possessions plays to the deeper idolatry of our selves — and in an endlessly consuming society, persons are always remaking themselves with new belongings.

These ongoing refabrications make the person's character increasingly pinched, more "inward-turned" as Martin Luther would say. Narcissistic attention only to one's own well-being leads to stinginess and an inability to understand life as service to others.

In such a world, the generosity and self-sacrifice of the people of God must be deliberately nurtured in a community that understands itself as an alternative culture and that resists society's materialism and greed. If Christian churches truly manifested the gracious self-giving of Jesus, that love would draw into the community many persons whose still-unfulfilled *Sehnsucht* has driven them to seek deeper and lasting satisfaction beyond possessions. Then, by a life-forming catechumenal process, such searchers can be helped to discover that their deepest yearnings are gratified as God fashions them to be selfless and truly themselves in relationship with him.

Experiential Consumerism

The aspiration to possess more things seems especially to characterize what is called the "boomer" generation (those now in their forties and fifties). Younger people, those called the "busters" or "Generation X" or "the blank generation," seem instead to have as their goal to accumulate experiences or adventures. This is the generation abandoned by their parents (see the last two idolatries discussed below) and raised by television. As a result, many of them seek only the next entertainment, the immediacy of fun. I run into this experiential consumerism often on airplanes, where I meet people in their twenties and thirties whose only interest is in their next ski trip or a concert for which they will fly halfway across the country.[3]

Attempts at deeper conversation with such people, however, often re-

---

3. For an excellent description of, and plea for, this generation, see Kevin Graham Ford, *Jesus for a New Generation: Putting the Gospel in the Language of Xers* (Downers Grove, IL: InterVarsity Press, 1995).

veal an inability to do any sort of spiritual contemplation or reflection about existential questions. Those who do yearn for something more are often at a total loss as to where to find it. Churches who make worship merely entertaining do them a severe disservice by fostering a consumerist stance toward faith and depriving them of what they truly need in character formation and a deeper relationship with the God who alone resolves their existential questions.

Instead, Christian communities that reject the superficial diversionary amusements of the world around them for the sake of earnest study and spiritual growth, for the pursuit of godly wisdom, will offer genuine meaning to those tired of their idolatry's fruitlessness. Instead of immediate gratification, they will cultivate — by a life-transforming educational process — what Eugene Peterson called *A Long Obedience in the Same Direction: Discipleship in an Instant Society.*[4]

Information Consumerism

I deliberately wrote *wisdom* in the previous paragraph because one of the disenchanting goals of our present society is the accumulation of information. The Church teaches details about God, to be sure, but that knowledge is rooted in a lived faith that acts on what it knows.

The society that surrounds us, in contrast, is overloaded with useless or contextless (though often interesting) information. We learned about the L.I.A.R. syndrome from Neil Postman in Chapter 6 — how television has trained us to hear and see tons of information about which we do not or cannot do anything. Thus, we have learned to receive data without really learning from it or acting on it. Think what that attitude does to sermons! And consider how that tendency is being aggravated by the World Wide Web! Ponder how it has made liars of us in the United States, that we know the sufferings of the poor in our world but do not change our consumption habits in order to change the inequities, or how it makes liars of us in the Church if we learn about the grace of God and do not live as a community that embodies it.

To those who chase after more and more information, only to discover in the end that they can never accumulate enough to satisfy the longing that burns within them, a vital Christian community has great gifts to offer in in-

---

4. See Eugene H. Peterson's study of the psalms of ascent, *A Long Obedience in the Same Direction: Discipleship in an Instant Society* (Downers Grove, IL: InterVarsity Press, 1980).

troducing them to the One who alone can appease their yearning as the Truth, the Way, and the Life. Then, by its formational training, the community immerses those searchers in a Life that acts on the information of faith, in a Way that brings wisdom out of knowledge, and in Truth that infuses everything with meaning and hope.

Idolatries of Autonomy and Power

Part of the reason why so many people in our society chase after information is that they think accumulating data will help them to be more in control of their lives — and perhaps the lives of others. The modern liberal state has fostered the idolatry of autonomy, that all individuals pursue their own personal happiness without much concern for the common good. The rebellions of the 1960s added a new dimension to this notion of independence in their rejection of all authority imposed on the person from the outside. Never before in the history of the world has there been such a visionless repudiation of the wisdom of elders, of the past, of traditions (in the best sense of that word). When they became parents, these rebellious boomers relinquished their mentoring role and left their children to their own devices and to the destructive formation of the media.

We see the results of this in my husband's fifth-grade classroom — children who are trying to figure out who they are, but who have no formed "web of reality" in which to locate their experiences. Many young people have no rooted story to give their lives meaning and, consequently, have no core of character out of which they act. The supreme demonstration of this amorphous incoherence is MTV, which has no plot, but only feelings and images endlessly spun out to entertain. Psychologists have recognized that this lack of a basic personhood is a major reason why so many young adults cannot make commitments — to jobs or to someone in marriage. They have no self to give to another.

Yet many people in our society do not realize that the very thing they need — trustworthy authorities beyond themselves who will nurture their moral and character development — is what they have with blind prejudice disdained. They keep chasing after a (false) freedom that actually enslaves them in their narcissistic selves.

Closely related to the idolatry of autonomy is the lust for power, for finding and being in control of one's own life is usually not enough to satisfy. Society has known for a long time that power corrupts and that absolute power corrupts absolutely, but in our time the drive for power is expressed with a new twist. Now frequently power is obtained by accentuating one's role as the "victim." Sometimes — and certainly this is a strong temptation in churches — power is accumulated in the guise of servanthood.

Contrarily, the authentic Christian community enfolds seekers in a gracious narrative, the story of God's loving care that has been passed on by a people ever since Sarah and Abraham. This is a Word that enables persons to find themselves truly by giving themselves first to God and then to others. Instead of clamoring for more dominating influence, those who crave power can dwell in and be trained by a community that practices vulnerability, consensus, and authentic servanthood after the model of Jesus. Instead of a greedy grasping for more autonomy to satisfy one's *Sehnsucht,* those who idolize independence can find the intensive mentoring care they need and the genuine home they most desperately want.

Idolatry of Intimacy

Perhaps the word *home* summarizes best the various goals we have considered here as people in our culture scramble, unsuccessfully, to relieve the haunting restlessness of *Sehnsucht.* The longing for the other world for which we were made is aggravated in our culture because so many persons have not experienced loving homes, familial support, genuine social intimacy. Too many have not been the beloved of anyone who was totally committed to them as spouse, parent, or friend — much less have they known that they are the beloved of God.

In obvious ways the other idolatries discussed thus far contribute to this lack of true intimacy. The endeavor to avoid suffering causes some people to betray their commitments. It is easier for parents to set their children in front of a television set than to spend time answering their constant questions. Extra hours of work to accumulate possessions often substitute for lap time and family games. The quest for diversionary amusements is contrary to the tedium of parenting. Selfishness about one's own rights negates the responsibility of genuine caring.

For all kinds of reasons, then, a large percentage of citizens in the United States are starved for genuine intimacy, which is a leading factor in the rife sexual immorality of our times and also in the ridiculous overkill that instantly brands the innocent hugs and kisses of little children as sexual harassment. Since the media so lopsidedly display genital sexual involvement as the only way to acquire intimacy, young people especially who are desperate for true love know nothing better than to jump into bed with someone to try to quench their insatiable *Sehnsucht*. Of course, genital union taken out of the context of God's design for it within the protected covenantal commitment of marriage will only intensify their voracious yearning for love.[5]

Each person's deep longing for love was implanted by a God who loves us perfectly and wants by our neediness to draw us to himself. The love of the Christian community, therefore, is the primary means by which the Church can inspire persons in our society to seek to follow Christ. For those who grope for love that lasts, but are never filled since *Sehnsucht* always yearns for more, God's love incarnated in a people is an irresistible gift. The catechumenal process of the Christian community teaches seekers that they are the beloved of God and then trains them in the way of selfless love, grounded in the freedom of grace. The Church teaches that genital union is a sign of the intimacy of God's love for us; thus Christian marriage symbolizes the ultimate fulfillment of our deep yearning for an even higher love. Furthermore, the Christian community imparts to and nourishes in searchers many other kinds of love — intelligent, purposeful love that does not require return; brotherly/sisterly love; and friendship-family love[6] — because the Church dwells in the love of God.

"If Ya Can't Fix It, Stuff It"

The previous sections have all identified aspects of our contemporary culture that display individuals' efforts to achieve some fulfillment for the deep yearning within them that cannot be assuaged by human means because at root it is a longing for God. Many give up striving to satisfy that yearning; some never try. Then the *Sehnsucht* must be repressed — and a wide assortment of methods are explored. None of them will ultimately work, because sooner or later the alcoholic stupor is over, the high bottoms out, the truth of oneself must be faced, the questions must be asked, or death will underscore the futility.

C. S. Lewis's schema is helpful for recognizing that people don't deal with their *Sehnsucht* in the same way, but their tools to satisfy it and their

---

5. To explore these themes more thoroughly, see Marva J. Dawn, *Sexual Character: Beyond Technique to Intimacy* (Grand Rapids: Wm. B. Eerdmans Publishing Co., 1993).

6. The Greek words for these three kinds of love — *agapē, philadelphia,* and *philostorgē* — all occur in verses 9 and 10 of Paul's description of the Christian community in Romans 12. See chapters 16-18 of Marva J. Dawn, *Truly the Community: Romans 12 and How to Be the Church* (Grand Rapids: Wm. B. Eerdmans Publishing Co., 1992; reissued 1997).

means to repress it frequently overlap as the same idolatries. The same erotic involvement could at some times be an attempt to quench the longing and at other times or by other persons be an effort to still it.

Techniques of repression are accentuated in the present world by the growing postmodern despair. I am not referring to postmodern philosophies or academic descriptions here, but to the postmodernism that has hit the streets, our homes, and our children with its (rightful) rejection of the modern myth of progress. However, the world around us has offered no hope in the place of that myth. Instead, young people especially believe postmodern slogans such as these: there is no such thing as truth except what you create for yourself; there is no meaning to life; all is random; everything must be mistrusted (the philosophers would say deconstructed) since it is all a power play; there is no story that is universally true; you only go around once so do it with gusto.

Consequently, those whose lives are perilously fraught with despair — or with devastating painkillers of all sorts to drown it — need a genuine and vital community with a compensatory process of life-formation in order to survive and thrive. Catechumenal training is one way to take more seriously the profound pain of the culture surrounding the Church.

Repression by What Is Harmful

When people cannot satisfy that deep, restless yearning of which they cannot understand the roots, postmodernism tells them only to push it under with whatever appeals to them. Sadly, those means are usually destructive, so that increasing numbers of U.S. citizens are caught in deadly courses of drugs, alcohol, promiscuous sexual involvement, and violence.

What do we expect when so many young people cannot find meaning or a home? Drug users often say that they are bored. Gang members participate in vicious crimes in order to belong to a community that will care for them. People of all ages look everywhere for new ways to ease the pain of living. The United States will never solve the problem of drugs and alcohol as long as we fail to address the spiritual issues that drive so many to use them — the hopeless attempt of many to repress the nagging *Sehnsucht,* their (unidentified) longing for God.

The Christian community offers hope, healing, and a home to those in bondage to addictive lifestyles. Social analysts recognize that rehabilitation programs centered on Christian faith have the highest success rate — which the Scriptures made clear to us long ago in all the passages about God as the one true liberator. The Church's catechumenal process is similarly a form of rehabilitation, a nurturing in an entirely new way of life. When the Church embodies and extends God's deliverance, those who follow Christ can bring those who are in captivity to the only One who can set them free from the ravages of their attempts to silence the profound yearning.

Repression by What Is Good

Some means that people use to muffle their restless yearning are good — gifts of God's superb creation meant for our enjoyment. The problem is that these excellent things are used to replace God as the true Stillness for our yearnings, instead of as pointers to his sufficiency. (These things also often become the means by which people gorge themselves in the idolatrous attempt to reach a satisfying goal.)

Truth, beauty, and goodness — wherever they are found — are means God uses to draw people to himself; they give a foretaste of the presence of God. Consequently, not only will they never entirely quiet our deep longing for more, but instead they will also stir up our *Sehnsucht*. Some films, for example, convey great truths, the archetypal myths that lead to fundamental understandings, but the insight or escape will never be enough. Beauty in music, art, architecture, or dance haunts us with its echoes of the eternal, so instead of subduing our yearning it whets our appetite for heavenly splendor. Some people even try to suppress their innermost restlessness with goodness, religious piety. They busy themselves with honorable Christian activities in the futile attempt (usually subconscious) to avoid facing and responding to their longing for God himself.

The Christian community makes its worship and communal life as full of truth, beauty, and goodness as possible in order to usher participants into the presence of God. These foretastes are not meant to satisfy our longing or to push it under, but to intensify it so profoundly that we search for its fulfillment only in the other world for which we were made, the kingdom of God.

We Are Made for Another World

Of course, all my descriptions of the Christian community are ideal — but they are not blind optimism, for they summarize the biblical vision of God's design for the Church. Not only do the needs and false goals and repressive techniques of the contemporary culture call for the catechumenal process to nurture in the life of faith those who yearn for God, but also the catechumenal process calls congregations truly to be Church, to be genuine communities. The vocation of God's people is to recognize the source of *Sehnsucht* and to offer the presence of God embodied in ways that draw seekers into hope and a home, a foretaste of the world for which we were all made. In a culture that chooses many idolatries to try to assuage or repress its restless hunger, the Church stands as an alternative society, incarnating — though imperfectly now — the kingdom of God for which everyone most deeply yearns. The Church's catechumenal process forms us all — both the new in faith and the more mature — to be a people who drink exuberantly of the satisfying Water of life to quench our deepest thirst. Then, in Joy-full response to the Giver of all good gifts, we worship God in the splendor of his holiness.

21

Forming the Character of the Church's Children by Nurturing Their Minds

> Train children in the right way,
> and when old, they will not stray.
>
> Proverbs 22:6

My urgent concern for the nurturing of the Church's children became so overwhelming two years ago that it nagged me into writing a complete book on the subject, one long chapter of which is on worship as a formative agent.[1] I will not repeat in this chapter what you can read there. Instead, I want only to add here a few very short pieces for further discussion as our churches try both to form our children for worship and to create worship that forms our children.

Nurturing the Mind

In a culture that is overloaded with information, but bereft of wisdom, Christian congregations need a piercing wake-up call to attend to the training of

---

1. See chapter 5, "The Heart of God Revealed in Worship," in Marva J. Dawn, *Is It a Lost Cause? Having the Heart of God for the Church's Children* (Grand Rapids: Wm. B. Eerdmans Publishing Co., 1997), pp. 64-88.

our children's minds. We need to give them a worldview that provides a framework for discerning and assessing what they hear and read, that gives them good reasons to be different from their peers, that gives them hope and motivation to make their lives count. Good worship is one key factor in developing such a life philosophy because it builds in them a sense of the meta-narrative, the master story of the creating/saving/empowering God, which frees them to develop their identity as the Trinity's beloved.

It is essential that we keep remembering in our churches that our response to God calls for the training of our minds. Ours is a faith not merely of emotions, but of loving the Lord your God "with all your heart, and with all your soul, and *with all your mind*" (Matthew 22:37). Only with trained minds can we trust God in the tough times, as Lamentations tells us in these verses:

> But this *I call to mind,*
>   and therefore I have hope:
> The steadfast love of the LORD never ceases,
>   his mercies never come to an end.
> they are new every morning;
>   great is your faithfulness.
>   (Lamentations 3:21-23)

Similarly, Isaiah 26:3 praises God because

> Those of *steadfast mind* you keep in peace —
>   in peace because they trust in you.
> Trust in the LORD forever,
>   for in the LORD GOD
>   you have an everlasting rock.

In several places the Scriptures call us to "let the *same mind* be in you that was in Christ Jesus" (Philippians 2:5) or to "*prepare your minds* for action; discipline yourselves; set all your hope on the grace that Jesus Christ will bring you when he is revealed" (1 Peter 1:13). Most appropriate for our concern here, the worship of our entire lives is linked with the renewal of our minds in Romans 12:1-2: "I appeal to you therefore, brothers and sisters, by the mercies of God, to present your bodies as a living sacrifice, holy and acceptable to God, which is your spiritual worship. Do not be conformed to this world, but *be transformed by the renewing of your minds,* so that you may discern what is the will of God — what is good and acceptable and perfect."[2]

2. See my explication of these verses in chapters 1-7 of Marva J. Dawn, *Truly the Community: Romans 12 and How to Be the Church* (Grand Rapids: Wm. B. Eerdmans Publishing Co., 1992; reissued 1997), pp. 1-64.

Because there is such emphasis in the Scriptures on Christianity being a knowing and a mindful faith, I am (I think rightly) gravely concerned that so many churches are robbing their youth (and adults) of intellectual content. It seems that every parent — and each member of our congregations if we truly want to raise Christian children — needs to hear the graduation speech that Martin Marty quoted in his newsletter, *Context*.

The address was given in 1997 by Richard Lee at Christ College, the honors program at Valparaiso University in Indiana. Lee urged the graduates to take seriously their calling to be thinkers in an age of overwhelming information, in which "less and less of it is weighed or judged or even *thought* about very much at all." He gave them this assignment:

> You may have the *added* task of getting a fresh hearing for reasoning that considers ends more than means, that discerns more than it calculates, that more often questions "why?" rather than "how much?" A post-intellectual society is one where few think critically and the rest do not listen to the few that do. It is a fraying democracy where the majority do not vote, fewer read, fewer discuss, and fewer care as education dumbs down, culture stupefies, and all that entertains is true. You may be entering a society of so many pleasing fictions that your first intellectual task may need to be the fresh invention of reality.
>
> A post-intellectual society is one where public relations substitutes for public policy, where one mass-media image can wipe out many careful arguments, where sound moral character means feeling good about yourself, and the increase of freedom means more consumer choices. It is, finally, a society where intellectuals are very comfortably kept thinking about what they are told to think about. I suppose the biggest difference in the past 30 years is that the intellectually gifted now have so many more places to sell out.

Lee urged the college students (and each of us) to rise to the challenge of *loving God with all our minds* in a culture where that does not seem to be an honored task — but he gave hope with this affirmation:

> Happily, to that weighty, yet delicate, task, many of you will bring the ballast of the Christian intellectual tradition. Most of you can steady your intellectual life without wandering off into idols and ideologies, fads and fashions. To your intellectual life, you bring a special understanding of the human condition, a view of the self and history, and finally a Providence which transcends all that you may think and do, which can save you from both sentimentality and despair.[3]

3. Richard Lee, "Don't Cry for Me, Valparaiso, The Truth Is *I Never Left You*," *The Spillikin* 14 (1997): 14.

Lee's comments make clear several reasons why the forming of our children's character requires training of their minds, including these: that they can claim the intellectual aptness of the Christian faith, resist the hype of our consumerist culture, and reject the lure of society's emphasis on "much" instead of "why." Worship is one critical part of the training processes. We will not be able to engage the children in educational experiences if worship keeps convincing them that they are not vitally useful.

What We Learn from Core Knowledge Schools[4]

Furthermore, if worship is intellectually stimulating, children will be more interested in matters of the faith and its application to their daily life. We can learn an extremely significant lesson from contemporary experiments with public education.

The Winter 1996-97 issue of *American Educator* (from the American Federation of Teachers) featured a set of articles on the new Core Knowledge Schools and how these innovative schools are increasing the level of achievement especially among disadvantaged children. The articles explore problems with schools in the United States these days and acknowledge that in most cases students aren't interested because the material is vacuous, abstract, boring, self-absorbed. Consider, for example, this sample social studies lesson:

> Needs are things people must have to live. We all need food to eat. We need clothes to wear. We need shelter. . . . We also need love and friendship. Needs are the same for everyone all over the world.
>
> Wants are important too. Wants are things we would like to have. Different people have different wants. What do you want?[5]

Do you find that lesson interesting? The students don't either because of the substance-less abstractions. The Core Knowledge Schools, in contrast (and there are now about 350 of them in 40 states), are focusing particularly on detailed, deep, substantial content; for example, a first-grade class learned about

---

4. This section contains a small portion of my keynote address, "Culture: Around, Against, In the Church's Worship," given on April 8, 1997, at the Institute of Liturgical Studies, held at Valparaiso University in Valparaiso, Indiana. That address will also appear in a compendium of proceedings from the Institute's three-year program on "Worship, Culture, and Catholicity," 1997-99. My thanks to director Dr. David Truemper for permission to use this adapted version here.

5. Editor, "Core Knowledge Schools Take Root across the Country," *American Educator* 20, no. 4 (Winter 1996-97): 4.

the people in ancient Egypt and how they buried the mummies. The children even learned the name of the jar into which the ruler's brains were put.

Researchers from Johns Hopkins University and the University of Memphis are discovering, in a multi-year evaluation of the schools, that the program lessens the need for reteaching, that students are more interested in learning and have a higher attendance average, that teachers are invigorated, that disadvantaged students are closing the gap between their achievements and that of higher-income students.[6] The interest is in the details!

The same is true especially of Christianity's worship. How dangerous it is if we evacuate our worship of substantive content! Then we have to increase the hype constantly in order to get people to pay attention. In contrast, if worship is rich and deep — with a large range of sounds and images and biblical details — it is invigorating to both participants and leaders. And would there be a higher attendance average?

In her wonderful book *Hearts and Hands and Voices: Growing in Faith Through Choral Music,* Sue Ellen Page, who directs nine choirs in Princeton, including one for inner-city youngsters, says this about choir music for children: "What we do must be effective, challenging, memorable, and distinctive."[7] That list could summarize why the Core Knowledge Schools are turning out to be so effective — and it is a great list of what our worship involves. We must practice the language of faith with content.[8]

Reasons for Being at Worship

Just as worship needs to be filled with details so that young people get a larger, more interesting view of God's splendor, so worship needs to be filled with reasons for them to be there. We have all heard the plaintive cry from kids, "Why do I *have to go* to church?" Here are some answers that I give them:

1. We're not *going to church;* YOU *are* the Church — and we go to worship so that we learn how to be Church.

2. We need you with us in worship because those who are old and tired need your smiles and vitality.

6. Editor, "Test Scores Rise, Enthusiasm Abounds," *American Educator* 20, no. 4 (Winter 1996-97): 21.

7. Sue Ellen Page, *Hearts and Hands and Voices: Growing in Faith through Choral Music* (Tarzana, CA: H. T. FitzSimons Company, 1995), p. 112.

8. A book that is concerned for groundedness and growth in worship and not only in choirs is Philip H. Pfatteicher's *The School of the Church: Worship and Christian Formation* (Valley Forge, PA: Trinity Press, 1995).

3. The congregation cannot get along without you. Just as your body needs every single part — like your eyes, your nose, your mouth, your hands and feet — so the church needs every single person to make it whole. Perhaps this Sunday some persons will need you to be eyes or hands for them.

4. You need the gifts of worship because you will learn things there that will make sense later. Almost every week I learn something that comes up in the days that follow.

5. If you pay close attention to the words of the songs and the Scripture readings and the liturgy, you will learn all kinds of new things about God. Since God is infinitely incomprehensible, all of life is an adventure in getting to know him better, but worship is especially rich with his presence.

6. Attending worship will teach you skills for your Christian life — skills like how to pray, how to sing, how to sit quietly in God's presence, how to study the Bible.

7. I need you to come to worship because I have cancer and am taking chemotherapy, which makes me too sick to sing, so I need you to stand beside me and sing for the both of us. (This is not an answer I give right now, but it was a very important answer for three-fourths of a year.)

8. The congregation needs the talents you bring to worship — your singing voice in the hymns, your ability to learn new songs quickly, your ability to read the Scripture lessons well, your help with the ushering, your warmth and friendliness in the "Passing of the Peace," the answers you give during the children's sermon, your modeling of reverence for the other children. (This point makes us realize how much more all our churches need to do to engage the children more practically in the actions of worship.)

9. When I preach, I need to watch you to see if what I am saying is understandable to people your age. I need you to give me critiques when the worship service is over.

10. Most important, God needs you there because he loves to be with you in his house.

22

"The Importance of the Word":
Two Children's Sermons*

Keep these words that I am commanding you today in your heart.
Recite them to your children and talk about them when you are at
home and when you are away, when you lie down and when you
rise. Bind them as a sign on your hand, fix them as an emblem on
your forehead, and write them on the doorposts of your house
and on your gates.

Deuteronomy 6:6-9

*These two texts approximate the messages given for children at Beautiful Savior
Lutheran Church in Vancouver, WA, on August 14 and September 6, 1998. These Sundays
were the 11th and 14th Sundays after Pentecost in Year C of the Common Revised
Lectionary. Because these sermons were not recorded, I have not been able to capture exactly how the interchange went with the children, so all that is given here is a rough fleshing out of my outlines. I pray that these might be useful, nonetheless, in suggesting two
possibilities for nurturing children in worship to know more about worship. Other recom-
mendations are briefly outlined in the appendix of *Reaching Out without Dumbing Down:
A Theology of Worship for the Turn-of-the-Century Culture* (Grand Rapids: Wm. B.
Eerdmans Publishing Co., 1995).

Sermon 1: Words about God

1. If we wanted to describe God, what words might we use? What is God like? [We spent a while considering them, and the children came up with words like "loving," "good," "strong," "almighty," "big."]

2. When we have said all those words, have we said enough about God? Do you think that God is bigger and more wonderful than we could ever say?

3. I brought some pictures today for our talking about words. What do you see in these pictures? [They answered "LOTS of books" — wall-to-wall bookcases filled with books.] All these books are about God! [That really surprised the children.] And if we read all these books, we still won't know enough about God.

4. Today in worship we are talking about the Word. We learn the best words about God from the Bible, and this book is often called "the Word." When I give the other sermon today, you could listen for how often I use that phrase, "the Word." [If there are plenty of older children, one could add here that Jesus is called the Word because he most clearly teaches us who God is.]

5. Every Sunday we hear words about God, don't we? One of the reasons why I like to come here for worship every Sunday is because every week we learn new words about God.

6. And did you know that we even sing words right out of the Bible? Do you remember when we sang, "Worthy is Christ, the Lamb who was slain"? We sang, "Blessing and honor and glory and power" and so forth. [This is from the hymn of praise, "This is the Feast of Victory for Our God."] Did you know that those words come right out of the very last book in the Bible, the book of Revelation? Many of the hymns that we sing use images from the Bible or phrases or special words. There are so many good words to sing — that is one of the things that makes our worship so wonderful!

7. The best part is that we sing God's words and speak God's words and listen to God's words when we gather together here for worship on Sundays, and those words help us to become the kind of people God wants us to be. Those words teach us how much God loves us, what it means to believe in God, and how to think about things in our everyday lives.

Let's thank God for all these good words:[1]

---

1. I usually end children's sermons with a prayer that I divide up into short phrases so they can repeat them after me. It is essential that we give children actual practice in praying. I know that I'm not very good at putting things in children's language, so I'm sure all of you reading this can vastly improve on these two messages for them — but I hope that these sketches give some ideas for emphasizing the importance of the Word for their lives.

Dear loving God, thank you for all the good words that tell us about you. Most of all, thank you for Jesus who came to teach us the best words about you. Help us always to learn new words and to thank you and to become like you. We love you and want to hear your words. Amen.

Sermon 2: Why Do We Hear All These Readings?

This morning we are going to talk about why we listen to so many readings on Sunday mornings when we are gathered here for worship.[2] Do any of you know how many different lessons we hear from the Bible each Sunday? [Help them discover that there are three; singing the Psalms needs to be discussed at another time lest this session get too long.]

Do you know why we have those three readings? Let me show you by means of this Bible I have with me. We hear three lessons every Sunday from three very different parts of the Bible — so let's think about what we heard today and where we could find those passages in the Bible instead of on our bulletin page.[3]

Our first lesson this morning was from the book of Deuteronomy, part of God's instructions to the Israelites before they entered into the Promised Land at the time of Moses. Have any of you heard about Moses in Sunday school? Did he live a long time ago? Before Jesus? Before King David?[4]

2. I think it is crucial that we avoid the language of "going to church" with children, but always speak instead of coming or gathering for worship. It is hard enough to teach them that Christianity is a way of life (especially if their parents do not understand that), so we must be very careful to help them know about being Church.

3. I believe it is essential that those who read the lessons in worship do so from an actual Bible, rather than off a worship folder page. That simple gesture is monumentally important for teaching children that what we hear is from *God's Word,* which we study in worship so that we can hear what God is saying and be formed by it. Furthermore, I wish we could develop the habit in all denominations of bringing our Bibles and seeing the lessons in their context rather than isolated on a bulletin page. The major advantage of having them printed in the bulletin is that I can more easily direct the adults to the same wording in the passages about which I am speaking in the main sermon of the day. However, I think it is easier to urge congregation members to try to hear the lessons as the first recipients of the letters or Gospels would have heard them if they do not follow along visually on any printed page. Each worshiping body needs to discuss how the community can best experience the power of texts to form us.

4. A woman told me after the service that an adult seated near her whispered to her neighbor, "I didn't know that Moses came before David." I think one important advantage of children's sermons is that it gives us an opportunity to deal with the biblical illiteracy of adults without as much embarrassment.

We can get a feel for when he lived by seeing where that lesson is in the Bible. Here it is, marked by the bookmark with the yellow tassel. That is quite near the beginning of the book, isn't it? Moses was one of the very first leaders of the Israelites — he helped them escape from being slaves in Egypt — and he lived more than a thousand years before Jesus.

Let's look at this Bible to understand the relation of Moses and Jesus. If this is where we first read about Moses in the book of Exodus [show them where that is], how far do you think we have to read in this Bible before we get to the part about Jesus? [Have the children turn the pages until we get to the Gospels.]

Did that surprise you that we went so far back into the Bible until we got to the story of Jesus? I think perhaps some of the adults at worship this morning might have been surprised by that too.[5] This great big part of the Bible — about four-fifths of it — we call the Old Testament or the First Testament. It tells us all about God's people, the Israelites, and how God took care of them. It tells us what happened when they disobeyed God and how wonderful it was when they trusted him. Our lesson from Deuteronomy this morning was about God giving them an opportunity to trust him and to live according to God's designs for their well-being. [See Chapter 28.]

All these stories and commandments and poems in all these pages were written to teach us about God, so that you and I can learn from them to be God's people. It is like when I heard the story about my grandmother and how her family kept going from country to country to find a place to live where they could worship God freely. I learned all about how she and her family loved God so much, how brave they were, and how they had to be so clever to stay alive, and I wanted to be like her. Each Sunday we learn more about God's care for us and how to love and trust him, and we learn it from the people who believed in God even before Jesus came. Their stories make us want to be like them in relying on God — and not like them when they disobey.

We have our second lesson each Sunday for the same reason — but this lesson comes from the New Testament, this last part of the Bible. Our second lesson every week comes from the books about the first Christians who lived after Jesus had risen from the dead and left the earth. Today we heard about a

---

5. I expected the children to be surprised by how much of the Bible is the First Testament, but I was quite unprepared for how overwhelmed they were by it. Several adults, too — including one very highly educated woman — commented after the service that they simply hadn't realized that there is so much in the Bible about the people before Jesus! Why don't we pay more attention to our Jewish roots in the Christian Church?

slave owner named Philemon. The apostle Paul wrote him a letter to tell him to treat his slave Onesimus like a brother instead.

Let's find that story — here it is, near the very back of the Bible, marked by the bookmark with the lavender tassel. We don't have slaves, of course, but the lesson is a good one to help us learn to treat everyone as if they were our brothers and sisters — even if we don't like them. Wouldn't that be great if everybody in the world took care of each other, instead of fighting?

Now we have seen why we have those two readings — one from the First Testament and one from the Second. You can see where those are in my Bible with the colored bookmarks. Those readings give us stories sometimes; other times they give us lessons on how to behave — but all the time they teach us new things about God and how much he loves us and cares for us and then what it means to believe in him and love him in response.

Now we'll check out this last bookmark with the white tassel. What other reading did we hear today — the one I read from the middle of the aisle? Yes, the Gospel. I walked down the aisle and stood in the center of the congregation when I read it, didn't I? The preacher does that every Sunday to remind us that Jesus lived right here on earth, right in the midst of people just like anybody else. But he wasn't just like anybody else, was he? Do you remember that you all stood up when I read the Gospel; why did we do that? We honor Jesus by doing that. It is like when you stand at your desks at school to say the Pledge of Allegiance to honor the flag and our country. We show Jesus how glad we are to listen to him by standing.

The Gospel is the most important lesson we read on Sundays — since it is because of Jesus Christ that we are Christians. So we are always glad to hear his words, like we did today — or sometimes we listen to part of the story about his life or his death or his rising from the dead. And all those lessons help us to know how much God loves us — so much that he sent Jesus to be our Savior and the most important person in our lives. That is the very best reason why we listen to the Bible, because we learn from it about who God is and how he cares for us.

God loves us so much that we want to be like Jesus — good and obedient and loving toward everyone. We want to do what Jesus says. And we have this wonderful book, the Bible, to learn what he says. Let's thank God for all the readings we have on Sundays.

Dear God, thank you for the Bible. Thank you that we listen to lessons from you every Sunday at worship. Thank you that you love us so much and tell us about your love in the Bible. Help us learn from the Bible how to be your children. Amen.

PART V

Being Church: Choices

Ascribe to the LORD the glory of his name;
worship the LORD in holy splendor.

Psalm 29:2

Worship is a moral matter — that is, some choices are better than others. If we are commanded to worship the LORD in holy splendor, then those of us who plan worship must choose what we do very carefully. We can't make our choices too narrow, for then we will lose many opportunities to waste our time royally in seeing new dimensions of God's splendor. On the other hand, worship planners need specific criteria — primarily biblical ones, since we are a people formed by the Revelation — by which to make our choices.

We dare never let our responsibilities for leading worship cause us to forget that what we do is not intended to be utilitarian, even though it is momentously significant. Remember Romano Guardini's definition of worship as *"zwecklos aber doch sinnvoll"* — "useless, but at the same time full of meaning" or "full of signs." If our worship is to be truly a waste of time in focusing on God as the Infinite Center, then that goal at the same time necessitates some practical choices about the meanings and signs that help us never lose sight of that paradox.

The initial sermon in this part is one of many that could have been chosen for this place. It simply illustrates the bringing together of this book's three themes: the splendor of worshiping God, being Church, and serving the world as we make choices in the stewardship of our lives as God's people. However, it does this by introducing the theme of eschatology — that is, that Christ has already brought us the kingdom of God, which someday will be completely fulfilled. After Parts I through IV of this book have laid the cultural and theological foundations of understanding our society, royally "wasting" our time in worship by focusing on our Infinite Center, building community, and forming character, now Parts V and VI will deal with more directly practical dimensions of making choices and facing the challenges of being Church for the world in our meanwhile times. The final chapter of this book will return to the theme of eschatology to underscore that living in the "already but not yet" of God's reign is the most important aspect of our being Church for the sake of serving our neighbors.

Chapters 24 and 25 give small examples of minor choices that have much larger consequences if we don't recognize their long-term effects. The first asks about a few words that are often misunderstood and thereby many times become the source of conflict or diminishment of all that the Church and its worship could be. Chapter 25, in contrast, deals with a specific, practical question: How do we best help the congregation sing?

Chapter 26 offers questions by which responsible leaders and committees can talk together about what a specific congregation does in worship.[1] These criteria are essential so that our worship is *"aber doch sinnvoll"* — full of signs by which all who participate can encounter the splendor of God.

Chapter 27 offers a few new hymn texts for worship. Those who have purchased this book are welcome to copy these and use them. The Pentecost hymn can be accompanied by piano or organ, although it was originally written for two clarinets (played by junior high students) or two recorders on the melody, cello on the bass line, and classical guitar and Celtic harp on plucked chords. Two hymns for weddings (written for the ceremony uniting Myron and me) are also included here, so that engaged couples who want their wedding to be God-centered might have a few more possibilities for congregational singing than most hymnbooks offer.

---

1. Though these questions expand the criteria offered in *Reaching Out without Dumbing Down: A Theology of Worship for the Turn-of-the-Century Culture* (Grand Rapids: Wm. B. Eerdmans Publishing Co., 1995), this chapter will be more helpful if the reader has already studied Parts IV and V of that book. Another resource that gives models of asking questions is Dori Erwin Collins and Scott C. Weidler, *Sound Decisions: Evaluating Contemporary Music for Lutheran Worship* (Chicago: Evangelical Lutheran Church in America, 1997).

23

*"Worshiping God and Being Church for the World"**

An Eschatological Sermon on Revelation 7:9-17
for Good Shepherd Sunday (the Fourth Sunday after Easter)

The Lord be with you. [Response: And also with you!][1]
Let us pray: Good Shepherd, we know that all your promises are already being fulfilled now and someday will be fulfilled completely. Thank you for the opportunity to deepen our language today so that we can know

---

*A sermon something like the following was given at Beautiful Savior Lutheran Church in Vancouver, Washington, on May 3, 1998. Since I do not preach from complete manuscripts, this approximation can not capture the Spirit of the moment, which is usually more powerful than would be possible if I wrote out sermons word-for-word. But this attempt to recapture what was said will, at least, set the theme for this section. Let me emphasize again that I'm not claiming any superior quality in my sermons; this one is included here simply to demonstrate the effort to make preaching formative for our daily life choices by keeping the focus on God (here specifically on God's reign as understood by different aspects of the doctrine of eschatology), so that we become Church (here specifically a people formed by that doctrine to manifest God's present reign) for the sake of the world (here specifically in living out the stewardship of our faith through the mission of the congregation and justice building for our neighbors).

1. In my hometown congregation, members have learned the significance of this ancient greeting, and they participate spiritedly and with physical gestures. See Chapter 2, 8, or 14 for the kind of explanation I make when I am in a parish other than my own.

better who you are, who we are, and how we can respond to your grace for the sake of our neighbors. Guide us in this sermon time that your Word would speak to each one of us afresh in your name, Christ Jesus our Shepherd. Amen.

I love Good Shepherd Sunday, don't you? The texts for the day include the comforting images of Psalm 23 and John 10, filled with elaborations of the motif that God, whose splendor overwhelms us in our worship, cares intimately for us as a Shepherd. I love the beautiful music that has been written to ornament the images. Through my mind flow such hymns as "My Shepherd Will Supply My Need" and "Savior, Like a Shepherd Lead Us," choir anthems like the well-beloved "Brother James Air" ("The Lord's My Shepherd") and, of course, the solo "He Shall Feed His Flock" from Handel's *Messiah*.[2] When I was invited to preach here today, however, three outside influences changed the way I heard the texts, so that my preparation for this sermon led me down different paths from the comforting ones I expected.

The first influence on my sermon preparation was Edward Farley's book *Deep Symbols: Their Postmodern Effacement and Reclamation,* which I am presently reading. This book discusses how our culture, with its increasing superficiality and surface treatments of every aspect of life, has stolen from us our words of power. In a world of sound bites in the evening news, barren political promises, vacuous busy-ness and bureaucracy, the constant hype of mega-stores for endless consumerism, and the inflated language of advertising, it is difficult to sustain rich words of power. Farley does not give us easy steps for repairing our deep symbols; instead, he urges us to engage in long times of extended conversation. It will take work on our parts to reinvest in weighty words.[3] One of the great gifts of the Church is that we gather here every week for worship to deepen and practice our language of faith, so that we can more truly become the Church and continue to live that language and its symbols as we go back into our daily lives in the world.

The second influence that changed the direction of my preparation for this sermon was a conference last week on eschatology and how that theologi-

---

2. In the aural version of this sermon, these pieces of music were mentioned by singing a few lines from each.

3. See Edward Farley, *Deep Symbols: Their Postmodern Effacement and Reclamation* (Valley Forge, PA: Trinity Press International, 1996). Jacques Ellul made an equally powerful case for careful words in *The Humiliation of the Word,* trans. Joyce Main Hanks (Grand Rapids: Wm. B. Eerdmans Publishing Co., 1985).

cal doctrine influences the way we worship.[4] Don't be worried if this word might be unfamiliar; simply, the doctrine of eschatology is named by the Greek word *eschaton*, which signifies "the last things" or "the end times." In the Church we have a special "take" on the notion of the last days because we believe that the future aeon has already come breaking in to our times. God's kingdom is not just "pie in the sky by and by when you die." Rather, the reign of God has already begun with Christ's triumph over the powers of evil at the cross and empty tomb, so we speak of God's rule happening "already, but not yet." The reign of God is present, but not entirely accomplished.

We sing about eschatology on Sunday mornings in our liturgy in the hymn of praise, "This Is the Feast of Victory for Our God." We taste that victory in the Lord's Supper, in anticipation of the final fulfillment in the promised wedding feast of heaven.

The third element influencing my preparation was that it is stewardship month — and I *hate* stewardship programs![5] That is, I have always hated them everywhere but here at Beautiful Savior. Most congregational stewardship programs appall me, because so often churches resort to gimmicks (like "the Pony Express," complete with saddlebags) to try to get everyone's attention. What impresses me about stewardship month here is that we do not engage in glitzy campaigns to try to entertain people into giving more money. Instead, we talk deeply about our lives as God's people and our mission as a congregation.

The second lesson for this Good Shepherd Sunday — Revelation 7:9-17 — pulls these three themes together: learning about the eschatological reign of God, we can recover in our faith many words of power that will help us more genuinely to BE Church in the stewardship of our lives; finding our lives changed by the shepherding reign of Christ, we can live more thoroughly for the sake of the world. Let's look closely at this text from the book of Revelation to learn seven lessons about eschatology so that our lives will be formed into deeper stewardship.

[Since I always invite the congregation to turn to the lesson in their worship bulletin so that they can follow along as I preach, I will print it here so that you have the complete text also:

4. See Chapter 31 of this book, which contains my keynote address from that event. In the aural version of this sermon at this point I also invited the children present to raise their hands every time they heard me say the word *eschatology* so that we could all pay attention to how the word is used and thereby learn its many implications for our lives throughout the sermon. Several children became quite actively involved after that and continued to raise a hand every time I mentioned the word.

5. This statement served its purpose for shock effect well. Some members of the stewardship committee especially told me they listened very closely after this sentence.

⁹After this I looked, and there was a great multitude that no one could count, from every nation, from all tribes and people and languages, standing before the throne and before the Lamb, robed in white, with palm branches in their hands. ¹⁰They cried out in a loud voice, saying,

> "Salvation belongs to our God
> who is seated on the throne,
> and to the Lamb!"

¹¹And all the angels stood around the throne and around the elders and the four living creatures, and they fell on their faces before the throne and worshiped God, ¹²singing,

> "Amen! Blessing and glory and wisdom
> and thanksgiving and honor
> and power and might
> be to our God forever and ever! Amen."

¹³Then one of the elders addressed me, saying, "Who are these, robed in white, and where have they come from?" ¹⁴I said to him, "Sir, you are the one that knows." Then he said to me, "These are they who have come out of the great ordeal; they have washed their robes and made them white in the blood of the Lamb.

> ¹⁵For this reason they are before the throne of God,
> and worship him day and night within his temple,
> and the one who is seated on the throne will shelter them.
> ¹⁶They will hunger no more, and thirst no more;
> the sun will not strike them,
> nor any scorching heat;
> ¹⁷for the Lamb at the center of the throne will be their shepherd,
> and he will guide them to springs of the water of life,
> and God will wipe away every tear from their eyes."]

Let us begin looking closely at this text with verse 10 (rather than 9) because there the hymn that the angels sing underscores the foundational gift of our faith: "Salvation belongs to our God who is seated on the throne, and to the Lamb!" Keeping in mind the lesson our children discussed,⁶ let us elabo-

---

6. I had already spoken in the children's sermon about how Jesus is both a lamb and a shepherd. We had considered this rich double symbol (though not in these words, of course) of both sacrifice and care. Only because Jesus freely gave up his life for us and became a lamb can he truly understand what we lambs are like and how to take care of us. Only by his willing sacrifice as the perfect Lamb could he be the Shepherd to rescue us truly from all dangers.

rate the lamb/shepherd images so that we can perceive more deeply all that God's salvation entails and why God must remain the Center of all our worship and worshipful lives. Many churches seem to have lost the multifold benefits of the Church's eschatological tradition — perhaps because the notion of salvation has been reduced simply to a reward for believers after death. The biblical description of salvation is much richer, as we can see in Psalm 23, which is the psalm assigned for this Good Shepherd Sunday. Think of all the aspects of God's reign opened up in this poem!

Because the LORD[7] is our shepherd we shall never want. Hebrew verbs don't have past, present, or future as do European languages; instead they are either "done" or "not done." The verb for not "lacking" is a continuing one — so when we say Psalm 23, we are proclaiming that we can always be free from every worry about any deprivation. Salvation includes God's constant provision, even as he cared for his people Israel in the wilderness. Furthermore, the Shepherd makes us lie down in green pastures — and thereby we are able to find the food and rest we need. He leads us beside the still waters — the waters of *menuhot,* which connotes tranquility, calmness in the midst of conflict or tension, peacefulness. God leads us beside the waters of harmony. Salvation results from God's having created peace with us, reconciling us to himself — and therefore we pass that salvation on whenever we reduce the tensions in our world.[8]

Time prevents me from expounding on other images in the psalm — the way our Shepherd leads us in paths of righteousness, restores our soul or true being, comforts us with the discipline of rod and staff, teaches us to feast with our enemies, anoints us for our calling, pursues us with goodness and steadfast love[9] — but all of these facets of shepherding teach us more about

---

7. I usually explain to congregations when I preach why it is the practice of our English Bibles to capitalize the letters in the word LORD— that this signifies that the Hebrew word to be translated is the name *YHWH*, often vocalized as *Yahweh* (formerly as *Jehovah*). That is the name by which the Lord revealed himself to Moses at the burning bush in Exodus 3:14-15. It is a term that distinguishes him from all the neighboring, false deities. He is not just a god, but he alone is the faithful covenant God, the great "I AM." We need to recover the promise of the name LORD in our eschatology, to learn the glory of the Lord's constant faithfulness to his covenant promises, his effective deliverance of his people from all their captivities, and the assurance that someday his cosmic reign will be universally fulfilled.

8. Concerning this notion of peace building, see chapter 28 of Marva J. Dawn, *Truly the Community: Romans 12 and How to Be the Church* (Grand Rapids: Wm. B. Eerdmans Publishing Co., 1992; reissued 1997), pp. 262-70.

9. Some of these images are explicated in Appendix B — "When Is a Rut Not a Rut? Hidden Promise in Psalm 23," in Marva J. Dawn, *I'm Lonely, LORD — How Long? Meditations on the Psalms,* 2nd ed. (Grand Rapids: Wm. B. Eerdmans Publishing Co., 1998), pp. 234-37.

our God, as does today's Good Shepherd Gospel text [series C — John 10:22-30] in which Jesus insists that no one can snatch you "out of the Father's hand."

The final line of Psalm 23 offers us this wonderful summary of our Christian eschatological hope: "I will dwell in the house of the LORD forever" (as we memorized it from the King James Version) or "I shall dwell in the house of the LORD my whole life long" (as it is printed in the New Revised Standard Version here). This sentence also contains a "not done" verb, so it is a continuing notion. We are already dwelling in God's presence. The kingdom has already begun; grace enfolds us, and we remain part of the Shepherd's constant working of salvation.

Our first clarification of eschatology, then, is a deepening of our sense of the greatness of salvation, which not only will be culminated in the future but also is already happening now. This certainly leads us into deeper stewardship, doesn't it? If salvation is not just one little piece of pie someday, then we have much more to respond to — all the aspects of God's salvation. We are invited to respond to all the ways in which the Shepherd provides — the multifaceted grace of God evidenced in his guidance, leading, discipline, comforting. Our stewardship becomes constant in response to the continual unfolding of the richly abundant aspects of God's salvation.

Second, let's turn back now to the first verse of our assigned text in Revelation 7:9: "After this I looked, and there was a great multitude that no one could count, from every nation, from all tribes and peoples and languages, standing before the throne and before the Lamb, robed in white, with palm branches in their hands." How glorious is this picture of all these people gathered together, from every ethnic group, all countries, every sort of culture, every tongue brought together in the unity of God's reign! This promised future unity of everyone forces us to ask now, How can we provide a foretaste of this gathering of all the people? We do practice that future gathering here every week when we celebrate the unity of various age groups and preferences and backgrounds in our worship.[10] Our congregation needs to grow, however, in welcoming persons from other ethnic groups or other social classes, but we have certainly begun that process by utilizing various sorts of musical styles, the faith expressions of diverse cultures. In our weekly gatherings, God who is the Subject and Object of our praise joins us together in practicing the great

---

10. Too many churches are dividing according to taste, a problem that Beautiful Savior has avoided by using a diversity of styles of music on alternate weeks, so that both services each Sunday are the same. See Chapter 15 on why it is destructive to divide our churches over matters of taste.

unity of the kingdom. Jesus speaks of this in the Gospel text for this Good Shepherd Sunday, when he declares, "The Father and I are one" (John 10:30). Our unity imitates the Tri-unity of the Godhead. God's oneness drives toward reconciling all the world as one.

As a congregation we practice that in our stewardship by constantly recognizing that our community encompasses a huge diversity of gifts, which are all needed. Every single person sitting in these pews is absolutely essential for the work of God in this place. You provide elements of the kingdom that are beyond my skills or training. I cannot do most of the things that you are able to do — that is precisely why we have to have each other. All of us are necessary for the working of the kingdom of God in and through and from this place of worship for the sake of the world around us. Our second lesson in eschatology, then, is that the future bringing together of all God's people in the fulfillment of his kingdom is initiated now and demonstrated here in the gathered stewardship of our lives.

For our third lesson, consider verse 11: "And all the angels stood around the throne and around the elders and the four living creatures, and they fell on their faces before the throne and worshiped God." We will contemplate their worship later, but at this point notice how this text hints at the entire story of the people of God. One of the worst aspects of our increasingly postmodern society is that it robs from people any sense of a master story.[11]

Our master narrative as the people of God begins with *YHWH* calling Abraham and Sarah to be the parents of a people who would be especially blessed in order to pass on that blessing to the entire world. This story of our roots goes on to tell about Isaac, Jacob/Israel, his twelve sons, and their tribes — how God gave his people promises, fulfilled his covenant by leading them out of their captivity in Egypt, bringing them into the promised land, instructing them to live there according to his designs for peace and justice, allowing them to be taken into captivity to Babylon when they violated that pattern and oppressed their neighbors and amassed wealth, delivering them once again from captivity, bringing them back to the land, restoring the Temple, and so forth. The high point of the entire narrative, of course, lies in the coming of Jesus the Christ to be the great fulfillment of God's promises; the grand culmination is the resurrection, which enables us to trust that God will fulfill all the rest of his promises for the future. Then the narrative continues with the multiplying of the disciples and God's protection over the growth of the Church, all the way into the present

11. This is emphasized especially by the postmodern philosopher Jean François Lyotard. See Chapters 3 and 4 above.

in which we became part of the story and into the future when God will culminate his reign in the return of Christ.[12]

Eschatology teaches us that the reign of God we will someday know in all its fullness has been hinted at throughout this great cosmic story, has been manifested in God's blessings upon his people and, through them, upon the world. This certainly affects our stewardship because when we gather every week for worship, we learn more and more about this master narrative, so that we can find our place in the story. Every one of us in the Church has an important part to play in this master story of being the people of God.

You might wonder how such a long discourse about God's master narrative could come out of a verse that mentions angels and elders and four living creatures. In the context of the entire book of Revelation we recognize that the twenty-four elders of verse 11 symbolize the whole people of God — the twelve tribes of Israel plus the twelve disciples who spread the gospel to all the ethnic groups grafted on to God's promises to the Jews. Similarly, the four living creatures take up symbolism from the First Testament, from the book of Ezekiel. By being built upon a multitude of images and accounts from the Hebrew Scriptures, the book of Revelation ties the cosmic story together, all the ways God has worked on behalf of and through his people — and now, at this place and time in the story, God works through you. The stewardship of our lives includes finding our place and tasks in the story.

For our fourth lesson in eschatology, we turn to verse 12, which records what the angels, elders, and creatures are singing. What a Joy it is in our Lutheran liturgy to join them in singing, "Amen! Blessing and glory and wisdom and thanksgiving and honor and power and might be to our God forever and ever! Amen." As we sing "This Is the Feast of Victory for Our God" on Sunday mornings from Revelation 5 and 7, we sing with all the people of God throughout time and space this particular one of the various sets of his attributes[13] that characterize the praise of heaven.

We could never name all the qualities that should be ascribed to God; so, since the number *seven* for the Jews symbolizes perfection, to list seven in this hymn is to represent all the other elements we could name. We specify honor and blessing and thanksgiving and glory to remind us that all of these belong only to God.

12. In the aural sermon all of this was traced on a timeline in the air as I walked across the front of the sanctuary. (Beautiful Savior does not have a pulpit, so sermons are given from a reading stand just in front of the communion rail.) This physical action made it possible to emphasize the particular place where we are part of the story and undergird that with a sense of the great history of the people of God.

13. See other sets of attributes in Revelation 4:8 and 11; 5:12-13; and 19:2.

Eschatology teaches us that there are no other gods in whom we can trust for the fulfillment of the cosmic future. This God, incarnated in Jesus Christ, is the true God who deserves all our praise and laudation. If we truly give him the adoration and devotion he deserves, just think how that will change our lives! If all homage goes to God, we won't honor possessions or position or power. Glorifying only God kicks out all other idolatries. If all thanksgiving goes to God, we can't be greedy. Gratitude and greed won't co-exist, for thanksgiving frees us from scrambling, enables us to relax in the provision of God. Obviously that will affect our stewardship, for if we don't deify money, we are set free to give it away for the purposes of God. If we are not greedy, we can more openly steward our lives by offering our gifts and whatever we have for the benefit of other people around us. Just think how singing "This Is the Feast" or other similar songs from the Scriptures in our worship services continually invites us to repudiate any other gods. Every Sunday morning we are reminded that we are part of the cosmic reign of Christ. The Lamb is on the throne, so we can gladly give over all of our lives — knowing that the Good Shepherd will care for us.

Our fifth lesson in eschatology appears in the dialogue of verses 13 and 14. Such an interchange is a great rhetorical device that the seer John uses at other places in the book of Revelation. The question and answer formula gets us interested in the answer to the inquiry, "Who are these, robed in white, and where have they come from?" The seer's deference, "Sir, you are the one that knows," highlights the angel's response. "Who are these?" we earnestly want to know because the angel's question to the seer implies that the answer includes him — and us. The NRSV's English translation of the angel's response is a bit inaccurate here, for the original Greek text uses a present participle to state that these are the ones "currently coming" out of the great tribulation. We, too, are often in the process of coming out of various tribulations as we move from the "already but not yet" of eschatology to the final fulfillment of God's reign in which our particular tribulations will be over. Of course, when the book of Revelation was first written, the phrase "the great tribulation" no doubt referred to the persecutions of the Roman emperor.

We must also focus on the clause "they have washed their robes and made them white in the blood of the Lamb," for the word *blood* is another very rich symbol that is often trivialized. In the Christian language, the word hints at the entire sacrifice of Christ — not only his excruciating suffering and death on the cross, though chiefly that, but also his total emptying of himself (as Philippians 2:6-8 declares) to be born in poverty, to live a marginalized existence, to put up with all the people clamoring for healing and those silly disciples who never understood him, to be so fleshed as to offer blood constantly throughout his entire life and death. In that blood — all Christ's sacrifices, all the work of atonement from birth to death and resurrection and ascension and the pouring out of the promised Spirit — we are set free. We are thereby enabled to come out of the tribulation. When the book of Revelation was written, the people who received it were going through great suffering under Roman rule, so the book is filled with assurances such as this that Jesus Christ has triumphed over the powers that afflict them and that someday they will share in his victory. The symbol of blood promises that someday they will come out of the present ordeal.

When I spoke with the children a short while ago, they eagerly told me that part of their care for the little lamb I showed them would be to protect it. Even so God's people are assured by the Lamb's blood in which they wash their robes and by their coming out of the great tribulation that their Good Shepherd has set them free from the powers of evil and continues to safeguard them. The Greek word for "tribulation" calls up the image of being pressed into a very tight situation, between a rock and a hard place. How many of us feel that we are caught in very tense positions, in the midst of difficult alternatives? The One who is the Center of our worship frees us from fear of the final result. We will indeed come out of that tribulation someday by means of the Shepherd's care — and that can help to free us in the meanwhile from fear.

The stewardship of our lives becomes liberated and, consequently, more liberal when we are not afraid. For example, if we don't have to be afraid of unemployment (because God will guide us in new directions and because the community will support us), then we don't have to hoard our money.[14] All the lavish sacrifices of God on our behalf free us from our fears about the future and enable us to make generous sacrifices also.

This leads to our sixth lesson in eschatology in the statement of Revelation 7:15 that those coming out, dressed in washed robes, are gathered "before the throne of God, and worship him day and night within his temple, and the one who is seated on the throne will shelter them." Earlier, verse 11 recorded that the angels fell on their faces to worship. I don't know about you, but I simply cannot miss worship on a Sunday. I need worship every week to encounter God, to be reminded of his promises and their fulfillment, to grow in my knowledge and practice of the language of faith so that it can then

---

14. This illustration arose because one member of the congregation, in giving a stewardship "temple talk" at the beginning of the worship service in which this sermon was preached, related how God had led him after a period of unemployment to a new job and how his giving for the congregation's mission had not declined during the interim.

guide all of the rest of my life in the daily routines and possibilities of care for my neighbors. Verse 15 captures in such a lovely way how worship brings us into the presence of God, for the original Greek literally declares that "the One who is seated on the throne will tabernacle over" his people. God pitches his tent over us to shelter us as we gather for worship,[15] and someday we will experience that tabernacling perfectly when the dwelling of God is with his own (Revelation 21:3).

In John 1:14, the evangelist graphically writes that when the "Word became flesh, he tabernacled among us." He pitched his tent to dwell among us. Someday we will know God face-to-face — this is the good news of our eschatology — but in the meanwhile God teaches us in our worship how he is tabernacled over us. When God remains the Center of our worship, we go out tented afresh to enter our daily lives of stewardship. Won't that change your life if every day you do your job and live in your neighborhood and care for your family in a tented way? If we keep remembering how God continues to tent over us, then we can live every moment of our lives in a worshipful way. We will BE Church in the excellence with which we work, in the way we care for those around us, in the way we steward our resources for the sake of the world. If we are encouraged by our gathering together, then we will more eagerly make everything we do worship-full.

Finally, as our seventh lesson in eschatology, the last two verses of our Revelation text underscore God's justice. All of the final promises in chapter 7 appear elsewhere in the master narrative — they come from Isaiah and the Psalms and Exodus. "They will hunger no more, and thirst no more; the sun will not strike them, nor any scorching heat; for the Lamb at the center of the throne will be their shepherd, and he will guide them to springs of the water of life, and God will wipe away every tear from their eyes." All these images reveal God's purpose to end poverty and suffering of every kind. Christian eschatology gives rise to the confidence that someday God's justice will reign entirely, but eschatology also always invites us into the "already but not yet" of that reign. Someday fully, but already to some extent now, God's justice reigns in the world — but how? The answer, of course, is through us. You and I are some of the agents of God's justice. What are the ways in which our congregation and you personally build that justice and reconciliation in the world?

Ultimately God does the feeding, since he is responsible for the growth

---

15. The sanctuary in which these ideas were preached on Good Shepherd Sunday is shaped somewhat like a sloping tent, so the very architecture underscored the presence of God in his tabernacling mercy and grace.

of food, but how will those of us gathered here for worship pass it on to others? Our congregation right now is collecting money, building houses, and making quilts for Habitat for Humanity; how might you participate in any of these projects? How might you be an agent to reconcile opponents in an office tiff or in a neighborhood disagreement? As we together sponsor two Bosnian refugee families, how will we collect the necessary furniture, pots and pans, linens, dishes, food, transportation, and money? How can all of us contribute to that gathering?

How can we all work for the end of hunger and thirst that this text promises? Sunstroke and scorching heat seem to me to be images of the overworking of those who are poor; let us keep considering as a congregation how we can build justice in our world and work for more equitable redistribution of the world's resources. How might we contribute to ending the suffering in places of horror like Rwanda and Bosnia? In all our actions, we are simply participating in the work that the "Lamb at the center of the throne" is doing in being all people's Shepherd, whose purpose is to "guide them to springs of the water of life." God will someday "wipe away every tear from their eyes." How will each of us participate in the "already" of God's amelioration of suffering, in anticipation of the "yet" of his final fulfillment? God's reign will someday prevail throughout the new heavens and new earth, but it has begun in the coming of the Lamb who was slaughtered for us — and, in the meanwhile, now it will be spread in the stewardship of our lives.

What a privilege is ours to live with this sense of eschatological stewardship! Worship immerses us in God's reign, which has already begun in the work of Jesus, our Good Shepherd. Let us go from this tabernacle back into our daily lives in a tented way — eager to see how we can extend that reign to our neighbors and our world — until we join the angels in singing the perfect praises of the heavens!

Let us pray about this: King of the cosmos, thank you for teaching us who you are, our Good Shepherd. Thank you for telling us about your reign in the Scriptures and for inviting us into the hope of eschatology — that someday you will do away with all evil and sorrow and tears. In the meanwhile, draw us into deeper stewardship of our lives so that we might be agents bringing your peace and justice into the world. We ask this confidently, because we know that you are Lord, and eagerly, wanting all our lives to be worship-full to give you the cosmic praise that you are worthy to receive. Amen.

24

What Do These Words Mean?

Do your best to present yourself to God as one approved by him, a worker who has no need to be ashamed, rightly explaining the word of truth.

2 Timothy 2:15

"We are what we eat," people say. More importantly, we are what we say. If we talk bad theology, we will live bad theology. I have already emphasized this in the introduction to this book, where I stressed that we are not "going to church" but "being Church." In a culture that does not have much care for words, it is essential that we think more accurately about how we handle not only the Word of truth in the Scriptures, but all words by which we wish to convey truths or to consider options to get closer to truth. In a world in which "stupendous," "amazing," and "exciting" refer only to the results of using the right kind of laundry soap and in which politicians routinely break their campaign promises or tell more and more lies to cover up earlier lies, it is essential that Christians take deep care to speak the truth as clearly as we can at all times.[1] In this chapter we will briefly consider four words or phrases related to worship that are being terribly misused, confused, abused, or over- or underused in churches.[2]

---

1. See the previous considerations of the importance of our words in Chapters 11 and 23 of this book. See also Jacques Ellul, *The Humiliation of the Word*, trans. Joyce Main Hanks (Grand Rapids: Wm. B. Eerdmans Publishing Co., 1985).

2. I would have included the phrase "church marketing" for discussion in this chap-

"Contemporary Worship" or "Contemporary Music"

As already mentioned in an earlier chapter, I taught a seminary course this year on "Music and the Arts in Worship." The school's catalog description stated that the course was to give an overview of music in the history of the Christian Church. While giving that overview I repeatedly explained that there are numerous kinds of "contemporary" music, but still one student said on his final evaluation that he wished there had been "more contemporary worship" in the course. I had included several current choruses, music from Taizé, a dramatic reading and song from the Iona community, contemporary music from Africa and Madagascar, new Spanish music, and some music by Marty Haugen published by GIA (see p. 291 n. 3). It made me realize again how much the words *contemporary worship* to most people mean one and only one style, although exactly what that style is varies from place to place.

I prefer to avoid the term altogether because it never ceases to cause trouble in churches. Often people use the term to complain or to divide the congregation into those who favor "it" and those who don't — never realizing that "it" has never been defined. What makes music contemporary? Much of what I have heard in "contemporary worship services" has been at least two to ten years old — sometimes it includes folk songs that go back to the 1960s. The truth is that in a way all music in worship is contemporary if we are engaging in it now.

Moreover, most people who use the term *contemporary* to define music mean by it songs that are played with guitars or folk/rock combos or tunes that are heard on the radio and performed with backup tapes. However, there are numerous living composers who are currently producing music in a hymnic style and for organ, choirs, bell choirs, orchestras, or congregational singing. Is their music not contemporary?

I'm sure that there is little need to say much more about this subject. Perhaps, though, you could join me in my campaign to get people to stop using the word (as well as the word *traditional,* which has become a word of opprobrium). Let us be clear about what we mean when we *discuss* the issues raised by confusion over the word. When people say they want more "contemporary worship," let us ask them to what they are specifically referring. Do they mean writing a new order of worship each week, jettisoning the hymnal, signing up for CCLI licensing permission, putting screens in the sanctuary, or using guitars instead of the organ? Do they mean paying attention to new

---

ter, but that has already been done superbly well by Philip D. Kenneson and James L. Street in *Selling Out the Church: The Dangers of Church Marketing* (Nashville: Abingdon Press, 1997).

global music, commissioning poets and composers to produce new works for the congregation, learning new skills for instrumental accompaniment? Clarity would be worth working for and might keep a community from splitting.

"Lent"

Clarity of terminology is essential if we expect worship to be truthful and constructively formative of character. Lent seems these days to be a season of the church year in which worship services are often becoming flimsy, if not flippant. The season was designed by our forebears to give us ample time to consider all that Christ did for us in his entire life of suffering, as that culminated in his death on the cross. Indeed, we cannot appreciate the immense triumph of Easter if we don't recognize the enormous cost it required.

In two forty-day seasons of exploring various Lutheran churches in my home area, I've run into the following mistreatments of Lenten worship: an introduction and Ash Wednesday worship service that suggested we observe a "joyful Lent" this year; sermons that spoke about our journey and our temptations without once mentioning Christ's; chancel dramas that told stories of biblical figures not at all related to Christ's work of Atonement or anything else Lenten; a reading of the story of Bel and the Dragon (from the apocryphal Daniel) as the main message; songs that were happy and "uplifting" on Good Friday; the sharing of "our stories," again without any reference to Christ; a discussion that focused on our feelings about people and how we can crank ourselves up to love them; and a children's sermon on burying the Alleluia during Lent, without a single statement as to why. Meanwhile, solid Lenten hymns or songs were sometimes rejected for "upbeat" tunes, and Marty Haugen's lovely evening vespers liturgy was frequently sung so fast that there was no time to think about what we were singing. In the latter, the canon (a round between two sides of the congregation) entirely fell apart one evening because the singers couldn't keep up with the pianist. Haugen's canon is written for the words of Psalm 141: "Let my prayers rise before Thee as incense." When it is sung, coherence would demand that we remember that the smoke of incense does not shoot upward, but wafts! How can one be reflective about prayer when the music is charging ahead at the speed of a tornado?

What has happened to LENT?

Can we be formed as a people willing to suffer if we do not reflect upon the willingness of Jesus to bear our sufferings? Are we able to refrain from making grace cheap if we do not pause to remember the agony of Good Friday and the days that preceded it?

I certainly don't want to advocate an overly morose Lent with funeral dirges similar to those some of us might have experienced as children in excessively sober Scandinavian or German congregations. But we *need* Lent! Our forebears were wise to put its forty days into the calendar to keep us mindful of the great sacrifice of Christ and the immense love of the Father, the overwhelmingly grace-full — and grotesque — sufferings of the Trinity. In these postmodern times, sin and failure are almost universally unacknowledged, though everyone experiences or is aware of disillusionment and despair. In response to this anguish, Lent and its fulfillment of the Promising God's forgiveness are great gifts the Church can offer the world around it.

Every season of the church year — and especially Lent — contains specific resources for carefully equipping the saints with the truths of faith so that they can witness to, and serve, their neighbors. The Church needs both preachers and musicians with great faithfulness to give worship participants what they need instead of what they think they need, to offer that which is needful instead of catering to neediness. Ultimately, this meat will be much more satisfying that the pabulum of a schmoozy Lent.

"Advent"

Sometimes the confusions are not so much about the meaning of a season, but about its timing and practice. Last year I attended a worship service during the season of Advent that raised my concern for how it should be observed. A group of pastors were tired of hearing complaints from people who wanted to sing Christmas carols in worship before Christmas actually arrived, so the churches they served decided to begin Advent two weeks earlier in order to celebrate two Sundays of Christmas before its date. After reading all the materials from these churches about the reasons for their decision, I compiled the following list to suggest some of the dangers of changing the Church's calendar. (Some of these comments will be relevant only to those churches who follow the common lectionary and its themes for various Sundays of the year.)

1. It is hard enough to help congregants realize that to be a Christian means that one is different from the world. The world plays Christmas music primarily to get us to buy things now (already in July?). The Church reserves Christmas music for the twelve days of Christmas in order to retain (against societal pressures) the highlighting of Christmas as the festival for which we've been *waiting*.

2. The purpose of Advent is to help people long for the coming Messiah. If they long to sing Christmas carols, that is actually teaching Advent's point.

3. It fits our psyche to observe the end of the church year, then Thanksgiving, and then the beginning of Advent. Perhaps our forebears in the United States purposely put Thanksgiving where they did — when Lincoln signed the order, who were his advisers? — because it forms a progression between the two church years.

4. Those who feel they don't get to sing enough Christmas carols could be encouraged to sing them at home for family devotions during the twelve days of Christmas. To fill a need for singing carols together as a larger community, the congregation could have carol festivals on the Sunday after Christmas and on New Year's Eve or carol in the neighborhood, at rest homes or hospitals, or for shut-ins, etc.

5. Let us consider why people are in a rush to sing Christmas carols anyway. Unfortunately, it is often merely for sentimental reasons or because they are not as morally convicting as are the texts of Advent. To rush the seasons is to cater to our penchant for instant gratification.

6. We also ought not to sacrifice the important lessons of the last Sundays of the church year (which these churches had done to move Advent up two weeks). All the Sundays after Pentecost teach important themes necessary for the entire language of faith, but the concluding Sundays consider the final judgment of God and then celebrate Christ the King and thus are essential for facing our death and relying entirely on grace.

7. If we confess that we believe in "one holy, catholic, apostolic Church," then we need to practice that Church's year — with all the other saints throughout space and time. Our forebears wisely understood that we needed four weeks in December, the darkest month, to think about our sins and to yearn for a Messiah. Of course, the dark and cold of this season of the year in the northern hemisphere don't apply in the southern hemisphere. However, in both hemispheres giving in to the world's schedule represents a destructive choice for the world over the Church.

8. The pastors who planned this change in the Advent schedule emphasized that they were trying to make Advent "more meaningful," but I don't believe that is possible if we put it wherever we want it to be. And we certainly won't make Christmas Eve more meaningful by "sort of" celebrating it for two Sundays before it happens. Instead, that takes away all the anticipation, all the yearning, all the waiting until the Holy Night. Christmas Eve was purposely put on the day when the ancients realized that sun time was increasing. (And John the Baptizer's day is on June 24, when they realized the sun time was decreasing, in keeping with John 3:30: "He must increase, but I must de-

crease.") To celebrate two Sundays of Christmas while the sun time is still decreasing is to detract from the coming of the Light of the World.

Most likely, those of you reading these pages could add other objections to this list. My basic point is simply that there are reasons why the Church has observed dates and seasons as it has for hundreds of years. We do not serve the people in our congregations well if we don't painstakingly consider those reasons before making decisions to change worship practices. I hope this list will help congregations who have altered the schedule to change their minds, return to the Church's calendar, and teach their people more thoroughly about Advent yearning and the resulting ecstasy of Christmas Joy that at last God's promises to send a Savior have been fulfilled.

"Hymn" and "Song" and "Reform"

My desire to be careful about these words arises from misconceptions I have heard proclaimed in the midst of debates about changes in worship styles. A speaker once included in her definition of the word *hymn* the false idea that they were always constructed of texts written by one person with melodies composed by another, whereas in songs, she said, both the text and the tune came from the same creator. Certainly there are some pieces that follow this pattern, but more often both older hymns and newer songs contradict her definition and occur in both combinations. Many poets write wonderful new texts for older melodies; many hymns were written long before their melodies. On the other hand, for a large proportion of both newer songs and older hymns the melody is composed in conjunction with the text, either by the same person or by a team. Martin Luther himself adapted folk melodies for some of his poems and wrote both tune and text for other hymns.

Luther's own musical work, however, achieved much more for the Church. Timothy Wengert, professor of the history of Christianity at the Lutheran Theological Seminary in Philadelphia, asserts that "Luther's most lasting contribution to Christian worship was the hymn." Luther did not invent the hymn form, but he made it central to worship. As Luther knew, hymns are immensely effective tools for worship because of the necessity for text and tune coherence. As Wengert describes it,

> Luther realized that he could not simply translate Latin chants into German, as Thomas Muntzer had done. His Germans sang songs; thus their German liturgy had to bend its Latin chants to German ballads and se-

quences, and its Latin hymns to techniques in familiar songs and trouba-
dour melodies. From that initial spark have come tens of thousands of
hymns in all kinds of languages and cultures from that time to the present.[3]

To secure help for preparing hymns Luther wrote in 1524 to George Spalatin,
a member of the Saxon court in charge of church affairs, as follows:

> [Our] plan is to follow the example of the prophets and the ancient fathers
> of the church, and to compose psalms for the people [in the] vernacular,
> that is, spiritual songs, so that the Word of God may be among the people
> also in the form of music. Therefore we are searching everywhere for poets.
> Since you are endowed with a wealth [of knowledge] and elegance [in han-
> dling] the German language, and since you have polished [your German]
> through much use, I ask you to work with us [Luther and others from
> Wittenberg] on this project.[4]

It is especially important to note that Luther wanted the best and the most
biblically faithful of poetry. In the same letter Luther urged Spalatin to undertake the work since he thought he himself did "not have so great a gift that I can
do what I would like to see done here." Luther advised the poets concerning
which psalms they should first adapt and urged them to read his commentary
in order to craft the adaptation well.[5] I wish that more poets in our time would
read commentaries to understand the biblical texts more thoroughly before
writing their new song verses. What makes Luther's hymns unique, Timothy
Wengert concludes, is that the Word of God is spoken in them all.

I introduce Luther into this discussion also because he offers a significant model for churches who are making reforms in their worship practices.
Luther actually had to contend for faithful Christian worship in two directions. On the one hand, he removed unbiblical accretions from the Roman
Catholic mass (it is wonderful that the Roman Church now values most of
Luther's work), and, on the other, he held the line against those who wanted
to throw out everything. In the process, Luther labored to counteract the idea
that worship was a duty to be performed.[6]

---

3. I am very grateful to Timothy Wengert for these insights and quotations from his
keynote presentation "The Theology of Worship in the Reformation," given on June 22,
1998, at the Association of Lutheran Musicians Region II conference at Lenoir-Rhyne College in Hickory, NC. He also directed me to other readings in *Luther's Works.*
4. Martin Luther, "To George Spalatin," trans. and ed. Gottfried G. Krodel, *Luther's
Works,* gen. ed. Helmut T. Lehmann, vol. 49 (Philadelphia: Fortress Press, 1972), pp. 68-69.
5. Luther, "To George Spalatin," p. 69.
6. This point is also from Timothy Wengert's keynote address.

Though Luther's statements were often quite strong and abrasive (please forgive any word choices that might be offensive to you in order to grasp the point of the following) this excerpt from his "Table Talks" is significant for the purposes of this book:

> The papists, the fanatics, and whoever they may be who set their own opinions against the gospel are already condemned with all their wisdom, holiness, and beliefs. For our wiseacres do nothing except to slander us and say, "Luther has indeed destroyed the papacy but he can't build a new church," that is, can't introduce a new form of worship and new ceremonies. These wretched [people] think that building up the church consists in the introduction of some sort of new ceremonies. They don't realize that building up the church means to lead consciences from doubt and murmuring to faith, to knowledge, and to certainty.[7]

How many of the present conflicts over worship could be avoided if everyone remembered that the issue is not new forms for their own sake, but faithfulness to the gospel and true building up of the Christian community by contributions to the people's growth in faith and knowledge and certainty!

---

7. Martin Luther, "Table Talk No. 3323b," from Spring 1533, recorded by Conrad Cordatus, trans. and ed. Theodore G. Tappert, *Luther's Works*, gen. ed. Helmut T. Lehmann, vol. 54 (Philadelphia: Fortress Press, 1967), pp. 195-96.

25

In Praise of the Harder Way:
Musings on Continuity, Ephemerality,
Change, and Faithfulness

> Honor and majesty are before him;
>   strength and beauty are in his sanctuary.
>
> Psalm 96:6

Recently at a clergy conference, my co-speaker's topic was what churches should be like in the twenty-first century.[1] At one point he cited as an illustration the initial founding of the Sunday school for the purpose of offering the possibility of literacy to poor children who did not have the opportunity to go to school. He lauded the churches' idea to give those children books as gifts since they were not supplied by the society around them; but then he seemed to mock churches who continue to give books to their children and suggested that today instead we should make computers available to children in our Sunday schools.

Later, in our panel discussion, when this speaker was asked how he envisioned what churches should be like in five years, he responded that we should have sanctuaries with large screens since this is a media world. One

---

1. I am refraining from naming this speaker not because this is not a specific, datable illustration, but because I wish not to malign a person, but to critique an idea.

observant clergywoman asked him whether he should be more consistent with his earlier comment about the alternativity (my word, not hers) of churches giving books to poor children who would not otherwise receive them. Since we cannot escape screens and computers in our culture and in our schools, she said, perhaps churches should continue to give books.

When the rest of the panel was similarly asked what we envisioned for churches five years from now, I felt compelled to respond that with all the changes and transitions of cultures one thing remained the same: the gospel always has to be incarnated. Children do not need the screens of videos and computers so much in Sunday school as they need walking, talking, hugging, caring human beings who incarnate the gospel and a kingdom way of life.[2]

Since that encounter I have continued to ponder the question of screens, especially in light of research on the effects of our contemporary cyberspace revolution in the United States. Specifically in this chapter let us ask which makes more possible the incarnation of the gospel during congregational singing: screens or hymnbooks.

Please don't stop reading this chapter if you don't like hymns. I didn't title these pages "In Praise of Hymnals," and I don't intend to talk about preferences; instead, I want to use this topic as an example in which we can explore more thoroughly the kinds of processes we need to think more carefully about long-term effects of the decisions our congregations make. I raise the issues of media for singing at this point because many congregations/denominations that formerly used hymnbooks are presently choosing instead to install screens at the front of their sanctuaries in imitation of faster-growing evangelical, Bible, or Pentecostal churches. My concern here — for all denominations across the mainline/evangelical/independent/Catholic/Orthodox spectrum — is to ask questions deeper than our surface reactions to one medium or another. Many of the practicalities of worship that we might at first decide quickly because they seem minor actually entail advantages and disadvantages on a larger scale that necessitate a more careful probing of the extended effects of our choices. For the mission of this chapter, then, we must ask about the reasons for congregational singing and what will best promote the honoring of God, the nurturing of believers' character, and the building up of the community.

2. See also Jeff Zaleski, *The Soul of Cyberspace: How New Technology Is Changing Our Spiritual Lives* (San Francisco: HarperSan Francisco, 1997), pp. 5-6.

The Purposes of Song

Lest we become too utilitarian with this word *purposes,* let me begin this section by emphasizing that the main reason to sing in worship is that God is so singable. More than fifty times in the psalms we are told to sing praises to God. Sometimes motives are offered, such as the one in these lines of Psalm 13:6: "I will sing to the LORD, because he has dealt bountifully with me." In a large proportion of cases, we sing simply because of who God is, as in this second half of Psalm 7:17: "[I will] sing praise to the name of the LORD, the Most High." Primarily we sing in worship to display, become more aware of, embrace, and respond to the splendor of God. It is a *royal* waste of time, this entering into the eternity of God's reign.

One result of our singing, if it is genuinely in response to God and not allowed to become a source of conflict, will be that our singing will knit us together as a community. The psalms invite us to think of the joining of the whole cosmos and the offering of a diversity of gifts in this global praise:

> Make a joyful noise to the LORD, all the earth;
>   break forth into joyous song and sing praises.
> Sing praises to the LORD with the lyre,
>   with the lyre and the sound of melody.
> With trumpets and the sound of the horn
>   make a joyful noise before the King, the LORD.
> Let the sea roar, and all that fills it;
>   the world and those who live in it.
> Let the floods clap their hands;
>   let the hills sing together for joy . . .   (Psalm 98:4-8)

Similarly, the poet David calls his fellow worshipers to respond to God's splendor with this invitation: "O magnify the LORD with me, and let us exalt his name together" (Psalm 34:3).

Psalm 34 also illustrates the second result of singing praise to God. Not only will it strengthen the community, but also the praise becomes a vehicle for passing on the faith to our children and thus nurturing their character as God's people. In verse 11 David welcomes them with "Come, O children, listen to me; I will teach you the fear of the LORD."

Comparably, Psalm 78 recounts many incidents in the history of Israel when they turned away from God and experienced God's anger, but then also were saved by God's mercy. The psalm ends with praise to the LORD, who chose his servant David from the sheepfolds "to be the shepherd of his people Jacob" (78:71). It is acknowledged that "with upright heart [David] tended

287

them, and guided them with skillful hand" (v. 72). The secondary result of this honoring of God is that the people will hear the teaching and thereby resist the rebelliousness of their ancestors.

> I will open my mouth in a parable;
>> I will utter dark sayings from of old,
> things that we have heard and known,
>> that our ancestors have told us.
> We will not hide them from their children;
>> we will tell to the coming generation
> the glorious deeds of the LORD, and his might,
>> and the wonders that he has done.
> He established a decree in Jacob,
>> and appointed a law in Israel,
> which he commanded our ancestors
>> to teach to their children;
> that the next generation might know them,
>> the children yet unborn,
> and rise up and tell them to their children,
>> so that they should set their hope in God,
> and not forget the works of God,
>> but keep his commandments;
> and that they should not be like their ancestors,
>> a stubborn and rebellious generation,
> a generation whose heart was not steadfast,
>> whose spirit was not faithful to God. (vv. 2-8)

As we think about the long-term effects of various visual media for singing, our primary foci for consideration must be these: that we sing to glorify God and respond to him, that as a result the community will be enhanced and the believers' character will be nurtured. By now I'm sure you are very aware of these three primary criteria under which I ask all worship questions, but it seems to me that better decisions would be made by congregations if these three purposes were constantly kept in mind.

The Atmosphere of Our Song

One crucial component remains to be mentioned. The psalms of praise and worship in the Scriptures pay a great deal of attention to the beauty or splendor of God. In addition to the verse at the head of this chapter, consider the following:

> One thing I asked of the LORD,
>> that will I seek after:
> to live in the house of the LORD
>> all the days of my life,
> to behold the beauty of the LORD,
>> and to inquire in his temple.   (Psalm 27:4)

> Out of Zion, the perfection of beauty,
>> God shines forth.   (Psalm 50:2)

All the themes of this section — our purposes for song and the beauty of God and of the place in which we worship — are brought together in these words from Psalm 96:

> O sing to the LORD a new song;
>> sing to the LORD, all the earth.
> Sing to the LORD, bless his name;
>> tell of his salvation from day to day.
> Declare his glory among the nations,
>> his marvelous works among all the peoples . . .
> Ascribe to the LORD, O families of the peoples,
>> ascribe to the LORD glory and strength.
> Ascribe to the LORD the glory due his name;
>> bring an offering, and come into his courts.
> Worship the LORD in holy splendor [or "the beauty of holiness" (KJV)];
>> tremble before him, all the earth.   (Psalm 96:1-3, 7-9)

Keeping these invitations from the Psalms in mind, let us set out some of the advantages and disadvantages of the visual tools we use for singing and ask especially about the long-term consequences of our decisions.

Using Screens for Congregational Singing

From questioning people who prefer using large screens at the front of the sanctuary for worship singing and from my own observations of numerous worship services that made use of screens, I think the following are the primary advantages claimed for this method of making songs accessible for the congregation to participate:

1. Using transparencies and screens is easier. Music can be used from multiple sources that do not have to be gathered into one place.

2. Using transparencies and screens is cheaper. Congregations do not have to invest in books that will quickly become outdated.
3. The congregation can always be using new music.
4. Having the words *up* on the screen gets people's noses out of a book and their heads up in the air.
5. Not having to hold a hymnal frees people to clap and raise their hands.
6. Hymnbooks are too heavy. A screen is accessible to everyone.
7. Screens are what people are used to in the rest of life.
8. Transparencies can be changed swiftly, so that the flow is not interrupted by turning pages.
9. Transparencies aren't so hard on the environment as using reams and reams of paper in handouts each week.
10. Many of the songs on the screen are texts from the Bible, so learning the songs in this way promotes memorization of Scripture.

Disadvantages of screens or reactions to the above list that various people have noted include the following:

1. Since songs on the screen rarely have the music notation in addition to the texts (or else the whole printing is much too small), people who do not know the melody cannot participate as well.
2. Similarly, since the notes aren't given, people cannot sing more complicated harmonies if they wish.
3. Those who are visually handicapped often cannot see screens. [My own visual handicaps prevent me from seeing them, whereas with magnifying glasses I can read hymnals.] The glare of screens is difficult for those with cataracts; in contrast, hymnals can be moved to the best light.
4. Congregants can be encouraged to get their noses out of the hymnal simply by teaching them how to hold the book up for singing.
5. The ephemerality of the screen gives no sense of the Church's continuity with the singing of the past.
6. The ephemerality of the words on the screen gives little opportunity for further reflection on the text of a song.
7. There is no way to take the words home to continue to teach them to our children and ourselves. [Those who advocate screens would respond that the song is memorized by learning to sing it in worship. Those who object would say that there is need for more substantive texts than can be memorized in one singing.]
8. The fact that screens are what people use most in the rest of life is a very good reason not to use them in worship.

9. There are several aesthetic reasons not to use screens — one is that they are ugly. One person said to me, "I have never yet seen a beautiful screen in a church building."

10. Often the screens are an aesthetic distraction that takes away worshipers' focus on the altar, the cross, the symbols, or the stained-glass windows.

11. Another aesthetic problem is damage to the art of singing. Songs that are simple enough to "pick up easily" do not usually have very complex melodies or harmonies and do not require much skill in melody, harmony, or texts. How will people stretch their abilities to praise God?

12. Correlatively, words on a screen do not entail much learning of doctrine, and we need doctrinal bones to keep the shape of the body of faith. (See Chapter 29.)

13. It is true that many of the songs projected on worship screens foster memorization of Scripture, but usually these songs are composed of only one or two Scripture verses, and they are often taken out of context.

Using Hymnals for Congregational Singing

Most of the advantages of using hymnals are no doubt obvious from the preceding lists.

1. Using hymnals is easier. Music in them has been gathered from lots of sources (especially in the newer denominational hymnals, which usually include more global music) and is already collected into one place. Secretaries do not have to type anything except a few numbers in the bulletin.

2. The expense of books is worthwhile because the hymnal gives a sense of the community over time and brings the resources of past eras to each worship service. Also there is no need for the expense of screens and projectors.

3. The congregation can always add new music with supplemental books or with handouts photocopied by permission from licensing agencies.[3]

---

3. Two excellent sources of good new music from which permission can be secured for reprinting are Oregon Catholic Press, 5336 NE Hassalo, Portland, OR 97213-3638; telephone 1-800-548-8749 and GIA Publications, 7404 South Mason Ave., Chicago, IL 60638; telephone 1-800-442-1358.

4. Holding a book together increases the sense of community. Younger people, especially the children, can hold the books for the elderly and feeble.
5. Screens are what people are used to in the rest of life; the hymnal underscores the continuity of the Church as the people of the Book.
6. The flow is already established by the progression of the hymnal's liturgy.
7. Hymnals aren't so hard on the environment because there is no plastic involved nor extra use of technological machinery.
8. The hymnal gives more space for a more complete rendering of texts from the Bible, so learning the songs and psalms in this way promotes more thorough memorization of Scripture.
9. Music notation is given so that those who read notes can learn more complex melodies and harmonies. Those who can't read notes can at least see if the melody lines go up or down, so they have more direction than they would get from a screen.
10. Large-print hymnals or photocopies can be made available for the visually impaired.
11. The relative permanence of books gives a greater sense of the stability of the Church.
12. A person can take the hymnal home or purchase one for further reflection on texts, for instruction of the children, or for devotional use.
13. Hymnals do not disrupt the beauty of the sanctuary. In fact, books can be beautiful.
14. Hymnals do not distract from the foci of the altar, the cross, the pulpit, and the symbols.
15. Hymns gathered in a hymnal together give a more thorough development of doctrine, which we need as the bones that keep the shape of the body of faith.
16. The hymnal links a church with other congregations using the same resource.

Besides the disadvantages of hymnals that are implied by the list of advantages of screens we must also add the following very significant disadvantages of hymnals:

1. Their lifespan is usually estimated to be about twenty years at most, and then the congregation incurs the expense of replacing them.
2. They can be confusing to the stranger.
3. They prevent free movement of the whole body.

4. They are heavy, easily dropped, burdensome.
5. Too many words in a text can be a barrier to encountering God in a song.
6. Sometimes denominational hymnals are a barrier to ecumenical relations.
7. Many times congregations limit themselves to the hymnal and thus get stuck in "traditionalist" ruts.
8. Notes on a page often prevent free harmonization and spontaneity.
9. Many object that hymns have "too many words" and are difficult for people in an age that is mostly image oriented.

However, this last point is a difficult problem for our churches because there are serious long-term consequences if we address it by eliminating serious and thorough words. We should instead answer the challenge by careful training in words, for we believe in a God who is the Word and who commands us not to worship images.[4]

Discussing the Matter as a Community

I have tried to be fair in compiling the lists above by asking numerous people for pros and cons of the two media, but I am sure that I have missed some important considerations. These will suffice, though, to illustrate the kind of carefulness I am advocating. If this chapter would continue the process, we would go through the lists again and add further responses and re-responses, as is done in #7 of the "disadvantages of screens" inventory above. My point is primarily to underscore that we ought not to make even these simple decisions too lightly, especially if we are concerned that what we do in worship will be beneficial in its longer lasting staying power.

We have to recognize, too, that many — if not most — of the advantages and disadvantages listed above depend entirely upon how the medium is used. Hymnals can get in the way of a congregation learning new music, or they can be the springboard from which to expand the repertoire. Screens can cover up the altar or can be placed more discreetly at the side. The point is this: Have we *thought* about that? The "harder way" that I am advocating is the *process of discerning* how best we will glorify God and strengthen God's people.

4. See Jacques Ellul, *The Humiliation of the Word,* trans. Joyce Main Hanks (Grand Rapids: Wm. B. Eerdmans Publishing Co., 1985).

Two Other Considerations

I did not list the following issues in the inventories above because I am not sure these two are genuinely connected with the question of the medium in worship. I raise them here as an addendum for our further reflection.

It seems to me that in general hymnals present a wider selection of viewpoints and perspectives. To see words only on a screen narrows the possibilities available to the worshiper for reflection. Remember this critique of the media in our culture by William Fore, whose thought we first considered in Chapter 6:

> They reflect the values in the culture, and they legitimate, circulate, and amplify them and thus, in reality, "create" them as potent values, through the process of resonance. By choosing to repeat and amplify some of the myriad of possible values, attitudes, and worldviews, and not to repeat or amplify others, the media become a powerful process that helps to create, maintain, and change our culture, and those who become expert at finding and amplifying these messages feel no moral responsibility for *what* is resonated, but only that it is done well.[5]

Of course, I am not at all suggesting that the situation is the same in worship (that is why I left this point off the above lists), for I don't doubt that most worship leaders prayerfully bear their moral responsibility for what is resonated. Furthermore, it is true that leaders choose what will be resonated out of the hymnal also. However, the book is still there to give the worshipers more options. I often read other hymns during the offering or before worship; I use several hymnals for my morning devotions. My concern is for whether the choice of projecting the congregation's song on the screen leads to too limited a resonancing, so it seems important to pose the issue for further consideration.

Similarly, I am not sure that the following concern applies either, but it seems important to raise it. Chapter 6 of this book began with two illustrations of the effects of our culture's technological milieu and our "screened-in culture" on persons' ability to experience and appreciate the immediate gifts of the senses. As more and more people spend more and more time in front of computer screens that connect them to the virtual reality of cyberspace, I wonder if screens don't aggravate the isolation of persons. Again, of course, they don't have to, but our culture is becoming less and less able to discern the

5. William F. Fore, *Television and Religion: The Shaping of Faith, Values, and Culture* (Minneapolis: Augsburg, 1987), p. 44.

"one-step-removedness" of their screen addictions. Since screens are connected in daily life with activities that are bodiless, will their use in worship begin to make us less aware of the Body and of our own bodies, which otherwise could touch the hymnal and see more fully the more lasting evidence of the Church's communal song?

26

Criteria by Which to Plan

Let the word of Christ dwell in you richly; teach and admonish one another in all wisdom; and with gratitude in your hearts sing psalms, hymns, and spiritual songs to God. And whatever you do, in word or deed, do everything in the name of the Lord Jesus, giving thanks to God the Father through him.

Colossians 3:16-17

We have seen in other chapters of this book some of the reasons why many congregations make bad choices about what to do in their worship services — perhaps from a confusion between evangelism and worship (Chapter 9), or because they have allowed worship to become a matter of taste (Chapter 15), or because of panic about the identity of the Church (Chapter 29). In this chapter we will consider several criteria that can be used to guide our decisions about music, liturgical forms, sermons — everything that we do and see and hear and taste and touch in worship. First, however, we must underscore two other primary problems that lead to bad decisions about worship.

Unwillingness to Work

Good worship takes effort — on the part of planners and participants alike. The first problem we must point out is that because many congregations have turned worship into what pleases people instead of "the work of the people" *(leitourgia),* they have given in to the consumers' wishes to be merely entertained, lazy, mindless, just like the world, successful, or rebellious against all that the Church has been. I know that I have overstated the case — purposely so because I am intensely troubled that so many church leaders seem to want never to demand anything of worshipers. Of course, I am not advocating the opposite extreme of making everything too hard for the people to participate. It is important, however, in between those two extremes, that congregations *do all they can to counteract the present idea* that we must do all we can to make worship easy for those who come so that they'll come back again. The best way to ensure that they will come back is to give them such a rich vision of God, with such warm hospitality, that they realize God is exactly whom they need.

To do this takes great effort on the part of worship planners, and, sad to say, fewer and fewer people in our times have the training it takes to do that well. Thus, the second major problem is that there are not enough persons qualified to do the hard work of planning. Carol Doran and Thomas Troeger discuss the massive changes that have taken place since the 1960s in worship music and bemoan that "the resulting lack of clarity about the professional identity of church musicians along with inadequate ecclesiastical recognition of their ministries and poor remuneration have led to a sharp decline in people acquiring the necessary skills." Then Troeger and Doran quote various musicians' organizations as they comment on how endangered a species organists are and how little is planned to attract young people into the profession.[1] Meanwhile, those who do have training as church musicians (not only organists) are frequently outvoted, outvoiced, outmaneuvered, or pushed out by councils or clergy with little understanding of what worship is or could be (see Chapter 17). Doran and Troeger comment, "We do not ask someone to coach who has no familiarity with the game, yet worship committees and pastors are frequently making musical judgments without any exposure to the elemental principles of music, including the seemingly simple act of listening."[2]

To learn to listen, to study the Church's worship throughout time and space, to explore new music and forms, to probe Scripture texts deeply, to

---

1. Carol Doran and Thomas H. Troeger, *Trouble at the Table: Gathering the Tribes for Worship* (Nashville: Abingdon Press, 1992), p. 86. For that reason the royalties of this book are being directed to the church music aspect of the Lutheran Music Program (which sponsors summer institutes for high school vocal and instrumental musicians). For more information, contact the executive director, Dr. Victor E. Gebauer, at 122 West Franklin Avenue, Suite 522, Minneapolis, MN 55404; phone (612) 879-9555; fax (612) 879-9547.

2. Doran and Troeger, *Trouble at the Table,* p. 49.

think theologically, to ask better questions, to converse together appropriately with others in leadership — these are all part of the effort that must be expended if we are to plan worship well. Once upon a time it was easy, when church denominations specified certain liturgies or the mass was done everywhere the same, but we live in times when great care and faithfulness are required to be *in* the world and accessible to it and yet not *of* the world and indistinguishable from it. Worship uses the tools of cultures (language and music and speech forms) to announce a different culture — that of the kingdom of God.

Expanding the Basic Criteria

Caring about the people in the culture that is around the Church, knowing that the Church is an alternative community that is often against the surrounding culture, and recognizing that elements of the culture provide tools for use in the Church's worship, what forms can we employ and what questions can guide our choices? In *Reaching Out without Dumbing Down* I focus on three basic criteria for all our choices: (1) Is God kept the Subject/Object? (2) Does worship nurture believers' character? and (3) Does it deepen the community?

Over the years since that book came out I have expanded the questions continually to try to find means by which pastors and musicians, the trained and untrained, the lovers of different styles, and people of different ages, backgrounds, classes, or races can talk together to end the conflicts that rage over what kind of worship we should have. My expansions have become a family joke because I like to underscore lists by including a symbolic number of items — so at one point there were ten questions on the list (since that is the Jewish number of completion), then twelve (the number of the people of God), then fourteen (doubly perfect, since seven is the biblical number for perfection). When my work on this chapter produced sixteen, I told Myron this would never do because that isn't a theological symbolic number. He responded that it was, since sixteen is four times four, and four is the universal number. Perhaps then the following list can symbolize a totally universal questioning as we talk together, so that the elements we choose for worship can be the best possible to hint at the splendor of God for the sake of nurturing the Church for mission to the world.

Let me assure the reader that I am not a closet "traditionalist," as some critics like to claim (see Chapter 11). There are many good gifts in the Church's heritage, but often churches have gotten stuck in ruts over it. There are also many good gifts in new music and forms for worship, but churches often choose them for the wrong reasons or don't choose them well. I certainly do not dislike "contemporary" music, even though I think that title is ill-defined (as discussed in Chapter 24). For worship I have played guitar and organ (and my recorders and harp), composed new anthems and songs, and directed choirs and instrumentalists in a wide variety of musical styles from a diversity of ethnic traditions and eras. The major problem in many churches is simply that, in many cases, worship planners don't realize how much carefulness is required to sort good new materials from the less than good, a process already quite well completed for worship elements that have been passed on in a tradition and therefore appear in hymnbooks. Hymns from past eras have stood the test of time usually because their content is strong and their music felicitous.

Questions of Propriety

Last year when I wrote an article on worship for *Christian Century* and suggested that we ask questions of appropriateness for worship,[3] some readers criticized me for setting myself up as an authority on what is appropriate. I have never claimed that, for the authority lies elsewhere — indeed, it is the authority of the larger community. Matters of integrity, coherence, craft, and biblical faithfulness are not so relative as our present culture wants to insist. There is consensus among biblical scholars over a great many aspects of God's character, among musicians over basic rules of aesthetics, among poets over fundamental principles of good writing, and among physiologists over the effects of certain kinds of music on the human psyche. Certainly persons with different tastes will react to songs in a variety of ways, but most would agree, for example, that a melody of three notes played in the same succession over and over is not musically interesting. Other aspects of musical effects are scientifically measurable.[4]

Research shows, for example, that there are serious implications for human bodies in the sympathetic vibrations or entrainment (that is, "dragging into itself") generated by certain frequencies. As Steven Halpern observes in

3. See Marva J. Dawn, "Beyond the Worship Wars," *Christian Century* 114, no. 18 (June 4-11, 1997): 550-52.

4. I am greatly indebted to Susan Palo Cherwien, who shared the information of the next three paragraphs with me through the research documented in her unpublished paper, "That Spoke So Sweetly and So Well: Music and the Body, Music and the Mind, Music and the Spirit."

Sound Health, "Imposed vibration can disrupt harmony and cause transformation at a molecular level."[5] Halpern reports on an experiment conducted by R. Murray Schafer in which students in both the United States/Canada and Europe were asked to sing the musical pitch that they felt predominated in themselves. The overwhelming majority of North Americans sang a B-natural, while the Europeans sang a G-sharp. The researcher wondered about this finding until he learned that those pitches corresponded to the cycles per second (cps.) of the oscillation of electric current in respective homes — 50 cps. for Europeans and 60 cps. for North Americans.[6] Correlatively, Andrew Watson and Nevill Drury wonder, "Is it not possible that musical vibrations, made by musical instruments or our own voices, can have an effect on how the cells of our body are arranged?"[7]

It is beyond the scope of this chapter to go into all of the possibilities researchers have investigated regarding music's influence on muscles (rock music actually makes muscles go weak), on the brain (the iambic meter of a great proportion of poetry imitates the "lub-dub" of our beating hearts and thus produces a unifying effect), on healing (certain kinds of music decrease the amount of anesthesia and the amount of recovery time needed), and on other elements of the whole person. My point is merely to emphasize that there are many reasons — physical as well as theological — why certain kinds of music might be more appropriate for worship, while other sorts might produce effects contrary to what is desired.[8]

Many have questioned, for example, the wide (and quite unexpected) popularity of the CD *Chant,* which records simply the singing of the Benedictine monks of Santo Domingo de Silos. Perhaps its prominence can be explained by this account documenting the effects on the body of such music:

> A Benedictine monastery, full of post–Vatican II zeal, decided to implement many changes in their prayer life. One of the things they discarded was the habit of rising in the middle of the night and chanting Matins. They substituted a spoken or even privately read divine office in place of the chanted and sung divine office.

---

5. Steven Halpern and Louis Savary, *Sound Health: The Music That Makes Us Whole* (New York: Harper and Row, 1985), p. 42.

6. Halpern and Savary, *Sound Health,* p. 7.

7. Andrew Watson and Nevill Drury, *Healing Music* (Sydney: Prism Books, 1987), p. 27.

8. A most amazing collection of articles concerning the neuropsychological foundations and neurobiologic functions of music is provided by Manfred Clynes, ed., *Music, Mind, and Brain: The Neuropsychology of Music* (New York: Plenum Press, 1982).

The monks began to complain about being tired. Their complaining brought a series of doctors to the cloister. The first doctor said that of course they were tired. After all, they got up in the middle of the night. . . . So the monastic schedule was changed. No longer did they even rise, much less sing or speak or read for an hour. The doctor overlooked the fact that these monks had been rising and chanting since the [sixth] century without complaint. The schedule change was to no avail.

Another doctor was called in . . . [who] knew at once the problem must be the lack of meat in their diet. It is clear these modern-day monks with heavy teaching schedules can't maintain their strength without meat. . . . [M]eat was added to their diet, again without noticing that these monks had gone without much meat for 1500 years with no harm. Thorough environmental, psychological and physical analyses were done.

Finally [French physician Tomatis] was brought in. He immediately restored the old schedule and diet and, most important, he restored the chant. Within 10 days he reported all fatigue was banished. Once they began to chant, they could give up their hour of sleep, forget the meat and still be able to enjoy the kind of vigor that makes the average life expectancy of a monk over 90 years.[9]

The album *Chant* has, no doubt, many reasons for its popularity — perhaps its holiness, its simplicity, its truth. It is also, indeed, healing for those who hear.

Questions for Worship Planning

The basic question underlying all of the following is whether or not what we choose for worship — our music, our liturgy, our prayers, our sermons, our architecture, everything — is appropriate[10] for the purpose of worship, which is for God.[11] If we ask worshipers what they believe is appropriate as opposed to what they want, we will hear entirely different answers. The questions in this chapter arise primarily because we need in our times to be more theolog-

9. Clarence Thompson, "The Sound of Healing," *Festivals* 6, no. 4, p. 5 (as cited in Susan Palo Cherwien, "That Spoke So Sweetly and So Well").

10. This word choice was suggested to me by the doctoral research of Barbara Resch, who studied youth from a diversity of locations and thirty-five religious groups including nonchurched youth; see "Adolescents' Attitudes towards the Appropriateness of Religious Music" (unpublished D.M.A. dissertation, Indiana University, 1996).

11. See chapter 5, "God as the Center of Worship: Who Is Worship For?" of Marva J. Dawn, *Reaching Out without Dumbing Down: A Theology of Worship for the Turn-of-the-Century Culture* (Grand Rapids: Wm. B. Eerdmans Publishing Co., 1995), pp. 75-104.

ical about worship. Catering to tastes has led to very human-centered worship.

Furthermore, these questions should be discussed in a community of discourse, a caring fellowship of those concerned for the well-being of the Church and its outreach to the world through faithful discipleship. We need to converse with each other more thoroughly to come to better understandings of truth, which usually lies beyond our differences of opinion. Remember that all our choices depend on our desire to be faithfully formed by God's Word. As we learned in the opening sermon of this book, our choices and creations must be guided by the exhortation in Colossians 3:16 that by our psalms, hymns, and spiritual songs the members of the community teach and admonish each other. Let us look then at questions to be discussed together as a community, and may that very discussion be a source of teaching, too.

1. *What is appropriate for displaying the character and interventions of God?* If God is the Subject, who makes it possible for us to worship him, then the elements we choose for worship must be faithful to who God is, as revealed in the Scriptures and through the community of his people over time. What kind of God do we have, and what tools for worship best reveal a diversity of God's attributes and the many ways he works in the world?

These days God's intimacy with us seems to be amply displayed, but how do we capture God's awe-fullness? or mystery? or wrath? Why is it, for example, that we rarely use the lament psalms in worship?

George Lindbeck has emphasized that Christianity is a language (see Chapter 29 of this book), a way of speaking about, and living in response to, God. Theological musician David Hendricksen, in a private conversation, helped me to see that we need to be like Shakespeare or Martin Luther, who virtually created the modern English and German languages, respectively. In a culture that is no longer Christian, we need to create a new bridging language that is both faithful to the biblical vocabulary about God and understandable to the people around us.[12] In evangelism, I think, we should veer a bit closer to the culture; in worship, on the other hand, we bend (and bow) closer to God to hear his language more faithfully (while still retaining accessibility). What we must take extra pains to avoid is translating the splendor of God into commercialized language, since that is the primary idiom of our milieu.[13]

---

12. See George R. Hunsberger and Craig Van Gelder, eds., *The Church between Gospel and Culture: The Emerging Mission in North America* (Grand Rapids: Wm. B. Eerdmans Publishing Co., 1996).

13. How best to bridge the faithful past and the searching future can lead to some

The ancient formula "In the Name of the Father and of the Son and of the Holy Spirit," which traditionally began worship services, positively demonstrates this first criterion and clearly reminds us that worship is for the Trinity — and that worship is possible only because God has called us there. One congregation at which I served as guest preacher underscored this perspective by inviting congregants to meditation before worship with these lines at the top of the worship folder: "We speak to God before the service. God speaks to us in the service. We speak to each other after the service. As you are seated in the pew, please bow in silent prayer."

Sometimes liturgies or songs are unsuitable because they trivialize God, as do these words from a congregational responsive reading I encountered elsewhere as a guest preacher: "and thank you, God, for the many savory guises of the lowly egg." I have tested that line with musicians and pastors at numerous conferences, and the community always agrees that this sentence sounds too much like someone trying to be clever and is too trite to be suitable for worship. The great advantage of using liturgies in hymnals or denominational worship resources is that they have stood the test of time or have been written and deemed appropriate by the larger Church and not just one individual.

2. *Are these lines appropriately written?* This question is simply one of excellence in poetic craftsmanship. If God is infinitely wonderful, we want to choose the best writing available to worship him. Often worship elements are inappropriate simply because the poetry is grammatically incorrect, it suffers from vain (or shallow) repetitions, or it contains unclear phrasing. Before the Gospel reading one Sunday when I was a guest preacher in a congregation divided into two different styles of worship (a practice questioned in Chapter 15), participants in the first service sang, "Lord, to whom shall we go? You have the words of eternal life" — Peter's response in John 6:68 after Jesus asked the disciples if they, too, would leave him. In contrast, the second service worshipers sang, "Open our days, Open our nights, to see the Way and the Truth and the Life." Do days or nights see? Though the poet probably meant that *we* would see Jesus in the ordi-

---

extremely difficult questions. A Ukrainian student whom I met at Westminster Choir College suffers deeply from the dialectical tension of treasuring the Orthodox music of his past heritage and wanting to reach out to a younger generation in the United States who are leaving their native language behind as they are assimilated into the customs of their new homeland. Since the particular music of this Orthodox heritage is inextricably connected to the Ukrainian language and the texts are thus untranslatable, what is needed are new composers and poets who can develop a similar richness in sound and vocabulary for Orthodox music that fits phonetically with the English language.

nary, the phrasing doesn't say that. Moreover, we were approaching not days or nights, but the Gospel lesson.

Superb poets such as Susan Palo Cherwien, Thomas Troeger, Jaroslav Vajda, and Brian Wren set excellent models of faithful crafting of texts. Of course, each church body has its favorite contemporary poets, but these four demonstrate that the texts we write must come out of our immersion in the splendor of God, our passion for worshiping him, and our involvement in his Church — and then the texts must be questioned by the Church for their suitability.

3. *Is this music appropriately written?* This question is the same as #2, except to deal with excellence in music rather than in texts. We can ask about melody, harmony, accompaniment, rhythm, tempo, complexity, movement of the line, and so forth. Numerous "styles" of music can be appropriate, but each piece must be judged respective to its own style for the caliber of its accomplishment. Some newer songs are just plain boring, circling around as little as three notes and two chords. Most monotonous hymns from previous epochs (though not all!) have already been thrown out. We want the best for God because God is worthy of our best.

Again, numerous composers could be mentioned from various church bodies who are exemplary in their crafting for the sake of revealing God's splendor. Music publishers have told me that across denominational lines there is great appreciation for the work of such people as David Cherwien, Marty Haugen, and Robert Hobby. These three, though very different in "style," model the same faithfulness we required of texts, for the music they compose has come out of their immersion in the splendor of God, their passion for worshiping him, and their involvement in his Church — and it has passed the testing of the Church with regard to suitability. Let me also emphasize the great gifts of those who are working to bring the music of global cultures into our churches.

4. *Are the music and text appropriately coherent?* Does the sound match the words? Is the tempo appropriate for the text? Is the piece honest? By that I mean does it avoid manipulation of emotions, in contrast to the commercial music of our culture? Cross-cultural studies have discovered nearly universal recognition of certain qualities of coherence. Almost everyone would agree that we cannot capture God's tenderness with blaring brass. In contrast, what kinds of sounds and vocabulary display the grandeur of God?

One frequently sung "contemporary" piece that seems to me incongruous is a setting of the psalm, "O Lord, our Lord, how majestic is your name in all the earth." The words are biblical, of course, but the music of that song isn't *majestic,* which, as dictionaries tell us, means to be very grand, dignified, lofty, stately. Nor does the melody match the original Hebrew adjective, which is also usually defined as great, mighty, noble, princely. This is not a matter of taste — I like the tune — but probably everyone who heard the melody without the words would agree that its timbre is more playful than august, more like frolic than nobility, more suited to penny whistles than to processional banners and kettledrums. No one would call the melody stately; the result of its constant use in churches is that many people, especially youth, no longer know what the word *majestic* actually means.

All kinds of music and forms — old and new — can sometimes be done in ill-suited ways. One Sunday I experienced the same kind of jarring incongruence when the fitting melodies from the hymnal version of *Kyrie Eleison* were played by the organist much too fast to let us acknowledge our need for the Lord's mercy. Similarly, the words of the prayers were rattled off by the pastor incredibly hastily, as if he were not thinking about them and didn't want to give us time to contemplate them either.

These first four questions emphasize that every piece that we sing in worship should be assessed for the propriety of its music, its words, and the combination of the two. Correlatively, we should ask about the coherence of tempo and tone with the words we say. Do these match what we are saying and singing about God or God's people or the world?

5. *What is appropriate for forming the character of the followers of Christ?* What kind of persons are the elements of our worship forming? Are we becoming the kind of people God calls us to be, imitators of Christ, reflecting his image?

One reviewer of my first book on worship criticized me for being "elitist" about head knowledge, whereas everyone, he said, should worship with the heart — but this comment misunderstands what Scripture passages about praising God with our whole heart mean (e.g., Psalm 9:1-2). The biblical word *heart* signifies the wholistic will, not merely the emotions, and thus emphasizes that we worship God intentionally, deliberately, mindfully — even when we don't feel like it — since God is worthy of our adoration. We live in a culture that overemphasizes emotion, in contrast to churches that in the past have understressed it. I do not deny the importance of our feelings, but we must recognize that formation of character often requires rechanneling our emotions, training them, submitting them to what we know and, more deeply, to what God has revealed about his will for us.

Moreover, to live our faith merely by our emotions is to ignore to our peril all the narratives of the Scriptures which demonstrate that the beliefs of Israel and the Church developed in response to a formative Word given to the community. Thus, Christian character is nurtured by the "renewing of [our] minds" (Romans 12:2), through the transformation of the Holy Spirit at work by means of God's Revelation and the wisdom of the Body.

Joseph Sittler memorably said, "Is the great catholic faith of nineteen centuries to be reduced to my interior dimensions?" Is worship forming us instead to be part of the whole people of God — caring about the world around us and reaching out to it in witness? Worship is not about feeling good; it is about becoming good.

6. *What is appropriate for developing a sense of the Church catholic?* How can what we do in worship give the participants a deeper awareness that they are part of the whole people of God throughout space and time?

It has been years since I have had the privilege of singing in worship the Church's ancient *Te Deum,* which I loved as a college student when we sang it regularly in the chapel Matins. The reason I long to sing it again is that it so fully names all the witnesses who worship with us on a Sunday morning. I don't know of any text that creates such an awareness as this:

> You are God; we praise you. You are the Lord; we acclaim you. You are the eternal Father; all creation worships you. To you all angels, all the powers of heaven, cherubim and seraphim, sing in endless praise: Holy, holy, holy Lord, God of power and might, heaven and earth are full of your glory. The glorious company of apostles praise you. The noble fellowship of prophets praise you. The white-robed army of martyrs praise you. Throughout the world the holy Church acclaims you: Father, of majesty unbounded; your true and only Son, worthy of all worship; and the Holy Spirit, advocate and guide. . . .[14]

What trinitarian splendor! What a mighty cloud of witnesses!

The great advantage of hymnbooks is that they convey a sense of the larger church body, united in worship according to the wisdom of all the people together. Using global music, saying the common creeds of the Church and the Lord's Prayer, singing the *Sanctus,* remembering that the Lord's Supper links us to all Christians everywhere, hosting joint worship services with other denominations or congregations of predominantly another race — all of these help to fix in our minds an awareness of being Church together with all the saints.

7. *What is appropriate for building community in this place?* How is our worship equipping us to be genuine community, a people who deeply care about each other, who bring diversity into unity, and who reach out to the

---

14. The entire text of the *Te Deum* (with modernized vocabulary) is included as the heading to chapter 10 of *Reaching Out without Dumbing Down,* p. 241.

world around us? How can what we use for worship counteract the ravages of our technological milieu, which pulls us apart from each other? How can our songs and sermons give more of a sense of *we*? How will we slow people down so that they can come away from a cultural environment that is too busy, too big, too misdirected, and filled with too many choices for the development of authentic intimacy? We must avoid cozy elitism, which leaves out the stranger, but we want instead to develop a public space in our worship into which all, including the stranger, may enter.

Let me cite a negative example. In one worship service for which I was the guest preacher, the opening call to worship included the congregational response, "We come in our different ways, walking in our own styles, at our own speeds, but we come to join the journey." That response puts all the initiative on us, rather than on God calling us to worship as emphasized by question #1 above — and it fractures the community by emphasizing our isolation in our own styles. I'm not saying that we shouldn't acknowledge our differences, but corporate worship is intended to bring us together in spite of them, to overcome (instead of to aid and abet) our culture's narcissistic individualism for the sake of uniting us in the common faith of the Church.

In contrast, let me hold up the example I know best, the primarily African-American congregation to which we belong. Under its grandfatherly pastor, now retired, this church had a deep sense of its place in the catholic community and of itself as a true community of diversity in unity. Worship utilized the liturgy of the Church, and — in contradiction of those who say that teenagers don't like liturgy — the students in this parish recited it with full voice. The key was that the pastor recognized the value of being part of the whole Church in the worship service, explained to the members why the liturgy is so valuable, and printed a complete statement of the week's theme at the beginning of the worship folder. Then he carried out the theme with all the "propers" of the early Church's liturgy, including the Introit, Collect, Gradual, and Gospel refrains, which many congregations leave out for the sake of time. He also utilized a range of music that was remarkably diverse. One Sunday we began by singing a theologically substantive contemporary chorus, "We Are Marching in the Light of God" from South Africa, and a refrain from Taizé. Other worship music that day included a Lutheran chorale, a Wesleyan pietistic song, and a soulfully sung African spiritual. Such diversity helps to form an inclusive community!

The great delight of this congregation is that everyone who comes is warmly welcomed; no one is a stranger. In these days of mega-churches, I keep realizing that smaller fellowships provide greater possibilities for genuine hospitality and true community, where the same persons remember you from week to week and care if you are missing. "Coffee hour" is not limited to a few minutes, but instead nurtures long communal conversation.

Two final comments are necessary on the subject of building community, and these arise in connection with my concern that the committee sorting through music by means of the criteria I am offering be genuinely open to the gifts of all eras and tastes. Since many of the persons reading this book are no doubt skilled musicians, I must emphasize that we cannot encourage others to be open to the music of the past unless we ourselves are open to the gifts and truths of new music.

If we remember the analogy of Diedra's restaurant at the beginning of Chapter 16, we might expand that parable to imagine that sometimes we might choose one of the chef's three entrés which we have never tasted before and discover that we don't like it. Since we know that she prepares things well and we trust her skill, we would not conclude that the dish itself is no good or that we should never return to the restaurant or that we should tell other customers not to order it. Similarly, there might be certain styles of music that we don't particularly prefer, but we will still respect the fact that these are probably appealing to others and have been chosen with attention to what fits the texts or reveals certain aspects of God and therefore that they are good for us. We can also be glad that they are prepared with the same carefulness and skill. I made this same point in Chapter 15 by saying that worship is not a matter of taste and that as part of the community it is my responsibility to sing songs I might not like for the sake of the whole Body.

8. *What is appropriate for the level of the congregation's ability to participate?* How do we make sure that everyone is enabled to sing the songs we use, partake of the blessings of the service, and share in the work of the people? For example, how can we take care so that everyone can receive the Lord's Supper — the elderly and others who find it difficult to move about; those who are confined to wheelchairs or are quadriplegic, as is a friend of mine, and need accessibility; those who are recovering alcoholics and so don't want wine; or those who are allergic to wine and grape juice. Are instructions clear so that strangers know how to proceed?

Similarly, the "work of the people" in singing often takes training. Our culture no longer teaches people to sing, so how can we make sure that worship participants can hear melodies clearly, can read the words, can find the materials needed to be involved? For one congregation split into two styles of worship (see Chapter 15) I had chosen the hymn "Wake, Awake, for Night Is Flying" to follow the sermon in both services since I know of no other song, old or new, that better recounts Matthew 25. To be hospitable I encouraged the "contemporary" service worshipers to open their hymnbooks to follow the musical score, even though the words were printed in their bulletins. (Even those who can't read music can tell if notes go up or down.) The organist introduced the melody by playing it in double octaves, and I left my microphone on for the first verse so that the congregation could clearly hear the melody. Though "Wake, Awake" is more difficult than most of the songs usually used in that service, a large number of congregants told me later how much they appreciated that hymn, thus confirming my belief that musical style is not the barrier when traditional elements are used for worship. Failures to teach and to lead are the impediments.

In fact, much of the rest of that same service had been inhospitable. Melodies for words printed in the worship folder could be found in a "Celebrate Book," but there was no copy of it where I sat. As I looked out over the congregation I noticed that quite a few people were not singing during those pieces. For some songs there was no printed music available, and the instrumentalists were not playing the melody. To leave people out of the singing in such a way frustrates Churchbeing.

In contrast, two weeks later in New Orleans the elderly gentleman sitting beside me hospitably explained before worship how to find the music — and later escorted me to make sure I could find the restroom. Also in that congregation the choir processed both at the beginning and at the end of worship, and their movement around the sanctuary strengthened the singing. (This was not an empty formalism because both times each member bowed reverently at the altar and gave us all a sense of God's preeminence.) Though this congregation was in an older, changing neighborhood, I noticed that *everyone* around me was singing — both the old people and the young. Participation in worship, no matter what the style of music, can be deepened by joyful leadership and good modeling.

9. *What is appropriate for including more of the gifts of the people in the worship space and time?* What new art can we use to evoke worship themes? What dance or symbols will display texts? How could we use new forms for Scripture readings that include more participants?[15] How can we help worship participants realize that their offerings include much more than their money? How can we prevent the elevation of some specific gifts or certain people to the exclusion of others? How can we best evoke the contributions of all the people? In what ways can the children be more actively engaged in the gifts of worship? What leadership can teenagers provide?

At one conference worship service for which I was preaching, I almost

---

15. For superb ideas regarding dramatic readings of texts, contact theater veteran Keith Titus at 514 E. Savidge, Spring Lake, MI 49456; office telephone (616) 842-1985.

missed utilizing a great gift in the congregation. I had been planning to sing snatches of "God's Gonna Trouble de Water" as part of my sermon on the healing of the man at the pool of Bethzatha (John 5:1-18), but only a case of laryngitis caused me to turn to someone else to help. The African-American woman who sang instead had a far richer voice, a vastly greater ability to improvise on specific words I wanted to highlight, and an immeasurably deeper understanding of the spiritual. What a great loss it would have been if I had sung myself instead of using her gifts!

10. *What is appropriate for envisioning the reign of God with all its truth, beauty, and goodness?* This follows #9 because churches being constructed these days seem to hide their Christian specificity since they are being told that their symbols are alienating to seekers. Contrarily, I am convinced that if the members of a congregation are hospitable and inviting, if they are equipped to explain what the symbols mean, the accoutrements of worship can be wonderfully enriching. How can our worship space display the splendor of God with the balancing of the philosophical trio of truth (in sermon and song texts), beauty (in the worship space), and goodness (in the hospitality on the part of the people)? Goodness keeps truth and beauty from being too overwhelming to the newcomer. (On the subject of beauty, refer again to Chapter 25.)

We must also pay attention to what fractures the splendor. This summer I suffered an injury to my good leg and attended a week-long conference in a wheelchair. At one worship service, the person who had removed my chair (which is a rather ugly shade of olive green) after I was seated in a pew left it at the front of the congregation in an open space — and the effect was jarring to me and to others. (The chair would not have been problematic if I had still been seated in it; then it would have underscored inclusivity for the physically impaired.) Several people commented to me after the service how much it helped the ambience when, at my urging, my pusher hid the chair behind an unused upright piano. Similarly, let us ask if anything is blocking the focus on God. At one service I attended, a screen was pulled down and subsequently hid both the cross and the altar for the entire worship time.

11. *What is appropriate to create a missional community?* How will what we do in worship immerse us in the language of the alternative community, so that we leave the service eager to carry God's reign into the world and to spread his presence throughout the following week? How will our worship encourage members of the community to offer their gifts to the world in daily life? (See especially Chapter 29 of this book.)

Do both songs and sermon give us the awareness that worship is not private coziness to make us feel good, but public equipping for our roles as disciples in a world that needs our service? How will our vision of the splendor of God stir in us God's love for his whole creation? What music and words, forms and elements in worship will prepare us to feed the hungry, clothe the naked, build homes for the homeless, visit the prisoners, act as agents of reconciliation, comfort the forlorn, and share with our neighbors the good news of God's reign in the world by means of all the actions of our daily life throughout the week?

12. *What is appropriate for the level of pain in the world?* How do our prayers, songs, and sermons keep us mindful of the needs to which we can minister?

During the year that I had cancer I found it impossible to worship in places that sang only happy songs (rather than genuine praise songs that focus on the character and interventions of God). Happiness alone is not congruent with the disequilibrium of our lives, nor is it faithful to God — our suffering God.

Once again this question is intended to motivate a balancing between the extremes of the kinds of morose worship many people experienced in the past and the constantly "upbeat" worship urged upon us these days. Worship that is true to both God and human beings will realistically face the sorrows and remember with hope the victory of Christ over all pain and suffering.

13. *What is appropriate for this time in the Church year?* How can our worship always give participants a sense of the whole meta-narrative and our particular place in it? The seasons of the Church year guide us to a wider sense of the master story of our faith.

One Sunday when I was preaching at a church split into two kinds of worship services I was very disappointed by how the "contemporary" service failed to take into consideration that it was the third to last Sunday of the church year. My sermon used the Gospel lesson from Matthew 25 (Jesus' parable of the ten virgins) and the First Testament reading from Amos 5:18-24 about the "day of the Lord," who declares, "I hate, I despise your festivals, and I take no delight in your solemn assemblies" — but none of the music or liturgy had matched the day's theme of judgment.

In contrast, in the traditional service that same day the end-times theme had already been set by the "Collect of the Day" from the propers that accompany the assigned pericope lists. This prayer appropriately correlated with the texts (and consequently my sermon): "Lord, when the day of wrath comes we have no hope except in your grace. Make us so to watch for the last days that the consummation of our hope may be the joy of the marriage feast of your son, Jesus Christ our Lord." Compare that with the following prayer used in the contemporary service: "O Holy Spirit, you are the breath that inspires and the fire that enlightens each word God speaks. As we walk into our ordinary days with our ordinary ways, send us out enlivened and enriched by God's word to be messengers of hope to the world." The second line might have suited the service's conclusion, but it didn't begin to prepare the listeners for a message about the last days and our worship as we wait. (Moreover, the first line is poorly verbalized, as questioned in point #2. Does the Spirit enlighten God's words or us? Did the poet mean instead that the Spirit inspires those who speak or record God's words?)

14. *What is appropriate for the texts of the day?* This question can free us from battles over style because a wide diversity of styles are appropriate if they express best the content of the texts. The key to using such diversity is that all the music must be taught well (as question #8 above emphasizes).

One Sunday in our primarily African-American congregation, the service wound up with a great diversity of styles of music, not because we intended it, but because each piece we sang captured best the related text. The first two songs were black spirituals, and LaVeta, who does soul music so well, played the piano. The First Testament lesson that day was Isaiah 12, so for the children's sermon the whole congregation learned the "contemporary" song "Behold, God Is My Salvation" (with its Hebrew melody), while I taught the children a Jewish dance. The Epistle lesson that day was about the immensity of God's grace, so next we sang the early American hymn "There's a Wideness in God's Mercy." For that song we tuned all the strings of a guitar to E's and B's, and one person strummed it to produce a droning while we sang Appalachian-style "call and response" for the verses.

My sermon that day was on Luke 15 — and I have never found a more wonderful setting of that Scripture passage than the Kevin Nichols' text "Our Father, We Have Wandered,"[16] the second verse of which ends, "In haste you come to meet us and home rejoicing bring, in gladness there to greet us with calf and robe and ring." These words are set to the melody "Herzlich tut mich verlangen," most often associated with the chorale "O Sacred Head Now Wounded," with a harmonization by J. S. Bach from the St. Matthew Passion. LaVeta doesn't read notes, so I played that hymn (we each wish we could play the way the other one does) and taught the congregation the melody first.

After worship several members commented to me how much they loved the Nichols/Bach hymn and the Jewish and Appalachian music. Certainly we had a great sense of the whole people of God in that service — simply because those songs fit the texts of the day so well.

---

16. This text is copyrighted by the International Committee on English in the Liturgy, Inc., and is available in *With One Voice* (Minneapolis: Augsburg Fortress, 1995).

15. *What is appropriate for this place in the worship service?* We certainly need different styles or timbres when we are confessing our sins as opposed to when we are celebrating the Lord's Supper or singing a hymn of praise. What is most fitting to gather a congregation together or to send it out?

One service I attended included a *Kyrie Eleison* that contained excellent verses asking for the peace of the world and the health of the church, for peace in this worshiping community, in hearts and homes — but the jolly music did not at all fit *Kyrie Eleison*. The melody sparkled — it would have suited a post-communion song quite well — but it didn't call us to intimate conversation with God, to meditation on peace.

16. *What is appropriate to evoke the recognition that we need more, to create a hunger and thirst for worship again next week?* How can what we do hint at the infinite more there is to know of God? Does what we do stretch the minds and souls of worship participants so that they know they have much more to learn in future services? Is there enough variety so that worship is not stuck in a rut, yet enough continuity so that there is a sense that this gathering together with the community to praise God is truly our home?

Perhaps if we continue to ask questions such as these concerning the propriety of our art, drama, music, liturgy, prayers, sermons, offerings — every dimension of worship — then we won't fight about the wrong things, such as style. Then we could perhaps use a wider host of gifts for the sake of experiencing the splendor of God and the fellowship of being Church together.

27

Pause to Wonder . . .
Choral and Hymn Texts*

A Gathering Hymn:
"Come Away from Rush and Hurry"
to the melody "Beach Spring"

Come away from rush and hurry
   to the stillness of God's peace;
From our vain ambition's worry,
   come to Christ to find release.
Come away from noise and clamor,
   life's demands and frenzied pace;
Come to join the people gathered
   here to seek and find God's face.

In the pastures of God's goodness
   we lie down to rest our soul.
From the waters of his mercy
   we drink deeply, are made whole.

*I have included a few of my hymn texts here to exemplify the crafting of songs for the Church. The gathering, Easter, and wedding texts are sung to familiar melodies. The Pentecost hymn arose in my mind with its new melody, and the Christmas text was set by a friend as a choir anthem. Those who have purchased this book are welcome to copy these hymns and use them.

At the table of his presence
    all his saints are richly fed.
With the oil of his anointing
    into service we are led.

Come, then, children, with your burdens —
    life's confusions, fears, and pain.
Leave them at the cross of Jesus;
    take instead his kingdom's reign.
Bring your thirsts, for he will quench them —
    he alone will satisfy.
All our longings find attainment
    when to self we gladly die.

A Christmas/Epiphany Anthem:
"Ceaseless My Rejoicing" (A Carol of Paradox)

Gentle comes the might of God;
Poor, the gen'rous Savior —
All of God wrapped in a child,
Mystery forever!

Humble shepherds angels call —
Magi at a manger,
Promised Rescuer so small,
Peace in spite of danger!

My frail heart can't take it in.
All is wrapped in splendor.
Once so captured, lost in sin,
Now I'm free to render

Praises! Praises burst my soul;
Songs, my gladness voicing.
Oh, the Christ Child makes me whole —
Ceaseless, my rejoicing!
Alleluia!

(David Hendricksen's setting of this poem for four-part
choir and piano ends with a sustained canon on the phrase
"Ceaseless, my rejoicing: Praises!" and then, after a crescen-
doing chorus of "Praises," the final "Alleluia!")

An Easter Hymn: "We Live, Too"
for the melody "Wie schön leuchtet"
("How Lovely Shines the Morning Star")

Christ is arisen — we live, too!
His rising makes the whole world new.
All evil's been defeated.
His work has done all that God willed.
The judgments we deserve are stilled,
Will never be repeated.
Now free, we'll be
Willing bearers, eager sharers of his graces.
Our lives filled with ceaseless praises.

Pentecost Hymn: "Tongues of Fire"

Enter, Holy Spirit; come with tongues of fire.
Stir us to commitment; fill us with desire.
When the seeds are planted, none can come to flow'r
Unless you guide the growing, watering with your pow'r.

Much in us needs changing; much is marred by sin.
You are the transformer — change us from within.
How we long for goodness! How we long to be
All that our God created. Spirit, set us free!

Come, renew our Church, sweet heav'nly dove of peace.
May our hearts be yearning, and our zeal increase
For your will and justice to be done on earth
Until we join the angels in celestial mirth.

Keep us strong and faithful, fervent in our prayer,
Sharing Christ's salvation through our words and care.
Holy Spirit, never leave us on our own
Until the Savior brings us to the Father's throne.

Pentecost Hymn: "Tongues of Fire"

En - ter, Ho - ly Spir - it; come with tongues of fire.
Much in us needs chang - ing; much is marred with sin.
Come, re - new our Church, sweet heav'n - ly dove of peace.
Keep us strong and faith - ful, fer - vent in our prayer,

Stir us to com - mit - ment; fill us with de - sire.
You are the trans - form - er; change us from with - in.
May our hearts be yearn - ing, and our zeal in - crease
Shar - ing Christ's sal - va - tion through the Word and care.

When the seeds are plant - ed, none can come to flow'r
How we long for good - ness! How we long to be
for your will and just - ice to be done on earth
Ho - ly Spir - it, nev - er leave us on our own

Un - less you guide the grow - ing, Wat - er - ing with your pow'r.
All that our God cre - a - ted. Spir - it, set us free!
Un - til we join the an - gels in ce - les - tial mirth.
Un - til the Sa - vior brings us to the Fa - ther's throne!

Pentecost Hymn

Pentecost Hymn for B-flat Clarinet

Wedding Hymn Text: An Opening Hymn
to the melody "Sine Nomine" ("For All the Saints")

Come, Triune God, this wedding feast to bless.
Forgive the sinfulness that we confess.
Draw us into Your love and tenderness.
　　Alleluia. Alleluia!

Come, heavenly Father, with Your loving care.
In gracious mercy, hear and bless our prayer.
Teach us to serve with Joy, our lives to share.
　　Alleluia. Alleluia!

Come, Bridegroom Christ, and call Your Church to be
Holy and blameless that the world may see
Your reign both now and through eternity.
　　Alleluia. Alleluia!

Come, Holy Spirit. Peace upon us show'r.
Draw us together; fill us with Your pow'r.
Stir our commitment in this worship hour.
　　Alleluia. Alleluia!

Wedding Hymn Text: A Closing Hymn
to the melody "The Ash Grove"
("Let All Things Now Living")

The wedding is ending, the Marriage beginning.
Lord Jesus, continue to guide and to bless,
For You are the focus, the meaning, the purpose;
All families are rooted in Your graciousness.
We leave now rejoicing — Our glad praises voicing,
For here in our worship Your message was heard.
Our vows You invited, Our lives You united —
Renewed in commitment to follow Your Word.

Come with us, dear Savior; live in us forever
That Your love may reach out through us to the world.
May You be the center of all that we enter;
May grace be the banner in our lives unfurled.
No matter our sorrows, in all our tomorrows
We know that Your purposes naught can destroy.
In confidence living and filled with thanksgiving,
We reach for the future with true Hope and Joy.

PART VI

For the World: Challenges

Ascribe to the LORD the glory of his name;
worship the LORD in holy splendor.

Psalm 29:2

How do we best reach the world? Much of this book is written to counter-act the claim that we should make our worship services as much like the culture as possible to attract people to Christianity. My thesis is that the world needs us instead to waste our time royally in worship and, consequently, to be Church, a people different from the world and thereby prodigally offering the gifts of the extravagant splendor of God. Genuine worship of God will send us out for the sake of the neighbor. We cannot ascribe to the LORD the glory of his name (that is, his character) without imitating him in lavishly establishing justice and peace in the world. We cannot keep our generous God as our Infinite Center without wanting our neighbors to be immersed in his opulent splendor, too.

Thus, this final section deals with caring for our neighbors by being Church. The initial sermon recognizes that to be God's people requires of us abundant obedience and profuse sacrifice — but that these lead to the truest fulfillment, as well as the most lavish love for the world around us.

Chapters 29 and 30 are especially concerned with congregational outreach to the neighbor. The former asks how our churches will convey to their members a better sense that everyone is called to mission in the world; the latter gives a short introduction to the weighty topic of specifically giving witness to neighbors who do not yet know our triune God. There are many excellent books on evangelism; my purpose is simply to introduce the practice as an outgrowth of worship.

Chapter 31 ties the ribbon to the gift package of this book's last two sections by returning again to the eschatological theme of Part V's initial sermon. This chapter is a modified version of my opening keynote address for the Institute of Liturgical Studies, for which I sketched the effects of the doctrine of eschatology on our worship decisions. This thorough summation will retrace the various parts of my thesis throughout this book of worshiping God and being Church for the world. May God be glorified as we reach out to our neighbors with the splendor of his holy grace.

28

"The Challenge of Discipleship":
*A Sermon**

Texts for the Fourteenth Sunday of Pentecost, Series C:
Deuteronomy 30:15-20; Philemon 1-21; Luke 14:25-33

The Lord be with you. [Response: And also with you!]
Let us pray: Jesus, your Word is truth. Sanctify us in that truth and set
us free to follow it. Make us your disciples by your grace, and open up our
hearts and minds to hear what you are teaching us this morning. Amen.

Yesterday I did an interview in a program about faith for a radio station in
Austin, Texas, to talk about my book *Keeping the Sabbath Wholly*. One of the
first questions the host asked was something like this: "Do we still have to
obey the Sabbath commandment when the New Testament did away with a
lot of the religious laws of the Jews?" That question is often asked. Why
bother to stop working an entire day when those Jewish laws don't apply any-

---

*A sermon something like the following was given at Beautiful Savior Lutheran
Church in Vancouver, Washington, on September 6, 1998. Because the sermon was not recorded, this printed version contains my remembrances of how my outline was spoken in
either or both of the two services. As with all my sermons there, the people at Beautiful
Savior responded warmly when they answered, "And also with you," to my initial blessing,
and they followed along with the printed text as I explicated the Scriptures.

325

more? In fact, the New Testament seems specifically to contradict them in Galatians 4:9-11 and Colossians 2:16-17.

I answered that God's commandments are not terrible burdens that we *have* to fulfill. They are gifts to us because they describe for us God's best design for our lives.

Think about this: Wouldn't it work really well in our world if there was no stealing? You would never have to lock your house when you go away or worry about being mugged in downtown New York City or Vancouver, USA. Wouldn't it work really well in our world if there was no murder or rape? We would never have to fear anymore. Thou shalt not kill; thou shalt not steal; thou shalt not commit sexual sin; thou shalt not bear false witness — if all of these commandments were obeyed, we could live freely. We would thoroughly enjoy living as God designed us to live. And the same is true of Sabbath keeping — what a delight it is that today I don't have to do any work. I can thoroughly enjoy worshiping here with my hometown congregation, picnicking with our guests who are coming, conversing deeply with these friends, relaxing in the beauty of Myron's gardens. God's commandments are a Joy to fulfill.

It is important that we realize this before we look at our texts for today because otherwise what God said in Deuteronomy, what Jesus said in Luke, and what Paul said in Philemon might sound like terrible burdens, instead of the goodness of discipleship.

Jesus tells us today to count the cost — and we must unquestionably recognize that it is indeed the cost of death to us, but it is also the gift of resurrection. There is no better life to live than that of discipleship, for we were created to love God and enjoy or serve him forever. But resurrection can't come without dying first.

Let's begin by turning to today's first reading from Deuteronomy 30:15-20. Part of the reason why I connected this morning's texts to God's creation design is the word translated "prosperity" by the NRSV in verse 15. The Hebrew word is *tov,* that wonderful word which Genesis 1 records God saying continually as he created the cosmos and everything in it. As verse 15 emphasizes, God sets before us the possibility of true life and goodness or prosperity. How is it that we can experience those, instead of death and adversity?

Verse 16 insists that if we obey the LORD's commandments, then we will live — but actually those words "if you obey" are not in the original Hebrew text. Instead, the Hebrew connects verse 16 to 15; this is how God sets before us life and prosperity: by commanding us to love the LORD our God, walk in his ways, and observe his commandments, decrees, and ordinances. In other words, he doesn't give us those words of instruction to spoil all our fun, but to help us find life! Notice that the name LORD is LORD in all capital letters, so it is the covenant God who is named — the great "I AM," the one who keeps his promises. Certainly what he commands will be good for us, will bring us true life.

For the Israelites to whom these words were spoken the promise meant the goodness of the land they were entering, the multiplication of their numbers in that land. That is why verse 17 is so important — because, in contrast to its warnings, their hearts did turn away; they did cease to listen to God; they were drawn astray to worship other gods and serve them; and the result was what verse 18 predicted. They did not live long in the land when they violated God's design for it. They were taken into captivity by the Assyrians and then the Babylonians. It wasn't that God wanted this to happen to them; the Israelites made the choice to practice injustice, to neglect God's blueprint for jubilee and the return of land so that no one would get rich while another became impoverished.

As the apostle Paul said about some other narratives concerning the Israelites, "These things happened to them to serve as an example, and they were written down to instruct us, on whom the ends of the ages have come. So if you think you are standing, watch out that you do not fall" (1 Corinthians 10:11-12). Just as the people of the First Testament ignored God's commandments to their own detriment and sometimes destruction, so when we violate God's designs we only hurt ourselves.

Deuteronomy 30:19 is a call to us. Heaven and earth are witnesses that God gives us the possibility of life or death. We certainly see that in our world, don't we? The earth is testifying that we have chosen death. Our lack of care for the earth continues to issue in all kinds of death — with various kinds of toxic substances causing illness and destruction to plants, creatures, and ourselves. If we had stewarded the earth according to God's designs, the world wouldn't be in so much trouble with acid rain, global warming, extinction of species, soil loss, water and air pollution.

Therefore, choose life, the LORD says, so that we and our descendants may live. If we really love the LORD our God, obey him, and cling to him, as verse 20 invites us, we shall indeed experience the truest life and the greatest possibility for length of days. For the Israelites God offered the covenant of the land promised to their ancestors. For us, the covenant fulfilled in Christ promises eternal life with God, already begun in our present experience of God's reign in our daily lives.

What a gift this is! Why would we want to choose anything but life?

The Gospel text for today gives several reasons why we might not choose God's life. For one, our family might not like it.

Luke 14:26 makes more sense to me because of an event that happened this past summer. I have always believed that Jesus is not *commanding* us to hate our families, but that he is identifying, and accentuating harshly so that we notice, the problems that result from discipleship and asking us if we are willing to pay that price. This summer at a camp in Minnesota several staff members from foreign countries demonstrated such a cost to themselves as they told of troubles they experienced with their families when they turned to Christ. There were students in the group from China, Japan, Latvia, Estonia, Slovakia, and Poland, and three or four of them expressed great sadness that their families had become very angry with them when they turned to Christ. Others had experienced dangers, mockery or suspicion from their peers, or other kinds of difficulties. Only the young man from Poland said that it was quite easy in his homeland to be a disciple because almost all the Polish are Christians — including most of the Communists.

Would we be willing to risk being ostracized within our own families to follow Jesus? A deeper question is posed by verse 26: Are we able to hate even our own life to be Christ's disciple? (Notice that it doesn't say that we hate *ourselves*, but that we are willing to give up life itself.) I heard a true story once about some Christians gathered together for worship at the time of the Communist enforcement of Soviet atheism. Suddenly some soldiers with automatic rifles burst into the room and demanded that anyone who insisted on being a Christian should line up against the wall; everyone else could leave immediately. Some of the people hurried out quickly; others began to move toward the wall. Once again the soldiers shouted, "If you are a Christian, line up against the wall! Anyone else can go" — and a few others sped away as the troops fixed their aim on those at the wall. After making their demand a third time, one of the soldiers went over to lock the door, while the remaining Christians, willing to hate life itself, looked into the rifle barrels pointed at them.

After the doors had been secured, and to the enormous surprise of the Christians awaiting death, the soldiers abruptly lowered their guns and said quietly, "Now that we know who the *real* Christians are, we'll tell you that we are, too, but we didn't want to risk betrayal by anyone who isn't seriously committed to Christ." Then they asked for the prayers of the saints for their difficult lives as believers in the midst of the military forces ordered to persecute them.

Would you have been standing against that wall? Would I have been? Do we hate our lives enough to lay them on the line as disciples?

Perhaps discipleship is not very strong in the United States because it has never been tested at gunpoint; few young people here have had to risk being disowned by their families; most likely none of us has lost our job or the possibility for education because of our faithfulness.

In verse 27 Jesus declares that if we don't carry our cross and follow him, we cannot be his disciples. I think we usually romanticize that harsh statement a bit too much. We wear pretty crosses and forget what an atrocious instrument of torture a cross is. What if we wore little electric chairs or gallows on a chain instead? We must remember that the only reason to carry a cross is to die on it.

I have often heard people say, "Oh, that is just the cross I have to bear," but they are usually not referring to anything that makes them die. For example, some might say that my physical handicaps are my cross, but they really aren't a cross, usually. However, sometimes a person will say something stupid to me like, "If you just prayed right, you wouldn't have such handicaps." Then keeping myself from slugging that person is a cross! I have to die to my impulse to tell that person off and instead find a way to be gracious and gentle. I have to find a way to die to my pride. To what do you — do I — need to die?

Maybe a better way to think about the cross we bear is to recognize that Christ calls us to give up our "druthers." I'd rather not write books. I'd much rather not get the flak. I'd rather spend my time conversing, visiting with friends, being with people, not dealing with computer hassles. But I *have to* write books! The Word becomes, as Jeremiah said, "fire in my bones — and I become weary of holding it in." Passion about a subject seizes me, and I feel compelled to write for the sake of the Church — but I'd really rather not. This text today forces me to ask, "Will I be obedient to God's call and stick with the nitty-gritty, the grunt work that is no fun at all?"

I use this example only to urge you to ask for yourself: To what might God call me to die? — to what I'd rather do? to my pride maybe, when people criticize? to my sense of confidence when I need to learn from those I dislike? to my own choices for how to spend my time? to *my* way of doing things, even when I know it is right?

After giving us two examples to show how important it is to calculate the cost of discipleship — the builder estimating whether he has enough money to finish the job and the king considering whether he has enough troops to wage war (vv. 28-32) — Jesus shocks us with another hyperbole. We can't be his disciples, he says, if we do not give up *all* our possessions.

People have never liked this text. Scholars like to say that it is simply Jewish overstatement, a way to emphasize the point that we should take discipleship seriously. But I don't think we should dilute it like that. People in the world are starving — and you and I have too much. Many people in our community have no home — and we are too busy to help with the Habitat for Humanity building project. Millions of people are dressed in rags — and our closets are far too full.

By now you might be thinking, "Whew! What's gotten into Marva? She's really hitting us hard today." But I would be doing you a major disservice if I let us escape this text by watering it down, if I did not preach this Word as strongly as Jesus gave it.

However, I would also be doing you a major disservice if I stopped now. If we struggle on, the difficulty of this text from Luke will lead us to two truths. (1) None of us can be a disciple of Jesus by ourselves. It is not merely too tough for us; it is impossible. And (2) Jesus did everything he asks of us. He was estranged from his own brothers and sisters, even his own mother (all of whom thought at times that he was crazy). Most importantly, he was willing to hate his own life, to lay it down to fulfill the work the Father gave him to do. He carried his cross and died on it. He gave up all his possessions, not only those on earth, but also all his heavenly powers and position. As Paul wrote to the Philippians (2:6-8), he emptied himself of everything he had and took on the form of a slave; he humbled himself all the way to dying on the cross, the most despicable of deaths.

He counted the cost of discipleship and paid it; and because he did, we are invited to count the cost and follow. One of the most important sentences in this text from Luke is verse 25, which tells us that Jesus proclaimed these harsh demands to the *large crowds* that were following him. Probably these severe words of Jesus sent some of the hangers-on scurrying away. This discipleship is not for the fainthearted.

But for those who stayed, there was a Resurrection — and after the Resurrection comes the Joy, the wild discovery that there is no more fulfilling way to live than as a disciple! Paul gives us just one example of that in our lesson from Philemon.

We don't have time to look at all the wonderful nuances of this text, but I urge you heartily to study the letter to Philemon sometime to notice the extreme grace with which Paul writes, how warmly he encourages Philemon and his household and church. He is enormously loving and lovable as he encourages Philemon to see that discipleship is really the best way to deal with this slave Onesimus. Let's look briefly at the central portion of today's reading.

The passage is actually delightfully funny. Paul uses a pun on the slave's name since "Onesimus" is Greek for "useful." The apostle writes in verse 11 that this slave had been useless — probably he had run away — but now had become useful. No doubt Onesimus had encountered Paul, probably in Ephesus, converted to Christianity, and subsequently had been very helpful to Paul in his imprisonment. Notice this tenderness with which Paul writes about the slave: "my child," he calls him, and then tells Philemon that he has become a father to Onesimus. His appeal to the former master is so beautiful. Close your eyes and listen to these words: "I am sending him, that is, my own heart, back to you . . . I preferred to do nothing without your consent, in order that your good deed might be voluntary and not something forced. Perhaps this is the reason he was separated from you for a while, that you might have him back forever, no longer as a slave but more than a slave, a beloved brother — especially to me but how much more to you, both in the flesh and in the Lord. So if you consider me your partner, welcome him as you would welcome me" (vv. 12, 14-17).

It is not necessary for me to make any comments about those verses; we simply need to hear them for us to tremble with delight and wonder. Do we really realize what a radical turnaround it sometimes is if we let God reign in our lives? Accept your slave as a beloved brother? Phenomenal!

Then Paul becomes droll once again. After all, he says ironically, "I say nothing about your owing me even your own self" (v. 19). Since Christ is in your life, Philemon, I know "that you will do even more than I say" (v. 21).

Paul is urging Philemon to give up his possession of Onesimus, to take up the cross of relinquishing ownership and die on it. Church history indicates that he did.

In Colossians 4:9 we read that Onesimus was sent with Tychicus to the church at Colossae. In that text he is called "the faithful and beloved brother, who is one of you." It seems that Philemon released his slave for service to Paul's mission; eventually Onesimus became an important leader in the early Church. Some sixty years later a man named Onesimus (the same one?) was bishop of Ephesus; several other bishops in later centuries had the same name. Evidently the slave Onesimus became so prominent that later leaders were named after him.

What remarkable gifts came to the Church because Philemon was willing to give up his possessions and die to his own position as master. I wonder what great gifts might result if you and I could take up the challenges of discipleship as Jesus named them for us today — not because we have to, but because we have realized that it is much better to choose life, to obey God's commands, to love the LORD our God and cling to him, to serve him and walk according to his designs. Only by taking up our cross to die to ourselves can we really choose life — the freedom and Joy of God's life in us.

Let us pray:

O Jesus, I have promised to serve you to the end;
be now and ever near me, my master and my friend.
I shall not fear the battle if you are by my side,
nor wander from the pathway if you will be my guide.

O let me feel you near me; the world is ever near:
I see the sights that dazzle, the tempting sounds I hear.
My foes are ever near me, around me and within;
but, Jesus, draw still nearer and shield my soul from sin!

O let me hear you speaking in accents clear and still,
above the storms of passion, the murmurs of self-will.
O speak to reassure me, to hasten or control,
and speak to make me listen, O guardian of my soul.

O Jesus, you have promised to all who follow you
that where you are in glory your servants shall be too.
And Jesus, I have promised to serve you to the end;
O give me grace to follow, my master and my friend.

Text: John E. Bode (1868), alt.
Tune: "Angel's Story," Arthur H. Mann (1863)

29

Worship to Form a Missional Community

"You did not choose me but I chose you. And I appointed you to go and bear fruit, fruit that will last . . ."

John 15:16

What would happen if everyone in our pews for worship on Sunday morning departed afterward with a deep understanding of all that Jesus meant by the sentences above? For that to happen, our worship would have to be remarkably filled with the sense that we did not choose to come, but that God is the Subject who has invited us here. Immersed in the wonder that God has chosen us for his purposes, appointed us specifically for our various ministries in the world, and equipped us to bear lasting fruit, we would depart with a vision for being Church the rest of the week.

As especially stressed in Chapter 9 above, my greatest disagreement with those who advocate turning worship into the congregation's evangelistic tool is that this notion removes the responsibility of all the members for reaching out to their neighbors by being Church, by bearing the fruit of discipleship. Furthermore, this is not an individualistic responsibility, for good worship also forms a *people* whose way of life is a warrant for belief.

The Alternative but Parallel Society

In *Reaching Out without Dumbing Down* and many others of my books, I especially stress that the Christian community must be an alternative society — offering its gifts of different ways to think and speak and be and behave to a world that is desperate for them. Lately I have been emphasizing the pun that to live this way is to recover true "altar-nativity" — the presenting of our church bodies as a living sacrifice on the altar (actually the Greek word means burnt offering in the invitation of Romans 12:1[1]) and then our rebirth into the new life of Christ in us.

From Mary Jo Leddy I learned another term besides *alternativity* for thinking about the uniqueness of the Church. She reported that the playwright-president of the Czech Republic, Václav Havel, was asked why the "Velvet Revolution" against the communists in the former Czechoslovakia was successfully nonviolent — and we might add, why it remains effective when so many other satellites of the former U.S.S.R. are presently in turmoil. Havel answered somewhat like this: "We had our parallel society. And in that parallel society we wrote our plays and sang our songs and read our poems until we knew the truth so well that we could go out to the streets of Prague and say, 'We don't believe your lies anymore' — and communism *had* to fall."[2]

In the midst of our post-Christian culture, the true Church must be a similar sort of parallel society. We gather together in worship to speak our language, to read our narratives of God at work, to sing the hymns of the faith in a variety of styles, to chant and pour out our prayers until we know the truth so well that we can go out to the world around us and invite that world to share this truth with us. In our worship, we are formed by biblical narratives that tell a different story from that of the surrounding culture. Since we thereby come to know the truth that sets us free, we are eager to share that truth with our neighbors; thus our worship must equip us for that mission with a deep vision of the extravagant splendor of God. Rather than being "a vendor of religious goods and services" that cater to people's tastes, the Church is called to be "a body of people sent on a mission."[3]

1. See chapter 2, "Two Kinds of Body Offerings," in Marva J. Dawn, *Truly the Community: Romans 12 and How to Be the Church* (Grand Rapids: Wm. B. Eerdmans Publishing Co., 1992; reissued 1997), pp. 11-18.

2. For the exact quotation, see Mary Jo Leddy, "The People of God as a Hermeneutic of the Gospel," in *Confident Witness, Changing World*, ed. Craig Van Gelder (Grand Rapids: Wm. B. Eerdmans Publishing Co., 1999), p. 311.

3. See George Hunsberger, "Sizing Up the Shape of the Church," *The Church between Gospel and Culture: The Emerging Mission in North America*, ed. George R. Hunsberger and Craig Van Gelder (Grand Rapids: Wm. B. Eerdmans Publishing Co., 1996), pp. 333-46.

We need both words, *alternative* and *parallel,* for describing the Church. To be parallel will deter us from being so alternative that we don't relate to our neighbors; to be alternative prevents our parallel line from moving closer and closer to modes of life alien to the kingdom of God. Rather than becoming enculturated and entrapped by the world's values of materialistic and experiential consumerism, of narcissistic self-importance and personal taste, of solitary superficiality, and of ephemeral satisfaction, members of Christ's Body choose his simple life of sharing, his willingness to suffer for the sake of others, his communal vulnerability, and his eternal purposes. When our worship gives us continual hearing of and deep reflection on God's Word, songs and prayers that nurture discipleship, and new visions of God's appointment of us to bear fruit, then we will gain God's heart for our mission and ministry of communicating the Christian story, of enfolding our neighbors in God's love, of choosing deliberately to live out the alternative Churchbeing of the people of God's kingdom.

Sociologists recognize that any alternative way of life that is substantively different from the larger society around it and that wants to maintain itself needs a language, customs, habits, rituals, institutions, procedures, and practices that uphold and nurture *a clear vision of how it is different and why that matters.* Are we as Christians committed to the alternative way of life described in the Scriptures and incarnated in Christ, so that we are willing to invest ourselves diligently in order to transmit this valued way of life to our children and neighbors? If so, our worship cannot be too much like the surrounding culture, or it will be impossible to teach altar-nativity.

We Are a *Christian* Community

In Chapters 6 and 24 I cited examples from the students' comments in my seminary course on "Music and the Arts in Christian Worship" to reveal some of the misconceptions about musical style and about multimedia that contribute to a destructive narrowing of possibilities for worship to display the fullness of God's splendor. Another student evaluator listed "more research on other religions" as a suggested change in the course, even though the seminary intended the course to be specifically about *Christian* worship, as indicated in the course's title. It seems to me that some of the major problems with *Christian* worship these days arise because of our frequent addition of elements from other religions (like the idolatries of speed, excitement, or any others listed in Chapter 19) and our failure to pass on faithfully the true identity of Christians. In this sense, we have to work hard to narrow our focus positively when we plan worship.

In a pluralistic world, what does it mean to participate in *Christian* worship? As we saw in Chapter 5, one of the wrong turns some congregations are making as society increasingly becomes more openly pluralistic and less supportive of Christianity specifically is that they blur their unique identity as the people of God, instead of accentuating it with loving commitment. If we understand ourselves to be a people sent on a mission as God's ambassadors in the world, then we can't become so much like the culture that we have nothing to offer.

Our Churches' Loss of Identity

Why is there such panic and confusion in churches these days over what it means to be the Church? Jesus never told us that we had to be big, successful, attractive to nonmembers, or like the culture in which we live. In fact, he said the opposite of all those things — that the way was narrow (Matthew 7:13-14), that the first shall be last (Mark 10:31), that we would be persecuted (Matthew 5:11), that we would be hated by all because of his name (Luke 21:17) — and he wondered whether, when the Son of man comes, he would find faith on earth (Luke 18:8). When I think about churches in our time and culture, I am haunted by Jesus' words, "Salt is good; but if salt has lost its taste, how can its saltiness be restored? It is fit neither for the soil nor for the manure pile; they throw it away. Let anyone with ears to hear listen!" (Luke 14:34-35). God have mercy on us, for we seem to have lost our savor!

On the other hand, Jesus never said that we should hide ourselves away from the world, ignore our neighbors' needs, keep silent about what we know, or be purposely elitist. Instead he told his disciples to let our light shine before others (Matthew 5:14-16), to heal the sick and announce the kingdom (Luke 10:1-9), to sell what we have to give to the poor (Luke 12:22-34), to proclaim repentance and forgiveness and to be witnesses (Luke 24:44-49). How, then, will we equip congregational members with a vision for this mission?

First We Need a Language

If our major question in this chapter is "What does it mean to be Christians in mission — and how are we equipped for that by worship?" we are greatly helped by George Lindbeck and other theorists of the "postliberal" ("Yale") school. Lindbeck insightfully proclaims that Christianity is not merely cognitive (that is, solely intellectual assent to a set of doctrinal propositions), nor is it simply experiential (engagement in uplifting religious experiences). Rather, Christianity is a cultural-linguistic system, by which we learn the language of faith.[4]

With regard to the plea for altar-nativity above — and in response to sociologists' recognition that a culture different from the dominant culture requires a language and habits and traditions to give a clear vision of how it is different and why that matters — Lindbeck wonders whether in our times "any religion will have the requisite toughness for this demanding task unless it at some point makes the claim that it is *significantly* different and *unsurpassably* true" (127, emphases mine). For that reason our triune language essentially includes the conviction that in Jesus we know the God who is the Truth and that by the Holy Spirit's power we are enabled to find a Way of Life that is momentously, transformingly, gratifyingly different from that of the world around us.

Lindbeck's perceptions are extremely important for our considerations about worship in a culture that specializes in feelings and experiences, for he explains that a cultural-linguistic approach to faith reverses the experiential-expressivist relation of inner and outer. An example related to this book's purposes is that some churches try to build faith in worship from the experiential side, by using music that creates emotions so that people feel "moved." In light of recent studies on the effects of vibrations on the human psyche, we must question if the people are moved by God or by the music's physical effects. Lindbeck's model of faith, on the other hand, supports the work of churches who focus instead on content. He gives this example:

> Thus, if one follows this account, Luther did not invent his doctrine of justification by faith because he had a tower experience, but rather the tower experience was made possible by his discovering (or thinking he discovered) the doctrine in the Bible. To be sure, the experience of justification by faith occasioned by his exegesis then generated a variety of fresh expressive symbolisms, among which Lutherans like especially to mention the music of Johann Sebastian Bach. Without such powerful experiences and their effective expression, the tradition would have neither started nor persisted, yet logically, even if not causally, a religious experience and its expression

4. See George Lindbeck, *The Nature of Doctrine: Religion and Theology in a Postliberal Age* (Philadelphia: Westminster Press, 1984). Page references to this book in the following paragraphs are given parenthetically in the text. See also Timothy R. Phillips and Dennis L. Okholm, eds., *The Nature of Confession: Evangelicals and Postliberals in Conversation* (Downers Grove, IL: InterVarsity Press, 1996).

are secondary and tertiary in a linguistic-cultural model. First come the objectivities of the religion, its language, doctrines, liturgies, and modes of action, and it is through these that passions are shaped into various kinds of what is called religious experience. (39)

Objectivities can be passed on, shared with another, whereas subjectivities cannot be transmitted. One of the problems arising from many congregations' emphasis on emotions is that it leaves out those who are at the moment struggling with the opposite feelings or encountering experiences that call those emotions into question. For example, if you tell me that I should get excited about Jesus when I am battling with anger at God because of a new physical malady, your invitation will only make me more depressed. If, on the other hand, you show me some objective truth about God that can produce in me hope for his presence in the midst of the new tribulation, then I might be able to move away from anger and into a more positive response. That is why the content of our worship music and preaching must proclaim primarily the splendor of God, rather than our feelings about him. (I'm not excluding feelings; but they simply aren't as important as the One whose splendor stirs them.)

Let us return to Lindbeck, for he offers profound wisdom for our correlation of our present situations with who God is and what his kingdom means. To stress a faith of feelings would mean to start with an account of our present experiences and adjust our vision of the kingdom of God accordingly (125). Lindbeck's postliberal approach reverses that order. He indicts churches for their destructive response to the

> rationalization, pluralism, and mobility of modern life [which] dissolve the bonds of tradition and community. This produces multitudes of men and women who are impelled, if they have religious yearnings, to embark on their own individual quests for symbols of transcendence. The churches have become purveyors of this commodity rather than communities that socialize their members into coherent and comprehensive religious outlooks and forms of life. (126)

The goal of our worship must be instead to give a clear vision of the reign of God so that participants are formed with the communal, coherent, comprehensive way of life that enables us to deal constructively with the perils of modernity and postmodernity.

If our worship truly immerses participants in the splendor of God and the way of life practiced by his people, then our entire direction of interpretation is reversed. What we do in worship and in educational processes is not to add bits of information to the piles of data people obtain elsewhere; instead, rich worship will convey the framework of faith in which everything is to be understood. In order for that to happen, worship cannot be superficial or merely entertaining; it must be full of as much God as can be put into it, and it must be formative of discipleship and community. If our language is both to form us and to be deepened in a never-ending spiral, we can't practice only a first-grade vocabulary, as illustrated in Chapter 11.

Moreover, as Lindbeck insists, it is not,

> as is often said in our day, that believers find their stories in the Bible, but rather that they make the story of the Bible their story. The cross is not to be viewed as a figurative representative of suffering nor the messianic kingdom as a symbol for hope in the future; rather, suffering should be cruciform, and hope for the future messianic. . . . It is the text, so to speak, which absorbs the world, rather than the world the text. (118)

This is a critical observation, for worship that is too much like the world can hardly redescribe it! How will our suffering be made cruciform if our worship does not form us to be an alternative society?

Lindbeck insists that the community of faith "is likely to contribute more to the future of humanity if it preserves its own distinctiveness and integrity than if it yields to the homogenizing tendencies associated with liberal experiential-expressivism" or (we could add) if it gives in to the contemporary push for worship that suits the culture. Our worship will be more practically relevant in the long run if churches do "not first ask what is either practical or relevant, but instead concentrate on their own intratextual outlooks and forms of life" (128). In other words, we are more helpful to the world if we concentrate on being Church for the world's sake.

What Lindbeck is saying and I am affirming, he admits, will not be popular with those who argue that the faith has to be translated into cultural idioms, with those

> chiefly concerned to maintain or increase the membership and influence of the church. This method [for reaching those outside the Church] resembles ancient catechesis more than modern translation. Instead of redescribing the faith in new concepts, it seeks to teach the language and practices of the religion to potential adherents. . . . In the early days of the Christian church, for example, it was the gnostics, not the catholics, who were most interested to redescribe the biblical materials in a new interpretive framework. (132)

Lindbeck is, of course, talking about the developments of contemporary doctrine, but his comments also apply to what we do in worship and in our catechumenal training that enables people to participate in the life of the Church (see Chapter 20). Are our worship services inviting people into the practice of the Christian faith or translating the faith into the framework of our present consumerist culture?

Lindbeck's insights are enormously helpful in the face of present confusions concerning the relationship between worship and outreach to the world. We must understand that the work of the Church is to teach people the language, the habits, and the practices of Christianity, so that people are both formed by the canonical texts of Scripture at the heart of the language of faith and then also sent out to bear the fruit of the discipleship thus nurtured. The rules of doctrine are the grammar, to guide our first-order speech of worship and life, so that we know how to converse as a people in this culture.

If worship is planned simply to entertain or appeal, will we be immersed in the language of faith? Especially if the main idioms of the Christian language are scriptural and we want our lives to be formed by the biblical narratives, can we conform ourselves too much to the language of the world around us?[5]

Immersing the Newcomer in a Way of Life[6]

We can learn some lessons about being a community that teaches to others the language and practices of faith from Bernice Johnson Reagon, a founder of the singing group "Sweet Honey in the Rock," a gifted *a cappella* ensemble that performs mostly music from African-American traditions. These singers are especially good at evoking audience involvement; when one of the members of this ensemble performed in the inner city of Portland, it was a stunning experience to sit in the middle of everyone's powerful participation in exquisite and soaring sound.

In an interview with *The Other Side* magazine, Reagon described the African-American tradition's understanding of being "given a sign," rather than

5. Bruce Shelley and Marshall Shelley make somewhat the same point in *Consumer Church: "Can Evangelicals Win the World without Losing Their Souls?"* (Downers Grove, IL: InterVarsity Press, 1992).

6. This section contains a small portion of my keynote address, "Culture: Around, Against, In the Church's Worship," given on April 8, 1997, at the Institute of Liturgical Studies, held at Valparaiso University in Valparaiso, Indiana. That address will also appear in a compendium of proceedings from the Institute's three-year program on "Worship, Culture, and Catholicity," 1997-99. My thanks to director Dr. David Truemper for permission to use this adapted version here.

being "born again." She said, "When this time came in your life, you didn't eat or drink. You fasted and prayed. When the sign came, it was a powerful experience for you and a real point of celebration for the whole community." Notice that this is a *community* concern. Reagon continued, "I became a member of the church and a Christian. After that, I didn't act the same. I was less frivolous in the way I conducted myself. I can also remember thinking that if I was *really* a Christian, I had to learn to sing more difficult songs."[7] Notice that this is Churchbeing, rather than a matter of taste or choice.

Reagon emphasizes that "the community is healthiest when it sings. Singing is the process of creating a communal voice. . . . Singing together expresses the community on a level that goes beyond anything you hear, see, or say." When she is giving a concert and is working to get everyone to sing, she wants everyone to feel that there isn't a choice. "I think I make people feel that if they don't sing they are going to die." That is the great possibility — and the challenge for our worship as people in our culture become more and more passive and thereby neglect the essence of *liturgy,* the "work of the people." Reagon declares, "I build a space that makes people feel very bad if they decide they don't want to sing. . . . It's a way of giving credit to the African American congregational tradition, which means you pass the audition when you walk in the door" (11). On her "Good News" album, she confesses these words from a traditional African-American song: "It was good news to lay down the world and shoulder the cross of Jesus. It's not a good time, but it is good news" (10).

Are our congregations conducting worship that is deep enough to equip people to lay down the world's follies and shoulder the cross, or do we simply seek a good time? Does our worship welcome us into the community and its way of life, its willingness to learn more difficult songs for the sake of Churchbeing? Does it equip us to be hospitable, welcoming the strangers into our songs so they feel that if they don't sing they will really miss the goodness of this way of life? Does our worship thereby strengthen us to be friends with our neighbors? Does it fill us with such Joy from the good news that we can bear the not-so-good times?

---

7. Bernice Johnson Reagon, interview with Sharon Anderson, *The Other Side's Faces of Faith: A Collection of Our Favorite Interviews,* p. 9. Page references to this article in the following paragraphs are given parenthetically in the text.

To Be an Outreaching People

The kind of Churchbeing that I am advocating, which requires learning a language of faith, is a potent argument against the present drive toward megachurches, for smaller communities with intimate mentoring and communal life are more able to train members in the constant particular acts of care that genuinely "love the neighbor." Wendell Berry's observations about nature lovers who only want to preserve the spectacular provide a parallel example. As Berry says, "it is going to be extremely difficult to make enough parks to preserve vulnerable species and the health of ecosystems or large watersheds."[8] These things can be done only if *everyone* participates in the small acts of care that ensure their preservation. So Christianity requires the gifts of all the members of the community to invite the world into our faith. Genuine outreach necessitates faithfulness on the part of everyone, rather than spectacle.

A similar case is made by Ferenc Maté's *A Reasonable Life: Toward a Simpler, Secure, More Humane Existence.* He discusses worker-owned companies and companies in which employers and employees live close by, and how much more caring they are about pollution, how much less fuel is wasted in commuting.[9] We might note some parallels with smaller, neighborhood churches. In such congregations, everyone can be more involved with each other and more personally caring; the members are able to be involved together in their neighborhood and serve their neighbors.

I am not advocating small churches for smallness's sake. I am simply wanting to counter the constant advocacy these days of largeness for its own sake. Both sizes of congregations offer particular advantages. Let us make sure that whatever quantity of people our churches involve, we equip all the members for the work of ministry, for participation in Churchbeing.

The Missional Church's Worship[10]

If the Church's worship as a royal waste of time is to result in equipping its members to be missional in their daily lives, it cannot be planned according

---

8. Wendell Berry, "Conservation Is Good Work," in *Sex, Economy, Freedom and Community: Eight Essays* (New York: Pantheon Books, 1993), p. 28.

9. Ferenc Maté, *A Reasonable Life: Toward a Simpler, Secure, More Humane Existence* (New York: Albatross Publishing House, 1993), pp. 77-85.

10. For excellent materials on the "missional church," see the following resources from the Gospel and Our Culture Network: Hunsberger and Van Gelder, eds., *The Church between Gospel and Culture* (cited in note 3 above); Darrell L. Guder, ed., *Missional Church:*

to what will appeal to those who do not even know the One who calls us into mission, those not yet committed to a life of Christian service and outreach. Questions about marketing and the appeal of musical style or liturgical form usually miss this point. Rather, the three criteria that I am constantly emphasizing establish essential foundations for worship:

(1) that the biblical God be the Infinite Center of worship, that worship enable its participants to waste their time immersed in all the fullness of God's splendor;
(2) that worship form believers to be disciples, following Jesus and committed to God's purposes of peace, justice, and salvation in the world;
(3) that worship form the congregation to be a genuine, inclusive Christian community linked to all God's people throughout time and space in worship, doctrine, fellowship, the breaking of bread, prayers, signs and wonders, communal care, and social involvement (see Acts 2:42-47).

These criteria will raise questions of integrity, propriety, coherence, and diversity to guide our choices of worship elements (see Chapter 26). Our goal will be to practice the language of faith by reading and preaching about the faith narratives carried in the Scriptures of the community, to sing our songs of faith (in all sorts of styles), to chant and pour out our prayers until we know the truth so well that we can go out to the world around us and invite it to participate with us in the reign of God.

If worship forms us to be a people who dwell in that reign, then we will carry God's kingdom wherever we go — and we will be equipped to reach out to the culture around us with words of gospel truth and deeds of gospel faithfulness. God grant our churches such worship — for his glory and for the love of the world.

A lovely hymn in the *Moravian Book of Worship* summarizes the intent of this chapter — that we become immersed in the splendor of God and thereby become more like God in our witness, that our mission for the world's sake is that of testimony undergirded by a way of life that warrants belief.

A Vision for the Sending of the Church in North America (Grand Rapids: Wm. B. Eerdmans Publishing Co., 1998); Van Gelder, ed., *Confident Witness, Changing World* (cited in note 2 above). For information on the Network itself, contact Judy Bos, Administrator, or Dr. George R. Hunsberger, Coordinator, The Gospel and Our Culture Network, 101 E. 13th St., Holland, MI 49423-3622.

May the mind of Christ my Savior live in me from day to day,
by his love and pow'r controlling all I do and say.

May the word of God dwell richly in my heart from hour to hour,
so that all may see I triumph only through his pow'r.

May the peace of God my Father rule my life in ev'rything,
that I may be calm to comfort sick and sorrowing.

May the love of Jesus fill me as the waters fill the sea;
him exalting, self abasing — this is victory.

May I run the race before me, strong and brave to face the foe,
looking only unto Jesus as I onward go.

May his beauty rest upon me as I seek the lost to win;
may they look beyond my witness seeing only him.

Kate B. Wilkinson (1925)

St. Leonards, Arthur Cyril Barham-Could (1925)[11]

---

11. This hymn can be found in *The Moravian Book of Worship* (Bethlehem, PA: Moravian Church in America, 1995), or if you do not know or have access to the melody "St. Leonards," you could sing these words to any other melody with the metrical structure 8 7 8 5.

30

Always Be Ready to Give an Account

"Going, make disciples of all nations, baptizing them in the name of the Father and of the Son and of the Holy Spirit, teaching them to be observing all things whatsoever I have commanded you; and behold! I myself am with you always until the consummation of the ages."

Matthew 28:19-20 (literal translation)

Since my primary reason for protesting the confusion of worship and evangelism that characterizes much contemporary discussion in churches is that it violates the biblical directives which form the Church (see Chapter 9), my purpose in this chapter is simply to look at a few biblical texts in order to sketch some principles for faithful evangelism. There are numerous excellent books on the subject, so we need no lengthy discourse here.[1] As throughout this book, I want to root our concern for and practice of evangelism in what it means to be the Church. Darrell Guder and his team of writers from the Gospel and Our Culture Network emphasize this, too, in this description of the present scene:

Church growth and evangelism models direct the attention of churches to reaching the unchurched and connecting with disaffected affiliates. A ma-

---

1. See, for example, Alan J. Roxburgh, *Reaching a New Generation: Strategies for Tomorrow's Church* (Downers Grove, IL: InterVarsity Press, 1993), and Kevin Graham Ford, *Jesus for a New Generation: Putting the Gospel in the Language of Xers* (Downers Grove, IL: InterVarsity Press, 1995).

jority of these approaches are technique and method driven. Generational studies and demographics are increasingly used as tools to develop effective strategies for reaching various groups in North America. Such tools are important resources, but they can become false substitutes for forming a missional identity. Often missing from their application is reflection on the nature of the church.[2]

Being Church means following a way of life, rather than resorting to techniques. Evangelism is not something that we strategize or plan to do in a certain way — although studying ways of talking about faith are certainly helpful. Rather, as the text above from the final teaching scene in Matthew's Gospel notes, evangelism happens *as we are going*. As we go about our daily lives — to work, to the grocery store, to school, to the neighbor's house for tea — we live the gospel. We speak it freely (see the discussion of 1 Peter 3 below). We incarnate it. We display a Joy in following Jesus and his Way that invites our neighbors to consider the Truth of his Life in us.

We possess that Joy because of the "behold!" in the Matthew text. Let this wake us up: Jesus is always with us, and someday he will bring to their consummation all the ages. Living in the light of that eternity, we have an entirely different perspective on everything — on the meaning and purpose of our lives, on our sense of identity and its place in a master story, on how and to whom we are beloved and how we therefore cope with the struggles of this life, on the values of this world, and on our hope for the future and its effect on our meanwhile (compare Chapter 3).

And we do not live this way alone. The only verb in the text above is plural. We make disciples as a community demonstrating this way of life by being Church — and thereby our corporate witness gives the neighbor warrant for belief. The task is making disciples — which we do while we go and which is followed by immersing them in the triune Name and instructing them in the triune life.

> . . . but in your hearts sanctify Christ as Lord. Always be ready to make your defense to anyone who demands from you an accounting for the hope that is in you; yet do it with gentleness and reverence. Keep your conscience clear, so that, when you are maligned, those who abuse you for your good conduct in Christ may be put to shame. For it is better to suffer for doing good, if suffering should be God's will, than to suffer for doing evil. (1 Peter 3:15-17)

2. Darrell L. Guder, ed., *Missional Church: A Vision for the Sending of the Church in North America* (Grand Rapids: Wm. B. Eerdmans Publishing Co., 1998), p. 201.

The third chapter of 1 Peter gives very precise instructions for evangelism to Christians who are being persecuted. After delineating the requirements for the character of believers in a non-Christian world in verses 8-14 (by quoting Psalm 34), the text specifies the following seven aspects of witness in verses 15-16. (I will first give the English phrases and then elaborate the emphases in the original Greek.)

1. "In your hearts [which means in biblical language not simply one's feelings, but one's intentional, deliberate will] sanctify [or reverence] Christ as Lord." The Greek text puts the word *Lord* first to accentuate it. If we really keep Christ as Lord over our will, feelings, attitudes, behaviors, habits, manner, and purposes, we will never be arrogant or imperious when we give witness to the salvation of God in Christ. Furthermore, Christ's Lordship will form in us a way of life that gives witness to his good news.

2. "Always be ready." This doesn't necessarily mean that we need all kinds of courses on evangelism, though some of them are useful. Simply, we will be ready to talk about Christ if we honor him as Lord of everything in our lives. Love is always ready to tell of the one loved. I never have trouble talking about my husband, Myron. Since he is the most important human being to me, his name and character and actions are always on the tip of my tongue. (He just brought in an arrangement of his flowers to brighten my study as I work.) We are always ready to give witness if we practice the presence of God — the promise of which we saw above in Matthew 28.[3] If our worship life is full of the splendor of God, we will regularly be reminded of the fullness of his presence with us and the immensity of his grace for us.

3. Constantly be prepared "to make your defense." The Greek text has no verb here, but simply says to be ready for *apologia*. That simplicity helps — for it seems to invite us not to worry about giving the reply, about making the defense. If we hear richly and learn deeply in our worship life, we will always be ready to give an account of God's splendor. We can easily promote the gospel, for the kingdom itself is its own warrant for belief.

We do not modify that good Word in an attempt to appeal to people. William Fore emphasizes that, if the purpose of evangelistic communication is to help people interpret their existence in light of what God has done for them in Christ,

This means that the purpose of Christian communication is *not* to ask, "How can we communicate the gospel in such a way that others will accept

---

3. See also the delightful book by Brother Lawrence, *The Practice of the Presence of God*, trans. Donald Attwater (Springfield: Templegate Publishers, 1981).

it?" This is the *wrong* question, the public relations question, the manipulative question. . . . Rather, our task is to put the gospel before people in such a way that it is so clear to them that they can accept it, or reject it — *but always for the right reasons.*[4]

4. Make your defense "to anyone who demands from you an accounting." At first I didn't like the NRSV rendering, "anyone who demands"; a more gentle "all the ones asking you" seemed to suffice. But these Christians to whom Peter was writing were being persecuted; this demand might have been their last chance before execution by some gruesome method. Perhaps our difficulty in giving witness to our faith arises because it has never threatened to cost us our lives. In our less threatening (and therefore perhaps more subtly dangerous) times, this phrase should at least prod us to consider whether our life provokes any question about the hope we display.

5. Give an answer to those who ask "an accounting for the hope that is in you." The source of that hope is accentuated in the reading of the Greek, for this phrase reads literally "a *logos* concerning the in-you hope." We who know Christ as the *Logos* or Word of God recognize that he is sufficient for our accounting. He *is* our hope. In our times when many possess only wishful thinking, Christians rejoice that our hope is a fact that never disappoints (Romans 5:5). We might not *feel* hopeful, but nonetheless the kingdom has already been initiated and will without doubt come to fruition. Much of our witness lies in living as people who possess such a hope.

6. "[Y]et do it with gentleness and reverence." This phrase begins with the stronger of Greek adversatives — almost as if to say, "but be sure" that you do it graciously. The bearing with which we speak our hope is essential, for the tone of the invitation determines its reception. We have no need to be anything but gentle when we tell others the good news of God's grace. The word rendered "reverence" could also be translated as "fear," which is an important possibility to consider. We need a profound sense of the immensity of God's grace as we invite others into it, and we cannot truly know grace if we don't know how little we deserve it.[5] Only when we discern the depths of our desperation do we genuinely experience the ecstasy of our escape from it.

---

4. William F. Fore, *Television and Religion: The Shaping of Faith, Values, and Culture* (Minneapolis: Augsburg, 1987), p. 49.

5. See my exposition of the biblical tension of fear and love in chapter 7, "Our Cry of Transience," in Marva J. Dawn, *To Walk and Not Faint: A Month of Meditations on Isaiah 40*, 2nd ed. (Grand Rapids: Wm. B. Eerdmans Publishing Co., 1997).

7. "Keep your conscience clear, so that, when you are maligned, those who abuse you for your good conduct in Christ may be put to shame. For it is better to suffer for doing good, if suffering should be God's will, than to suffer for doing evil." Some might revile us for what we believe, might slander our uprightness in Christ. This text reminds us that whenever we suffer evil it is easier to bear the troubles if there is no guilt and regret mixed in.

These seven themes from 1 Peter 3 form us to be witnesses without co-ercion, evangelists without condescension, apologetes without animosity. Most important, they nurture mission that arises out of Churchbeing, which in turn arises out of reverencing Christ as Lord. Worship leads to being Church, which leads to witness for the sake of the world.

Lest this chapter become too lengthy, let me comment only briefly on the third text in groups of stanzas rather than line by line. Psalm 145, entitled "a Psalm, of David," provides us with an excellent overview of a life that speaks and practices a witness to God, our King.

> I will extol you, my God and King,
>   and bless your name forever and ever.
> Every day I will bless you,
>   and praise your name forever and ever.
> Great is the LORD, and greatly to be praised;
>   his greatness is unsearchable.

Notice the different words for speaking about God — extolling him to others, blessing God himself, praising him — and all of this speaking is due to God's character, which is too immense for us ever to capture sufficiently. Our wit-ness is not for the purpose of making our congregation grow; it is simply be-cause God is worthy of our worship and praise and witness.

> One generation shall laud your works to another,
>   and shall declare your mighty acts.
> On the glorious splendor of your majesty,
>   and on your wondrous works, I will meditate.
> The might of your awesome deeds shall be proclaimed,
>   and I will declare your greatness.
> They shall celebrate the fame of your abundant goodness,
>   and shall sing aloud of your righteousness.

Again, the reason for speaking is the greatness of God, though these verses add a wonderful list of his deeds and attributes. Several important new themes are introduced.

One of the first responsibilities of our witness is to our children.[6] By telling the youth of the Church how God works in our lives and in the world, we invite them to share our faith and to participate in the community of God's people. If we continue to meditate on God's splendor in his demeanor and deeds, then we will have more to proclaim and declare. The result will be that others ("they") will join in the celebrating and singing of God's grace and justice.

> The LORD is gracious and merciful,
>> slow to anger and abounding in steadfast love.
> The LORD is good to all,
>> and his compassion is over all that he has made.

These lines are a Hebrew creed, repeated in many places in the First Testament. They give important precedent to our tradition of saying creeds, universally agreed upon by the people of God. We invite our children and our neighbors and strangers into this language of our faith. We derive our identity from such testimony about our God.

> All your works shall give thanks to you, O LORD,
>> and all your faithful shall bless you.
> They shall speak of the glory of your kingdom,
>> and tell of your power,
> to make known to all people your mighty deeds,
>> and the glorious splendor of your kingdom.
> Your kingdom is an everlasting kingdom,
>> and your dominion endures throughout all generations.

Once again, we hear (psalms are meant to be read aloud) many words for our speaking and for God's attributes and actions. Overwhelmed by God's splendor, how can we help but give thanks and tell others?

A momentous addition in these stanzas is the word *kingdom*. We are the people who practice God's reign, who live in this world as it is redefined by another (see the previous chapter). It is this dominion of God into which we invite our neighbors; God's sovereignty is our good news. In our culture, which is enslaved to other powers, it is good news indeed.

> The LORD is faithful in all his words,
>> and gracious in all his deeds.

6. See Marva J. Dawn, *Is It a Lost Cause? Having the Heart of God for the Church's Children* (Grand Rapids: Wm. B. Eerdmans Publishing Co., 1997).

350

> The LORD upholds all who are falling,
>   and raises up all who are bowed down.
> The eyes of all look to you,
>   and you give them their food in due season.
> You open your hand,
>   satisfying the desire of every living thing.
> The LORD is just in all his ways,
>   and kind in all his doings.
> The LORD is near to all who call on him,
>   to all who call on him in truth.
> He fulfills the desire of all who fear him;
>   he also hears their cry, and saves them.
> The LORD watches over all who love him,
>   but all the wicked he will destroy.

What an eloquent list of ways in which the faithfulness and graciousness of the LORD are manifested — in emotional, physical, and spiritual ways; with justice and kindness and generosity; with support and answers and presence!

These stanzas take us into the responsibility for our way of life, for if our LORD is like this, then we his people will want to be just and kind and generous also — supportive of our neighbors, listening to their cries, and incarnating for them the love of God.

Our testimony to God's character and conduct is thus given credence if we embody who he is in who we are becoming and what he does in how we live. The more we observe God (the great gift of our worship and educational practices and community life), the more we are transformed into his likeness, from one degree of glory to another (2 Corinthians 3:18). The best warrant for belief is our altar-nativity (see the previous chapter).

Notice, moreover, that these verses also add the concept of fear. The immensity of God's love cannot be seen unless we know how little we deserve it. The deservedness of our destruction enables us to comprehend how good the LORD's good news really is.

> My mouth will speak the praise of the LORD,
>   and all flesh will bless his holy name forever and ever.

These final lines in the poem reiterate our goal: we want to tell the LORD's praises so that everyone can know his character and bless it.

The more we know who God is, the more we have to tell others. That is why our worship must manifest the splendor of God in as great a fullness as possible. We are concerned that all flesh — these mere mortals, including ourselves, who desperately need God's grace — will not merely be attracted for the moment, but will become engaged in living God's holy name, his character, forever.

Just as the texts from the Scriptures above can form us to speak God's praises, so may singing the hymn below nurture our zeal — for certainly it is good news we share with the world, this news of Christ:

> Christ high-ascended, now in glory seated,
> throned and exalted, victory completed;
> death's dread dominion finally defeated — we are his witnesses.
>
> Christ from the Father ev'ry pow'r possessing,
> who on his chosen lifted hands in blessing,
> sends forth his servants still in faith confessing — we are his witnesses.
>
> Christ, who in dying won for us salvation,
> lives now the firstborn of the new creation,
> to win disciples out of ev'ry nation — we are his witnesses.
>
> Christ in his splendor, all dominion gaining;
> Christ with his people evermore remaining;
> Christ to all ages gloriously reigning — we are his witnesses.
>
> As at his parting, joy shall banish grieving,
> faith in his presence strengthen our believing;
> filled with his Spirit, love and power receiving, we are his witnesses.
>
> Timothy Dudley-Smith (b. 1926), © Hope Publishing Co.
> Christe Sanctorum, Paris *Antiphoner* (1681)[7]

---

7. The punctuation in this hymn has been modified slightly. If you do not know or have access to the melody "Christe Sanctorum," this hymn can be sung to any tune with the metrical structure 11 11 11 6.

31

*Asking New and Old Questions as We Remember the Future**

> And they, continuing daily with one accord in the temple, and breaking bread from house to house, did eat their meat with gladness and singleness of heart, praising God, and having favor with all the people. And the Lord added to the church daily such as should be saved.
>
> Acts 2:46-47 (KJV)

Let us remember that we are working together as a community while you read what I have written in order to grow in our knowledge and love of the Lord and in our service to God and God's Church. To remind us, I love to use this refrain from the Church's communal heritage, which has been cherished for hundreds of years: "The Lord be with you; and also with you." I would like to encourage those of you reading this chapter to respond to my blessing with deliberate intentionality — for I cannot continue to think and

---

*This is an edited transcript of the opening keynote address for the conference "Worship, Culture, and Catholicity: Remembering the Future," sponsored by the Institute of Liturgical Studies at Valparaiso University on April 21, 1998. All the papers from the institute's three-year series on "Worship, Culture, and Catholicity" can be obtained from the Institute of Liturgical Studies, Valparaiso University, Valparaiso, IN 46383. With the permission of Dr. David G. Truemper, Director, this chapter appears as an adaptation of one of my papers in that collection.

write as a scholar for the Church unless we all continue to participate together actively, searching for God's truth in our desire to be faithful as his people.

The Lord be with you! (And also with you!) Let us pray: Merciful Father, Covenant God, we thank and praise you that you led your people — our forebears — out of Ur and Haran, out of Egypt, out of Babylon, and into the land and the future that you provided. In the person of our resurrected Lord, Jesus Christ, you have led us out of slavery to sin and death and into all the privileges and responsibilities of sonship in your kingdom. We eagerly await Christ's coming again when we will at last perfectly worship you face to face, when we will at last be perfectly faithful as your people. In these days between the comings of Christ, pour out upon us your Holy Spirit that we may worship you eschatologically in the midst of all the tensions of this meanwhile. Triune God of the past, the present, and the future, be present in our midst as we listen and learn together — that we may grow in wisdom and insight, in commitment to you and to our neighbors, that we may love you and glorify your Name now and forevermore, into the ages of the ages. Amen.

My title, "Asking New and Old Questions as We Remember the Future," arises because my training is in biblical ethics, and therefore my approach to various worship issues centers on *asking questions* (the proper work of ethics) about how our worship practices form us to be God's people. In this final chapter, my concern is to ask what the Church's "eschatological tradition" has to say about worship. As we think about the biblical witness regarding the "end times," the kingdom of God as it breaks into the present, and how God's great future affects our present way of life, we will discover that the more new questions we ask, the more they will drive us back to the old questions. Indeed, "there is nothing new under the sun," for always, throughout human history, people have been strung between the times, between who we have been formed to be by our past and what we might become, especially if we consciously and deliberately orient our present toward the future. Moreover, ever since the resurrection of Christ, which provides the ultimate definition of our Christian faith and life, God's people have always lived — whether we realize it or not — in the midst of the tension of "already, but not yet."

The problem is that in recent times many Christians individually and corporately have not realized that this eschatological tension defines us. It is essential that our congregations, pastors, and every member of our churches recover this fundamental Christian tradition — and I mean the word *tradition* in its best sense. My purpose in this chapter is primarily to pose many questions to spark your deeper reflection concerning issues of the Church's eschatological tradition in relation to its worship. Some of the questions in the next pages might be painful — they have driven me to shame and repentance as I have thought about them — but the questions are necessary and urgent if we are going to recover the eschatological tradition of the Church, if we want its truths to guide our worship, and if we intend to take seriously our calling as present participants in God's kingdom and therefore as servants of God and of God's Church for the sake of the world.

Why Has the Church Forgotten Its Eschatology?

This first question is essential if we would recover the Church's eschatological tradition for the sake of its worship. I first began noticing our loss of eschatology in table prayers. When I was a child we always sang, "these mercies bless and grant that we may feast in Paradise with thee." Now at camps, congregational dinners, and family events we seem only to sing, "these mercies bless and grant that we may strengthened for thy service be." Of course, there is nothing wrong with asking for strength for our labors today, but why is it that we seem to be ashamed to think about feasting in Paradise? Why do we so rarely sing about the future anymore?

When was the last time you heard a sermon about heaven? Even at funerals, messages usually degenerate into proud acclamations of the dead person's personality and a recital of the beloved deceased's accomplishments, often greatly aggrandized. Why are we and our churches somewhat embarrassed about the topic of God's great future? We *must* ask why.

Some of our reasons for shying away from eschatological talk are very good ones. For example, it was terrible that churches used "heaven" as a message to console those we oppressed. Many seemed to think, "Give the slaves a hope for glory and their masters can continue to exploit them now" — never realizing that the slaves knew far better than their owners that God's great future has radical repercussions on the present. So African-American spirituals evolved that unfold, and enfold us in, true eschatology — songs about Moses to teach us that the prophecies of the past foretell a better future, songs about crossing the Jordan in the future to represent the rivers to be crossed on the freedom trail now. From spirituals, then, we can often learn a better eschatology than that which was distorted by churches in order to maintain their power.

Space prohibits mentioning all of our other reasons for ceasing to talk about eschatology, but consider these: in many churches and books ideas about "heaven" were stretched far beyond the biblical testimony; the book of Revelation was turned into a calendar by which human beings could outwit God; ethics for the end times became an excuse for immorality now; or, in Nietzsche's critique of churches, eschatology became a means for denying the natural world or escaping our responsibilities for it. We are faithful if we reject these unbiblical, untheological, unethical eschatologies.

But why have we discarded genuine biblical eschatology as faithfully understood in the Church's heritage? Some of our reasons for ceasing to talk about eschatology have been devastating to the community and its gifts to the world. As we look at Christian history, we discover that we gave in too much to modernity; we allowed the Enlightenment project of proving everything scientifically to dissuade us from our proclamation of the reign of God and of how that reign has come crashing in to our epoch.[1] Why did we let extreme uses of historical-critical tools atomize texts until they were no longer capable of forming a people who live in the present by remembering God's past provision and therefore believing God's promises for the future?

Hans Frei's insightful book *The Eclipse of Biblical Narrative*[2] warns us about what we are doing. Whereas formerly the Scripture texts judged our human experience and our understanding of the world, we in the modern epoch allow the interpreter's experience and worldview to judge and criticize the text. This is a paradigm shift that we must regret, and if we ask our first question diligently — why have Christians forgotten their eschatology? — it will expose our idolatries.

When we look at the history of the development of modern thought, beginning with Descartes, Spinoza, Hobbes, Locke, Hume, Kant, and others, focusing especially on Feuerbach, Nietzsche, Marx, and Freud, and continuing all the way to the present postmodern philosophers such as Foucault, Lyotard, and Derrida, we recognize the progression culminating in the current abhorrence of anything approaching transcendence.[3] (We were extremely blessed at the gathering where this chapter was first presented to have

---

1. I use the word *crashing* instead of the more usual verb, *breaking*, for its wake-up effect. God's reign usually does come more quietly, but we are so lulled by enculturation that we don't recognize the kingdom's presence and don't live its present way of life against the inimical "values" of the society around us. See Marva J. Dawn, *Is It a Lost Cause? Having the Heart of God for the Church's Children* (Grand Rapids: Wm. B. Eerdmans Publishing Co., 1997).

2. Hans Frei, *The Eclipse of Biblical Narrative* (New Haven: Yale University Press, 1974).

3. See especially Brian D. Ingraffia, *Postmodern Theory and Biblical Theology: Vanquishing God's Shadow* (Cambridge: Cambridge University Press, 1996).

had Jürgen Moltmann with us, for he was one of the great leaders to expose the fallacy of Christians' rejection of eschatology.[4])

My first point, then, in raising questions concerning the relationship of eschatology and worship is to urge us to ask personally, corporately, and ecclesiologically why we have failed to keep God's future prominent in our theology and in our lives, and to recognize in that omission many of the idolatries that are now destroying the worship of the Church.

Why Do Our Neighbors Turn to False Eschatologies?

It is ironic that even as churches have rejected eschatological thinking, many of our neighbors — in all age groups — have turned to it with eager zealousness. In the annual *Word and World* lecture at Luther Seminary on September 23, 1997, Gustav Niebuhr, senior religion correspondent at the *New York Times*, asked, "Why does millennialist prophecy hold a particular appeal now? . . . Could it be that a certain level of pessimism in contemporary American culture gives a permission to end-of-the-world thinking?"[5]

Niebuhr acknowledges that "talk of massive social decline is fairly well accepted as fact." He lists some of the common concerns as follows: "Start with a near collapse in standards of civility, move to concern that educational standards are falling, then to fear that family life is deteriorating, and finally to the worry that the environment is being permanently degraded." On the positive side, he notes a cultural change "in which personal faith seems suddenly more public, in which the general atmosphere seems more friendly to its expression" (8).

However, this turn to thinking about the end times because of social decline plus a cultural environment more sympathetic to religiosity has not added up to more effectiveness on the part of our churches. Niebuhr comments,

> The poll numbers tell us that the will to believe is alive. But they offer no evidence that religious institutions have the same degree of influence over

---

4. See especially Jürgen Moltmann, *Theology of Hope: On the Ground and Implications of a Christian Eschatology*, trans. James W. Leitch (Minneapolis: Augsburg Fortress, 1993), and *The Coming of God: Christian Eschatology*, trans. Margaret Kohl (Minneapolis: Fortress Press, 1996).

5. Gustav Niebuhr, "American Religion at the Millennium's End," *Word and World* 18, no. 1 (Winter 1998): 7. Page references to this article in the following paragraphs are given parenthetically in the text.

people's lives than they exercised 30 years ago, or that many people have kept up an attachment to the denominational bodies that served to organize and guide religious life throughout much of this century. A problem for national church organizations these days is that we live in a time suspicious of institutions and their authority. (9)

Consequently, churches are not trusted for — and often do not offer, as we recognized in the first point of this chapter — an eschatology that deals with the reality of social decline. This attitude of "more general distrust of or alienation from sources of authority" also "coexists with a heightened sense of spiritual individualism" (9) that "places the satisfaction of personal needs above maintaining traditional loyalties. Herein lies a major challenge for the churches" (10). Congregations are not ministering to our society's panic and fears, especially because we have rejected or hidden our eschatological tradition, in favor of meeting (supposed) immediate needs.

One of the best ways in which we can see our society's millennialist panic and apocalyptic thinking is in the literature of the younger generation. Let me highly recommend to all pastors, musicians, and other church leaders Douglas Coupland's book *Generation X*. Reading this novel, which is subtitled *Tales for an Accelerated Culture*, I found myself sobbing over the pain expressed by the three main characters — all of whom have given up on their previous jobs and lives to move to the desert and tell each other stories. In one of their conversations (recorded also in Chapter 3 of this book), two of the principals admit the following:

> "You know all of this sex gossip and end-of-the-world nonsense, I wonder if they're really only confessing something else to each other."
> "Like?"
> "Like how scared sick they all are. I mean, when people start talking seriously about hoarding cases of Beef-a-Roni in the garage and get all misty-eyed about the Last Days, then it's about as striking a confession as you're ever likely to get of how upset they are that life isn't working out the way they thought it would."[6]

What a great grief it is that our churches are not responding to the discouragements and frustrations of people in their twenties and thirties in the society around us!

In fact, eschatological yearnings have been expressed throughout the

---

6. Douglas Coupland, *Generation X: Tales for an Accelerated Culture* (New York: St. Martin Press, 1991), p. 37.

cultural breakdown of the last half of the twentieth century.[7] That is one of the reasons why postmodernism has arisen (as explained in Chapter 4). There is no longer any basis for truth since the idolatries of science, technology, and economics have failed us by not solving all the world's problems, as many claimed they could. What we have reaped instead are the terrors of world wars, political and economic chaos, rampant immorality, government deception, and so forth. Responding to the atrocities and horrors of world war, William Butler Yeats penned these lines in his oft-quoted poem "The Second Coming":

> Things fall apart; the centre cannot hold;
> Mere anarchy is loosed upon the world,
> The blood-dimmed tide is loosed, and everywhere
> The ceremony of innocence is drowned;
> The best lack all conviction, while the worst
> Are full of passionate intensity.
>
> Surely some revelation is at hand;
> Surely the Second Coming is at hand.
> The Second Coming! Hardly are those words out
> When a vast image out of *Spiritus Mundi*
> Troubles my sight . . .[8]

There is indeed an enormous need in our society for an eschatology that can give hope in the face of the world's mayhem. How would it affect ministry to our neighbors if the Church could recover its true eschatology — made clear in, and also therefore making clear, the Church's worship? That leads to our third question.

What Happens to "Spirituality" without Eschatology?

What has happened in many churches is a lot of degeneration into pop spiritualities. Cynthia A. Jurisson, professor at the Lutheran School of Theol-

---

7. See also chapters 6 ("The Revenge of the Sacred in Secular Culture"), 12 ("The Death of Utopia Reconsidered"), and 18 ("Revolution — A Beautiful Sickness") of Leszek Kolakowski's *Modernity on Endless Trial* (Chicago: University of Chicago Press, 1990), pp. 63-74, 131-45, and 215-24.

8. William Butler Yeats, "The Second Coming," in *Chapters into Verse: Poetry in English Inspired by the Bible,* ed. Robert Atwan and Laurance Wieder, vol. 2: *Gospels to Revelation* (Oxford: Oxford University Press, 1995), p. 376.

ogy in Chicago, writes of "Pop Spirituality" in *Word and World* and names it as the attempt at self-improvement that it really is. In most of contemporary spirituality's various forms Jurisson recognizes "foolproof coping mechanisms to deal with the hassles of modern life that hinder the pursuit of success." She underscores that "Unlike the earlier self-help literature, however, which had an implicit eschatology, much of the current popular literature, despite its use of terms like 'spiritual awareness,' lacks any eschatological dimension."[9] Throughout the country and across the denominations I have heard countless sermons that were only therapeutic, that offered merely suggestions for self-improvement, instead of faithful proclamation of the reign of God.

Why is it that our churches deliver human remedies, instead of proclaiming God's hope and God's salvation (in the fullest sense of that term)? Why do we fall into the most popular of eschatological replacements and the worst substitute for heaven of all — materialistic consumerism? Philip Rieff, in his book *The Triumph of the Therapeutic: Uses of Faith after Freud*, laments that "Religious man was born to be saved, [modern] psychological man is born to be pleased."[10] How dangerous it is, then, if churches let their worship degenerate into whatever is pleasing.[11] Why do churches not stand mightily against the ethos of the United States? As God's people, formed by God's reign, we know better than to chase after the god of Mammon. Why have we let the idolatry of consumerism invade our churches, as is evidenced by worship that caters to instant gratification or simply offers music that sells?

9. Cynthia A. Jurisson, "Pop Spirituality: An Evangelical Response," *Word and World* 18, no. 1 (Winter 1998): 15-16.

10. Philip Rieff, *The Triumph of the Therapeutic: Uses of Faith after Freud* (London: Chatto & Windus, 1966), pp. 24-25.

11. I would highly recommend that pastors and musicians and other worship leaders read some of the literature written in protest of U.S. consumerism. From a non-Christian and sometimes very cynical perspective, Ferenc Maté's *A Reasonable Life: Toward a Simpler, Secure, More Humane Existence* (New York: Albatross Publishing House, 1993) awakens us to how dissatisfying and false the "salvation" of consumerism is. Maté gets quite vitriolic at times because he doesn't have the hope of the reign of God, but many of his suggestions are quite practical as he asks why we let ourselves be turned stir-crazy by our endless pursuit of stuff. From a Christian perspective, Wendell Berry's *Sex, Economy, Freedom and Community: Eight Essays* (New York: Pantheon Books, 1993) and Rodney Clapp's "The Theology of Consumption and the Consumption of Theology: Toward a Christian Response to Consumerism," in *The Consuming Passion: Christianity and the Consumer Culture*, ed. Rodney Clapp (Downers Grove, IL: InterVarsity Press, 1998), pp. 169-204, call us to Christian discernment of, and responses to, the lures of our advertising and inundating materialist society.

How Will Eschatological Thinking End the Confusions of Evangelism and Worship?

What might a recovery of the Church's eschatological tradition contribute to clarifying the difference between evangelism and worship? (As emphasized especially in Chapter 9 of this book, the confusion of these two in many churches has led to the detriment of both.)

Some of the confusions are illustrated by Walt Kallestad's book *Entertainment Evangelism: Taking the Church Public*.[12] They are helpfully summarized in a review of Kallestad's book by Frederick J. Gaiser in *Word and World*.[13] Let me emphasize three aspects of the Church and the Church's worship that are presented in destructively unbiblical or theologically mistaken ways in Kallestad's book and that could be rectified by faithful eschatological thinking.

First, in Kallestad's book — and in much of the literature that confuses worship and evangelism — there is no significant discussion of the relation between style and subject matter. The result is that, in Gaiser's words, there is no concern for how "adopting an entertainment style baptizes the content of a culture of diversion" (104). If our worship merely offers a diversion, we have lost the eschatological call to involvement in the world's needs and investment of ourselves for the sake of God's ministry purposes. Instead of being distracted from the needs of our society, eschatology plunges us into them because the reign of God gives us the courage, the strength, the tools, and the power of the Spirit at work through us already to care for our neighbors' sufferings. Worship is not to escape, but to encounter. As we worship we are changed, so that when we leave the worship service we go out to change the world.

Second, Gaiser points out that Kallestad does not deal with the problem of a "star clergy" and the "cult of personality." He asks, "Is the system itself compatible with a New Testament notion of Christian community?" (105). This question is critical these days because worship in so many churches and at larger gatherings has turned increasingly to what I call "patter" — small talk that makes the worship leader sound like a radio talk-show host. The great gift of liturgy (in whatever style of music we use) is that it takes our consciousness off the person leading it and focuses our attention instead where it

---

12. See Walt Kallestad, *Entertainment Evangelism: Taking the Church Public* (Nashville: Abingdon Press, 1996).

13. Frederick J. Gaiser, review of *Entertainment Evangelism: Taking the Church Public* by Walt Kallestad, in *Word and World* 18, no. 1 (Winter 1998): 102-6. Page references to this article in the following paragraphs are given parenthetically in the text.

belongs — on the God whose words we speak and sing. Preachers with a charismatic personality who confuse worship and evangelism concentrate on how they can attract people with what they do in the corporate gatherings and forget that worship is intended to praise God and to equip the congregation to introduce their neighbors to Christ. Rather than creating a "cult of personality," those who serve to enable others to worship ought to be like Paul's old "clay jars" (2 Corinthians 4:7), so that "it may be made clear that this extraordinary power belongs to God and does not come from us." Eschatological thinking always reminds musicians and pastors that it is the reign of God which draws people to Christ and not the star organist, guitarist, or preacher. It is the Word of God that speaks to hearts, and not the manipulative chatter of human beings.

Third, Gaiser points out that Kallestad's book contains no serious mention of sin and evil (105). Many of the worship services that I encounter in my travels focus on "happiness" instead of offering the true Joy of sins forgiven. As Walter Brueggemann asserts, "The problem with a hymnody that focuses on equilibrium, coherence, and symmetry . . . is that it may deceive and cover over. Life is not like that. Life is also savagely marked by disequilibrium, incoherence, and unrelieved asymmetry."[14] Faithful eschatology enables us to confront sin and to look evil straight in the face. We are changed by the forgiveness of God and set free by grace to renounce sin, resist evil, conquer oppression, and endure suffering. Our present participation in God's future kingdom gives us the courage to be realistic about the present workings of the principalities and powers in our world, for we know that they are already defeated and that someday God will annihilate them forever.

How Can We Relearn the Language of Eschatology in Our Worship?

Since eschatological thinking is a critical aspect of our identity as Christians, how will we recover its language? What educational methods can we use? How will worship help us recover the language, and how will that recovery deepen our worship?

In order for the Church — or any other community that nurtures an alternative way of life substantively different from the larger society — to maintain itself, sociologists recognize that we will need rituals, procedures, prac-

14. Walter Brueggemann, *The Message of the Psalms: A Theological Commentary*, Augsburg Old Testament Studies (Minneapolis: Augsburg, 1984), p. 51.

tices, habits, customs, and, most of all, a language that tell us who we are, that remind us of our identity, that uphold and nurture our vision of how we are different and why that matters. Are we passing on to our children and to our neighbors in our worship such a language of faith? (See Chapter 29.)

Edward Farley's profound book *Deep Symbols: Their Postmodern Effacement and Reclamation* uses the eschatological notion of hope as his final example of a "word of power" that has been eroded, diminished, and allowed to atrophy in the modern and postmodern world. Building on his previous discussion of tradition, obligation, the real, and law as other deep symbols infected and affected by the culture around us, he writes,

> Again, the word of power is not the term itself but the deep symbol that finds its way into a variety of expressions: the kingdom of God, Messiah, second coming, the promised land, resurrection, utopia, the new aeon. Along with faith and love, hope is part of Paul's trilogy of Christian existence. One form of hope, prophetic eschatology and the theme of Messiah, is at the heart of the faith of Israel. Some [such as Paul Ricouer, whom Farley cites] maintain that hope is the very core of the Christian kerygma. For Kant, "What can I hope?" is one of the three great questions human beings ask.
>
> If this word of power is now threatened, everything else is threatened with it.[15]

Farley's is not a "self-help" book; he's not going to give you six easy lessons (remember that six is the biblical number for sin) in deep symbol repair. Farley will not help us quickly manufacture a technological fix to enable the language of faith to convalesce. But he calls our attention to the need for major efforts on our part to recover our faith tradition's "words of power." I am sure that you are aware of how few persons in our culture understand the deep signs and expressions of Christianity.

For example, last week at a regional church gathering I met for a while with the youth convocation and asked the young people — since I had been thinking about eschatology in preparing this chapter — why we don't talk about heaven anymore. Their answers included the fear that they would be laughed at by their peers, so I asked them whether heaven is a place or a time. Their response was wonderful; it was quiet for a moment of stunned silence, and then several said, "That is a *good* question!" Because of previous destructive inflections of the idea of heaven as a place, we have lost the sense of it as

15. Edward Farley, *Deep Symbols: Their Postmodern Effacement and Reclamation* (Valley Forge, PA: Trinity Press International, 1996), p. 95.

an epoch, as God's reign breaking into the present aeon, as eternal life already begun and someday enjoyed completely (however God prepares it) as the "tabernacling" of God. We can recover these deep symbols, as Farley urges us, if we center on, sort out, and embody them again[16] in new ways appropriate to the times in which we live.

The Church's historic liturgy and new liturgies help us recover the deep symbol of eschatology. This is not to argue for a certain style of music, but I love the *Lutheran Book of Worship* settings of the ancient *Sanctus* (sung by angels in Isaiah 6 and by the children when Jesus entered Jerusalem) and of Revelation 5 in the hymn of praise, "Feast of Victory." When we teach people where these hymns of praise are found in the Scriptures, what they mean, why we need to envision God's reign in both the future and the present, and with whom we are singing, we will enable those we teach to love songs like those, too. Similarly, in our sermons we do not have to be afraid of our identity; we need not think that sermons have to provide instant gratification, but we can instead instruct richly and thereby recover the substance of the Church's deep symbols. Young people especially are starved for deeper content.

Children's sermons also provide a great opportunity to recover deep symbols. We can teach eschatology on Palm Sunday by asking the children how they would welcome Jesus if he walked into our sanctuaries. Imagine what we might do for "Christ the King" festival, throughout all of Advent, and on Transfiguration Sunday in teaching the children about the reign of God both now and in the future. Every Sunday is rich with potential for recovering both eschatological hope and other deep symbols of the faith. We have a powerful tradition, but it needs to be recovered within our heritage of expressions and practices.

How Do the Heavens Worship?

Another way to pose this question might be to ask what we can learn from cosmic praise. So many of the biblical psalms suggest that our praise will always be inadequate — so we have to encourage the trees to clap and the mountains to dance, too. Numerous passages in the First Testament call on the heavens to join us in praise or urge us to chime in with the worship of the whole cosmos, for, indeed, God's worthiness requires all the forces of the heavenly hosts to contribute to his adoration. Consequently, in these texts we get a sense of the "already, but not yet" of worship. Eschatological visions per-

16. Farley, *Deep Symbols*, pp. 39-41.

vade both testaments of the Scriptures; for example, one of the assigned texts for my devotions this morning was Psalm 2, which reminds us that the King is already on the throne.

When we look carefully at how the heavens respond to God's reign, we find many hints for how we might worship now in practice for the ultimate fulfillment of God's promises. What can we learn from angels' worship of God? What do they express in their songs, and how might that teach us about true praise?[17]

How Will Eschatological Worship Convey the True God?

In my earlier book on worship, *Reaching Out without Dumbing Down,* I emphasize that the most important question we must always ask about any element in our worship is whether it keeps God as the Subject and Object of our corporate gathering. This will never change: our fundamental criteria must always be how what we do in worship enables us to encounter the true and living, reigning God.[18]

In recent times the eschatological dimension of our faith has often been missing, so we have lost an awe-full lot of God. We miss much of God's grace when we fail to envision his reign; we displace his power. We turn our sermons into therapy instead of proclamation. We discuss our "journey," but forget that it is dependent upon God's journey to us. Don't tell me what I must do to make my journey better or more enjoyable; remind me instead of how graciously and compassionately God has come to us, how his powerful and merciful reign has broken into our world. The result of that will be the formation of my journey, but we will wander aimlessly or along the wrong paths if we are not first changed by God's advent and then transformed into his way of life.

---

17. Notice especially that the angels never sing about themselves or their feelings, but always about the character of God. See Marva J. Dawn, *Joy in Our Weakness: A Gift of Hope from the Book of Revelation* (St. Louis: Concordia Publishing House, 1994).

18. See especially chapter 5, "God as the Center of Worship: Who Is Worship For?" in Marva J. Dawn, *Reaching Out without Dumbing Down: A Theology of Worship for the Turn-of-the-Century Culture* (Grand Rapids: Wm. B. Eerdmans Publishing Co., 1995).

How Will Eschatological Worship Form Us, Personally and Corporately?

This question points to the other two major criteria I offered in *Reaching Out without Dumbing Down;* besides keeping God as the focus of our worship, we who lead it also craft its elements and forms in order to nurture the character of the followers of Jesus and to upbuild the community to reflect God's ways in our corporate life.[19]

If our worship is oriented by the present and future reign of God, it will form us to be dependent on him — in contrast to our culture, which always wants to be in control. We will be formed to be churches that are humble, instead of competing to be successful. We will be nurtured to be people who are repentant, Joy-full in our forgiveness, and eager for direction — aware of our insignificance and yet of our critical importance for God's purposes, aware of the immensity of God's sovereignty and yet of his intimate care for us. For example, what might it mean to worship a God who can hold all the waters of the earth in a single palm and yet gently carries the lambs in his arms? How does it change us to worship a God who can name the stars and call them out so that not one of them is missing?[20]

How would it form us if our worship imbued us with the eschatological sense that all of us carry the reign of God wherever we go? This question is intended to call for a major paradigm shift in our churches. I want every single person in our pews to know that when we leave this place, we all go out to *be Church.* We don't "go to church"; we *are* the Church. How would it affect the society around us if all the people in our congregations knew that wherever they go they bring with them the presence of God in proleptic envisioning of the fulfillment in glory and power of all his promises? We go to the grocery store differently if we know that; we get on the bus with an alternate sense of things if we remember that. We live distinctly if we live eschatologically. How will our worship equip us, personally and corporately, for that eschatological way of life?

---

19. See especially chapters 6 ("The Character of the Believer: Having Content or Being Content?") and 7 ("The Character of the Church as Christian Community: What Is at Stake?") in *Reaching Out without Dumbing Down.*

20. See chapters 11 ("The Cry of *YHWH*'s Gentleness"), 12 ("Our Cry of Wonder"), and 26 ("The Cry of Personal Significance") in Marva J. Dawn, *To Walk and Not Faint: A Month of Meditations on Isaiah 40,* 2nd ed. (Grand Rapids: Wm. B. Eerdmans Publishing Co., 1997).

How Will the Recovery of Eschatology Extricate Our Churches from Our Destructive Battles Over Taste?

A corresponding question might be "Is heavenly worship for everyone?" Recently I received an invitation for an evangelism conference that is going to feature worship one evening oriented to "boomers" and another night to "X-ers." What sort of model and preparation for heaven is our worship if we cannot sing together now across generation lines? Perhaps we have to rewrite Galatians 3:28 these days to stop this division of our churches according to tastes. Instead of "there is neither Jew nor Greek, male nor female, bond nor free," now perhaps Paul would declare, "there is neither boomer nor X-er, neither traditionalist nor lover of jazz, neither guitarist nor organist, neither young nor old, neither black nor white, but everyone has gifts to contribute to the praise of God and the well-being of the communion of saints." (See Chapter 15 of this book.)

Why Is Eschatological Worship a Royal Waste of Time?

We have to question the present emphasis on utilitarian worship, evidenced by frequent comments concerning what we "get out of" a particular worship service. The preface to this book tells the story of the origin of this volume's title and this question. The phrase "a royal waste of time" (see Chapter 2) is intended to contradict the notion of worship that is created to be like Burger King because, according to the review cited in Chapter 5, that "meets the needs."

How will we reteach our congregations that worship is not intended to accomplish anything? How will we learn again simply to stand in the presence of God and to bask in the immensity of God's reign over all of life and the future? Furthermore, by God's grace our future will be perfect and lived fully in the presence of God; consequently, all our present worship is inadequate and a waste of time. It won't change God's opinion about us at all. It won't earn us any points with God; he will gift us anyway with the kingdom.

Does that cause us to give up? Does that allow us to think that anything goes? Or does that challenge us always to respond by growing in constantly developing excellence, to praise this immensely gracious God with the very best that we can offer?[21] Because the future is present and operative, how can we best imagine it? What does that say about Burger King–style worship?

21. For a bracing championing of excellence, see George Steiner, *Errata: An Examined Life* (New Haven: Yale University Press, 1998).

Why Is Sabbath Keeping Important for Eschatological Worship?

Since Sabbath keeping is preparing for the final rest of God's reign, a foretaste of eternity, there is a very deep need for the Church to recover Sabbath keeping as the daylong setting of our morning worship. My book on the subject came out almost ten years ago and still results in letters and comments from people who say that practicing Sabbath keeping has changed their lives. It is essential that we encourage members of our congregations to continue remembering that the whole day of Sunday is a day for God; then we could end the worship service's enslavement to the clock. Perhaps we could demand that everyone take off his or her watch when entering the sanctuary, and then we won't hear any beeps telling us that the time is up.

In our culture there is a frantic need — with emphasis on the word *frantic* because our technological milieu constantly increases its pace — for true rest, for a genuine ceasing from the madness and frenzy of our society, for a better set of values and way of life to embrace, for an unfeigned feasting that is true celebration and not merely an attempt to suppress the profound pain of our lives.[22] How will we plan and participate in worship so that members of our congregations recognize the worship service as only one part — albeit the most important part — of an entire day of getting ready for the future by practicing now the traditions of the past and the reign of God in the present?

How Well Do Our Sacramental Practices Reflect Our Eschatology?

Since the sacraments practice the presence of the future, this question will lead us to important reflection on how often we savor the Lord's Supper, on how well we highlight it as a major mark of our identity. Weekly eucharistic celebrations can be an important means of tasting the splendor of God.

We must also contemplate the place of baptism in the context of our worship services and congregational life. Do we understand baptism as the beginning of the eternal reign of God in the individual's life, as welcoming that person into participation in the kingdom of God, and therefore as a

---

22. See Marva J. Dawn, *Keeping the Sabbath Wholly: Ceasing, Resting, Embracing, Feasting* (Grand Rapids: Wm. B. Eerdmans Publishing Co., 1989).

transformation of the baptized person's life and a responsibility for the whole community to nurture an eschatological way of life?[23]

How Will Eschatological Worship Deal with Suffering?

How will we deal with suffering in our worship services if we know that in the future, which we begin to experience now, all sorrow and sighing will flee away? In the confusions about what worship really is that characterize many churches in our times, worship services often suppress or ignore suffering in the singing of "happy songs" — rather than engaging in honest, genuine lament and rather than recognizing that God's reign changes the way we approach and deal with suffering. If we could only learn a theology of weakness — one piece of the more comprehensive theology of the cross — rather than reverting to the theology of glory that pervades many worship services these days, we would be more faithful to the God of the Scriptures, the way of life of God's people, the realities of our broken world, and the truth of God's ultimate victory over pain and sin and death at the close of time.[24]

How Will Eschatological Worship Convey the True Hope of the Gospel?

We live in an age desperate for lasting hope, struggling to find some basis for hope. How can we capture more thoroughly in our worship the hope of God rather than human hopes and opinions?

Many of the sidebars in Douglas Coupland's *Generation X* (which we looked at in Chapter 3) poignantly illustrate the hopelessness of many young adults who wonder how to find meaning and a future in a nuclear-threatened, consumerism-drowned, technologically frenzied, relationship-bereft society. In one conversation concerning their parents, Andy concludes his comments to Dag with these words:

> Sometimes I'd just like to mace them. I want to tell them that I envy their upbringings that were so clean, so free of *futurelessness*. And I want to

23. I have not said much about the sacraments in this book primarily because there are so many differences between denominations in celebrating them, and therefore they can best be studied in the denominational literature.

24. See Dawn, *Joy in Our Weakness.*

throttle them for blithely handing over the world to us like so much skid-marked underwear.[25]

This is the cry of many people in their twenties and thirties as they look at the political and economic chaos in our world, at the lack of job possibilities in their chosen profession, at environmental degradation, at the loss of all moral authority: How can we carry on when you have left us such a messed-up world? They are starved for hope.

Let's not simply give them phony pats on the back and manipulate their feelings into coziness. Let's instead give them the true hope that is not entertainment, nor escapism, nor diversion, nor a consumerist appeal to taste, but that teaches us instead a realistic appraisal of sin and evil, that reminds us of the victory of Christ over sin and evil at the cross and empty tomb, that enfolds us in the presence of God's reign in the world now, that challenges us to participate in that reign in ministry to our world, and that assures us of the truth that someday God will usher in his kingdom in all its fullness. Let us recover the Church's eschatological tradition, worship richly in light of that tradition, and thereby give such a hope to our neighbors who are yearning for it!

Let us pray: O God of infinite splendor, as we ask these questions, help us turn to you and your Word and your community throughout space and time for answers. May the Scriptures and the eschatological wisdom of your Church be formative of our lives and of our worship, so that we might offer to the world around us the gospel in all its truth, and beauty, and goodness. We ask this confidently because we have seen that you are always faithful to keep your past promises to us in the present, and so we can trust you for the fulfillment of our future in yours. Guide each of your people and all of us together in our wrestling with the questions of this chapter and this book so that personally and corporately we can become the Church that you have designed us to be — to your honor and glory and praise into the ages of the ages, and for the sake of a world longing for your reign. Amen.

---

25. Coupland, *Generation X*, pp. 85-86.

For Further Reading

Allen, Diogenes. *Christian Belief in a Postmodern World: The Full Wealth of Conviction*. Louisville: Westminster/John Knox, 1989.

Aronowitz, Stanley; Barbara Martinsons; and Michael Menser, eds. *Technoscience and Cyberculture*. New York: Routledge, 1996.

Barber, Benjamin R. *Jihad vs. McWorld: How Globalism and Tribalism Are Reshaping the World*. New York: Ballantine Books, 1996.

Bass, Dorothy C., ed. *Practicing Our Faith: A Way of Life for a Searching People*. San Francisco: Jossey-Bass, 1997.

Berry, Wendell. *The Memory of Old Jack*. New York: Harcourt Brace Jovanovich, 1974.

———. *Sex, Economy, Freedom and Community: Eight Essays*. New York: Pantheon Books, 1993.

Blanchard, Tsvi. "After Eden: The Search for the Holy in a Consumer Society." In *The Consuming Passion: Christianity and the Consumer Culture*, pp. 91-106. Edited by Rodney Clapp. Downers Grove, IL: InterVarsity Press, 1998.

Brook, James, and Iain A. Boal, eds. *Resisting the Virtual Life: The Culture and Politics of Information*. San Francisco: City Lights, 1995.

Brooke, Tal, gen. ed. *Virtual Gods*. Eugene, OR: Harvest House Publishers, 1997.

Brueggemann, Walter. *The Message of the Psalms: A Theological Commentary*. Augsburg Old Testament Studies. Minneapolis: Augsburg, 1984.

———. *Theology of the Old Testament: Testimony, Dispute, Advocacy*. Minneapolis: Fortress Press, 1997.

Campbell, Charles L. *Preaching Jesus: New Directions for Homiletics in Hans Frei's Postliberal Theology*. Grand Rapids: Wm. B. Eerdmans Publishing Co., 1997.

Capon, Robert Farrar. *The Foolishness of Preaching: Proclaiming the Gospel against the Wisdom of the World*. Grand Rapids: Wm. B. Eerdmans Publishing Co., 1998.

Cherwien, Susan Palo. *O Blessed Spring: Hymns of Susan Palo Cherwien*. Minneapolis: Augsburg Fortress, 1997.

Clapp, Rodney. *A Peculiar People: The Church as Culture in a Post-Christian Society*. Downers Grove, IL: InterVarsity Press, 1996.

———. "The Theology of Consumption and the Consumption of Theology: Toward a Christian Response to Consumerism." In *The Consuming Passion: Christianity and the Consumer Culture*, pp. 169-204. Edited by Rodney Clapp. Downers Grove, IL: InterVarsity Press, 1998.

Clynes, Manfred, ed. *Music, Mind, and Brain: The Neuropsychology of Music*. New York: Plenum Press, 1982.

Collins, Dori Erwin, and Scott C. Weidler. *Sound Decisions: Evaluating Contemporary Music for Lutheran Worship*. Chicago: Evangelical Lutheran Church in America, 1997.

Coupland, Douglas. *Generation X: Tales for an Accelerated Culture*. New York: St. Martin Press, 1991.

———. *Life after God*. New York: Simon and Schuster, 1994.

Dahlstrom, Paul T. *Worshiping: Present and Future Hope*. Lima, OH: Fairway Press, 1996.

Dawn, Marva J. "The Concept of 'The Principalities and Powers' in the Works of Jacques Ellul." Ph.D. dissertation, University of Notre Dame, 1992.

———. *I'm Lonely, LORD — How Long? Meditations on the Psalms*. Revised edition. Grand Rapids: Wm. B. Eerdmans Publishing Co., 1998.

———. *Is It a Lost Cause? Having the Heart of God for the Church's Children*. Grand Rapids: Wm. B. Eerdmans Publishing Co., 1997.

———. *Joy in Our Weakness: A Gift of Hope from the Book of Revelation*. St. Louis: Concordia Publishing House, 1994.

———. *Keeping the Sabbath Wholly: Ceasing, Resting, Embracing, Feasting*. Grand Rapids: Wm. B. Eerdmans Publishing Co., 1989.

———. *Reaching Out without Dumbing Down: A Theology of Worship for the Turn-of-the-Century Culture*. Grand Rapids: Wm. B. Eerdmans Publishing Co., 1995.

———. *Sexual Character: Beyond Technique to Intimacy*. Grand Rapids: Wm. B. Eerdmans Publishing Co., 1993.

———. *To Walk and Not Faint: A Month of Meditations on Isaiah 40*. Second edition. Grand Rapids: Wm. B. Eerdmans Publishing Co., 1997.

———. *Truly the Community: Romans 12 and How to Be the Church*. Grand Rapids: Wm. B. Eerdmans, 1992; reissued with new title in 1997. (Formerly published under the title *The Hilarity of Community: Romans 12 and How to Be the Church*.)

————. "What the Bible *Really* Says about War." *The Other Side* 29, no. 2 (March-April 1993): 56-59.

Dawn, Marva J., trans. and ed. *Sources and Trajectories: Eight Early Articles by Jacques Ellul That Set the Stage*. Grand Rapids: Wm. B. Eerdmans Publishing Co., 1997.

Doran, Carol, and Thomas H. Troeger. *Trouble at the Table: Gathering the Tribes for Worship*. Nashville: Abingdon Press, 1992.

Ellul, Jacques. *The Humiliation of the Word*. Translated by Joyce Main Hanks. Grand Rapids: Wm. B. Eerdmans Publishing Co., 1985.

————. *The New Demons*. Translated by C. Edward Hopkin. New York: Seabury Press, 1975.

————. *The Technological Bluff*. Translated by Geoffrey W. Bromiley. Grand Rapids: Wm. B. Eerdmans Publishing Co., 1990.

————. *The Technological Society*. Translated by John Wilkinson. New York: Vintage Books, 1964.

————. *The Technological System*. Translated by Joachim Neugroschel. New York: Continuum Publishing Company, 1980.

Farley, Edward. *Deep Symbols: Their Postmodern Effacement and Reclamation*. Valley Forge, PA: Trinity Press International, 1996.

Farnsworth, Kirk E. *Wounded Workers: Recovering from Heartache in the Workplace and the Church*. Mukilteo, WA: WinePress Publishing, 1998.

Forbes, Bruce David. "Why Clergy Should Not Ignore Television." *Word and World* 18, no. 1 (Winter 1998): 34-43.

Forbes, Bruce, and Jeffrey Mahan, eds. *Religion and Popular Culture in America*. Berkeley: University of California Press, 1998.

Ford, Kevin Graham. *Jesus for a New Generation: Putting the Gospel in the Language of Xers*. Downers Grove, IL: InterVarsity Press, 1995.

Fore, William F. *Television and Religion: The Shaping of Faith, Values, and Culture*. Minneapolis: Augsburg, 1987.

Frei, Hans. *The Eclipse of Biblical Narrative*. New Haven: Yale University Press, 1974.

Gaddy, C. Welton. *The Gift of Worship*. Nashville: Broadman Press, 1992.

Gaiser, Frederick J. Review of *Entertainment Evangelism: Taking the Church Public* by Walt Kallestad. *Word and World* 18, no. 1 (Winter 1998): 102-6.

Gay, Craig M. "Sensualists without Heart: Contemporary Consumerism in Light of the Modern Project." In *The Consuming Passion: Christianity and the Consumer Culture*, pp. 19-39. Edited by Rodney Clapp. Downers Grove, IL: InterVarsity Press, 1998.

Grenz, Stanley J. *A Primer on Postmodernism*. Grand Rapids: Wm. B. Eerdmans Publishing Co., 1996.

Groothuis, Douglas. "It Takes More Than a Virtual Village." *Books and Culture* 3, no. 3 (May/June 1997): 13-14.

————. *The Soul in Cyberspace.* Grand Rapids, MI: Hourglass, 1997.

Guder, Darrell L., ed. *Missional Church: A Vision for the Sending of the Church in North America.* Grand Rapids: Wm. B. Eerdmans Publishing Co., 1998.

Halpern, Steven, with Louis Savary. *Sound Health: The Music That Makes Us Whole.* New York: Harper and Row, 1985.

Healy, Jane M. *Endangered Minds: Why Our Children Don't Think.* New York: Simon and Schuster, 1990.

Hunsberger, George R. "Sizing Up the Shape of the Church." In *The Church between Gospel and Culture: The Emerging Mission in North America*, pp. 333-46. Edited by George R. Hunsberger and Craig Van Gelder. Grand Rapids: Wm. B. Eerdmans Publishing Co., 1996.

Hunsberger, George R., and Craig Van Gelder, eds. *The Church between Gospel and Culture: The Emerging Mission in North America.* Grand Rapids: Wm. B. Eerdmans Publishing Co., 1996.

Ingraffia, Brian D. *Postmodern Theory and Biblical Theology: Vanquishing God's Shadow.* Cambridge: Cambridge University Press, 1996.

Job, Rueben P., and Norman Shawchuck, eds. *A Guide to Prayer: For Ministers and Other Servants.* Nashville: The Upper Room, 1983.

Johansson, Calvin M. *Discipling Music Ministry: Twenty-first Century Directions.* Peabody, MA: Hendrickson Publishers, 1992.

Jurisson, Cynthia A. "Pop Spirituality: An Evangelical Response." *Word and World* 18, no. 1 (Winter 1998): 14-23.

Kenneson, Philip D., and James L. Street. *Selling Out the Church: The Dangers of Church Marketing.* Nashville: Abingdon Press, 1997.

Kolakowski, Leszek. *Modernity on Endless Trial.* Chicago: University of Chicago Press, 1990.

Lathrop, Gordon W. *Holy Things: A Liturgical Theology.* Minneapolis: Augsburg Fortress, 1993.

Lawrence, Brother. *The Practice of the Presence of God.* Translated by Donald Attwater. Springfield: Templegate Publishers, 1981.

Lears, Jackson. *Fables of Abundance.* New York: BasicBooks, 1994.

Lewis, C. S. *The Abolition of Man.* New York: Simon and Schuster, 1996.

Liesch, Barry. *The New Worship: Straight Talk on Music and the Church.* Grand Rapids: Baker Book House, 1996.

Lindbeck, George A. *The Nature of Doctrine: Religion and Theology in a Postliberal Age.* Philadelphia: Westminster Press, 1984.

Luther, Martin. *Letters.* Translated and edited by Gottfried G. Krodel. Volume 49 of *Luther's Works.* Helmut T. Lehmann, general editor. Philadelphia: Fortress Press, 1972.

————. "Those Recorded by Conrad Cordatus, 1532-1533." In *Table Talk*, pp. 167-200. Translated and edited by Theodore G. Tappert. Volume 54 of *Lu-*

ther's Works. Helmut T. Lehmann, general editor. Philadelphia: Fortress Press, 1967.

Lyotard, Jean-François. *The Postmodern Condition*. Translated by Geoff Bennington and Brian Massumi. Theory and History of Literature, 10. Minneapolis: University of Minnesota Press, 1984.

Marty, Martin E. "Cross-Multicultures in the Crossfire: The Humanities and Political Interests." In *Christianity and Culture in the Crossfire*, pp. 15-27. Edited by David A. Hoekema and Bobby Fong. Grand Rapids: Wm. B. Eerdmans Publishing Co., 1997.

Marty, Peter W. "Beyond the Polarization: Grace and Surprise in Worship." *Christian Century* 115, no. 9 (March 18-25, 1998): 284-87.

Maté, Ferenc. *A Reasonable Life: Toward a Simpler, Secure, More Humane Existence*. New York: Albatross Publishing House, 1993.

McKibben, Bill. "Returning God to the Center: Consumerism and the Environmental Threat." In *The Consuming Passion: Christianity and the Consumer Culture*, pp. 40-50. Edited by Rodney Clapp. Downers Grove, IL: InterVarsity Press, 1998.

Middleton, J. Richard, and Brian J. Walsh. *Truth Is Stranger Than It Used to Be*. Downers Grove, IL: InterVarsity Press, 1995.

Miller, Patrick D. "Good-bye Seinfeld." *Theology Today* 55, no. 2 (July 1998): 147-51.

Mills, Stephanie, ed. *Turning Away from Technology: A New Vision for the 21st Century*. San Francisco: Sierra Club Books, 1997.

Moltmann, Jürgen. *The Coming of God: Christian Eschatology*. Translated by Margaret Kohl. Minneapolis: Fortress Press, 1996.

———. *Theology of Hope: On the Ground and Implications of a Christian Eschatology*. Translated by James W. Leitch. Minneapolis: Augsburg Fortress, 1993.

Myers, David. "Money and Misery." In *The Consuming Passion: Christianity and the Consumer Culture*, pp. 51-75. Edited by Rodney Clapp. Downers Grove, IL: InterVarsity Press, 1998.

Myers, Kenneth A. *All God's Children and Blue Suede Shoes: Christians and Popular Culture*. Westchester, IL: Crossway Books, 1989.

Niebuhr, Gustav. "American Religion at the Millennium's End." *Word and World* 18, no. 1 (Winter 1998): 5-13.

O'Leary, Stephen D. "Cyberspace as Sacred Space: Communicating Religion on Computer Networks." *Journal of the American Academy of Religion* 64, no. 4 (Winter 1996).

O'Neill, John. *The Poverty of Postmodernism*. London: Routledge, 1995.

Page, Sue Ellen. *Hearts and Hands and Voices: Growing in Faith through Choral Music*. Tarzana, CA: H. T. FitzSimons Company, 1995.

Palmer, Parker. *The Company of Strangers: Christians and the Renewal of America's Public Life*. New York: Crossroad, 1986.

Peterson, Eugene H. *The Contemplative Pastor.* Second edition. Grand Rapids: Wm. B. Eerdmans Publishing Co., 1997.

————. *Five Smooth Stones for Pastoral Work.* Second edition. Grand Rapids: Wm. B. Eerdmans Publishing Co., 1997.

————. *A Long Obedience in the Same Direction: Discipleship in an Instant Society.* Downers Grove, IL: InterVarsity Press, 1980.

Pfatteicher, Philip H. *The School of the Church: Worship and Christian Formation.* Valley Forge, PA: Trinity Press, 1995.

Phillips, Timothy R., and Dennis L. Okholm, eds. *Christian Apologetics in the Postmodern World.* Downers Grove, IL: InterVarsity Press, 1995.

————. *The Nature of Confession: Evangelicals and Postliberals in Conversation.* Downers Grove, IL: InterVarsity Press, 1996.

Postman, Neil. *Amusing Ourselves to Death: Public Discourse in the Age of Show Business.* New York: Viking Penguin, 1985.

————. *Technopoly: The Surrender of Culture to Technology.* New York: Alfred A. Knopf, 1992.

Resch, Barbara. "Adolescents' Attitudes towards the Appropriateness of Religious Music." D.M.A. dissertation, Indiana University, 1996.

Rieff, Philip. *The Triumph of the Therapeutic: Uses of Faith after Freud.* London: Chatto & Windus, 1966.

Roof, Wade Clark. *A Generation of Seekers: The Spiritual Journeys of the Baby Boom Generation.* San Francisco: HarperCollins Publishers, 1993.

Roxburgh, Alan J. *Reaching a New Generation: Strategies for Tomorrow's Church.* Downers Grove, IL: InterVarsity Press, 1993.

Salerno-Sonnenberg, Nadja. *Nadja: On My Way.* New York: Crown Publishers, 1989.

Sampson, Philip. "The Rise of Post-modernity." In *Faith and Modernity,* pp. 29-57. Edited by Philip Sampson, Vinay Samuel, and Chris Sugden. Oxford: Regnum Books, 1994.

Sass, Louis A. *Madness and Modernism: Insanity in the Light of Modern Art, Literature, and Thought.* New York: BasicBooks, 1992.

Schultze, Quentin J. *Winning Your Kids Back from the Media.* Downers Grove, IL: InterVarsity Press, 1994.

Schwehn, Mark R. "Christianity and Postmodernism: Uneasy Allies." In *Christianity and Culture in the Crossfire,* pp. 155-68. Edited by David A. Hoekema and Bobby Fong. Grand Rapids: Wm. B. Eerdmans Publishing Co., 1997.

Shelley, Bruce, and Marshall Shelley. *Consumer Church: "Can Evangelicals Win the World without Losing Their Souls?"* Downers Grove, IL: InterVarsity Press, 1992.

Steiner, George. *Errata: An Examined Life.* New Haven: Yale University Press, 1998.

Stewart, Sonja M., and Jerome W. Berryman. *Young Children and Worship.* Louisville: Westminster/John Knox Press, 1989.

Thiselton, Anthony. *Interpreting God and the Postmodern Self: On Meaning, Manipulation, and Promise.* Grand Rapids: Wm. B. Eerdmans Publishing Co., 1995.

Tocqueville, Alexis de. *Democracy in America.* Translated by George Lawrence. Garden City, NY: Doubleday/Anchor, 1969.

Torvend, Samuel, and Lani Willis, eds. *Welcome to Christ: A Lutheran Introduction to the Catechumenate.* Minneapolis: Augsburg Fortress, 1997.

Van Gelder, Craig, ed. *Confident Witness, Changing World.* Grand Rapids: Wm. B. Eerdmans Publishing Co., forthcoming.

Van Leewen, Arend. *Christianity in World History.* Edinburgh: Edinburgh Press, 1964.

Watson, Andrew, and Nevill Drury. *Healing Music.* Sydney: Prism Books, 1987.

Webb-Mitchell, Brett. *Christly Gestures: The End of Christian Education.* New York: Crossroad Publishing Company, forthcoming.

———. "Crafting Christians into the Gestures of the Body of Christ." In *Human Disability and the Service of God: Reassessing Religious Practice.* Edited by Nancy Eiesland and Don Saliers. Nashville: Abingdon, 1998.

———. "A Protestant View of Physical Gestures in Church Life." *New Oxford Review* 62, no. 8 (October 1995): 18-21.

Weber, Max. *The Protestant Ethic and the Spirit of Capitalism.* Translated by Talcott Parsons. New York: Charles Scribner's Sons, 1958.

Westphal, Merold. *Suspicion and Faith: The Religious Uses of Modern Atheism.* Grand Rapids: Wm. B. Eerdmans Publishing Co., 1997.

Wilson-Dickson, Andrew. *The Story of Christian Music: From Gregorian Chant to Black Gospel.* Minneapolis: Fortress Press, 1996.

With One Voice: A Lutheran Resource for Worship. Minneapolis: Augsburg Fortress, 1997.

Wright, N. T. *The New Testament and the People of God.* Minneapolis: Fortress, 1992.

Wuthnow, Robert, ed. *Rethinking Materialism: Perspectives on the Spiritual Dimension of Economic Behavior.* Grand Rapids: Wm. B. Eerdmans Publishing Co., 1995.

Yancey, Philip. *What's So Amazing about Grace?* Grand Rapids: Zondervan Publishing House, 1997.

Yeats, William Butler. "The Second Coming." In *Chapters into Verse: Poetry in English Inspired by the Bible.* Edited by Robert Atwan and Laurance Wieder. Volume 2: *Gospels to Revelation,* pp. 376-77. Oxford: Oxford University Press, 1995.

Zaleski, Jeff. *The Soul of Cyberspace: How New Technology Is Changing Our Spiritual Lives.* San Francisco: HarperSanFrancisco, 1997.